ACADEMIC INTEGRITY IN THE CARIBBEAN

ACADEMIC INTEGRITY IN THE CARIBBEAN

Plagiarism Policies, Perception, Prevalence and Possible Solutions

Ruth Baker-Gardner

The University of the West Indies Press
Jamaica • Barbados • Trinidad and Tobago

The University of the West Indies Press
7A Gibraltar Hall Road, Mona
Kingston 7, Jamaica
www.uwipress.com

© 2022 by Ruth Baker-Gardner

All rights reserved. Published 2022

A catalogue record of this book is available from the National Library of Jamaica.

ISBN: 978-976-640-921-0 (print)
978-976-640-922-7 (ePub)

Cover design by Robert Harris

The University of the West Indies Press has no responsibility for the persistence or accuracy of URLs for external or third-party internet websites referred to in this publication and does not guarantee that any content on such websites is, or will remain, accurate or appropriate.

Printed in the United States of America

My Story for Your Glory.

—Jeremiah 29:11

Contents

List of Tables \ xiii

List of Figures \ xv

List of Acronyms and Abbreviations \ xvii

Acknowledgements \ xviii

Foreword \ xix

Preface \ xxi

Part 1 Academic Integrity and Plagiarism

1. Understanding Academic Integrity \ 3
Introduction \ 3
Academic Integrity Defined \ 3
ICAI \ 4
The Role of Education \ 9
The Education System as an Open Social System \ 12
Academic Dishonesty \ 14
Plagiarism: The Most Popular Form of Academic Misconduct \ 17
Conclusion \ 19

2. Defining and Understanding Plagiarism \ 20
Introduction \ 20
Defining Plagiarism \ 20
Types of Plagiarism \ 25
Plagiarism across the Globe \ 28
What's so Wrong with Plagiarizing? \ 29
Contract Cheating \ 34
Conclusion \ 36

3. Causes and Prevalence of Plagiarism \ 37
   Introduction \ 37
   Why Students Plagiarize \ 37
   Plagiarism and the Internet \ 42
   Factors Impacting Plagiarism among Academics \ 44
   Prevalence of Plagiarism \ 45
   Conclusion \ 48

4. Detection and Consequences of Plagiarism \ 50
   Introduction \ 50
   Detecting Plagiarism \ 50
   Consequences of Plagiarism for Students \ 54
   Consequences for Plagiarism among Academics \ 56
   Deterrents to Plagiarism \ 57
   Conclusion \ 58

Part 2 Research on Academic Integrity in the Caribbean

5. Background to the Caribbean \ 61
   Introduction \ 61
   Defining the Caribbean \ 61
   Overview of Education in the Caribbean \ 64
   Funding Education in the Caribbean \ 66
   Regional Educational Institutions \ 68
   Conclusion \ 73

6. Methodology \ 75
   Introduction \ 75
   Research Objectives \ 75
   Research Design \ 76
   Content Analysis \ 76
   Descriptive Survey \ 81
   Ethical Concerns \ 84
   Secondary Data \ 84
   Conclusion \ 84

7. Snapshots of Plagiarism from across the Caribbean \ 85
   Introduction \ 85
   Background \ 85
   Review of Literature \ 86
   Presentation and Analysis of Data \ 87
   Discussion of Findings \ 93

8. Maintaining Academic Integrity in Secondary Education in the Caribbean \ 94
   Introduction \ 94
   Background \ 94
   Review of Literature \ 97
   Data Presentation and Analysis \ 99
   Discussion of Findings \ 110

9. Academic Integrity and Plagiarism Policies of Caribbean Higher Education Institutions \ 112
   Introduction \ 112
   Background \ 112
   Review of Literature \ 113
   Data Presentation and Analysis \ 114
   Discussion of Findings \ 132

10. Academic Integrity, Accreditation and Plagiarism in Higher Education \ 135
    Introduction \ 135
    Background \ 135
    Review of Literature \ 137
    Accreditation in the Caribbean \ 138
    Data Presentation and Analysis \ 140
    Discussion of Findings \ 149

11. Undergraduate Students' Perceptions of Plagiarism: Analysis of Quantitative Data \ 152
    Introduction \ 152
    Background \ 152
    Review of Literature \ 153
    Data Presentation and Analysis \ 154
    Discussion of Findings \ 161

12. In Their Own Words – Undergraduates' Perception of Plagiarism \ 163
    Introduction \ 163
    Background \ 163
    Data Presentation and Analysis \ 163
    Discussion of Findings \ 175

13. Perceptions of Plagiarism by Academic Discipline and Gender \ 177
Introduction \ 177
Background \ 177
Review of the Literature \ 178
Data Presentation and Analysis \ 183
Discussion of Findings \ 194

14. Perception of Plagiarism by Age and Academic Maturity \ 196
Introduction \ 196
Background \ 196
Review of Literature \ 197
Data Presentation and Analysis \ 199
Discussion of the Findings \ 205

15. Conclusions Drawn from the Research \ 207
Prevalence of Plagiarism in Education in the Caribbean \ 207
HEIs Presentation and Treatment of Plagiarism in Their Policies \ 210
Undergraduates' Perception of Plagiarism \ 212

Part 3   Developing a Culture of Academic Integrity

16. Regional and National Framework for Academic Integrity \ 217
Introduction \ 217
The State of Academic Integrity in the Caribbean: Findings and Recommendations \ 217
From Plagiarism Policies to a Culture of Academic Integrity \ 219
Regional Approach to Academic Integrity \ 223
National Academic Integrity Programmes \ 224
From a Punitive Approach to a Culture of Integrity \ 226
Ethical Issue, Moral Dilemma or Educational Challenge? \ 229
Conclusion \ 231

17. Institutional Context for Academic Integrity \ 232
Introduction \ 232
Triad for Developing Academic Integrity within Higher Education Institutions (HEIs) \ 232
Institutional Framework \ 235
The Role of the Library in Promoting Academic Integrity \ 241
Conclusion \ 247

18. Roles and Responsibilities of Faculty and Students \ 248
Introduction \ 248
Faculty as Critical Partners \ 248
Strategies for Developing and Practising Integrity \ 251
Graduate Education on Academic Integrity \ 258
Discipline-Specific Approach to Plagiarism \ 259
Role of the Student \ 259
Barriers to Engagement of Faculty and Students \ 263
Conclusion \ 266

19. Elements of the Academic Integrity Programme \ 267
Introduction \ 267
Elements of a Programme Designed to Develop a Culture of Integrity \ 267
Mitigation \ 268
Strategies for Prevention \ 272
Managing Allegations of Misconduct \ 274
Rehabilitation \ 277
Reporting Systems \ 278
Honour Systems \ 279
Ongoing Programme Evaluation \ 281
Conclusion \ 283

20. Education and Training for Academic Integrity \ 284
Introduction \ 284
The Need for Training and Education in Academic Integrity in the Caribbean \ 284
Academic Integrity Instructions at the Pre-University Level \ 286
Education for Integrity at the Primary and Secondary Levels \ 290
Developing Academic Integrity among Students in HEIs \ 293
Methodology for Use in Academic Integrity Education \ 298
Developing Academic Integrity among Faculty \ 302
Conclusion \ 303

21. The Way Forward \ 304
Introduction \ 304
Background \ 304
Building a Culture of Integrity \ 308
Conclusion \ 311

Appendices

    Appendix 1: Questionnaire \ 315

    Appendix 2: Confessions of a Plagiarist \ 318

References / 323

Index / 363

Tables

Table 1.1   Plagiarism among graduate and undergraduate students \ 18
Table 2.1   The plagiarism spectrum as presented by Turnitin \ 26
Table 2.2   Top ten cases of plagiarism in 2016 \ 30
Table 5.1   Percentage of G.D.P. spent on Education by Territory \ 67
Table 5.2   Number of students sitting CSEC in May/June 2018 by territories \ 70
Table 5.3   The UWI enrolment by nationalities for the period 2012–2017 \ 72
Table 6.1   Distribution of sample across facilities \ 82
Table 7.1   Number of cases of plagiarism reported in online newspapers for the period 2002–2017 \ 88
Table 7.2   Number of articles published by sector in each territory for the period 2002–2017 \ 91
Table 7.3   Types of plagiarism in articles \ 92
Table 9.1   Institutions with online academic integrity and plagiarism policies \ 115
Table 9.2   Elements present in Caribbean plagiarism policies and guidelines \ 120
Table 10.1 Population and number of cases of plagiarism for the period 2004–2017 \ 144
Table 11.1 Perception of the factors which exacerbate plagiarism \ 156
Table 11.2 Students' responses for justification for plagiarism \ 158
Table 11.3 Responses for the severity of and penalty for plagiarism \ 160
Table 13.1 Relative levels of cheating among graduate students in the United States and Canada \ 180
Table 13.2 Gender difference as it relates to the overall plagiarism scale \ 184
Table 13.3 Independent samples test for the entire plagiarism scale \ 185
Table 13.4 Gender difference as it relates to the factors of plagiarism subscale \ 186
Table 13.5 Independent samples sub-test for the factors of plagiarism subscale \ 187
Table 13.6 Gender difference as it relates to justification for plagiarism subscale \ 188

Table 13.7 Gender difference as it relates to independent samples *t*-test for justification for plagiarism subscale \ 189
Table 13.8 Gender difference as it relates to severity of and penalty for plagiarism subscale \ 190
Table 13.9 Independent samples test for severity and penalty subscale \ 191
Table 13.10 Mean differences on the plagiarism scale as it relates to faculty \ 192
Table 14.1 Number of participants by year group \ 199
Table 14.2 Mean differences in age as it relates to the four scales \ 201
Table 14.3 Mean differences as it relates to years in school \ 204
Table 18.1 Comparison of principles of academic integrity and principles for good practice \ 252

Figures

Figure 1.1   An open system with reference to educational institutions and systems / 12
Figure 2.1   Synonyms for plagiarism / 22
Figure 5.1   Map of the Caribbean / 62
Figure 6.1   Data sources / 76
Figure 7.1   Number of articles on plagiarism published annually from 2002 to 2017 / 89
Figure 8.1   Number of articles on academic misconduct in secondary education by territories / 99
Figure 8.2   Cases of suspected plagiarism in CSEC subjects for the period 2006–2018 / 106
Figure 8.3   Cases of suspected plagiarism by CAPE subjects for the period 2010–2016 / 107
Figure 8.4   Number of suspected cases of plagiarism for the period 2006–2018 / 108
Figure 9.1   Location of academic integrity and plagiarism policies / 116
Figure 9.2   Comparison of codes used for analysis of Caribbean policies with Hu and Sun's codes / 118
Figure 10.1 Average number of reported cases of plagiarism for three institutions for the period 2010–2016 / 145
Figure 10.2 Comparison of reported cases of plagiarism for three institutions for the period 2004–2018 / 147
Figure 10.3 The number of cases of plagiarism by year groups at Institution 2 / 148
Figure 12.1 Qualitative data respondents by year groups / 164
Figure 12.2 Qualitative responses by themes / 165
Figure 13.1 Line graph showing mean of factors of plagiarism subscale / 193
Figure 13.2 Line graph showing mean of justification for plagiarism subscale / 193
Figure 13.3 Line graph showing mean of severity of and penalty for plagiarism subscale / 194
Figure 14.1 Age of participants / 200

Figure 14.2 Perception of factors of plagiarism by age groups / 202
Figure 14.3 Mean of justification for plagiarism subscale by age / 203
Figure 14.4 Mean of the severity of and penalty for plagiarism by year group / 205
Figure 17.1 Triad for academic integrity / 234
Figure 17.2 Roles of teaching librarians / 245
Figure 17.3 Information Literacy and Integrity Model / 246
Figure 19.1 PACT model showing elements of an academic integrity programme / 268
Figure 19.2 Core elements of exemplary academic integrity policy / 269
Figure 19.3 Academic integrity toolkit of Notre Dame University / 273

Acronyms and Abbreviations

ACRL	Association for College and Research Libraries
ANOVA	Analysis of Variance
CANQATE	Caribbean Area Network for Quality Assurance in Higher
CAPE	Caribbean Advanced Proficiency Examination
CARICOM	Caribbean Community
CHEA	Council for Higher Education Accreditation
CMU	Caribbean Maritime University
COSTAATT	College of Science, Technology and Applied Arts of Trinidad and Tobago
CSEC	Caribbean Secondary Examination Certificate
CXC	Caribbean Examination Council
EMCVPA	Edna Manley College for the Visual and Performing Arts
EU	European Union
GDP	Gross Domestic Product
HEIs	Higher Education Institutions
ICAI	International Center for Academic Integrity
JIE	Josephson Institute of Ethics
JTS	Jamaica Theological Seminary
LIS	Library and Information Studies
MIL	Media and Information Literacy
MUC	Mico University College
NCU	Northern Caribbean University
PACT	Prevention, Mitigation, Assessment and Curation of Academic Integrity Based on Values and Taxonomy
SBA	School-Based Assessment
UCC	University of the Commonwealth Caribbean
UCJ	University Council of Jamaica
UG	University of Guyana
UNESCO	United Nations Educational, Scientific and Cultural Organization
UTECH	University of Technology
UWI	University of the West Indies

Acknowledgements

I take this opportunity to express gratitude to a number of persons who made this project possible. I want to thank my mentor Dr Cherrell Shelley-Robinson who provided feedback on the manuscript in the early stages and assisted with the editing of the final draft. Kudos also to my former lecturer Ms. Rosemarie Runcie who assisted with the referencing. My gratitude to Ms. Angella Wilson who initially proofread the manuscript. Thanks to my colleagues in the Department of Library and Information Studies at the University of the West Indies, Mona, Jamaica, for the many ways they supported me from the beginning to the completion of this project. I also want to thank Ms. Sharlett Thomas and Mr. Eraldo Truman who assisted with the formatting of the manuscript, and Ms. Nadina Shorter, Mrs. Natoyna Garwood and Ms. Marsha Jack, who assisted with the data collection.

I am grateful to the students who so willingly participated by responding to the questionnaires. Special thanks to the University administration that gave me permission to conduct the study and the lecturers who were willing to allow me into their classes to collect data. My gratitude to the institutions across the Caribbean which provided data and documents for analysis and responded to the many queries for clarification.

I want to thank my lifelong friend Mrs. Claudia Allen-Hutchinson for ongoing moral support throughout this project and assistance with the collection and preliminary analysis of the data used in part 2. Her unwavering support helped me to believe this project was possible. I must also make mention of Mr. and Mrs. Musa Laing, who so ably took care of my son during the times I needed to focus on writing. Commendations also to those who prayed for me during this two-year journey. To my family who always believed in my dreams and encouraged them, please know that having you in the wings cheering me on has helped tremendously.

Foreword

I am pleased that Dr. Ruth Baker-Gardner reached out to me to write the foreword for this first book about academic integrity in the Caribbean area. I have been active in academic integrity since 2008 with most recently being the president of the International Center for Academic Integrity (ICAI) from 2020 to 2023.

I first interacted with Dr. Baker-Gardner in the summer of 2018 as she was just beginning writing this book. She was contacting me as a leader in the ICAI with the hope to be able to share her ideas for this book with other members at the spring, 2019 annual conference. I then had the pleasure of meeting Dr. Baker-Gardner in person at that conference in New Orleans, Louisiana, United States, in March 2019 as she presented the beginnings of this work. We have since continued our connection as I have remained in the leadership of ICAI.

During this time period (2018–2020), there was little to no writing about academic integrity in the Caribbean. The ICAI strives for an international presence; however, Dr. Baker-Gardner was our first contact with the Caribbean. With that being said, her work in this book is monumental while also showing her extreme dedication to the field.

As you will note, this book gives a thorough overview of what academic integrity is and provides an understanding of plagiarism including its detection and consequences. This is followed by research to show the actual areas of concern regarding plagiarism in the Caribbean, and concludes with practical tips and recommendations for institutions to uphold academic integrity.

Dr. Baker-Gardner has followed the mission of the ICAI by explaining academic integrity in terms of the six fundamental values and having the goal for institutions to create a culture of integrity. Tricia Bertram Gallant (2011) in her white paper entitled *Building a Culture of Academic Integrity: Based on the Magna Online Seminar, 'Helping Students Learn from Ethical Failures,'* explains the change of approach to academic integrity over time. When academic integrity accountability first began, the approach was one of rule compliance, focusing on following rules in a judicial or legalistic way. Over time, the approach of most academic integrity enforcement offices has moved to an integrity approach, focusing on the values, honour and ethics of a student. This approach tends to be more educational and proactive. Dr. Baker-Gardner successfully defends this educational approach and gives readers practical ways to implement it at their own institution.

While Dr. Baker-Gardner's background is focused on the Caribbean, readers from all over the world will benefit from her writing. The ICAI does not promote one specific structure to hold individuals accountable, but ICAI does highly encourage institutions to have some way to do so. As Dr. Baker-Gardner explains, this structure must bring in the voices of students, faculty and administrators to truly create a culture of integrity.

In conclusion, it is clear that Dr. Baker-Gardner has written this book not for it to sit on the bookshelves of researchers or administrators. This book has been written to show the concerns specifically in the Caribbean, but then is a call for all readers across the globe to make real change at their own institutions based on the practical advice and examples she gives. I encourage you as a reader to take notes and attempt to make those changes in order to continue to enhance and promote the fundamental values of academic integrity and build a culture of community.

Camilla J. Roberts, Ph.D.
Kansas State University
President, ICAI

Preface

The academic environment of the Caribbean is shrouded in silence for the most part when it comes to academic integrity, but occasionally this tranquillity is punctuated by serious cases of academic breaches which bring the matter to the forefront for a short period . . . then it is soon forgotten. Academic integrity is essential to higher education institutions (HEIs) globally as it helps to ensure the qualifications obtained by graduates are representative of the knowledge and skills acquired. With this in mind, these institutions have sought to establish programmes aimed at developing a culture of academic integrity. Caribbean HEIs are still at the rudimentary stages, with the majority having policies for plagiarism and academic integrity. They have no established programmes aimed at holistically developing students' knowledge and skills enabling them to come to a better understanding of academic integrity.

On encountering plagiarism in students' work at the tertiary level, the researcher became curious about whether this was intentional or if it was due to ignorance. She teamed up with a colleague and conducted a mixed-methods study among Library and Information Studies (LIS) students. This group was important because as information professionals, they are responsible for teaching information literacy believed to be an effective strategy in combatting plagiarism. The findings from that study indicated that although LIS students possessed general knowledge of plagiarism, that knowledge was not adequate and some had plagiarized unintentionally (Baker-Gardner and Smart 2017).

The finding which intrigued the researcher most from this preliminary study was the absence of literature on plagiarism in the Caribbean. This absence was glaring, seeing that plagiarism was studied extensively in other countries. In addition, anecdotal evidence showed students in the Caribbean were plagiarizing, and universities were applying penalties based on their policies. This stimulated the interest to conduct further research on the topic that culminated in this book, which presents an overview of academic integrity in the Caribbean. In addition, it examines ways that HEIs can move from plagiarism and academic integrity policies to establishing programmes for academic integrity tailored to the particular needs of each institution.

This work represents a significant contribution to the literature on academic integrity in the Caribbean. It lays a foundation from the literature on plagiarism and provides empirical data on acts of academic misconduct within the region. It goes where other works have not gone by examining the prevalence of plagiarism using secondary data and makes a call for the establishment of a system of academic integrity in the Caribbean. This book is divided into three parts. Part 1 presents an overview of the literature in the field of academic integrity, which forms a foundation for the next two parts. It explores the concept of academic integrity and describes how academic misconduct nullifies the ideals of education. It then focuses on plagiarism, the most common type of academic misconduct identified in the literature. The author then explores the causes, prevalence, detection and consequences of plagiarism based on literature mainly from developed countries.

Part 2 presents research aimed at drawing conclusions about academic integrity in the Caribbean. This includes a content analysis of newspaper articles on plagiarism from across the English-speaking Caribbean. The author then continues by examining academic integrity in secondary education, as this is likely to impact any attempt to understand and develop academic integrity in higher education. It then focuses on academic integrity in higher education from a variety of perspectives. First, it presents a content analysis of plagiarism and academic integrity policies to get the views of HEIs on academic integrity. This is followed by a content analysis to determine the extent to which academic integrity is evident in the accreditation standards of Caribbean countries, and an examination of plagiarism data for a fifteen-year period from four universities. Presentation and discussion of the data on students' perception of plagiarism gathered from 1,039 undergraduate students follows. This data is discussed from the perspective of academic discipline, gender, age and academic maturity. The survey also yielded qualitative data which are analysed using the Creswell (2007) data analysis spiral. Part 2 closes with a summary of the findings of various studies, arranged according to the research objectives.

Part 3 begins with the findings from the data analysed, presented and discussed in part 2. In addition, it presents recommendations on how regional institutions can advance from policies and guidelines to developing and implementing programmes for academic integrity. It explores the need for both regional and national policies on academic integrity and then details the institutional framework needed for the implementation of these programmes, and the role of the academic library in their development and implementation. The roles of faculty and students in developing and practising academic integrity are then examined. Using the Preventation, Mitigation, Assessment and Curation of Academic Integrity Based on Values and Taxonomy (PACT) model developed by Siaputra (2019), which illustrates the elements and sub-elements of an effective academic integrity programme, the author explores the elements needed in the programme. She then provides suggestions for the development of educational interventions on academic integrity. This part concludes by outlining the way forward, a call for stakeholders to begin the process of transformation to a culture of academic integrity.

This work is intended for students who are at the centre of the programme for academic integrity, administrators at both the secondary and tertiary levels, and faculty and staff of HEIs. It should serve to stimulate discussion on academic integrity, breaking the silence on a topic that is well researched elsewhere in the world but is just beginning to emerge in the Caribbean. For administrators, it is expected to provide information on how HEIs in other jurisdictions are managing academic integrity and the need to elevate this topic to the agenda of their institutions. For administrators vested with responsibility for examination and assessment processes, it will provide insights into the perceptions of students and the factors that cause plagiarism. This should help them to evaluate their roles and functions and ensure academic integrity issues are dealt with fairly, effectively and efficiently. For faculty, it is expected to stimulate reflection on current practices and challenge some existing beliefs. It should also help them to evaluate their roles in helping students develop and practise academic integrity and stimulate them to adopt best practices. It should provide students with a better understanding of academic integrity and apprise them of their roles and responsibilities in this regard.

Academic integrity is important to the Caribbean and should be seen as a priority, given the devastating impact that academic misconduct can have on the reputation of the regional education system as a result of its interconnected nature, especially at the secondary and tertiary levels. The author hopes that this book will be both a stimulant for future research and a source that other researchers can refer to as they conduct further explorations on the topic. This work aims at lifting a corner of that blanket of silence to begin the discussion of what is a very important subject in the region.

Part 1

Academic Integrity and Plagiarism

Overview

Although not always explicitly stated, academic integrity is the ideal of all higher education institutions (HEIs), and those in the Caribbean are no different. In this part the author explores the definition of academic integrity and discusses its importance in education. The discussion is situated within the concept of the school as an open system responsive to the forces at work in the wider society. The author also examines the role of schools within this open system as agents of transformation and explains how academic integrity is central to ensuring the outputs of the system have met the requirements as evidenced through the certification awarded to them. The author then introduces the International Centre for Academic Integrity, an institution with a mandate for promoting integrity in higher education globally.

Academic misconduct, the opposite of academic integrity, occurs at various points in the education process. Plagiarism is the most common form of academic misconduct. Its impact and prevalence are so pervasive that it has captured the attention of researchers and administrators at the tertiary level and is beginning to emerge in research in the Caribbean. In this part, the author presents and discusses the various definitions of plagiarism and explains its prevalence. It includes a discussion of the ten most common cases of plagiarism across the globe for 2016 to show that plagiarism is not just a challenge in higher education. The author then explores why plagiarism is wrong and the many contributing factors to students' plagiaristic behaviours. It includes a differentiation between plagiarism and contract cheating, an emerging phenomenon often incorrectly labelled as plagiarism.

In this part the author also explores detection of plagiarism with a focus on text-matching software that is currently being used by HEIs in the Caribbean. The researcher then examines the consequences of plagiarism for both faculty and students. This part ends with a discussion of the motivating factors preventing students who did not practise academic misconduct from engaging in dishonest behaviours.

Chapter 1

Understanding Academic Integrity

Introduction

This chapter situates academic integrity within the context of the purpose of education and explains how academic misconduct, which includes plagiarism, nullifies the ideals of education. It begins by examining the general view of the role of education worldwide before defining academic integrity and establishing the connection between this and the purpose of education. The discussion extends to the six fundamental values of academic integrity of the International Center for Academic Integrity (ICAI) which are then contrasted with the "Six Pillars of Character" advocated by the Josephson Institute of Ethics (2009). The definition of academic misconduct and its many manifestations in the education system from the admission stage to the award of degrees are also examined.

Academic Integrity Defined

"The integrity of men is to be measured by their conduct, not by their professions" (Junius Quotes 2020). This suggests that one's conduct is a window into one's character, revealing more about a person than what is said. *Cambridge Dictionary* defines integrity as "the quality of being honest and having strong moral principles *that you refuse to change.*" Based on this definition, one either has or does not have integrity since it is not situational nor dependent on circumstances. A similar approach should be taken with regard to academic integrity which deals specifically with the formal pursuit of education, research and scholarship and is a term commonly used within post-secondary education and discourses.

The term academic integrity was popularized by Don Macabe, founding president of the Center for Academic Integrity (Academic Integrity 2020), and in terms of its definition, while there are many, only two will be focused on. The first is Tauginiene et al.'s which is succinct in covering the major aspects of the concept by stating that it is "[c]ompliance with ethical and professional principles, standards and practices by individuals or institutions in education, research and scholarship" (2018, 7–8). The second is that of the ICAI which identifies the values that the concept embodies by defining it as "commitment, even in the face of adversity, to six fundamental values: honesty, trust, fairness, respect, responsibility, and courage" (International Center for Academic Integrity 2014, n.p.). These two definitions are strikingly different with regard to what is emphasized as Tauginiene, and colleagues do not allude to the motivation behind the display of integrity, but rather focus on compliance which could be the result of the pressure from outward systems or inner motivation. Further differences are observed when Tauginiene and colleagues separate the ethical principles from the professional ones. In reality, the differences between these two sets of principles could be questioned as there is such a concept as professional ethics.

Looking at Taugiene et al.'s definition, it could also be argued that ethics are not separated from self, even to the extent that it is difficult to separate the person from the profession. These authors also contextualize academic integrity as being pertinent to education, research and scholarship. Additionally, they are of the view that academic integrity is not just the purview of the individual but also of the institutions (2018). ICAI, on the other hand, provides a broader definition which lacks the contextual elements of education, research and scholarship and proposes that academic integrity goes beyond compliance to commitment, signalling an inner drive to act ethically. This is based on the centre's six fundamental values of academic integrity which will now be discussed.

ICAI

No discussion of academic integrity would be complete without reference to the ICAI founded by Don McCabe in 1992, and originally called the Center for Academic Integrity (International Center for Academic Integrity 2019). Describing itself as a "consortium of 200 colleges and universities" (International Center for Academic Integrity 2014, n.p.), this centre was initially founded "to combat cheating, plagiarism, and academic dishonesty in higher education," and has evolved to where it now has an international mandate and serves its constituents through assessment services, resources, consultations and an annual conference (International Center for Academic Integrity 2019). In 2014, the centre had over 1,200 members at 250 universities in 19 countries worldwide (International Center for Academic Integrity 2014). ICAI noted that higher education institutions (HEIs) have traditionally focused on academic dishonesty at the expense of academic integrity. It further states that it is not often that they "identify and describe their commitment to the principles of integrity in terms that are at once positive and practical" (2014, n.p.). The centre has sought to correct this imbalance by positing what it refers to as the fundamental values of academic integrity – honesty, trust, fairness, respect, responsibility and courage (which was later added to the original five principles). ICAI believes if institutions focus on developing these principles, the negative focus on academic misconduct will decrease (International Center for Academic Integrity 2014). The six values are worth exploring in order to build a common understanding of what is involved in academic integrity from the perspective of ICAI, and to provide a better understanding for individuals and institutions that desire to move away from punitive measures for those who act dishonestly.

Honesty: Considered the cornerstone of the other values, honesty is difficult to define without mentioning the other virtues listed by ICAI. A compromise is therefore made by citing the attributes of an honest person as listed by the Josephson Institute of Ethics (JIE), which states that an honest person "tells the truth, is sincere, doesn't deceive, mislead, act devious or tricky, doesn't betray a trust, doesn't withhold important information in relationships of trust, doesn't steal, and doesn't cheat" (n.d.). ICAI advocates that honesty is important, considering that academic dishonesty "jeopardizes the welfare of academic communities and violates the rights of its members; it can also tarnish the reputation of the institution and diminish the worth of the degrees it grants" (International Center for Academic Integrity 2014).

JIE states that truthfulness, sincerity and candour are the three dimensions of honesty and that individuals should seek to be honest in both communication and conduct. It further explicates that honesty in communication is speaking the truth as best as we know it, while honesty in conduct is following the rules (n.d., 104). ICAI advocates that in learning, research and teaching, there should be a constant search for honesty, which should be reflected in academic policies and community practices (International Center for Academic Integrity 2014). This perspective is shared by Ahearne (2011, 3) who believes honesty is the best policy for both the individual and the long-term health of the research community as it is a requisite for science to advance. JIE advocates that cheating, which breaches the principle of honesty, is wrong because it deceives and also puts at a disadvantage those who are being honest (n.d., 104).

Trust: ICAI is of the view that trust, defined by *Oxford Dictionary* as a "firm belief in the reliability, truth, or ability of someone or something," thrives where honesty is practised. JIE agrees that honesty is an integral component of trustworthiness, which they describe as the most complicated of the six core values, and that when there is trust there is little need for monitoring as it is expected that obligations will be met (n.d., 104). According to ICAI, trust is developed by institutions and promoted by faculty when the former set clear, consistent academic standards and the latter clear guidelines for assignments and assessment (2014, n.p.). ICAI believes students are an important component in this relationship as they are expected to produce work that is thoughtful, honest and genuine (2014). Many benefits accrue when there is a culture of trust in the academy which makes individuals willing to use the works of others. Trust is also important as it provides the atmosphere for collaboration and information sharing without fear of this information being used in an unacceptable manner (Kucharska 2017).

Outside of the academy, trust is also important as it encourages others to "believe in the value and meaning of scholarly research, teaching, and degrees" (International Center for Academic Integrity 2014), and Thornton (2014) posits that trust cannot exist without ethics and vice versa. Žalec advocates that trust is important in education as "trust in teachers and faith in educational institutions is a necessary condition for their proper functioning" (2013, 65), and in concurring with its importance Schlesinger, Cervera and Pérez-Cabañero identified trust as one of the antecedents of alumni loyalty (2017, 2178). Institutions will therefore have to give careful attention to developing trust as an institutional value in order to ensure that they are effective in executing their mandate.

Fairness: JIE acknowledges that although overall there is little disagreement that we should practise fairness, applying this principle daily can be challenging because it is "probably more subject to legitimate debate and interpretation than any other ethical value" (n.d., 107). According to ICAI, whereas fairness is firstly concerned with being fair, consistent and reasonable, it also requires the appropriate responses when an individual breaches the acceptable code of behaviours (2014), and therefore JIE posits that fairness involves process, impartiality and equity (n.d., 107). ICAI further advocates that there are many aspects to fairness. For example, faculty has a right to expect fairness from colleagues and also from students. Students are expected to be fair to each other, alumni, faculty and also administrators, who demonstrate fairness when they develop and implement policies that help to create an atmosphere conducive to developing and practising academic integrity (2014). Hooker opines that the word fair is used in many different contexts and that fairness "depends on a wide range of considerations" (2005, 350). In spite of this lack of precision with regard to the word, he contends that its absence is easily noticeable as there is likely to be inconsistent application and interpretation of rules (329).

Respect: Respect for self and others engaged in the scholarly community is vital for beneficial and successful interactions among its members because the "most dynamic and productive learning environments are those that foster active engagement, including rigorous testing, spirited debate, and lively disagreements over ideas tempered by respect for those who voice them" (International Center for Academic Integrity 2014, n.p.). JIE states that respect embodies the notions of "civility, courtesy, decency, dignity, autonomy, tolerance and acceptance" and describes a respectful person as one who "treats others with consideration, and doesn't resort to intimidation, coercion or violence except in extraordinary and limited situations to defend others, teach discipline, maintain order or achieve social justice" (n.d., 106).

Middleton advocates three reasons we should care about respect, including self-respect. These are self-respect is an integral part of the image of our self; social respect mediates our social interactions; and respect matters because it links to social justice (2004, 227). On the one hand, ICAI states that students show respect by participating in discussions, doing their best, owning their learning and seeking after new knowledge. The Center opines that faculty need to respect students and their ideas and value their perspectives even though they might differ from theirs (2014). O'Grady speaks to the importance of respect in the research process, indicating that students feel respected when they contribute to research by providing data, and the researcher conveys appreciation (2016, 229). He believes the respect accorded to research participants is exemplified through courtesy, listening and sensitivity, and these likely result in truthfulness in research responses (250).

Responsibility: According to JIE, life is full of choices, and this calls for responsible actions which means "being in charge of our choices and, thus, our lives. It means being accountable for what we do and who we are. It also means recognizing that our actions matter and we are morally on the hook for the consequences." A responsible person is accountable, pursues excellence, exercises self-restraint and is able to respond to expectations (n.d., 106). Different actors on the academic stage have different responsibilities for academic integrity. ICAI advocates both personal responsibility and shared concern.

Responsible individuals are expected to ensure that they do what is right while simultaneously "standing up against wrongdoing, resisting negative peer pressure" (International Center for Academic Integrity 2014) in order to ensure that academic honesty is not compromised. In their discussion about how to build shared responsibility for student learning, Conzemius and O'Neill (2001) identified focus, reflection and collaboration as central components, explaining that shared responsibility is an ongoing process which is built from within when stakeholder groups accept their roles and possess the knowledge, skills and opportunities to make student learning a reality.

Courage: This last addition to the fundamental values was made in 2013 and is defined as "the capacity to act in accordance with one's values despite fear" (International Center for Academic Integrity 2014). This carries the expectation that learners will not only hold themselves to high moral and ethical standards but that they will also hold their colleagues to these same high standards. Although there is the possibility of reprisal or negative consequences, one is expected to do the right thing and this should be manifested even in situations that test one's beliefs. Woodard and Pury note that research on courage is limited despite its wide acceptance and so they deem it the "overlooked core virtue" (2007, 135). They advocate that one reason for this scant attention is the difficulty of defining courage and present various types such as: moral, social, physical, vital and psychological. The type of courage that concerns this discussion of academic integrity is moral courage, which is "often identified in situations where there is a morally desirable goal" (Woodard and Pury 2007, 137).

ICAI acknowledges the challenges in translating these values into action; however, it believes that through various programmes and activities, students can be taught these fundamental values that are important not just for higher education. The centre, therefore, provides a range of resources that institutions can use to help in the process. In reinforcing this call to action, Nannerl Keohane, president of Duke University, states that "[r]aising the level of student academic integrity should be among our highest priorities on college and university campuses" (International Center for Academic Integrity 2014).

Six Pillars of Character: As established previously, integrity is intricately linked to a person's character. The JIE postulates that there are six pillars of character: trustworthiness, respect, responsibility, fairness, caring and citizenship. A comparison of ICAI's six fundamental values of academic integrity with the six pillars of character identified by the JIE demonstrates the overlapping relationship between ethics and academic integrity. Four of the six values advocated by the JIE are the same as those proffered by ICAI. JIE is described as a nonpartisan, nonsectarian organization located in Los Angeles, California, and its six values were articulated in the Aspen Declaration and were identified by a group of youth development experts in 1992 as "core ethical values that transcend cultural, religious and socioeconomic differences" (2009). The shared elements on the ICAI and the JIE's lists are trustworthiness (called trust by ICAI), respect, responsibility and fairness. The differences arise in that whereas ICAI has courage and honesty, the JIE has caring and citizenship. The last two can be explained as reflective of the wider social and global mandate of JIE when juxtaposed with the academic mandate of the ICAI.

JIE describes caring as the heart of ethics and explains that it is concerned with good relations between and among people. It goes beyond loving humanity to loving individuals and being able to empathize and sympathize with others. JIE advocates that caring speaks more to motives than to actions (n.d., 107). Heater posits that citizenship has legal, social and political rights and responsibilities (1999), and JIE focuses on the social facet of citizenship which is concerned with our relationship to the community to include civic virtues and duties and our behaviour. JIE advocates that good citizenship not only goes beyond knowing and obeying the law but also includes volunteerism, staying informed and doing all that can be done to preserve the current society, and seeking to ensure a legacy is left for future generations (n.d.).

An understanding of these virtues as postulated by ICAI and JIE is important to Caribbean institutions that desire to develop academic integrity programmes. However, what is evident from the brief discussion is that institutions will have to ensure that they have a good understanding of what these are and how they can be developed.

The Role of Education

All societies engage in some form of education which Roser and Ortiz-Ospina (2016) describe as a fundamental resource usually considered a duty that the government is expected to perform for its people. With the expansion in education over the past two centuries (Roser and Ortiz-Ospina 2016) comes the need to ensure the quality mandate is given careful attention as a lack of balance will defeat the purpose of education. Academic integrity is central to the purpose of education which Foshay (1991) states is to "bring people to as full a realisation as possible of what it means to be a human being" (277). He contends that subsumed within this broad statement is the idea that education develops human intellect, serves social needs, contributes to the economy, creates an effective workforce, prepares the young for careers or jobs and promotes political and social ideologies. Miller, in describing education as an intentional social activity, notes that it is designed to serve social purposes and that it is the tool by which "a society and a people construct their future" which should be "consistent with the long-term and survival and perceived destiny of a people" (2005, 67–68).

In discussing the goal of education, Leo-Rhynie notes that graduates must be prepared for employability that is very complex, involving myriad skills, subskills, attitudes and attributes. She fulsomely goes on to say:

> The development of students' learning skills are central, with emphasis and importance being placed on learning to learn, involvement in autonomous learning, critical thinking and problem solving, accomplishing the transfer of theory to practise, and knowing how organisations work. As important, however, are the attributes of self-understanding, self-reliance, conflict management, flexibility and teamwork as well as being able to manage transitions, deal with numerous and complex life choices and commit to lifelong learning. . . . Employability facilitates the preparation of graduates for self-employment and encourages the development of an entrepreneurial spirit, and an approach to work that sees business development and ownership as a viable career option. (2007, 12)

This detailed enumeration of what should be attained through the process of transformation reveals the importance of placing emphasis on the process so as to achieve these outcomes.

Given the significant role of education in society, most societies expend significant efforts on their institutions of education in the form of establishing policies and legal frameworks for their operation and through the investment of significant financial and human resources. The following examples from the Caribbean illustrate the extent of financial and human resources commitment that make an education system function. With the average years of compulsory schooling in the Caribbean Community (CARICOM) being approximately 10.3 (George 2016), students in this region spend a considerable part of their youth being educated and this comes with a hefty price tag. For example, for the 2018–19 fiscal year, the Jamaican government ministry which received the second-largest amount of money was education ($104.6 billion), surpassed only by the Ministry of Finance (Barnes 2018), and this represents a $2.7 billion increase over the previous year (Patterson 2018). In addition, in July 2018, approximately 5.5 per cent of the Jamaican workforce was employed in education (Statistical Institute of Jamaica 2017).

In 2009, the education sector in Barbados, the fifth highest employer of labour, employed 6.8 per cent of the persons in the workforce (Barbados n.d.). In 2017, St Vincent and the Grenadines was listed among the top twenty countries in the world which spent most of their gross domestic product on education, whereas Jamaica was listed at number thirty-three and Barbados at number sixty-two (Education Spending, Percent of GDP

– Country Rankings 2021). This high investment in the education sector, the importance of education in determining the future of society, and the number of persons who benefit from the offerings are evidence of the government's commitment to the education sector. Institutions, especially those at the secondary and post-secondary levels, have to implement systems to ensure the transformation process is effective in creating the kind of output that will be beneficial to advancing the cause of society. This would justify the amount of money spent on education in the Caribbean.

Examinations, which are a feature of the global education system, are "a major and universal means" to assess achievement, select qualified individuals and distribute limited opportunities (Hallak and Poisson 2007, 231). Examinations are able to effectively meet this need because they provide the information on which objective and neutral decisions can be made (231) within a global marketplace where migration of labour from one country to another is the norm. This is true in the Caribbean where those who are deemed to have met the requirements of the system are awarded the credentials. These certificates indicate the individual has achieved at least the minimum level of education and serve as evidence that transformation has taken place. Due to the critical nature of education in the transformation process, and the importance placed on these examinations, it is paramount that the process is conducted with integrity which means having in place systems for ensuring this.

Access to education for all has become one of the goals of higher education in the twenty-first century and it is also a matter of great concern to the governments of the region (Grant-Woodham 2007, 135). Holding and Burke advocate that access will require increased attention to the development and maintenance of standards as these are important to the reputation of HEIs in the Caribbean. In addition, they believe that these standards are one way of assuring employers that certificates and degrees awarded by institutions are of the required quality (2005). So critical is the role of these tertiary institutions in the region, the Honourable P.J. Patterson, former prime minister of Jamaica, stated "[a] large part of the economic success of the future resides in the hands of the U.W.I. and other universities and tertiary institutions" (Patterson 2003, 10).

In discussing the tension between shrinking public funding for universities and the increasing need for university education, Clayton raises a valuable question regarding maintaining the quality of education while increasing access. He inquires, "How is it going to be possible to increase the scale of provision of higher education on the basis of reduced resources, without sacrificing quality?" (2003, 138). Part of the quality that Clayton mentioned would be ensuring that certification awarded to graduates represents their own efforts and is an indication that they have met the standards established by the global, regional and local education systems. Academic integrity is one set of standards that all academic institutions must give attention to as a way of "maintaining the reputation of tertiary and higher education institutions in the region" (Holding and Burke 2005, 417).

The Education System as an Open Social System

Educational institutions, and by extension education systems, can be described as social systems. They conform to the definition of a social system as "an organization of individuals into groups or structures that have different functions, characteristics, origin or status" (Social System 2020). Hoy and Miskel also agree that academic institutions are social systems (2005, 18) characterized by the interdependence of parts, clearly defined population, differentiation from their environments, a complex network of social relationships and their own unique culture (22). Figure 1.1 presents a graphical representation of the open social system model made relevant to individual institutions at the basic level and national, regional and global systems of education at a more advanced level. This model was originally developed by Hoy and Miskel and was adapted for this work to

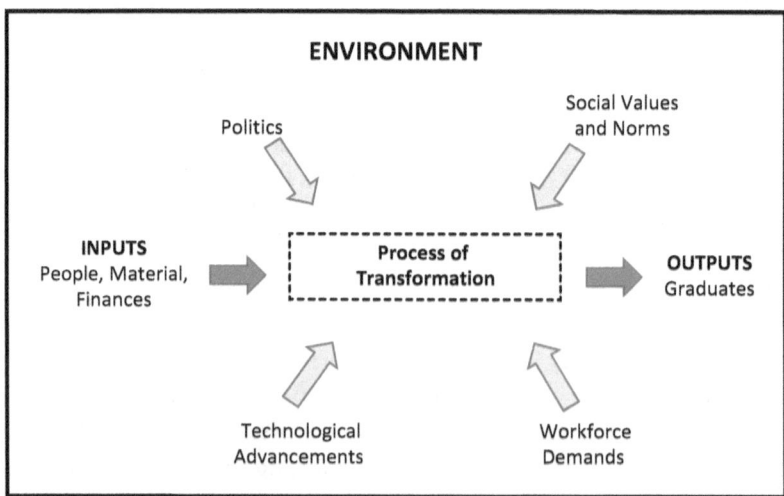

Figure 1.1. An open system with reference to educational institutions and systems.

show the dynamic environment in which the school exists and the many forces impacting its operation.

Hoy and Miskel postulate that schools are open systems because they are impacted by the values, history, politics and the availability of resources of the society in which they exist (2005, 22–23). In addition, technological dynamism and the demands of work also impact the knowledge, skills and competencies required by the workplace and in turn determines what is taught in schools. As an open social system, the school uses human, financial, physical and information resources (called "inputs" in figure 1.1) from the environment. Transformation or learning is accomplished through the use of technology and the administrative functions and is a product of the interactions between students and teachers (Lunenburg 2010). Figure 1.1 demonstrates that the school uses these resources from the environment to provide education within a system impacted by the political will and decisions as well as by the values and norms of society, technological advancements and workforce demands.

Social systems are peopled by individuals who engage with these systems based on their needs as well as roles (Hoy and Miskel 2005, 22). These individuals are one category of inputs into the education system and are involved in the process of transformation as both the raw materials (students) and processors (teachers, lecturers, administrators). Students exit the system as graduates, possessing the knowledge, skills and attitudes that will serve them in executing their roles as responsible citizens contributing to society. The environment, which includes social, political and economic forces, is critical to the success of the school, and school administrators have to "manage and develop 'internal' operations while concurrently monitoring the environment and anticipating and responding to the 'external' demands" (Lunenburg 2010, 3). Failure to do so might result in a product that does not meet the needs of the environment. Feedback within the system is important to maintaining stability and critical to the existence and survival of the system (The School as an Open System 2014).

Due to the normative nature of social systems, formal and informal rules and regulations prescribe acceptable behaviour. The rules within the system are usually reflective of the values and norms of the wider society, and when the prescribed norms are breached in social systems, penalties are effected because social systems are sanction-bearing, a concept that is at the heart of this work. Hoy and Miskel note, "[N]orms for behavior are enforced with reward and punishment" (2005, 23). Academic integrity can be viewed as one prescribed norm, and academic dishonesty, the breach of the prescribed norm, usually results in the application of the stipulated penalty. Within this system, there is ongoing synergy between the parts and the whole. Dynamism in the whole will affect the parts and vice versa, and in figure 1.1, this is represented by the arrows.

Social systems have boundaries that differentiate them from their environment (Hoy and Miskel 2005). These allow a constant flow of ideas, information, resources and personnel, among other things, between the environment and the system as represented by the broken boundary lines in figure 1.1. What flows across this boundary depends on the synergy between the environment and the system. However, central to the system is the transformation process, and the education system is responsive to the needs of the environment even while it is being shaped by the dynamism of the social environment within which it exists.

Academic Dishonesty

Academic integrity is central to research and scholarship and globalization has highlighted the need for trusted and objective academic systems. Implementing systems and measures to ensure academic integrity is a challenge in both secondary and post-secondary institutions. Breaches of academic integrity and the compromise of quality control mechanisms are likely to have negative consequences. Despite the importance ascribed to academic integrity, individuals and institutions sometimes fail to live up to the tenets of ethical behaviour. Hallak and Poisson (2007) advance the view that no country is exempted from academic fraud, while Pincus and Schmeklin state that "[o]ne of the main issues that emerge from the literature relates to inconsistencies in the definition of academically dishonest behaviors and the lack of consensus and a general understanding of academic dishonesty among all members of the campus community" (2003, 196). This observation was made almost two decades ago and has not changed since then as the definitions and classifications that have been proffered are broad and ambiguous (Louw 2017; Kokkinaki, Demoliou and Iakovidou 2015).

Academic dishonesty, which is the antithesis of academic integrity, has been defined as "[m]orally culpable behaviours perpetrated by individuals or institutions that transgress ethical standards held in common between other individuals and/or groups in institutions of education, research, or scholarship" (Tauginienė et al. 2018, 7, quoting from Jordon 2013). Another word sometimes used in discussions about academic dishonesty is academic fraud defined as:

> any prescribed action taken in connection with an examination or test that attempts to gain unfair advantage (or in some cases to place a candidate at a

disadvantage). This action might be taken by an examination candidate, a teacher, a supervisor, an official, an employee of an examination authority, or anyone with an interest in the performance of a candidate. But the scope of academic fraud goes beyond examination or test issues: It also covers credentials, diplomas, research, academic journals and publications (Hallak and Poisson 2007, 231)

There is a legal connotation to the use of the term "fraud" not conveyed by the term academic dishonesty, which carries a moral and ethical tone. Academic dishonesty is manifested in many forms and is practised by students at all levels of the systems, and by academics who are expected to understand the importance of practising academic integrity. Following are some examples of academic dishonesty among scholars.

Retraction Watch presents a list of the top 10 retractions of 2017, and some of the cases are cited here as examples of academic misconduct among scholars or members of the academy. In 2017, more than one thousand items were retracted from Medical Literature Analysis and Retrieval System Online (MEDLINE), a bibliographic database containing information on articles from academic journals in the fields of medicine, nursing, pharmacy, dentistry, veterinary medicine and health care. In addition, *Retraction Watch* also recorded that in one day a total of 107 entries were retracted from the journal *Tumor Biology* as a result of fake peer review. Upon investigation, it was discovered that five hundred Chinese scientists were guilty of academic misconduct and the journal was delisted from the Web of Science database.

Another reported case of academic dishonesty involved the resignation of the entire editorial board of the *International Journal of Occupational and Environmental Health* due to interference in the journal's operations. This was because a paper written by an editor was withdrawn without adequate explanation. There was also the case of a paper written by two Swedish researchers that was retracted due to the fabrication of research results. The retraction of papers written by two Nobel Prize winners also made the top 10 list due to the inability of the researchers to reproduce the results of the research (Top 10 Retractions of 2017).

Impact of Academic Misconduct: Hallak and Poisson noted that cheating has personal, institutional and global impact. In the first instance, it negatively impacts student learning and raises questions about the quality of the credentials and the integrity of credential holders. Next, it can result in significant damage to an institution's reputation, and, globally, it can create doubt about the assessment systems and academic degrees and create distrust in addition to endangering the education export business (2007, 233–34). One of the cases of academic dishonesty which shows the dangers of acting unethically is that of Japanese researcher Yoshihiro Sato. He falsified research results that were later used as the basis for new clinical trials and developing treatment guidelines for patients with bone issues. The findings of the studies based on fabricated data negatively affected many lives. Kupferschmidt records the extent of this deception and reported that Sato committed suicide when the deception was revealed (2018). It is, therefore, not advisable to dismiss academic integrity as an insignificant issue as to do so might have far-reaching consequences. Whereas institutions cannot make individuals act ethically, they are expected to harness and deploy the required human and other types of resources to help their constituents develop integrity. This will ensure that the transformation process achieves the expected outcomes as elucidated by Leo-Rhynie (2007, 12).

Cheating in high school can be an indicator of possible dishonest behaviour in adulthood. A study conducted by the JIE found that those who admitted to cheating on a test in high school are "far more likely as adults to lie to their spouses, customers and employers and to cheat on expense reports and insurance claims" (2009). Nonis and Swift, in attempting to discover the connection between academic dishonesty and workplace behaviour, surveyed a sample of 1051 business students from six campuses. They found that those who practised academic dishonesty at school were more likely to do the same at the workplace. Harding, et al. also supported this finding; however, their results went beyond the action of the participants. They found "substantial commonalities . . . between the elements of the decision-making process with regard to academic dishonesty and unethical behavior in professional practice." They also found a "strong relationship between self-reported involvement in prior academic dishonesty (high school) and self-reported involvement in present dishonest behavior (college and workplace) of engineering students" (2004, 318).

The implications of these findings cannot be lost on a prospective employer or those in academia whose responsibility is to ensure that academic honesty is the norm and not the exception. These findings seem to suggest that students who cheated in high school are likely to cheat in college and will continue this unacceptable behaviour in the workplace. Institutions which are in the business of preparing individuals for the workforce, therefore, have the responsibility to ensure they employ all the necessary strategies to stem this unethical behaviour.

Some forms of academic dishonesty such as plagiarism, copying from someone else's examination script, purchasing term papers, stealing a test or forging of a university document are apparent to everyone. Other more questionable forms of academic behaviours are still debated among faculty, students and administrators. These include collaborating on homework and take-home examinations when individual work is specified, handing in the same work for two separate classes, or inappropriately utilizing the services of a tutor or a writing centre (Fass 1986). To get a better understanding of the types of academic misconduct, a compilation was made of the lists from the top ten universities globally for 2018. By far the most popular form of academic dishonesty was plagiarism, cited by the ten universities. The second most popular forms of academic dishonesty based on their listings were unauthorized collaboration and facilitation. At the bottom of the list were behaviours mentioned only once, that is by one of the ten institutions under examination: cheating; revising and resubmitting work without permission; representing another person's work as your own; receiving and giving aid which is not allowed; tutoring schools and term paper companies; falsification; deliberate, dangerous, reckless or negligent deviations from research practices; impersonation and academic fraud. This listing points to the lack of agreement among HEIs with regards to the behaviours that constitute academic misconduct including plagiarism.

Plagiarism: The Most Popular Form of Academic Misconduct

The volume of literature available on plagiarism is an indication of the interest it has generated in academia. Plagiarism is practised by graduates and undergraduates as well as faculty, and the topic has been studied by all academic disciplines and examined from the perspective of gender and geographical locations as researchers seek to get a better understanding of the phenomenon and how to stop or reduce its occurrence. The continued development of information technology has made this even more difficult by providing additional opportunities for cheating, although it has also made detection easier (Marsden 2014; Nilsson 2015). Don McCabe in his survey of over 63,700 US undergraduate and 9,250 graduate students over the course of three years (2002–5) unearthed the findings displayed in table 1.1. The information was self-reported and should be interpreted against the background that self-reporting is impacted by the honesty/image management, the introspective ability of participants, varying understanding and interpretation of the items, and respondents' interpretation of the rating scale used (Hoskin 2012, 1).

Based on table 1.1, undergraduate students plagiarized more than graduate students with the most prevalent type of plagiarism being copying and paraphrasing without giving the required credit (38 per cent graduate

Table 1.1. Plagiarism among graduate and undergraduate students

Actions	Undergraduates (%)	Graduates (%)
Paraphrasing/copying few sentences from an internet source without footnoting it	36	24
Paraphrasing/copying few sentences from a written source without footnoting it	38	25
Fabricating/falsifying a bibliography	14	7
Copying materials "almost word for word from a written source without citation"	7	4
Turning in work done by another	7	3
Obtaining paper from term paper mill	3	2

students, 25 per cent undergraduate). The use of the internet to facilitate cheating was also high as 36 per cent of the undergraduate students engaged in this behaviour compared to 24 per cent of the graduate students. Additional findings showed that undergraduates were twice as likely to engage in falsifying or fabricating a bibliography, copying word for word and not providing a citation, and submitting work done by someone else. Obtaining a paper from a term paper mill, considered contract cheating in the literature, was done by a small number of the sample with only 3 per cent of the undergraduate students and 2 per cent of the graduate ones admitting that they engaged in this practice.

Plagiarism is also evident in secondary education, although this has not received the same level of attention as in higher education. McCabe's surveys of over seventy thousand high school students at over twenty high schools in the United States demonstrated that 64 per cent of students admitted to cheating on a test, 58 per cent admitted to plagiarism and 95 per cent said they participated in some form of cheating, whether it was on a test, plagiarism or copying homework (Plagiarism Facts and Stats 2017).

Given the pervasive nature of plagiarism, it is therefore important to begin to investigate the phenomenon from a Caribbean perspective. This should motivate educators to gather data to arrive at an informed perspective on the topic in order to develop programmes and policies aimed at assisting students to appreciate the importance of academy integrity and to practise it. An examination of the websites of universities in the Caribbean revealed an awareness of plagiarism evidenced by the inclusion of plagiarism policies and guidelines aimed at assisting students to practise academic honesty. Newspaper articles from across the Caribbean provided anecdotal references to cases of plagiarism in education as well as in other sectors of Caribbean society. Considering that plagiarism is such a significant challenge to education systems internationally, there is a need for the exploration of the manifestations of this phenomenon in the region.

Conclusion

As open social systems, schools are tasked with the social responsibility of moulding individuals capable of shaping the future of the society in which they live. Based on the importance and uniqueness of their roles, these systems are expected to reflect the norms and values of the societies within which they exist, and the students are expected to abide by certain prescribed guidelines. In cases where institutions or individuals fall short of these ideals, they are likely to face sanctions, as this is one of the characteristics of the social system. Academic integrity represents one of the ideals of global education embodying principles of trust, honesty, fairness, respect, responsibility and courage as advocated by the ICAI. While these principles are expected to guide the actions of members of the academic community, some academics and students sometimes fail to practise the ideals of academic integrity by engaging in academic misconduct. This is likely to have personal and institutional repercussions such as sullying the character of the individual academic, possibly destroying his career and bringing the institution into disrepute. Plagiarism has been identified as the most widely practised form of academic misconduct, and it is present in the Caribbean; hence, the following chapters will explore its manifestation globally as reported in the literature, while part 2 will present studies on plagiarism in the region.

Chapter 2

Defining and Understanding Plagiarism

Introduction

This chapter sets out to clarify the concept of plagiarism by first discussing the various definitions of the term, which the author then uses as a foundation on which to create a new and more comprehensive definition. Afterwards, the chapter delves into the various types of plagiarism, giving special attention to intentional, unintentional and self-plagiarism before going on to present some of the notable cases of plagiarism worldwide. It concludes with a discussion of contract cheating, sometimes mistaken as plagiarism, the new phenomenon that is that is on the increase as a result of the creation and use of the internet.

Defining Plagiarism

All members of the scholarly community are expected to practise intellectual honesty and transparency, which means giving due respect to the originators of the ideas, data and works consulted in the process of carrying out academic work. Failure to do so through a lack of proper referencing or a display of other forms of poor scholarship indicates a serious gap in the members' learning process and can often result in unethical conduct, like plagiarism, which can be detrimental to their future careers. Even if the plagiarism was unintentional, it is of serious concern mainly because academic work necessarily builds on what has gone before. There is thus an overwhelming need to learn how to appropriately use and cite others' work. Hence, this is a key skill every scholar should learn (Why Does Academic Integrity Matter 2015).

An examination of the etymology of the word "plagiarism" is instructive for the reader to arrive at an understanding of the term and the practice. Bailey (2011b) reports that the word "plagiarus" was first used by the Roman poet Martial, who lived in the first century, to describe individuals who were using his work without ensuring that he benefitted financially. Bailey (2011b) further notes that prior to this, the word was used to describe the kidnapping of slaves or the enslavement of a free person. According to the

Online Etymology Dictionary, the word "plagiarism" came into the English language in 1620. It originated from the Greek "plagion" and found its way into Latin as "plagium," meaning "a kidnapping." The word "plagiarus," derived from "plagium," was later used to refer to a kidnapper or seducer (Literary Discourse: Plagiarism in Academic Writing 2014). The word found its way into the English language as "plagiarism," a combination of the term "plagiary" and the suffix "ism," and was first recorded in the English dictionary in 1755 (Bailey 2011b). Although the word has since lost the original meaning of kidnapping, it still has a negative connotation (Berlinck 2011, 368) and is now used to mean or imply "literary theft" (Wrobel 2011, n.p.).

One critical and recurring issue evident in the research and discussion of plagiarism is the challenge of finding a generally accepted definition (Louw 2017, 116) as there is a lack of agreement on what actually constitutes plagiarism (Glendinning 2014, 214), which is often confused with other forms of academic misconduct, including contract cheating. This is likely to perplex students entering university based on the varying interpretation of what is meant by the term. Adding to the confusion could be their understanding of plagiarism gained from their primary and secondary education which often allows them to cut and paste without much emphasis on citing the sources of their information. Baker-Gardner and Smart discovered this to be so in the findings of a study conducted among Library and Information Studies students in Jamaica (2017, 197).

This lack of an agreed definition of plagiarism will also have implications for the creation of programmes aimed at developing academic honesty among students. Indubitably, there is a need for an agreed-on definition of plagiarism and academic dishonesty (Kokkinaki, Demoliou and Iakovidou 2015, 1), but until this is accomplished, this current research will discuss some definitions provided in the literature and use them as the foundation to articulate a fairly comprehensive definition which will serve to guide this work to ensure a common understanding among the readers.

Definitions of plagiarism are many and varied with some focusing on the "what" of plagiarism, while others on the effect. Moulton and Robinson, emphasizing both the "what" and the effects of plagiarism, boldly state that "plagiarists steal the work of others, taking for themselves the credit of ownership and thereby depriving the original authors of this benefit" (2002). In its syllabus for Electronic Document Preparation and Management, the Caribbean Examination Council (CXC), the regional body which administers examinations taken in the final years of secondary education, focuses more on the "what" of plagiarism. It is defined as "the use of someone's intellectual property without giving appropriate credit" (2012, 17). Here, the idea of stealing is softened, and this definition undoubtedly requires an understanding of what is meant by "intellectual property" and "appropriate credit," especially for students at the secondary level. This is the only way they will grasp the nature of these concepts in order to avoid plagiarism and act with integrity.

The generic definition of plagiarism provided by CXC is expanded by the University of the West Indies (UWI). It defines plagiarism as "the unacknowledged and unjustified use of the words, ideas or creations of another, including unjustified unacknowledged quotation and unjustified unattributed borrowing" (University of the West Indies 2011, 2). Whereas the terms "unjustified unacknowledged quotation" and "unjustified unattributed borrowing" might require some clarification for undergraduate students, the policy includes examples of what falls into these categories. The University of Cambridge goes beyond just the act of plagiarism in its definition and also focuses on intent, defining plagiarism as "submitting as one's own work, irrespective of intent to deceive, that which derives in part or in its entirety from the work of others without due acknowledgement" (2018). This definition advances the premise that ignorance of the rules of good writing and a lack of knowledge of acceptable citation practices will not negate the fact that a person has plagiarized.

Synonymous terms used for plagiarism are captured in figure 2.1, a graphic organizer, which shows similarities and differences as taken from Oxford University Press (Plagiarism 2018) and Thesaurus.com (Plagiarism 2018). Both sources agree to some synonyms for plagiarism such as

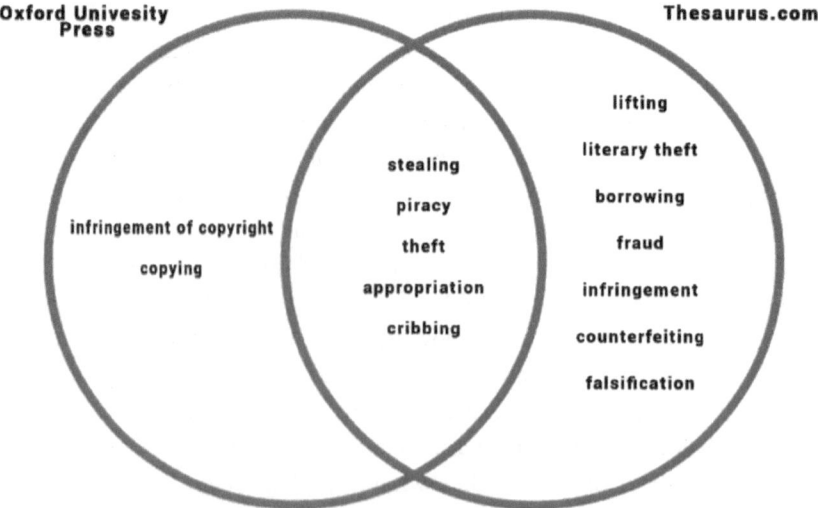

Figure 2.1. Synonyms for plagiarism.

stealing, piracy, theft, appropriation and cribbing (informal term). They also use other terms that are not shared, such as copying and infringement of copyright advocated by Oxford University Press, and counterfeiting, falsification and borrowing suggested by Thesaurus.com. The lack of agreement about the synonyms for plagiarism is again symptomatic of the challenges inherent in defining and understanding it. For the most part, synonyms such as fraud, falsification and counterfeiting can have other meanings apart from those conveyed by the word plagiarism.

Given the challenges in defining plagiarism, some institutions provide a description of the behaviours to ensure that confusion is reduced. Others enumerate the types of work that can be plagiarized, like the University of Cambridge (2018) providing the following categories of materials:

- text, illustrations, musical quotations, mathematical derivations, computer code and so on;
- material downloaded from websites or drawn from manuscripts or other media;
- published and unpublished material, including lecture handouts and other students' work.

This institution includes unpublished material which is not always given consideration when plagiarism is discussed.

The following is a list of the behaviours described as plagiarism by ETH Zurich, an institution listed in the top ten universities internationally for 2018 (Top Universities in the World 2018). ETH Zurich states a person plagiarizes when the person:

- uses extracts from another author's work without citing the source. This includes using material from the internet without citation;
- takes extracts from another author's work and changes (paraphrases) them slightly without citing the source;
- translates texts or extracts from foreign-language documents and submits them as his/her own work without citing the source (translation plagiarism);
- submits a paper in his/her name which he/she has actually commissioned another person (a ghost writer) to write;
- submits the work of another author in his/her own name (full plagiarism); and
- takes an extract from someone else's work, paraphrases it and indeed cites the original author, but somewhere other than in the context of the extract the source is hidden away.

(ETH Zurich 2021)

This list presents information in a manner that should be comprehensible to students, even those just entering higher education. However, it must be noted that this institution considers the practice of outsourcing assignments (referred to as contract cheating) as plagiarism, emphasizing the lack of a common understanding of plagiarism across institutions and jurisdictions.

A definition of plagiarism cannot be properly arrived at without a basic understanding of the concept of copyright as people sometimes tend to confuse the two. The latter is defined as "[t]he right of literary property as recognized and sanctioned by positive law [...] granted by statute to the author or originator of certain literary or artistic productions, whereby he is invested, for a limited period, with the sole and exclusive privilege of multiplying copies of the same and publishing and selling them" (What Is Copyright n.d.).

In discussing the differences between plagiarism and copyright violation, Bailey (2011b) notes that copyright is applicable only to works that are in a fixed format, while ideas, facts and general plot elements cannot be copyrighted, although they can be plagiarized. Bailey continued by stating plagiarism is an offence against the author, while copyright infringement is a violation against the copyright holder, who is not always the author. In copyright violation, the sole victim is the owner of the work, but plagiarism has two victims: the creator who was not given due credit for his work and the audience who is deceived into thinking the work belongs to the plagiarizer and in some cases might attribute credit to him unworthily (2013). Thus, we can conclude that plagiarism is largely considered an ethical and moral issue, hence, the labels "academic dishonesty" and "academic misconduct." On the other hand, copyright has legal connotations because the breach of these rights deprives creators of the financial benefits of their labour, so avoiding plagiarism is about properly apportioning intellectual credit, while copyright infringement is about collecting revenue.

The examination of the various definitions is instructive in helping the author arrive at an extended definition of plagiarism, encompassing the six common elements advocated by Pecorari (quoted in Nushi and Firoozkohi). These are "(1) an object (i.e., language, words, text), (2) which has been taken (borrowed, stolen, and so on)[,] (3) from a particular source (books, journals, Internet), (4) by an agent (student, person, academic), (5) without (adequate) acknowledgement and (6) with or without intention to deceive" (2017, 2). Plagiarism can be defined as the use of ideas or tangible intellectual products (words, graphics, images and so on) of a creator, whether published or unpublished, by another individual, intentionally or otherwise, without giving due credit to the creator using the established guidelines. This definition, though compact, is written in language that makes it understandable to students at both the secondary and the tertiary levels.

An individual could present ideas without necessarily writing these down, and these can then be copied. The term "tangible intellectual products" is inclusive enough for various categories of works. Although plagiarism is usually concerned with copying a published work, if an individual copies unpublished work, it follows the same principles and breaches the same rules as if the work was published. Using an established set of guidelines to indicate the source of the cited work or ideas is essential to the way scholars communicate and will minimize the chances of plagiarism occurring. Following these guidelines ensures that when individuals write, their ideas are clearly distinguishable from the works of others that have been used. Contravening established citation rules can and will lead to the incorrect use of the works of others resulting in plagiarism.

Types of Plagiarism

Plagiarism has been classified in a variety of ways, and several types of plagiarism have been identified in the literature. Firstly, plagiarism has been classified based on intent, resulting in intentional plagiarism also known as direct plagiarism (Bowdoin College n.d.). Secondly, there is also unintentional plagiarism (Shreiber 2018; Tabor 2013; Ison 2012; Baker-Gardner and Smart 2017). Thirdly, plagiarism is classified based on how it is done and this has resulted in the types of plagiarism as listed on the Plagiarism Spectrum advocated by Turnitin (White Paper: The Plagiarism Spectrum 2012). Turnitin, founded in 1998 in the USA, is currently used "by more than 30 million students at 15,000 institutions in 150 countries" and has offices in Mexico, the USA and Korea (Turnitin 2021). Students upload their papers to the database and receive an originality report which "shows the paper's text highlighted with any text that matches sources found in the Turnitin databases containing vast amounts of web content, previously submitted papers, and subscription-based journals and publications" (Does Turnitin Detect Plagiarism? 2013).

Based on the findings of a survey of nine hundred educators in secondary and higher education, Turnitin identified ten types of plagiarism and organized these on the plagiarism spectrum based on the levels of severity. These are displayed in table 2.1.

An assignment or any piece of writing might display a combination of two or more of the practices mentioned in the table. The spectrum is very valuable to help readers get a clear understanding of the various types of plagiarism.

Table 2.1. The plagiarism spectrum as presented by Turnitin

Rank	Name	Description
1	Clone	Submitting another's work, word-for-word, as one's own
2	CTRL + C	Work contains significant portions of text from a single source without alterations
3	Find-Replace	Changing keywords and phrases but retaining the essential content of the source
4	Remix	Paraphrases from multiple sources made to fit together
5	Recycle	Borrows generously from the writer's previous work without citation
6	Hybrid	Work combines perfectly cited sources with copied passages without citation
7	Mashup	Mixes copied material from multiple sources
8	Error	Includes citations to non-existent or inaccurate information about sources
9	Aggregator	Includes proper citation to sources, but the paper contains almost no original work
10	Retweet	Includes proper citation but relies too closely on the text's original wording and/or structure

Finally, plagiarism can be categorized based on what is plagiarized, such as ideas plagiarism (Office of Research Integrity 2018). The various approaches to categorization of plagiarism reflect the lack of discipline specificity which creates the opportunity for various individuals to examine it from varying perspectives since it is not "owned" by any one discipline. Plagiarism has also been classified based on whose work is being used, for example, self-plagiarism. An attempt will now be made to explain the major types of plagiarism for a better understanding by the reader.

Intentional Versus Unintentional Plagiarism: Sutherland-Smith notes the issue of intention is one of the focal points of the plagiarism debate (2008, 27). Ignorance or intent was investigated by Baker-Gardner and Smart in the Caribbean, and the findings showed that students were plagiarizing largely due to ignorance (2017, 196). Comparing the prevalence of these two types of plagiarism was not feasible because very little information was found in the literature about this. However, Gabriel makes reference to a study at the University of California which discovered that the majority of the 196 cases of plagiarism involved intent (2010b).

The University College of London acknowledges that plagiarism can be accidental and extrapolate the following causes of unintentional or accidental plagiarism:

- misunderstanding standard citation procedure;
- over-reliance on the original source material;
- following practices encouraged or accepted in the previous educational experience or culture;
- not fully understanding when group work ceases and individual work begins;
- compensating for poor English language skills; and
- poor note-taking practice. (n.d.)

The issues on the list can be successfully dealt with through educational interventions.

Some institutions take a zero-tolerance approach to plagiarism, believing that the severity of the penalties should not be influenced by the intent. Therefore, students who deliberately or unintentionally plagiarized are assigned the same penalty. Sutherland-Smith states that some teachers argue that intention should not be considered because students know that plagiarism is wrong and, therefore, they ought to be punished (2008, 22). Where this zero-tolerance approach exists, robust support systems must be in place to assist students in developing academic integrity, thus lessening the possibility of plagiarism due to ignorance. In some instances, it is believed that acts of plagiarism exist along a continuum from the least to the most serious, consequently, the penalties usually reflect the gravity of the offense (Walker and White 2014, 3).

Self-Plagiarism: Self-plagiarism defined as "any attempt to take any of your own previously published text, papers, or research results and make it appear brand new" (Mudrack 2018) is a highly contested concept that leads to arguments about whether one can "steal" from oneself (Lederman 2010). It is described by Gnanavel as the "latest ethical dilemma" (2014, 448), and as noted by the definition, is generally confined to published works. According to Ithenticate, one of the suite of products marketed by Turnitin, self-plagiarism can include not just the entire work but also portions of the previous work (2011). Mudrack, writing on behalf of American Journal Experts, proffers three reasons for self-plagiarism being wrong. He asserts that since the expectation is that a new publication will provide new knowledge, self-plagiarism defeats this outcome. In addition, it might be a breach of copyright and may result in a delay in the publication of the journal as publishers and editors conduct their investigations (2018).

Roig cites specific behaviours which can be considered self-plagiarism. These include dual publication and data aggregation and disaggregation. Dual publication is the appearance of the same article in more than one journal. This can be ethically done when the work is translated from one language to the next, with the knowledge of the editors and with both items being listed as duplicate publications (Roig 2015, 18). Data aggregation, disaggregation and segmentation are also practices that Roig encourages researchers to avoid in an attempt to ensure that the ethical guidelines governing plagiarism are not breached. Although the general understanding is that self-plagiarism is concerned only with published materials, Roig mentions that when students re-submit assignments for another course or class to get a grade, this is considered "double dipping" and is unethical (17).

Plagiarism across the Globe

From the literature, it can be concluded that plagiarism is ubiquitous irrespective of the state of development of the country, the type of the educational institution or the prestige it carries, even as Berlinck insists that plagiarism is also evident in public institutions and government (2011, 8). Dias and Bastos found that it was a widespread problem in secondary education in Europe "growing hand in hand with the increase of new technologies and easy access to information" (2014, 2530). The case seems to be the same at all levels of the education system in both the United States and the United Kingdom (Walker 1998, 89) and also in Vietnam (Tran, Huynh and Hòa 2018).

With regard to the developing world, Heitman and Litewka cite research which indicates the "high rates of perceived plagiarism and other misconduct in emerging research environments and developing nations" (2011, 105). This would suggest that Caribbean territories are likely to face similar challenges. Reports confirming the widespread nature of plagiarism show that elite institutions are not exempted either as the University of Oxford, in its supplement of March 2016, reported that the majority of disciplinary cases were for plagiarism, with most of the thirty cases involving graduate students in taught master's programmes. These were classified as "less than able" students who were guilty of cutting and pasting and paraphrasing the content without providing the required citations (University of Oxford Gazzette 2016, 391).

McCabe, founding president of International Center for Academic Integrity, contends that cheating behaviours are not only prevalent, but they are also on the increase in the USA with the percentage of students who plagiarized increasing from 10 per cent in 1999 to 40 per cent in 2006

(Bibliography – Academic Integrity 2006). This conclusion was drawn from data collected from a comprehensive survey which included fifty thousand undergraduate students from more than sixty universities. McCabe points to internet plagiarism as a concern, deducing that its prevalence might be due to a lack of knowledge of what "constitutes acceptable internet use" (Bibliography – Academic Integrity 2006). This is another facet of the discussion regarding unintentional plagiarism.

While the issue of plagiarism is of grave concern in HEIs, the top ten plagiarism stories of 2016 as reported by Bailey (2017) show the pervasiveness of plagiarism in other sectors of society worldwide. These ten cases are shown in table 2.2.

Of the ten cases identified, only four came from academia which indicates that, although plagiarism is largely classified as academic misconduct, it is present in all sectors of society. The politicians involved in three of the four cases listed in table 2.2 suffered no long-lasting consequences for their acts of plagiarism. This outcome is contrary to that of many others including Austrian minister Christine Aschbucher (France-Presse 2021); Hungarian president Pat Schmitt (Karasz 2012); and Petr Krcal and Tatna Mala, former government ministers in the Czech Republic (Second Czech Minister Resigns over Plagiarism 2018).

Whereas plagiarism in academia is viewed with disdain, Yusof is of the view that, outside academia, it does not carry the same weight (2009). He argues that ghostwriting and bureaucratic authorship are two practices that, based on the definition of plagiarism, would normally be construed as such. However, they do not carry the negative connotation that is evident in academia. He further explains that in politics and business, persons make speeches which are written by others as if they were the originator of the ideas, and usually the writer is not acknowledged. He further states some companies use researchers to conduct the formal research but use ghostwriters to prepare the report or article for publication. Enago Academy defines a ghostwriter as a "professional writer, whose contribution to producing a paper will be excluded in the final publication." In order to avoid problems with issues of authorship, Enago encourages authors to avoid ghost authorship and not to include the names of individuals who made no contribution to the research (2018).

What's so Wrong with Plagiarizing?

According to Bretag, "Plagiarism is one of the most vehemently derided breaches of academic integrity because it undermines the premise that scholarly work will make an original and honest contribution to an existing

Table 2.2. Top ten cases of plagiarism in 2016

Ranking	Alleged plagiarists	Details	Outcomes
1	Melania Trump	Ghostwriter Meredith McIver plagiarized parts of a speech previously delivered by Michelle Obama	Speechwriter attempted to resign, but this resignation was rejected
2	*New York Daily News*	Attribution in an article was "edited" out by the editor	The editor was fired
3	Two hundred professors from fifty universities in South Korea	Allegations of book plagiarism in which academics going up for promotions colluded with publishers to get their names on books they didn't write	The matter was taken to court. Both plagiarists and original authors were fined and in some cases sent to jail
4	Peruvian presidential candidate Cesar Acuña	Evidence of plagiarism found in his doctoral thesis	Investigations ongoing at the time of writing
5	Appa Rao Podile, former vice-chancellor of the University of Hyderabad, India	Was listed as a co-author on three papers that contained plagiarized passages	Requests were made for his removal from office by students
6	Kenny Florian sports commentator in the USA	Copied information verbatim from a YouTube video to write an analysis for an upcoming fight	Apologized and was suspended but later rehired
7	Mexico's president Peña Nieto	It is alleged that approximately 29% of his law thesis was plagiarized material	No negative repercussions
8	Nic Cavell	Copied the work of Christina Larson, a freelance reporter in China without giving credit	He was fired from his job

(Continued)

Table 2.2. (Continued) Top ten cases of plagiarism in 2016

Ranking	Alleged plagiarists	Details	Outcomes
9	Joanne Clancy	Made superficial adjustments to the novels of Ellis O'Hanlon and Ian McConnell from Northern Ireland and published these with new titles	Amazon removed the account of the alleged plagiarist, but the author whose work was plagiarized suffered emotional effects
10	Nigerian president	Plagiarized President Obama's speech	Scandal had no lingering effect on his political career

Source of information: Bailey (2017).

body of knowledge" (2013a, 1). One school of thought, though not very popular, proposes that it is impossible to steal the words and ideas of another person since the author still has ownership of the words that were plagiarized (Lynch 2006). However, this view is not representative of the majority of individuals who see plagiarism as wrong because it takes away from another person's original work and undermines academic and moral values (Xavier University Library n.d.), and students who plagiarize are depriving themselves of valuable opportunities for learning and achievement (Xavier University Library n.d.; Foust 2016). Another significant reason forwarded as to why everyone should be concerned about plagiarism is that students who believe that dishonest actions are acceptable are more likely to practise them while studying (Carpenter, Harding and Finelli 2006) and to perpetuate such dishonest behaviours in the workplace (Nonis and Swift 2010, 69; Josephson Institute of Ethics 2009). By so doing, they create a serious predicament for employers and organizations that need workers with integrity.

URKUND, the European company that provides text-matching software to secondary schools, HEIs and businesses, advances a more comprehensive response as to why plagiarism is wrong. The five reasons given are legal problems, academic integrity, knowledge, fairness and the working environment (URKUND 2005). Firstly, it notes that plagiarism can be a legal problem if inappropriate use is made of copyrighted materials. Secondly, plagiarism chips away at the very foundations of the intellectual process as it compromises the trust society has in its educational institutions. Thirdly, there is an expectation that an academic qualification is a reflection of knowledge and skills acquired through the process of education and training. Through plagiaristic behaviours, individuals circumvent the process of learning and acquire these qualifications for which they do not have the corresponding knowledge and expertise. Fourthly, plagiarism breaches the principle of fairness as it creates an uneven playing field by giving some individuals an unfair advantage over others. In cases where promotion and scholarships are dependent on grades and publication output, individuals who have not expended the required effort might be rewarded at the expense of others (URKUND 2005). Foust (2016) concurs, claiming the plagiarist receives undue credit. Finally, there are psychological effects from the unhealthy working environment for those involved, as faculty might still be required to teach students they previously reported.

Given that plagiarism is generally considered an ethical issue, in addition to the academic penalty the offender might also suffer what Ithenticate refers to as "reputational damage" such as a ruined reputation as a student, a professional or an academic as well as having to face the legal and financial repercussions. In the case of plagiarized medical research, the outcome can even include the loss of lives (Ithenticate n.d.). Wangaard presents a comprehensive listing of how cheating impacts both individuals and the institution. For the former, he notes that cheating is harmful because cheaters:

- rationalize the cheating which leads to more cheating;
- compromise their moral and ethical codes;
- fail to engage the authentic learning and mastery of academic materials;
- harm their reputation and they face consequences; and
- reduce the enjoyment of accomplishments earned through genuine effort (2016, 9).

For the institution and society, Wangaard notes that cheating:

- creates an environment of broken trust which will negatively impact the relationship between faculty and students;
- normalizes cheating which leads to more cheating and a lowering of institutional standards;
- challenges the moral authority of school leaders through lowered standards;
- awards cheaters through scholarships and other benefits; and,
- places pressure on honest students to protect their work from those who cheat (2016, 9).

These reasons make it important for individuals to avoid cheating, and for institutions to have structures in place to deter its occurrence.

Rothschild, in discussing the issue of plagiarism in China, explains that its negative effect goes beyond the individual and the institution by having the potential to damage the reputation of an entire country (2011). This is because the research community is not confined to geographical boundaries but is global and depends on research produced by various countries. The severity of this problem is captured in the words of Yang Wei, director of the National Natural Science Foundation of China, who is quoted in the *China Daily USA* as saying that research misconduct "is compromising academia and exerting a negative impact on the sound development of science and technology" (Academic Misconduct Cases Disclosed 2013).

Plagiarism in grant proposals and research writing is noted by Rothschild as one of the "large obstacles" to ensuring integrity in China (2011). Lim notes that, in the case of China, plagiarism has hindered the country's ability to advance scientifically by damaging its reputation. This has resulted in part, from "traditional Chinese culture, which values rote memorization and repetition and holds that copying a teacher's work is a way of learning." She also notes that money and politics add to the problem of culture to create a situation which has become challenging to change even though the consequences are obvious and impactful (Lim 2011). From all these reports, little doubt exists that the practice of plagiarism can and does have a negative impact on an individual's scholarship and reputation, the advancement of an academic discipline and even the reputation of a country.

While it is acknowledged that plagiarism undermines independent thought, shows a decline in moral or ethical standards and is as bad as cheating in examinations, students display ambivalence towards it. In research conducted by Howard, Ehrich and Walton, the students indicated that plagiarism was not "a big deal" and should be ignored in an otherwise high-quality paper, and they admitted that they could not write a good paper without plagiarizing (2014, 376). However, these responses are mild compared to those obtained by Hosny and Fatima (2014) in their study involving 144 graduate and undergraduate students of computer and information sciences attending a Saudi Arabian university. Although 72 per cent of the undergraduate students knew what plagiarism was, approximately 32 per cent of them paraphrased texts without noting the sources, and 40 per cent used direct materials from the works of others without quotation marks or citing the sources. These researchers also found that 35 per cent of the undergraduate students thought plagiarism was ethical, while 25 per cent of the graduate students shared this perspective.

These findings reveal that students are ambivalent in how they regard plagiarism, even when they know it is wrong, which would make it seem that the benefits that accrue make the fight against it more difficult, despite its deleterious effect in the short and long term on the individuals and their institutions. Institutions and even governments are making serious attempts to decrease the incidence of plagiarism due to its harmful effects. However, there are others who think lightly of the matter and seem to plagiarize due to the benefits, financial and otherwise (Chen 2018).

Contract Cheating

Contract cheating is a "form of cheating where a student submits work to a higher education provider for assessment, where they have used one or more of a range of services provided by a third party, and such input is not permitted" (The Quality Assurance Agency for Higher Education 2018, 3). Lancaster and Clarke identify the third parties as essay writing services; family, friends and other students; private tutors and copyediting services; agency websites and reverse classified. They explain that essay writing services operate on a large scale, are usually online and therefore are available across geographical boundaries, and so they are an immediate threat to academic integrity (2016, 3). On the other hand, family, friends and other students are easy to find and, although they have good intentions, they may cross the boundary between acceptable and unacceptable behaviours just like private tutors (Lancaster and Clarke 2016, 4). Copyediting services may be contracted to review and improve writing styles; however, the finished work may not reflect the students' effort as there is a thin line between editing and providing original work (Lancaster and Clarke 2016, 4). Another source of contract cheating is agency websites where students post details of the work they want to be done and interested contractors bid for the jobs (Lancaster and Clarke 2016, 4). In reverse classified, the final type of contract cheating, students advertise work and interested parties contract them privately (5).

The products of contract cheating are not limited to essays but in some cases involve theses or dissertations. In research conducted by Don McCabe for the period 2002–2005, 3 per cent of over 63,500 students admitted to having "obtaining a paper from a term paper mill" (Plagiarism Facts and Stats 2017).

The Quality Assurance Agency for Higher Education (QAAHE citing Beckham and Lam) states that the two driving factors behind contract cheating are motivation and opportunity (2018, 10) facilitated largely by the ubiquity of the internet which brings goods and services closer to the user. Sureda (2008) found that about 3.3 per cent of his sample of Spanish students admitted to engaging in contract cheating at some stage of their academic lives, and this is very similar to Newton's 3.5 per cent arising from a meta-analysis of studies from across the globe which were available online (2018, 6). This kind of academic cheating seems to be escalating over time in keeping with the increase in other forms of academic misconduct (Newton 2018, 5).

Bretag argues that, contrary to what some universities might think, contract cheating is not plagiarism (2018a). She supports her argument by explaining that students plagiarize when they use the works of others and fail to give credit. However, when students commission work, "no use by the submitting student is involved. There is no effort, no learning, and therefore no attempt at justifying a claim for academic credit" (2018a, 9). She further argues that contract cheating is especially dangerous as it "has ramifications for an individuals' learning outcomes, institutional reputations, educational standards/credibility, professional practice and public safety, particularly if it is somehow normalised as an acceptable way for academic work to be accomplished" (2018b).

There are several obvious challenges inherent in dealing with contract cheating. Firstly, it is difficult to detect as work is usually original (Lancaser and Clarke 2016, 9) and so cannot be detected by text-matching software, such as Turnitin. Secondly, it is difficult to prove that students have actually cheated, and so the burden of proof might deter faculty from reporting suspected behaviour. QAAHE advocates that the more the students escape detection, the more likely it is that the practice will continue. Given these challenges, Carroll believes universities should treat contract cheating in the same way they treat other cases of fraud (2016, 9). Lancaster and Clarke also recommend the following responses: staff development aimed at helping faculty become more aware; carefully designing assignments so they are unique and cannot easily be done by a person outside the learning environment; the use of Turnitin as a teaching tool so students have more than one working copy of the assignment; and alternatives to course work such as tests and presentations (2016, 9).

As contract cheating emerges as one of the new threats to the integrity of higher education elsewhere, it is expected that this trend will eventually find its way into higher education in the Caribbean, if it has not already done so based on newspaper reports. Based on anecdotal evidence, the researcher concludes that many Caribbean nationals, including students, have a strong online presence which include shopping and studying. Given the aggressive nature of online advertising, students will most likely be exposed to opportunities to engage in contract cheating. HEIs in the Caribbean, therefore, need to be cognizant of this threat and take preemptive steps before they are confronted in a significant way with this challenge. They can begin with opening up the conversation about the topic and the likely approaches to handling the matter based on best practices from elsewhere.

Conclusion

Plagiarism, the most commonly practised form of academic dishonesty, is present in all sectors of society, at all levels of the education system, and affects all levels of students and faculty to varying extents. Although plagiarism is difficult to define and identify, many universities have developed clear-cut behaviours that exemplify it. Most if not all academic institutions regard plagiarism as academic misconduct not only because it deprives the author of credit, but it also deceives the public into giving credit to an individual who is undeserving. Plagiarism is committed in many different ways with the top ten types presented in the plagiarism spectrum developed by Turnitin with a clear description of each. This should prove beneficial to those interested in understanding and avoiding plagiarism. Contract cheating has become the newest challenge to academic integrity, and although there is a clear distinction between it and plagiarism, this is sometimes not fully recognized. To discourage students' involvement in contract cheating, Caribbean academic institutions need to begin to explore this new phenomenon, given the many already existing opportunities for cheating and the lack of academic integrity programmes in HEIs in the region.

Chapter 3
Causes and Prevalence of Plagiarism

Introduction

The causes and prevalence of plagiarism are well researched, and this chapter presents a review of the major findings from the literature review. The reasons for plagiarism tend to fall under three main types of factors – student related, teacher related, and institutional, usually the university. Additional factors include a lack of knowledge of the concept and its manifestations, and the contribution of the internet to the problem. All these are discussed along with the prevalence of plagiarism from the perspective of the students, graduate and undergraduate, and the faculty.

Why Students Plagiarize

Many reasons have been postulated as to why students plagiarize with Bretag identifying five general causes for this, namely: the higher education landscape, individual factors, peer influences, the nature of the consequences for cheating and the role of the teacher (2018a). Vázquez-Recio and her colleagues' investigation of plagiarism among undergraduate Spanish students also linked it to these same student, teacher and institutionally related factors (2016, 5711). Therefore, based on the rest of the literature, the author found these three categories of factors useful for framing the discussion.

Student-Related Factors: A broad scan of the literature on the factors contributing to plagiarism revealed that the majority of these were student-related and could be classified as either personal or academic. Recurring personal factors which lead students to plagiarize are a lack of time (Sisti 2007, 222; Kayaoglu et al. 2015, 1), procrastination (Vázquez-Recio et al. 2016, 5709; Sureda-Negre, Comas-Forgas and Oliver-Trobat 2015, 109), a lack of proper organization and bad time management skills (Vázquez-Recio et al. 2016, 5711; Sureda-Negre, Comas-Forgas and Oliver-Trobat 2015, 109; Dias and Bostos 2014, 2528). Additional personal factors include inadequate planning and lack of motivation (Vázquez-Recio et al. 2016, 5710) and the friend factor (Sisti 2007, 221; Howard, Ehrich and Walton 2014, 31). Broeckelman-Post also notes that students are more likely to engage in academic dishonesty if they believe their peers are doing so (2008, 206), a finding also supported by Carpenter, Harding and Fineli (2006). Laziness also contribute to a student's decision to plagiarize (Baker-Gardner and Smart 2017, 197; Vázquez-Recio et al. 2016, 5711). Attempts to reduce the incidence of cheating among students must take into consideration these personal factors and devise strategies to lessen their effects.

Academic reasons influencing plagiaristic behaviours are the pressure to obtain high grades (Wilkinson 2009, 103; Carpenter, Harding and Finelli 2006, n.p.; Power 2009, 649), while, strangely enough, some students said copying provided inspiration for them to do their work (Howard, Ehrich and Walton 2014, 31). In reality, this could be due to other factors like a lack of critical analytical skills (Dias and Bostos 2014, 2528) as well as a lack of interest in the paper, and a feeling of inability to complete the task on their own (Sisti 2007, 222). Weak academic writing skills are also listed as a factor in plagiarism (Kayaoglu et al. 2015, 1), in addition to students cheating because they thought the benefits outweighed the chances of being caught (Dias and Bastos 2014, 2529) and that plagiarizing was easy (Power 2009, 649). Some students cheated because of the satisfaction they received from beating the system (Bahadori, Izadi and Hoseinpuorfard 2012; Sisti 2007, 222).

There are some additional academic reasons students plagiarise. Gabriel (2010a) theorized that students plagiarize because of a lack of understanding of authorship, and Comas and Sureda believe that students plagiarized due to a lack of documentation strategies such as poor notetaking (2008, 3). However, Carpenter, Harding and Finelli (2006) cite the importance of context as a factor in plagiarism as they noted that the number of students who would cheat in examinations (15 per cent) was far less than the number who would plagiarize on assignments (45 per cent). The number of factors presented might not all be manifested in each institution. Given the possible impacts of context on students' plagiaristic practices, research will be important in guiding any educational programme aimed at mitigating the academic reasons students plagiarize.

Cleary presented the top ten reasons students plagiarize and starting at number 10 her list reads: laziness; panic; lack of confidence, thinking they need to reproduce what experts have written; difficulty integrating source material in their writing; lack of understanding of the need for citation; sloppiness; ignorance of the need to cite sources for facts, figures and ideas; them being learners; and finally, because they produce knowledge collaboratively (2017). Additional reasons for cheating include previous educational experience (Barrett et al. 2004, 5), the second language factor and culture (East 2016, 3; Kayaoglu et al. 2015). Blum also noted that students' focus on success and achievement may lead them to plagiarize as well as having limited understanding of originality in a culture where sharing is strongly promoted and there is not much value placed on the process of learning (2009, para. 8). In discussing plagiarism, Carroll identified three groups of students who were most likely to cheat based on their circumstances – those who have changed disciplines, returned to studying after a protracted absence or have moved between systems, for example, from the secondary to the tertiary level (2016, 5).

Students are central to the education process, and any system designed to develop and maintain academic integrity must be developed with an understanding of the factors which influence them to act both honestly and dishonestly. Therefore institutions must expend time and resources in developing an understanding of how these factors are manifested and the interrelatedness between them in order to launch successful initiatives. Interventions that are developed based on research and which include the involvement of students at various levels are most likely to succeed.

Teacher-Related Factors: Vázquez-Recio and colleagues (2016, 5711) as well as Sentleng and King (2012, 63) found that students plagiarized due to factors linked to the teachers and the teaching models and methodologies they used. According to Sentleng and King, 36 per cent of their student sample claimed doing this, and Vázquez-Recio et al. expanded their observation by stating that students plagiarized when they knew teachers did not check for plagiarism, when assignments lacked creativity, or information and communication technology was inappropriately used by teachers, and there was a lack of clarifications about assignments from the faculty. Students also resorted to plagiarism when there was scarce or superficial monitoring (2016, 5711) so they might not be caught (Power 2009, 649). In addition, if they had a large number of assignments, were given theoretical ones to do, and had lecturers who lacked interest in their work (Vázquez-Recio et al. 2016, 5711) they were likely to plagiarize. When faculty assigned "busy work" to students (Power 2009, 649), this also encouraged them to plagiarize. McCabe (2011) found that when students are faced with little possibility of being reported they are likely to plagiarise.

Sisti (2007) also mentioned that students will cheat when the lecturer does not explicitly warn against plagiarism (221), a conclusion also made by Broeckelman-Post (2008, 209). An additional factor that may be overlooked in the discussion of plagiarism was the lack of knowledge by the teachers which might encourage this behaviour. Dant found that 15.6 per cent of the 309 participants reported that they were encouraged by teachers to copy

(1986, 82). However, Carpenter et al. warned that students believed "that it is primarily the instructor's or the institution's responsibility to limit cheating and not the students" (2006, 192). This might explain why they cheated when they were not explicitly warned not to do so. Slovene students surveyed by Jereb et al. indicated that the teaching factor was the second most important one fuelling plagiarism by students (2018b, 11).

These teacher-related factors place the spotlight on how institutions view academic integrity. Those institutions that take a proactive approach to the issue are likely to provide education and training to faculty within a system that promotes academic integrity and provides the necessary support so that they are able to effectively carry out their roles. Institutions that are reactive are likely to take a punitive approach, by responding to breaches of academic integrity and applying sanctions as deemed appropriate. In this kind of context, faculty's role may be reduced to identifying and reporting breaches. This reactive stance is likely to result in a thriving culture of academic misconduct.

Institutional Factors: Certain institutional factors are known to influence whether or not students plagiarize. Vázquez-Recio et al. believed that when the educational system stressed the search for high qualifications without caring about the means of achieving them, plagiarism was likely to occur (2016, 5711). Similarly, students cheated when there was a lack of policy or processes in place to serve as a deterrence (Bahadori, Izadi and Hoseinpuorfard 2012) since students were more likely to cheat if they believe they can get away with it (Sisti 2007, 222; Howard, Ehrich and Walton 2014, 31).

There has also been a shift in perspective in academia to treating students as clients rather than students (Comas and Sureda 2008, 3), and this has also been cited as an institutional factor which might encourage plagiarism. Additionally, Furedi opined that universities were culpable for the number of students who plagiarize since they fail to educate them about the importance of scholarship (2017). Power agrees that universities were partially responsible for students' plagiarism as students sometimes receive mixed messages, for instance, when they are expected to regurgitate facts in examinations without citing the persons responsible for these facts. On the contrary, they are encouraged to be reflective and critical when providing their own answers and interpretation of what was being presented by faculty (2009, 653) while completing term papers.

Blum found that "[f]aculty members in various disciplines differed vastly in their expectations concerning citation and quotation. In engineering, for instance, quotation is not considered desirable, while in the humanities it is expected" (2009). This might result in unintentional plagiarism for those students in other faculties who take humanities courses in which they are expected to follow citation rules. Farahian, Parhamia and Avarzamani examined reasons for plagiarism in theses and found "motivation, social environment, self-efficacy, institutional regulations, supervision and control of theses, culture, creativity, education, technology, and socioeconomic status, respectively, are the underlying factors affecting plagiarism." In addition, differing perceptions among faculty based on ranks are also contributory factors to plagiarism (2020, 1). Carpenter et al. went beyond the university to suggest that maybe the education system itself was a factor in students' cheating behaviour (2006, 192). The many institutional factors when combined reveal that HEIs need to be cognizant of how they approach the issue of academic integrity. They will therefore need to adopt practices that reinforce academic integrity as it is possible for institutional practices to have the opposite effect.

Factors External to the Education System: Scholars like Comas and Sureda have identified factors extraneous to the education system that are also contributory to plagiarism, and these include the belief that what is on the internet belongs to everyone and can be used indiscriminately; the desire of the "video clip" generation to accomplish tasks in a short time; and declining ethics in the wider society which might lead students to conclude that unethical behaviour is acceptable (2008, 3). Another important factor that Sureda proffers is that of "[s]ocial models and schemes based on the culture of reproduction rather than on the reproduction and production of culture" (2008, 3). In the former, plagiarism is committed as the norm, while for the latter, the students are versed in using the works of others ethically in the production of new information instead of regurgitating the available content. An oral tradition that practises repeating what was said may also be another social factor contributing to plagiarism (Blum 2009).

Lack of Understanding of Plagiarism: A seemingly obvious, and maybe often overlooked, factor that can also contribute to the prevalence of plagiarism is ignorance or a lack of understanding of the concept and nature of the act. This does not fit neatly into any of the categories advocated by Vázquez-Recio et al. (2016), and this ignorance can be a result of a personal, faculty or institutional deficiency. Sutherland-Smith makes it clear that plagiarism "is a complex notion – and deceptively so. Although it appears easy to define the terms and allocate a range of penalties for the act – that approach ignores the layered reality of the issue" (2008, 3). Insufficient knowledge is one such layer identified as a contributory factor in the literature (Husain, Al-Shaibani and Mahfoodh 2017, 167), and for some, the confusion about it is even regarded as one of the greatest contributors to plagiarism (Gullifer and Tyson 2010; Ismail 2018). Ali, Ismail and Cheat (2012) reported that although students believed that plagiarism was wrong, 40 per cent were of the view that "copying from friend's assignments, buying assignments from seniors and changing statements from the sources obtained without acknowledging the original authors/writers were not considered plagiarising acts" (610). This lack of understanding was not just a problem among undergraduate students, as Ramzan et al. (2012) found low levels of awareness of plagiarism among 365 graduate students in several universities in Pakistan (80). Such a finding strongly supports the idea that a lack of knowledge or insufficient knowledge and confusion actually play a role in causing students to commit unintentional plagiarism.

Pincus and Schmelkin stated that it should not be assumed that all students come to the classroom with the same belief system (2003, 197), and other researchers discovered that nationality and cultural practices may also impact students' knowledge and understanding of plagiarism (Glendinning 2013; Jereb et al. 2018b; Thompsett and Ahluwalia 2010). Berlinick ascribed this lack of understanding to the way students are educated (2011, 367). He believed students are educated in a system which requires them to "repeat pre-established fact," and so they are confused when required to write and give appropriate credit since this is not how they were taught. This was also found to be true regarding students in the Caribbean (Baker-Gardner and Smart 2017, 197), and Dant (1986) noted a high correlation between a lack of knowledge and the number of cases of plagiarism (83). Kokkinaki, Demoliou and Iakovidou observed that there was a "lack of clear understanding among Cypriot university students regarding the definition of plagiarism" (2015, 10); thus, Power sums up this situation by stating that, generally, students understood the definition of plagiarism, but their understanding was superficial and this impacted their ability to avoid plagiarism (2009, 650).

Education has been touted by researchers as the most effective strategy in combatting plagiarism, and this can be understood given the lack of understanding regarding the issue. This author also supports education as a strategy that should be employed in the process of developing academic integrity. As such, an entire chapter in part 3 of this book is devoted to discussing how educational programmes can be developed and implemented to this end.

Plagiarism and the Internet

Sutherland-Smith admits that there is an ongoing debate about the connection between plagiarism and the internet (2010, 11), and Ison describes the relationship as complicated (2015). This latter conclusion is warranted given that some studies are inconclusive about the impact of technology on plagiarism, while others show a strong correlation between them. Although plagiarism was around before the internet, there are empirical data to support the position that advances in technology have increased the opportunities for students to plagiarize (Carpenter et al. 2006, 184). Jered et al. found that new technologies and the web were the main factors which drove plagiarism (2018b, 11), and Yeung et al. (2016) similarly discovered that the internet facilitated it among secondary students. In addition, Sureda-Negre, Comas-Forgas and Oliver-Trobat found cyber-plagiarism (plagiarism committed with the use of the internet) was more frequent among secondary students than that done by the "traditional" means of copying from printed sources (2015, 105). These findings support the conclusion of some of the college presidents in the United States who believe plagiarism is on the increase and the internet is largely to be blamed (American Society of Business Publication Editors Staff 2014).

On the contrary, McCabe reported in 2011 that there were no differences in the percentage of his sample who plagiarized through traditional means versus those who used the internet (2011). Ison, in a comparison between studies done prior to and during the internet age, found that there was no statistical difference between the amount of plagiarism present in 384 dissertations examined (2015, 151). This concurs with the findings of Kayaoglu et al. who concluded that the internet was not a major player in the results of their cross-cultural study of plagiarism (2015, 1). Bailey contends that what might seem like a significant rise in the number of cases of plagiarism might be partially due to the increased detection of the behaviour facilitated by technology (2011a).

The internet is seen as a significant variable in plagiarism because it provides opportunities to quickly and easily locate, copy and paste information (Sureda-Negre, Comas-Forgas and Oliver-Trobat 2015, 107) which ends up saving a considerable amount of the person's time (Bailey 2015). This explains why it would appeal to students who are lazy, lack time, procrastinate and have poor time management skills. Bailey lists five effects, good and bad, of the internet on plagiarism as: making it easier to carry out, but at the same time easier to detect; facilitating the growth of contract cheating; the creation of new citation standards for new web-based resources; and, opening up the conversation about plagiarism and the internet (Bailey 2017). The listing of contract cheating as a form of plagiarism by Bailey is a position not shared by Bretag (2018b) who, along with others, considers it as a separate category of misconduct. To combat some of the negatives, Davies and Howard favour an educative approach to plagiarism, instead of the current one which focuses on the use of text-matching software for detection, leading to punitive measures (2016, 1).

Factors Impacting Plagiarism among Academics

The literature is replete with empirical data on the factors which cause students to plagiarize, but the information on those that influence cheating among academics is sparse. Parmley postulates that plagiarism by academics is fuelled by the "publish or perish" mandate which is a feature of the academic culture of most institutions (2000). In agreeing, Löfström notes "the pressure to publish could lead to unethical behaviours, such as tweaking data and 'improving' or falsifying outcomes, and may affect implementation of research protocols" (2016, 5). In their policy paper on plagiarism in the scientific work of sixty-five Albanian academics, Lamallari, Madhi and Shpuza also identified some of the major factors which contribute to plagiarism among academics, such as a lack of professionalism and an academic culture; impunity with regard to plagiarism; a lack of research infrastructure in universities; the existence of quantitative parameters only in obtaining an academic title; limited financial resources for scientific research and dormant ethics boards in universities (2016, 21).

The factors which are posited by Lamallari and colleagues are worth considering, given the many anecdotal references to cases of plagiarism among academics which find their way into the mass media, mostly outside the Caribbean. However, there was at least one reported incidence of claims of plagiarism by an academic reported in newspapers in the Caribbean. On March 15, 2014, the *Daily Express* of Trinidad and Tobago reported on the case of a university lecturer who allegedly plagiarized the contents of a nursing curriculum. Based on the report, when asked for comments on the issue, Rhoda Reddock, the UWI vice-principal, stated, "It was an inadvertent failure not to have acknowledged the source of some of the data and examples used in this specific curriculum document." The curriculum in question was not used and instead, the UWI Mona's programme was implemented at the other campus. In addition it was reported that "an official apology was made to the head of the institution from which this information was taken" (Concerns at UWI over Plagiarism Claim 2014).

In addition to the institutional factors which influence faculty to plagiarize, several personal variables were identified among faculty who submitted essays to be considered for tenure track positions in a medical department in a university. Segal et al. stated them as "previous residency or fellowship; lack of research experience, volunteer experience, or publications; a low United

States Medical Licensing Examination Step 1 score; and non-membership in the Alpha Omega Alpha Honor Medical Society." Geographical location was an important variable as there was a higher prevalence of plagiarism by faculty outside North America (2010, 112). Needless to say, for every case of plagiarism that is made public, there are likely to be many others that do not leave the walls of the institutions concerned.

Prevalence of Plagiarism

Plagiarism is a common feature of the educational landscape, and Parmley (2000) notes that it is more prevalent than anyone suspects. According to Hughes and McCabe, research indicates that "the majority of U.S. undergraduate students have engaged in some form of misconduct while completing their academic work, despite knowing that such behaviour is ethically or morally wrong" (2006, 49). As established previously, plagiarism is practised at the secondary and tertiary levels of the education system, by graduates and undergraduates across disciplinary boundaries and by faculty as well as by persons outside academia. The following section presents a brief review of the literature on the prevalence of plagiarism among these groups.

Plagiarism among Undergraduate Students: The literature reveals that students' cheating behaviour at one level is a predictor of future cheating (Carpenter, Harding and Finelli 2006, n.p.). Thus, evidence of cheating at the secondary level suggests that it is likely to occur at the tertiary level. To support this claim, Church (quoted in McCabe, Butterfield and Trevino 2006) stated that cheating behaviour among college students developed before they enrolled in college, and they were likely to use the same styles of cheating while in college. The website *Check for Plagiarism* reported on statistics from *Psychological Record Study*, which stated that in 1997, 36 per cent of undergraduates reportedly plagiarized written material (Cyber Plagiarism and Statistics 2020). Additionally, 62 per cent of 71,300 undergraduate students surveyed by McCabe cheated on assignments (Statistics 2017). With plagiarism being the most commonly practised form of cheating (St Petersburg College 2019), it is expected that the majority of the 62 per cent of students in McCabe's study who admitted to cheating, actually plagiarized.

Based on empirical data, plagiarism among undergraduate students is widespread and on the increase, even as Kelly reports that 55 per cent of the college presidents said that plagiarism in student papers had increased over the past ten years (2011). The University of California-Berkeley found evidence that cheating increased by a huge 744 per cent from 1993 to 1997 (Know the Emerging Plagiarism Trends to Keep Your Content Unique

2021). From their research among undergraduate students in South Africa, Sentleng and King (2012) concluded that cheating among second and third-year students was "fairly common" (57). Using data generated from the Turnitin database, Watters noted that whereas more secondary than undergraduate students copied from social and "content sharing" sites, the percentage of the latter using cheat sites, paper mills and news sites was higher (2011). Evidence shows there is prevalence of plagiarism among undergraduate students although it is not clear if the incidence is increasing.

Plagiarism among Graduate Students: Graduate students, like all others, are guilty of plagiarism, and Mahmud and Bretag (citing the Academic Integrity Standards Project 2010–2012) noted that one in five Australian postgraduate research students reported they had never heard of academic integrity, and two out of five said that they did not know whether their university had an academic integrity policy (2013). Rosentiel's report, based on data collected by PEW Research Center, tells of the extent of the problem when he noted that 56 per cent of the more than five thousand Master of Business Administration students "acknowledged that they had cheated at least once" (2006). Ramzan et al. found that approximately 19 per cent of 365 graduate students reported that they cited their sources every time, creating the assumption that the remaining almost 81 per cent were possibly plagiarizing (2012).

There is a lack of agreement in the literature as to whether cheating among graduate students was increasing; however, the statistics from the ASBPE showed that the rate of plagiarism among graduate students was lower than among the undergraduate (ASBPE Staff 2014). This finding was supported by Plagiarism Facts and Stats (2017), even as McCabe also noted that the rate of plagiarism among graduate students had decreased from 43 per cent in 2002 to 39 per cent in 2011 based on data collected as part of the US Academic Integrity Assessment. These figures included cheating both in tests and term papers but did not include institutions with honour codes, which could be assumed to have lower levels of cheating (McCabe 2011). Two conclusions can be drawn from the findings of these studies. Firstly, there is significant plagiarism among graduate students. Secondly, when compared to undergraduate students, the prevalence of plagiarism among graduates seem to be less. Until more research is done, it cannot be clearly decided whether the rate of plagiarism among graduates is on the rise or the decline.

Plagiarism by Faculty: Ultimately, some graduate students become faculty; therefore, based on the trend, plagiarism among graduate students should be an indicator that there is likely to be some level of cheating among faculty. Turner (2017) presents an interesting situation arising out of the United Kingdom in which research assistants and lecturers were involved in contract cheating – earning additional income by writing papers for students through paper mills. This situation was so dire that it prompted a commission of inquiry and resulted in an upgrade to the basic requirements that universities had to meet in order to maintain their status. Statistics on cheating among academics are sparse when compared to the robust empirical data for students, so much of what is known tends to come from anecdotal references to cases of plagiarism in the media and from the few empirical works available.

Stripling contends that plagiarism among faculty is minuscule when compared to that among students. He cited statistics from the University of Florida which showed only twenty investigations of plagiarism among faculty in twenty-two years, with two persons who were found to have breached the university's ethical guidelines, representing approximately 10 per cent of all these cases. This compares with only 7 per cent of 466 students being cleared of plagiarism allegations over a two-year period (2008), although the disparity between the number of staff and students must be borne in mind when drawing conclusions from this finding. Gillis (2011) contends that the fewer number of cases reported among academics is not that they do not plagiarize, but there is a "blanket of silence" that covers these cases as a means of damage control by the institutions. He cites Irving Hexham saying that this was done due to the institutions' desire to protect their research grants and reputation.

Segal and colleagues attested to low rates of plagiarism among faculty in the United States as they found out that it was present in only 5.2 per cent of 4,975 essays submitted by faculty for tenure track positions in Pharmacology Department at a university (2010, 112). Similarly, Honig and Bedi, in their examination of 279 papers presented at a management conference, found that only 13 per cent of the papers had a "considerable amount of plagiarism" and 25 per cent had "some amount" (2012, 101). A higher rate of plagiarism (26 per cent of all abstracts) was discovered among graduates from institutions in North America by Hodges et al. who analysed conference submissions made by international faculty. They also found a higher level of text matching among senior faculty (2017, 12).

Although the rate of plagiarism among faculty seems to be low, one practice that contravenes the rules of academic honesty is guest authorship, also known as honorary authorship, which has received little attention in the literature (Moffatt 2011, 76). Honorary authorship involves giving credit to individuals who have not contributed to a work by having their names listed on the paper. Greenland and Fontanarosa cite research which revealed that "honorary authors were attached to 25% of research reports, 15% of review articles, and 11% of editorials published in six major medical journals in 2008" (2012). Jahangier pointed out some of the advantages and disadvantages to this practice for both parties involved. Whereas senior academics benefit from an additional publication, if the quality of the work is poor, their reputation might suffer. In addition, although junior staff members or graduate students might benefit from the association due to the reputation of the honorary author, it might be construed that the work belongs to the person who made no significant contribution (2017). The person who makes no contribution to the work is still given credit without the concomitant effort, so this could be considered a subtle form of cheating.

Conclusion

Plagiarism among students is due to a number of factors that are mainly personal, academic, teacher-related and institutional. The personal factors seem to be heavily skewed towards poor time management, low motivation to do the right thing and not being well organized. The academic factors had to do mainly with writing skills and a lack of knowledge and understanding of what constituted plagiarism and proper citation practices. The teacher-related factors included the faculty's lack of vigilance, failure to warn students about the issue, poor assignment design and lack of clear rules. Institutional factors included low detection, lack of clear policies, guidelines and rules on plagiarism and lack of education about plagiarism. Finally, there is the challenge posed by the internet which has become a tool that provides many opportunities for students to copy and paste content, even though it simultaneously allows for easier detection of such activity. With regard to faculty, although done on a smaller scale than students, plagiarism is largely driven by the "publish or perish" syndrome found in HEIs which requires faculty to publish in order to remain employed and get promotions.

Although plagiarism does not feature prominently in the research literature of the Caribbean, the statistics and findings from elsewhere would seem to lead to the conclusion that the region is not likely to be exempted from this problem. Based on the research findings and the similarities in the approach to education generally, it is not difficult to conclude that the nature of the plagiaristic acts and the reasons for committing them would be approximately the same for both students and faculty in the Caribbean. Plagiarism is no doubt a global problem which demands that more research is conducted to establish its nature and practice in the Caribbean and the many contributing factors. The findings of such research would help institutions to develop effective policies, guidelines and educational programmes to minimize its occurrence.

Chapter 4

Detection and Consequences of Plagiarism

Introduction

Detection is an important aspect in the fight against plagiarism, and so this chapter delves into the use of text-matching software to help to detect the possible cases of plagiarism. It examines the features of these software packages and the research investigating their effectiveness, followed by the consequences of plagiarism for both faculty and students. It ends with an exposition of reasons some students tend not to cheat but to practise academic integrity.

Detecting Plagiarism

The reputation of educational institutions, which takes so long to build, can be easily destroyed by one substantial case of plagiarism. This makes it absolutely important for them to take whatever steps are necessary to prevent this from happening, hence the need for the development of academic integrity which provides a high degree of protection against plagiarism. Before the age of technology, plagiarism was not hard to detect with the "word for word" kind being the easiest (Martin 1994, 37). In addition, lecturers were more than likely familiar with the sources from which the students copied. The SEO Tool Station website identifies three ways for the possible detection of plagiarism without the use of technology. These are inconsistent font style, inconsistent and incorrect citations and inconsistent and very professional narration styles (Admin 2017) which usually are not reflective of the student's ability. However, these are not enough in this technologically diverse environment where students, many of whom are digital natives (Prensky 2001), have superior technological skills and are able to mask some of the evidence.

While technology has led to an increase in plagiarism, it has also made it easier to discover and investigate it due to the prevalence of tools like search engines and online plagiarism checkers as well as the publicity opportunities afforded by social media (Marsden 2014). Bailey describes two types of plagiarism detection tools – the originality verification ones that check whether the individual's work shows elements of similarity to existing works, and the infringement detection tool that checks whether a known work is being plagiarized (2013). Detection tools may be free or subscription based with some being quite sophisticated, as in the case of Ephorus, which supports twenty languages (Naik, Landge and Mahender 2019, 18). After analysing seven open detection tools and eight commercial ones, Nahas concluded that the best tool was *iThenticate* provided by Turnitin, only that it was also the most expensive (2017, 53). In 2006, the UK was hailed as the country which led in plagiarism detection through the establishment of the Plagiarism Advisory Service which provided access to online plagiarism detection for institutions (Maurer, Kappe and Zaka 2006, 1054).

One text-matching software that is now being used in the Caribbean is Turnitin, described as a "anti-plagiarism most popularly used system. Turnitin stores and computes unique fingerprint for a given document. It computes detailed document similarities for a selected set of documents with similar fingerprint. Internal document storage is composed of archived student papers, journals, periodicals and books. The document storage is being enlarged by automatic web page crawling" (Naik, Landge and Mahender 2019, 475). When papers are uploaded to Turnitin, they are matched against sources in the database and online. The system then highlights the similarities (if any) between the papers that are uploaded and the sources. Papers which show substantial levels of matching text would then have to be scrutinized by a lecturer or editor to determine whether or not the author had plagiarized. Turnitin does not detect plagiarism but highlights matching text so that detection is made easier (Turnitin 2013a).

When institutions are seeking a text-matching software to implement, Kovtun advises that they look for the following eight features:

- security;
- multiple sources to check against – web, public and private repositories;
- multiple file formats;
- comprehensive plagiarism report;
- smart plagiarism checker with the ability to analyse citation sequence;
- downloading and sharing reports;
- custom library which allows the user to check submitted articles against each other for similarity; and

- free checks or trials before making a decision to purchase (2016).

Evaluation of the software by experienced and knowledgeable individuals is vital for ensuring that institutions acquire the one that best meets their needs.

Despite the popularity of text-matching software, Weber-Wulff is concerned that the many promises made by the companies in their advertising such as instant identification of plagiarism may mask other issues (2016). For example, in a study comparing the effectiveness of five brands of text-matching software, Ali, Abdulla and Snášel noted each tool had advantages and limitations (2011, 171). They, therefore, recommended that instead of placing so much emphasis on detecting plagiarism through the use of these tools, it would be better to focus on educating students about plagiarism. There have been significant advancements in technology since this 2011 discovery by Ali and his colleagues; however, recent findings also show a significant disparity in outcomes when different kinds of software were compared. Longcroft, in a report about a comparison between SafeAssign (described as in-built "tools" within Blackboard virtual learning environment) and Turnitin, found out that, in some cases, the difference in the percentage of matching text for the same document was as high as 52 per cent (2016, 8) when checked in both systems. Findings like these should signal to the institution that extreme care needs to be taken when using these tools.

In an evaluation of text-matching software, Nancy Johnson, blogger and middle school teacher, did an extensive analysis of fifteen software options and noted the best was Grammarly which she rated five out of five. She analysed each product based on price, vendor support, text length limit, reports and examination. She listed the following benefits of using Grammarly: "plagiarism percentage; downloadable report; automatic grammar, spelling and punctuation proofreader; synonym suggestions and citation generator" (Johnson 2020). Plagramme, Playscan, Unicheck and Turnitin were rated four out of five. Turnitin was highly rated because it provides "plagiarism percentage; customizable and downloadable report; citation and reference exclusion; doc vs doc comparison; and feedback option." An added advantage was that it also allowed for a number of file types such as "doc, docx, txt, pdf, rtf, ps, wpd, html, htm" (Johnson 2020).

Proffitt raised some additional issues with the use of text-matching software. The first was the high cost, and given the financial challenges facing HEIs in the region, they might find it difficult to pay the usual per capita cost for use. Second, Proffitt cited the use of students' work for profit by these companies to create their databases without compensating the students. The third point he made was the sense of distrust that the mandatory use of the software causes as it presupposes that students are cheaters and need to be cleared of wrongdoing by the software (2012).

In spite of the popularity of Turnitin, the research on its impact for stemming plagiarism are mixed. Those who subscribe to the use of this software must be aware that for maximum results, it should be part of a larger framework for ensuring academic integrity. Chapman et al. found that the temptation to cheat was reduced by the threat of discovery as their study showed that cheating on a web-based examination fell from 42 per cent to 14 per cent when this element was introduced (2004, 243). Turnitin introduced this "threat of discovery" which has been successful to some extent in stemming plagiarism in higher education (Bailey 2014) and at the secondary level (Turnitin 2013b). On the contrary, Goh reported that although Australian undergraduate hospitality students had to submit papers through Turnitin, they still plagiarized (2013, 307). These observations would seem to suggest that although the use of Turnitin and other such software might help to decrease plagiarism, it is not sufficient to significantly decrease the practice in some instances nor eliminate it and the context within which it is used will help to determine its effectiveness. Therefore, the need exists for a more comprehensive approach to deal with plagiarism.

This need for a more comprehensive approach was confirmed by Atkinson and Yeoh's findings after conducting a mixed-methods study that examined the perception of staff and students regarding the use of Turnitin. Six students and six staff members were interviewed in addition to a survey of 176 students. The researchers found that the students believed that detection software makes it easier for lecturers; it is fair to use "detection software; students support its use; and it will have some effect in preventing plagiarism" (2008, 222). On the other hand, the "students were concerned about being caught for unintentional plagiarism; teaching staff placing too much emphasis on detection results above student ability; and the accuracy of the software at detecting plagiarism" (222). Staff expressed concerns about the time required for running the students' scripts, the extra workload involved and the fact that the assignments were being matched only against online resources. In this same study, 53 per cent of the students felt it was fair for staff to use detection software, while 34 per cent thought it unfairly targeted students. Forty-five per cent of the students supported its use, and 44 per cent believed it was effective in preventing plagiarism.

Wan and Scott noted that Turnitin was usually promoted in schools as a "policing, rather than a teaching, agent" (2016, 5). Some HEIs in the region use Turnitin, and in 2012, Caribbean Examination Council (CXC) indicated its intention to implement the use of such software (CXC Touts Introduction of Software to Arrest Plagiarism 2012). Although text-matching software has been predominantly employed for the detection of plagiarism, it can also be used as a tool to guide students in the development of good writing skills. An example of this approach was reported by Cassandra Sachar, an assistant professor of writing at the Bloomsburg University of Pennsylvania. She explained that she gave her students multiple opportunities to submit their work through Turnitin. Then, based on the percentage of text matching found, they can make adjustments to the assignment and re-submit to Turnitin for another check. She also taught her students to use the filter feature which allows them to check the percentage of matching text without checking the quotations (Sachar 2018). However, an investigation into the use of Turnitin as a guide for producing plagiarism-free assignments showed that there was no significant difference between the draft assignment and the final version (Halgamuge 2017, 1). Further research is therefore needed on this aspect of the use of text matching software.

Any decision to use text-matching software should be informed by the research regarding its effectiveness. There should also be an understanding of the purpose for which it was designed and an acknowledgement that by itself, it does not serve to detect plagiarism. Implementation of text-matching software should also be complemented with training for both faculty and students in how to interpret the results as Keuskamp and Sliuzas found students did not understand the report produced by the software (2007, A-96), and so its use as a deterrent to plagiarism might not be as effective as expected by the university administration. This ignorance could be combatted by education.

Of note also is the reality that Turnitin might identify the symptoms of plagiarism, but it does not deal with the causative factors. The University of Toronto includes a "Frequently Asked Questions about Plagiarism Detection Tool" on its Centre for Teaching Support and Innovation's website (University of Toronto n.d.). This should be a helpful guide to students who have questions regarding its use. The University of Indiana stresses the importance of students' understanding how to interpret the percentages indicated on the Turnitin report and provides training for both students and faculty (University of Indiana 2019). This kind of training would also be necessary for faculty and students in Caribbean HEIs.

Consequences of Plagiarism for Students

Berlinck (quoting McDonald and Carrol, 2006) states that prior to applying penalties for plagiarism, four factors should be given consideration: the extent to which plagiarism was committed; the level of the student; the student's knowledge of institutional rules and norms and the disciplinary rules of the institution (2011, 369). Berlinck further states that while faculty is of the view that sanctions are to be applied in cases of plagiarism, there is little "consensus on how, when and the way to apply such sanctions" (368). While faculty views it as a serious matter, the penalties they apply when it occurs do not usually correspond to their views on the matter (Robinson-Zañartu et al. 2005). *iThenticate* takes a firm stance on the penalty for plagiarism and states, "Neither ignorance nor stature excuses a person from the ethical and legal ramifications of committing plagiarism" (n.d.). However, as a commercial text-matching software provider, their position can be easily understood. Harvard University takes the high ground, signalling its intolerance of plagiarism by not considering intent or the lack thereof as a mitigating factor, nor the type of assignment or the frequency with which the student plagiarized (Harvard University Extension School 2017).

The following were the penalties applied for plagiarism in the "Academic Misconduct Benchmarking Research Project (AMBeR) [which] sought to investigate the range and spread of penalties available for student plagiarism, as stated in the regulations of UK Higher Education Institutions (HEIs)" (Tennant and Duggan 2008, 4). The research was extensive involving 168 HEIs in the United Kingdom. Penalties were informal or verbal warning or reprimand; formal or written warning or reprimand; fine; resubmission of assessment with no cap on the mark; marks deducted from assessment grade above pass; assessment mark reduced to a pass; resubmission of assessment for a pass mark; assessment mark reduced to a fail or zero with no resit; marks deducted from module grade above pass; resit of module for a pass mark; module mark reduced to a fail or zero with no resit; suspension; reduced or capped final degree mark or classification; resit of the academic year for a pass mark; reduced qualification; and failure or expulsion from the programme. The most popular penalties applied were resubmission of assignment for a pass mark and the formal or written warning or reprimand. The penalties least applied were fines and marks deducted from module grades above pass (Tennant and Duggan 2008, 13). Carnero et al. found that in the case of epidemiology students enrolled in a master's programme in Peru, implementation of what was described as a "zero tolerance" policy resulted in no repeated offences (2017, 1183), suggesting that punishment coupled with intervention can effectively deter plagiaristic behaviour but sanctions alone might not achieve this objective.

The many sanctions and consequences for plagiarism furnished by the literature might not be consistently applied across institutions (Tennant and Duggan 2008), and this in part is due to differences in how institutions deal with plagiarism and faculty-related factors. Thomas discovered that the faculty did not report instances of plagiarism due to psychological discomfort, time constraints, the efforts involved in following due process and the lack of clarity about it. She also indicated that in cases where faculty were sometimes involved in academic dishonesty themselves, they might be less inclined to report their students (2017, 103). Thomas' findings are supported by McCabe who surveyed ten thousand faculty and found that 44 per cent of them did not report students who plagiarized (Bibliography – CAI Research 2006). Students indirectly corroborated the findings on faculty's unwillingness to report plagiarism by stating that even when they plagiarized, nothing happened as reported by 30 per cent of the sample surveyed by Dias and Bastos (2014, 2529). Similarly, Boyle, Boyle and Carpenter (2016) found that only approximately half of the students caught plagiarizing were reported. This lack of reporting by faculty only encourages students to act unethically, and this is likely to lead to an increase in the number of cases of plagiarism (39).

Other contributory factors which can reduce the reporting of plagiarism are the cost in terms of the amount of time the faculty member will have to spend looking through documents as well as the psychological impact of proving guilt (Marsden 2014). Marsden cites Jeremy Duns, who claims that in an attempt to prove plagiarism, individuals and institutions might make themselves vulnerable to legal action by the perpetrator. A situation like this could help to explain why faculty are reluctant to report cases of plagiarism. An example to illustrate the "cost" of dealing with plagiarism is the case of Gabrielle Napolitano which was reported by Checkforplagiarism.net (Plagiarism Consequences n.d.). After being found guilty of plagiarism by the Princeton University Committee on Discipline, it was recommended that her diploma be held for a year. After a second hearing with the same outcome, she sued the university. The initial decision was upheld by the courts. This case garnered much publicity and was reported by the *New York Times* (Plagiarism Consequences n.d.).

Consequences for Plagiarism among Academics

Academics are also subject to consequences for plagiarism. In addition to the reputational damage cited earlier by *iThenticate* (n.d.), there can be a "warning, public apology, suspension of activities for a specified period and even dismissal. The consequences in these cases can be a profound loss of a career for professionals who can be literally annihilated" (Berlinck 2011, 369). In addition, Xinhau notes that in China, faculty can be disqualified from projects or be mandated to pay back research funding (2013). The seriousness with which plagiarism is viewed in some institutions and countries is evident in the case of Phillip Baker, dean of the University of Alberta Medical School. He plagiarized parts of a speech he made to graduates and lost his administrative position but kept his job as a professor (Gillis 2011). Hexham (as cited by Gillis 2011) is also of the view that cheating on the part of faculty is a serious matter, given that their expertise in specialist areas is sometimes needed in order to make critical decisions. This point was borne out in the case of Yoshihiro Soto which was previously discussed. Plagiarism, in this context, may mean that the expertise that is being called on is not available, as the process which leads to the acquisition and creation of new knowledge might have been circumvented.

Retraction from databases and loss of academic degrees are two other possible outcomes of plagiarism for faculty. Grieneisen and Zhang conducted a comprehensive survey of 4,232 scholarly publications retracted from databases during the period 1928–2011. They found approximately 18 per cent of these retractions were as a result of plagiarism (2012, e44118). Other reasons the articles were retracted included fraudulent or fabricated data, duplicate publication, authorship issues, and unspecified copyright issues. Retraction of articles has significant implications, not just for the authors but also for the journals. Almeida et al. (2016) noted that the majority of papers that were retracted from Latin American/Caribbean databases were a result of plagiarism therefore, plagiarism by academics is likely to be a reality in this region.

Deterrents to Plagiarism

Although some students found reasons to justify their cheating behaviours, there are those who chose to display academic honesty. Evidence of this is that the percentage of students who admitted they plagiarized in the literature is consistently less than 100 per cent. Making allowances for instances of false reporting, it is still possible to find a subset of students who do not cheat. Academic honesty does not receive the same amount of attention as academic dishonesty, but the following explanations for not plagiarizing were identified. Some students who chose not to plagiarize gave ethical reasons to explain their positions (Andrews et al. 2007; Sisti 2007; Power 2009). In the sample surveyed by Andrews et al., one-third of the respondents reported that they had not cheated or gave a "Not applicable" response to that item. Fear of consequences if caught proved a deterrence to some students (Andrews et al 2007, 1032). The secondary school students in Sisti's study explained that plagiarism was not fair and deprived them of opportunities to learn (2007, 226). Additional factors cited in Power's research that inhibited cheating were the ease of doing the assignments, the enjoyment of doing the work, the desire to avoid feelings of guilt and the inability to afford the cost of the paper from paper mills (2009, 650–51). Understanding these motivating factors is important in developing academic integrity programmes.

Conclusion

Advancements in technology have been described as a double-edged sword (Nilsson 2016, 1), because of their ability to both increase the frequency of plagiarism and detect it. Many brands of free and commercial software are on the market that can assist in plagiarism detection, and choosing the best one requires specialized knowledge. In a bid to stem plagiarism, some Caribbean regional institutions have invested in text-matching software; however, evaluation of the effectiveness of this kind of software in identifying possible cases of plagiarism has shown the promises made by vendors do not always materialize. In addition, issues such as the cost, possible copyright breaches and their effectiveness in stemming plagiarism make the decision to use text-matching software much more difficult than initially considered.

With regard to members of educational institutions committing plagiarism, there are consequences for students as well as faculty. For students, the consequences may range from a warning to expulsion. The severity of the penalty usually reflects the seriousness of the offence. The outcomes for faculty can have negative professional implications, such as the loss of research funding and retraction of articles from databases. It may also result in destroyed professional reputations. There are students and faculty who choose not to cheat. For students, this may be due to both extrinsic and intrinsic factors. The extrinsic factors include fear of being caught, while intrinsic factors include the pleasure of completing assignments and the desire to avoid feelings of guilt. Finally, the act of plagiarism is not about to disappear any time soon, especially in this age of increasing technological developments that are likely to make it harder to detect. In light of this reality, educational institutions, especially at the higher level, must be vigilant and do all within their power to ensure the maintenance of academic integrity.

Part 2

Research on Academic Integrity in the Caribbean

Overview

The absence of empirical data on plagiarism in the Caribbean necessitated preliminary investigation to inform this work. This part presents original research on academic integrity in the Caribbean. The aim of the research was to describe the state of academic integrity in the Caribbean and propose solutions aimed at developing a robust system for ensuring academic integrity. The research was guided by the following objectives:

- determine the prevalence of plagiarism in various sectors of Caribbean societies and responses to its manifestation;
- investigate the prevalence of academic misconduct in secondary and tertiary education in the Caribbean;
- evaluate HEIs' presentation and treatment of plagiarism in their policies;
- determine undergraduate students' perception of the causative factors and penalties for plagiarism;
- examine undergraduate students' perception of the justifications for plagiarism;
- investigate the inclusion of academic integrity in accreditation policies and guidelines of member territories; and
- propose strategies aimed at assisting institutions to develop a culture of academic integrity.

Part 2 begins by providing a background to the Caribbean. It then presents a detailed discussion of the methodology used to collect and analyse data from six sources: academic integrity and plagiarism policies; accreditation standards and guidelines; articles from newspapers; secondary data from the Caribbean Examination Council and four regional universities, and a survey of undergraduate students.

The research in this section is relevant for several reasons. Given the scarcity of research on academic integrity and plagiarism in the Caribbean, it will begin to fill this gap. It is intended to stimulate discussions on academic integrity and plagiarism and should also result in future research. It is hoped that this work will provide HEIs with the impetus to begin seeking solutions to develop academic integrity and stem the problem of plagiarism.

Chapter 5

Background to the Caribbean

Introduction

This chapter gives a background against which the research presented in this section can be interpreted and understood. It provides geographical information about the Caribbean and describes its education system from the early childhood to the tertiary level before examining the roles of two Caribbean Community (CARICOM) institutions which have contributed significantly to education in the Caribbean. They are the Caribbean Examination Council (CXC) and the University of the West Indies (UWI), both of which impact education in all the territories and cater to students at the secondary and tertiary levels.

Defining the Caribbean

Although it is generally agreed that there is no one way to define the Caribbean, a definition is important as it serves as a means to contextualize and interpret the discussion contained in these pages. Vargas and Hugo posit the "Caribbean proves slippery and elusive in the face of any attempt to define it correctly" (2017), a position shared by Blake (2000, 46). This work therefore presents some definitions proffered in the literature, which can be political and geographic (Blake 2000, 47; Hepburn 2017); cultural (Blake 2000, 47); or geological, historical or diasporic (Hepburn 2017). The geological and diasporic Caribbean are the easiest to define. The geological definition, which is least used, speaks to the region resting on the Caribbean plate. However, this definition excludes the territories of Guyana, The Bahamas and much of Cuba (Hepburn 2017). The political Caribbean is made up of independent states, colonial dependencies and associated states, while the diasporic Caribbean refers to the large number of Caribbean people who live elsewhere in the world but still identify with the region (Hepburn 2017).

Complexities arise when attempts are made to define the geographic and historical Caribbean. The geographic Caribbean is usually defined using the coordinates of longitude and latitude. Though this sounds simple enough, there is a lack of agreement as to the exact coordinates. Regardless of the coordinates that are used geographically, the Caribbean lies southeast of North America, east of Central America and northwest of South America. Blake states that the sea is central to any physical or geographic definition of the Caribbean (2000, 46) as is shown in figure 5.1, which presents a typical map of the Caribbean.

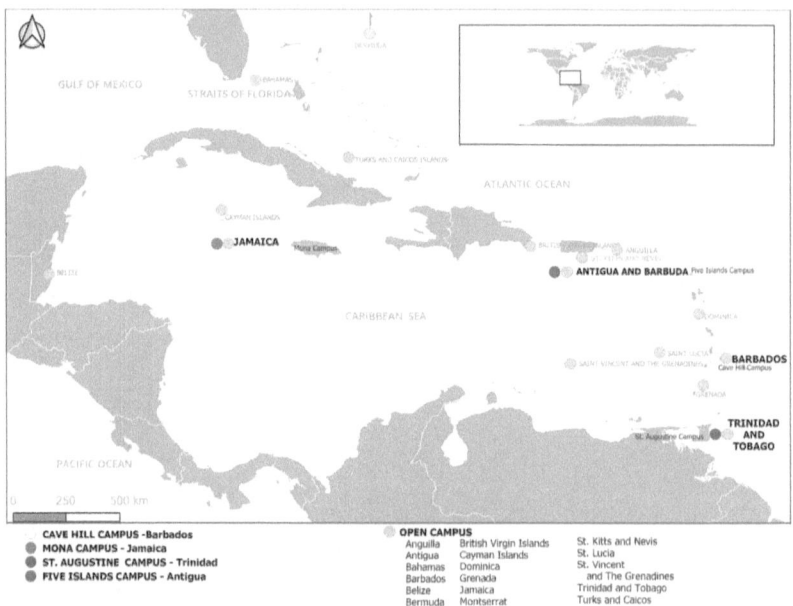

Figure 5.1. Map of the Caribbean.

With reference to the map, the region consists of the Caribbean Sea, more than seven thousand islands, keys, islets and reefs and the surrounding coast. The islands form an archipelago with the Caribbean Sea on one side and the Atlantic Ocean on the other (Caribbean 2019). The archipelago itself extends from the south of Florida in the United States to the mainland of South America. Briney, using a conservative estimate, reports that the region is 2,754,000 square kilometres (2018), and it is home to over 44 million people (Caribbean Population Live 2019) who speak six official languages (How Many Languages Are Spoken in the Caribbean 2019). The region has a shared socio-economic, political and cultural history as a result of its common colonial experiences (Vargas and Hugo 2017).

Given the challenges involved in adopting any one definition as the foregoing discussion reveals, the writer adopts the position taken by Blake.

He suggests that the definition of the Caribbean that one chooses will depend on the user and the purpose (2000, 48). The subject of this treatise is the Core Caribbean, which consists of those countries formerly colonized by Britain, with English as the official language, and holding membership or associate membership in CARICOM. As such, both the historical and political definitions are most relevant to this discussion. The political designation is informed by the historical experiences that have shaped the education system, and from which vestiges of colonial influences still echo (Miller 1999).

The political definition resounds with this work for two reasons. Firstly, CARICOM is a political organization comprised of independent member territories and dependent territories which are associate members. These independent countries are Antigua and Barbuda, Barbados, Belize, the Commonwealth of Dominica, Grenada, Guyana, Jamaica, Montserrat, St Kitts and Nevis, St Lucia, St Vincent and the Grenadines, the Commonwealth of The Bahamas and the Republic of Trinidad and Tobago. All the preceding countries, except for Monserrat, are members of the British Commonwealth and would be in the group categorized as the Core Caribbean. The associated members of CARICOM are Anguilla, Bermuda, British Virgin Islands, Cayman Islands and Turks and Caicos Islands. These are British Overseas Territories, and as such, would also be a part of the Commonwealth, and thereby part of the Core Caribbean. Haiti and Suriname are members of CARICOM but were left out of this discussion because the focus was on the Anglophone Caribbean. The official language of Haiti is French and Dutch is spoken in Suriname.

Another significant reason for this political categorization being relevant is that these members and associate members of CARICOM are all contributing territories to the UWI, which is the regional institution tasked with educating the Caribbean workforce. The only exception is Bermuda, which though an associate member of CARICOM does not make any financial contribution to the UWI. Additionally, the majority of the countries under discussion are also served by the CXC. This is the regional body established by regional governments with the responsibility for certifying secondary school leavers and administering exit examinations for secondary schools.

The historical definition of the Caribbean is relevant to this discussion since it centres around the Anglophone Caribbean, which has a common language and a history of being colonized by Britain. This has resulted in these territories all having an education system built on the British model (George 2016) in which colonial influences are still evident (King n.d.).

Overview of Education in the Caribbean

Education in the region has come a long way since the Negro Education Grant of 1835 which was as a part of the Act of Emancipation and was so named because it was earmarked to provide education for the newly freed slaves of the colonies. According to Whyte, initially, this was a sum of £30,000 for the entire English-speaking Caribbean and was to be allocated based on the number of free slaves in each territory. The grant was used to build schools and remunerate teachers, but it ended in 1845, and the financing of education for the newly freed slaves became the purview of the legislature and the church (Whyte 1977). Responsibility for education later changed hands, and although the government currently manages the system, both private and government-funded institutions coexist. The region currently has a four-tiered education system with institutions at the early childhood, primary, secondary and post-secondary levels. The Anglophone Caribbean has an average literacy rate of 94.8 per cent, a figure calculated by the researcher based on data from the United Nations Educational, Scientific and Cultural Organization (UNESCO) Institute for Statistics.

Early Childhood Education: Early childhood education is provided to children between the ages three to five years. The document *Guidelines for Developing Policy, Regulation and Standards in Early Childhood Development Services* is aimed at aligning and standardizing early childhood education provision across CARICOM. This attests to the regional approach to education even at the early childhood level. Based on the document, early childhood education is provided in "day care centres, preschools, infant schools and family homes" (CARICOM n.d., 9). The United Nations International Children's Emergency Fund, in its global report, states that a "child born in the Latin America and the Caribbean region, for example, is more than twice as likely to be enroled in pre-primary education as a child born in Eastern and Southern Africa or West and Central Africa" (2019, 27). This gives an idea of how the Caribbean compares with other parts of the world in terms of access to early childhood education.

Primary Education: Primary or elementary education is provided to Caribbean students from the age of five years to twelve. Compulsory education begins at five for the majority of countries and ends at age twelve for Jamaica and Grenada. Based on the data from UNESCO, the average enrolment in primary education for Latin America and the Caribbean was 93.7 per cent in 2018. Average enrolment ranged from a low of 81 per cent for Jamaica to a high of 97 per cent for Barbados (UNESCO Institute for Statistics 2019). Average percentage enrolment in primary education for the Caribbean was approximately 92.1 per cent, 1.6 per cent below the combined average for Latin America and the Caribbean. This average was calculated by the researcher; however, the available data for territories such as Grenada and Trinidad and Tobago were dated 2008 and 2010 respectively, and so this figure might not be truly reflective of the current enrolment.

Secondary Education: Students transition from primary to secondary education at approximately twelve years old after at least six years of formal schooling. During their final year in primary school, they sit an exit examination known by various names, such as the Barbados Secondary School Entrance Examinations, Secondary Entrance Assessment (Trinidad and Tobago) and Primary Exit Profile (Jamaica). Although some countries in the Caribbean have achieved universal access to secondary education, there are still challenges. According to UNESCO, the average enrolment in secondary education in Latin America and the Caribbean in 2018 was 78 per cent, a significant improvment from 59.3 per cent in 1986 (UNESCO Institute for Statistics 2019). In all territories except for St Kitts and Nevis, enrolment in primary education surpassed that of secondary education. The Bahamas had the lowest percentage of enrolment (67 per cent), while Barbados (94 per cent) and St Kitts and Nevis (98 per cent) were the only two territories with secondary enrolment percentages in the nineties (UNESCO Institute for Statistics 2019).

Bhoendradatt Tewarie, a former government minister of Trinidad and Tobago, goes beyond enrolment figures and states that more than half of the students who pursue secondary education fail to achieve the requirements for graduation within the expected five years (Tewarie 2007, 38). This situation is of concern given that for 2018, only "approximately 55 per cent of the candidates achieved Grades I–III" in English language (Caribbean Examination Council 2018). This subject is a core requirement for entry into tertiary education and employment. The region has therefore made significant strides in providing access to secondary education. However, there are still concerns regarding outcomes at the secondary level, as high completion rates for secondary education remain an elusive target (Fiszbein and Stanton 2018, 13). The Global Monitoring Education Review notes higher completion rates for girls when compared to boys (2018, 12). There is also evidence of inequity in the provision of education at the secondary level with some students being privileged to a higher quality than others (Miller 1999).

Higher Education: Higher education is "any of various types of education given in post-secondary institutions of learning and usually affording, at the end of a course of study, a named degree, diploma, or certificate of higher studies" (Higher Education 2016). Institutions at the tertiary level include "not only universities and colleges but also various professional schools that provide preparation in such fields as law, theology, medicine, business, music, and art. Higher education also includes teacher-training schools, junior colleges, and institutes of technology" (Higher Education 2016). The tertiary education sector in the Caribbean is made up of a number of local, regional and international institutions which combined provide training in every skill and profession. These institutions offer qualifications from post-secondary certificates to professional and doctoral degrees.

Access to higher education in the region is also increasing. From as early as 2010, the UWI noted the increased competition in the tertiary market due to the new opportunities for students to access online education from HEIs across the globe, a move further facilitated by technology (Challenges in Higher Education: Annual Report n.d., 44). Fiszbein and Stanton note the average enrolment rate of tertiary education in the Caribbean has grown by 20 per cent since 2000, and in 2015, the average tertiary enrolment was 44.3 per cent, a growth rate which was faster than most regions in the world (2018, 18). The higher education sector is most likely to be impacted by academic integrity and its nemesis academic misconduct. Fiszbein and Stanton further note the expansion in tertiary education has not been matched with quality and efficiency (2018, 18), a matter that needs to be given due consideration.

The quality of higher education in the region has a direct impact on the quality of the human resources in each territory. Given the symbiotic relationship between the workplace and the higher education sector, it is important that quality is maintained in HEIs. Cheng notes HEIs "are increasingly under public pressure to demonstrate their educational quality and to implement quality mechanisms within each institution" (2016, ix). Most HEIs subscribe to a quality framework which includes institutional policies and procedures and accreditation agencies. Whereas there is an ongoing discussion as to what quality in education entails, Cheng (2016) writes that the most frequently cited definition of quality in tertiary education concerns fitness for purpose but contends even this definition is being debated. Regardless of the definition of quality presented, if institutions fail to uphold certain standards that are generally acceptable to the wider society this is evidence that there are weaknesses in the systems. This might also signal that the output from this system is not fit for the intended purpose.

Funding Education in the Caribbean

The US International Trade Commission cited a 2005 World Bank report which states Caribbean countries spend "considerable resources" on education, but the returns on this investment are compromised because of a number of reasons including high migration, size of each country and high poverty rates (2008, 3–30). The average spending on education in the region at that time was 6.5 per cent of GDP, signalling the region's commitment to education. This sum exceeded investment in education by Latin America and the Organisation for Economic Co-operation and Development (United States International Trade Commission 2008, 3–30). The Commission further states that post-secondary education is negatively impacted by low return on investment due to ongoing migration of the educated (3–31). Table 5.1 shows Caribbean governments' spending on education by territories. Population data was taken from World Bank (2019) and economic data from World Bank (2021). The expenditure stood at a low of 1.5 per cent for Bermuda in

Table 5.1 Percentage of G.D.P. spent on Education by Territory

Territory	Population[1]	% of Overall[2] Govt. Spending	Year of Data
Anguilla	15.045	--[3]	--
Antigua & Barbuda	103,554	2.5	2009
Barbados	286,556	4.4	2017
Belize	385,971	7.6	2018
Bermuda	61,070	1.5	2017
British Virgin Islands	31,719	2.5	2018
Cayman Islands	62,348	--	--
Dominica	74,308	5.6	2019
Grenada	108,507	3.2	2017
Guyana	784,240	5.5	2018
Jamaica	2,902,539	5.2	2019
Montserrat	5,203	--	--
St. Kitts and Nevis	55,850	2.6	2015
St. Lucia	180,003	3.3	2018
St. Vincent & Grenadines	110,368	5.7	2018
The Bahamas	401,132	--	--
Trinidad & Tobago	1,374,277	3.1	2003
Turks and Caicos	38,191	2.9	2018
TOTAL	6,965,851		

[1]Population data source: World Bank 2019.
[2]Economic data Source: The World Bank 2021.
[3]No data available.

2017, to a high of 7.6 per cent for Belize in 2018. Other countries which were spending above 5 per cent included Dominica (5.6 per cent), Guyana (5.5 per cent), Jamaica (5.2 per cent) and St Vincent and the Grenadines (5.7 per cent). The current economic climate seemed to be adversely impacting spending on education. Some countries such as St Vincent and the Grenadines and St Lucia, which previously experienced spending of over 8 per cent of GDP, have decreased spending (World Bank 2021). This expenditure is a valuable investment in the process of transformation that is intended to secure the future of Caribbean societies. There was no data available for Anguilla, Cayman Islands, Montserrat and The Bahamas.

Regional Educational Institutions

The region boasts two institutions which deserve focus in this chapter for two reasons: they are integral to the provision of education for the citizens of the region, and they are featured in this work. The CXC is the institution which manages assessment primarily at the secondary level through a variety of examinations. Standing at the pinnacle of the education system is the UWI with campuses in Jamaica, Barbados, Trinidad and Tobago, Antigua and Barbuda, in addition to the Open Campus which offers online programmes. CARICOM states these two regional giants "have served the Region well for decades to advance the skilled free movement agenda" (CARICOM HRD Strategy 2018, 26). So close is the relationship between these two institutions that at the time of writing, Professor Sir Hilary Beckles, the vice-chancellor of the UWI, was chairman of CXC. The following section will briefly examine the roles and contributions of both CXC and the UWI to the regional educational mandate.

The CXC

CARICOM identifies CXC as one of its member institutions, and Griffith states the establishment of the regional examination was tied to the move for independence from Britain (2013, 16). The agreement for the establishment of CXC was signed in 1972 by fifteen territories, and seven years later in 1979, the first examinations were administered (Caribbean Examination Council 2020b). The Caribbean Secondary Examination Certificate (CSEC) replaced the General Certificate of Education Ordinary Level education, which originated in Europe and did not meet the needs of Caribbean students. In expressing this ideal, Kenneth Hall stated, "CXC was expected to facilitate the development of the human resources for Caribbean development, provide the training for the leaders of the Region and serve as the intellectual and ideological apparatus to nurture our identity as a Caribbean people" (2013, 6). Hall was a Caribbean historian, former pro-vice-chancellor, and principal of the Mona Campus of the UWI and also served as chairman of CXC for four years. This ambitious goal was achieved, and eight years after its implementation, CXC subjects were being accepted for matriculation to tertiary institutions not just in the region but also in the United States, the United Kingdom and Canada (Caribbean Examination Council 2020b), countries with significant Caribbean populations.

One of the goals of the CARICOM Regional Education Policy was to provide a post-CSEC examination to replace the General Certificate of Education A-level (Carrington and the Caribbean Community Secretariat 1993, 18), which was been offered out of Britain. This would give the region complete autonomy in providing students with matriculation qualifications to universities. This became a reality as the Caribbean Advanced Proficiency Examination was successfully piloted in 1998 (CXC 1998–2008: A Period of Consolidation and Expansion 2013).

The Council currently offers thirty-three CSEC subjects and serves sixteen participating territories which are members of the Council. In addition, it caters to three external territories, namely Suriname, Saba and St Maarten (Caribbean Examination Council 2020a). The Council is governed by vice-chancellors of the Universities of the West Indies and Guyana, three additional representatives of the UWI and another from the University of Guyana, representatives from each country and a member of the teaching profession (Caribbean Examination Council 2021). The close relationship between CXC and the UWI makes a partnership in the matter of academic integrity highly possible.

The vision of the regional examination body is "to assure the global human resource competitiveness of the Caribbean through the provision of quality assurance in education and comprehensive certification" (Caribbean Examination Council 2019). As such, ensuring and maintaining academic integrity is central to the examination processes of the organization, which has the legislative authority to "regulate the conduct of any such examinations and prescribe the qualification requirements of candidates and the fees payable by them" (Caribbean Examination Council 2021).

The impact of CXC is evident in the number of students who register for examinations which are held twice annually. A total of 127,897 students registered for the May/June 2018 sitting of the CSEC examinations, a marginal decrease of 1,691 from the previous year. Table 5.2 shows the number of students from each territory. These data were taken from the Council's 2018 annual report.

Table 5.2. Number of students sitting CSEC in May/June 2018 by territories

Territory	Number	Percentage
Anguilla	343	0.27
Antigua and Barbuda	2,356	1.84
Barbados	7,557	5.91
Belize	3,775	2.95
British Virgin Islands	345	0.27
Cayman Islands	964	0.75
Dominica	961	0.75
Grenada	2,500	1.95
Guyana	12,272	9.60
Jamaica	63,471	49.63
Montserrat	102	0.08
St Kitts and Nevis	1,483	1.16
St Lucia	2,777	2.17
St Vincent and Grenadines	2,716	2.12
Trinidad and Tobago	25,518	19.95
Turks and Caicos	466	0.36
External territories	291	0.23
Total	127,897	100.5*

Source: Tull (2018).
*Data added up to more than 100 per cent due to rounding off.

The number of students registering for the examination is proportionate to the secondary population from each territory. By virtue of its size and population, Jamaica registered approximately half of the 127,897 entrants for the examination. This was followed by Trinidad and Tobago with approximately 20 per cent. There were no entrants from The Bahamas and Bermuda as these territories have alternative exit examinations for secondary schools. External territories are Saba, Suriname and St Maarten.

The UWI

The UWI describes itself as the "region's premier educational institution" (The University of the West Indies 2021b) and rightly so. The 2020 World University Ranking named it the top university in the Caribbean. In addition, it was placed among the top 2 per cent of universities in Latin America and the Caribbean, and the top 4 per cent of universities in the world, making it one of the top 600 institutions in the rankings (The University of the West Indies 2021a). The institution, which began in 1948 in Kingston, Jamaica as a college of the University of London, opened its second campus in Trinidad and Tobago in 1960 and achieved full university status in 1962. The third campus in Cave Hill, Barbados, was opened in 1963 (The University of the West Indies n.d.). The establishment of a university in the region was a significant milestone as it brought an end to the region's need to "import university graduates from Great Britain to serve as senior staff in secondary schools" (Jamaica – History and Background n.d.).

The distance and size of the territories, in addition to advances in technology, make a compelling case for online education in the region. This need is partially met by the Open Campus, which is headquartered in Kingston, Jamaica and has forty sites in sixteen territories (The UWI Open Campus 2019). Figure 5.1 shows the location of the physical campuses and the Open Campus sites across the region. Open Campus sites are strategically located in every territory, emphasizing the regional nature of the university. Administration and examinations for students enroled in the Open Campus are done at these sites, in addition to examinations for online students who are attached to the Mona Campus.

The UWI commands the highest number of students enroled at the tertiary level in CARICOM, and it offers programmes leading to the award of degrees from the undergraduate to the doctoral level. The UWI is still in expansion mode with its new campus in Antigua and Barbuda which was opened in 2019. Table 5.3 shows the total number of students enroled in the four campuses of the University from each territory for the period 2012–2017. Enrolment does not include data from the Five Island Campus.

Although the population of Jamaica is more than twice that of Trinidad and Tobago, it had less students enroled for the period under consideration. This could be attributed to the fact that some students in Trinidad and Tobago are able to obtain up to a first degree free of cost to them (Education System in Trinidad and Tobago 2018). Based on table 5.3, the number of students enroled in the UWI has shown a marginal decline of 5 per cent, mainly attributed to a decline in enrolment figures for Barbados which resulted from the introduction of university fees in 2014 (Alleyne 2018). Organisation of Eastern Caribbean States countries are Antigua and Barbuda, St Kitts and Nevis, Montserrat, Anguilla, British Virgin Islands, Dominica, St Lucia, St Vincent and the Grenadines, and Grenada and Martinique.

The UWI produced an annual average of 10,137 graduates for the five-year period 2012–2017, which is approximately one-fifth of the students enroled in its various programmes across the four campuses. The influence of the UWI in the region is pervasive. At the time of writing, it had among its

Table 5.3. The UWI enrolment by nationalities for the period 2012–2017

Nationality	2012–2013	2013–2014	2014–2015	2015–2016	2016–2017
Trinidad and Tobago	20,700	20,885	20,363	19,877	19,636
Jamaica	16,225	16,232	15,905	16,586	16,989
Barbados	7,634	7,607	5,900	5,200	4,774
OECS[1]	3,452	3,437	3,190	3,676	3,882
Other Caribbean	1,101	1,180	1,304	1,382	1,598
International	1,070	805	733	783	712
Total	50,182	50,146	47,395	47,504	47,591

Source: The University of the West Indies Statistical Digest (2018).
[1] Organisation of Eastern Caribbean States (OECS) countries are Antigua and Barbuda, St Kitts and Nevis, Montserrat, Anguilla, British Virgin Islands, Dominica, St Lucia, St Vincent and the Grenadines, and Grenada and Martinique.

distinguished alumni, twenty-three heads of state across the region (UWI Alumni Online n.d.), in addition to distinguished academics and world-renowned industry leaders. In spite of these outstanding gains, UNESCO points to significant challenges in the delivery of tertiary education in the region when progress is evaluated against the six goals of Education for All. These include an unequal expansion trend in higher education; a need for strengthening institutions to generate more scientific and technological output; and a need to better connect to the development needs of the society. It describes the latter as a chronic problem, citing that the school system is an apt setting for research, which could support school improvement and reform to benefit society (UNESCO 2014, 25).

Migration continues to be a feature of West Indian life, and Zong and Batalova state there were approximately four million Caribbean persons (referred to as the diasporic Caribbean) living in the United States (2019). This is one of the preferred destinations for Caribbean migrants (Migration in the Caribbean: Current Trends, Opportunities and Challenges 2017). Other countries with significant Caribbean populations are Britain and Canada. Byron (citing Chamberlain 2002) states, "[F]ew if any people are more global and more migratory than those from the Caribbean" (2000, 80). The ease with which Caribbean migrants are able to obtain gainful employment overseas will depend on the premium placed on the educational qualifications which are acquired in the region. Academic integrity is vital to ensuring the qualification attained in the region can be accepted without question as Caribbean people continue to forge new global trails. Both The UWI and CXC are central to this mandate.

Conclusion

Defining the Caribbean can be challenging given the need to select a definition from a range including historical, diasporic, geopolitical, political, geographic and geological. However, Blake's advice to choose the definition which best meets one's need led to the decision to define the region based on the political designations as members of the British Commonwealth. The shared history of the territories, based on their colonization by Britain, has brought the education systems together despite the diversity of each territory. A four-tiered system of education exists, beginning at the early childhood level, progressing through to the primary and secondary levels and terminating at the tertiary level.

The cooperation among the territories is best exemplified through the CXC and the UWI. Together, both ensure a cadre of highly qualified workers for the region, whose education matches up to international standards. This is evidenced by the high migration of skilled workers trained in the region to first-world countries. The significant place occupied by these two institutions means that they are gatekeepers, charged with the challenging task of ensuring the integrity of the system of education in the region. This not only has implications for the trust that the international community places in the regional education systems, but it is vital in terms of ensuring that graduates possess the requisite skills, knowledge and competencies represented by the certifications that they hold. Any additional attempts at ensuring that academic integrity is developed and practised will further bolster the image of these institutions.

Chapter 6

Methodology

Introduction

This chapter presents a discussion of the methodology used to collect and analyse data for the research done, the details of which are presented in Chapters 7–14. The choice and appropriateness of undertaking a content analysis to arrive at the answers sought are explained along with the steps in the process. It then focuses on the application of the content analysis methodology to the newspaper articles, institutional policies for academic integrity and plagiarism and national accreditation guidelines and policies. A detailed discussion of the procedures utilized for the survey is also presented, including a description of the questionnaire used for data collection and an explanation of the sample selection and data analysis procedures. The researcher then outlines the ethical procedures followed.

Research Objectives

The researcher sought to gather data to meet the following objectives:

- determine the prevalence of plagiarism in various sectors of Caribbean societies and responses to its manifestation;
- investigate the prevalence of academic misconduct in secondary and tertiary education in the Caribbean;
- evaluate HEIs' presentation and treatment of plagiarism in their policies;
- determine undergraduate students' perception of the causative factors and penalties for plagiarism;
- examine undergraduate students' perception of the justifications for plagiarism;
- investigate the inclusion of academic integrity in accreditation policies and guidelines of member territories; and
- propose strategies aimed at assisting institutions to develop a culture of academic integrity.

Research Design

The research which is reported in this section utilized a combination of qualitative and quantitative methods to carry out six small scale studies to meet the research objectives. Qualitative content analysis was used for plagiarism and accreditation policies, while quantitative content analysis was used for newspaper articles. Quantitative data were also collected using a cross-sectional survey. Based on the objectives, data were gathered from the six sources outlined in figure 6.1. Triangulation was a feature of this research as data were obtained from content analyses and a survey, in addition to four universities and the Caribbean Examination Council which provided secondary data for analysis.

Content Analysis

The researcher utilized content analysis in three ways to collect the data. Articles on plagiarism published in newspapers in the Anglophone Caribbean for a period of fifteen years (2002–2017) were analysed, in

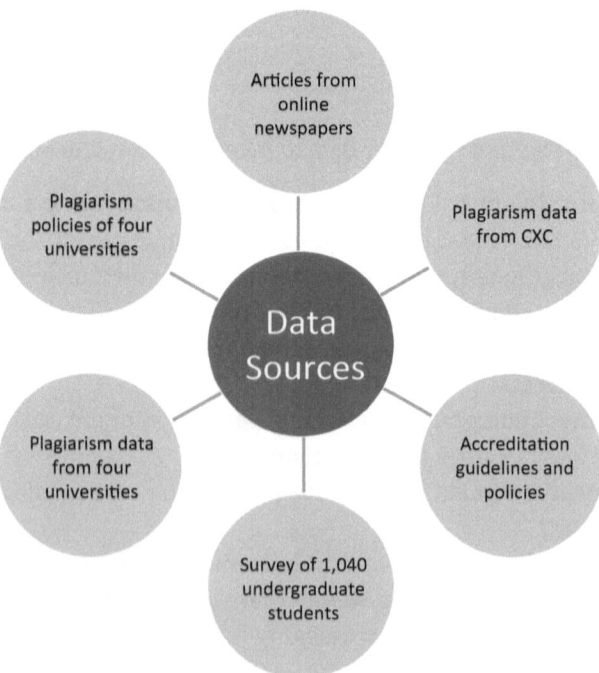

Figure 6.1. Data sources.

addition to national accreditation policies and guidelines, and the academic integrity and plagiarism policies of HEIs. Content analysis, classified by Neuman (2006, 323) as nonreactive research, is defined as "a detailed and systematic examination of the contents of a particular body of material for the purpose of identifying patterns, themes or biases" (Leedy and Ormrod 2019, 235). Content analysis has been applied in many disciplines such as literature, history, journalism and political science and can be used for the analysis of talk, conversation and mediated content which represents the essence of human behaviour (Krippendorff 2013, 5). Other resources that can be analysed are books, newspapers, films, television, art, music, videotapes of human interactions, internet blogs and bulletin board entries (Leedy and Ormrod 2019, 235).

Krippendorf agrees that content analysis is a useful means of providing new insights into a phenomenon while increasing the researcher's understanding of what is being studied (2013). This justifies its use for this research which seeks to provide insights into plagiarism, a phenomenon not yet studied in a significant way in the Caribbean. Much of the information being sought required the consultation of primary sources for which content analysis is particularly suited. Freankel and Wallen explain that content analysis allows the researcher to:

- obtain descriptive information about a topic;
- formulate themes that help to organize and make sense of large amounts of descriptive information;
- check other research findings;
- obtain information useful in dealing with educational problems; and
- test hypothesis. (2009, 474)

The wide scope of content analysis makes it suitable for use in this research where a large volume of text must be studied "at a distance," and when the messages are difficult to observe (Neuman 2006, 324). In this case, these documents consisted largely of newspaper articles and institutional policies. Furthermore, content analysis is widely used in educational research to describe prevailing policies (Ary et al. 2005, 464), exactly what this research aims to do.

Content Analysis Procedure: Fraenkel and Wallen identify nine main steps to be followed when conducting content analysis. They are:

1. determine objectives;
2. define terms;
3. specify the unit of analysis;

4. locate relevant data;
5. develop a rationale;
6. develop a sampling plan;
7. formulate coding categories;
8. check reliability and validity; and
9. analyse the data (2009, 472–75).

Adhering to these steps ensures that the content analysis is conducted in a systematic manner which will further strengthen the reliability and the replicability of the research. Some advantages of content analysis are flexibility, transparency, unobtrusiveness, the relative ease with which it allows longitudinal analysis as well as its ability to facilitate the collection of information about social groups to whom it would otherwise be difficult to gain access (Bryman 2016, 302–3). In addition content analysis is simple and economical (Fraenkel and Wallen 2009, 483). These guidelines posited by Fraenkel and Wallen were followed for this project, thus the advantages were achieved.

Sampling: The researcher used purposive sampling to select the newspaper articles, accreditation policies and guidelines, and academic integrity and plagiarism policies. According to Burns, this sampling technique involves selecting a case which serves the "real purpose or objectives of the researcher of discovering, gaining insight and understanding into a particularly chosen phenomenon" (2000, 465). Krippendorff, in writing about content analysis, uses the term relevance sampling, a type of purposive sampling that aims to "select all the textual units that contribute to answering given research questions" (2013, 120). Based on the number of available textual units for analysis for this research, relevance sampling was considered as the most appropriate.

Content Analysis of Newspaper Articles

In order to select the textual units for analysis, a list of criteria was established. Articles had to be written from 2002 to 2017, published in an online newspaper in a CARICOM member country or associated territory, and focused primarily on plagiarism. The researcher believed a period of fifteen years would provide an adequate number of articles that would give a reasonable picture of plagiarism in the Caribbean. The articles used for this research enabled the researcher to gather multiple points of view from the various territories and the persons written about in the articles. In addition, they provided the opportunity to examine cases of plagiarism in the various sectors within the society, such as politics, education, entertainment and religion.

To facilitate the analysis, the researcher developed codes defined by Neuman as "a set of instructions or rules on how to systematically observe and record content from the text" (2006, 324), a critical element in content analysis. It helps the reader to understand the conversion from text to quantitative data. The content was coded by year of publication, territory of origin, sectors in which they were found (such as education, politics and so on) and type of plagiarism. Neuman explains that one way of using newspapers is to identify and count key events, and this study is an example of such, although other techniques were used. He postulates that newspapers are an important means of measuring social events across time (2006, 333), thus they proved useful in this context.

The researcher decided to analyse newspaper articles after considering the following advantages outlined by Ohio State University Libraries which explains that newspapers provide the opportunity to:

- see how people viewed an event when it happened;
- provide multiple points of view about an issue;
- permit researchers to trace the historical development of subjects over time;
- examine issues in the context of their time; and
- give a snapshot of a time period (2020).

The advantages were realized in this study as the various voices were identified and discussed; the articles provided multiple points of view from various countries and sectors; and the time span allowed for the examination of the number of cases over time. One limitation to the use of online articles was the possible omission of valuable articles published in another medium. The study of plagiarism is beginning to emerge in the research of the Caribbean; therefore, it is important to lay a foundation on which further research on the topic can be done. The use of newspaper articles was a practical way of achieving this making it possible to get an overview of the situation in the Caribbean with regard to the prevalence of plagiarism and the sectors which were being affected.

Content Analysis of Plagiarism Policies

For the content analysis of plagiarism policies, the researcher searched institutional websites to locate policies and guidelines using the following search strategies:

- search for handbooks on the institutions' websites and search within these handbooks;

- search under forms, policies and documents where these options existed;
- combine the name of institutions with the term "handbook" or "catalogue" and use the search engines;
- combine the name of the institution with the term "plagiarism", "academic misconduct", "academic integrity", "cheating" or "academic dishonesty" and use search engines.

The researcher used handbooks for the current year where these were available, but in their absence, she used whatever was available. In the majority of cases, the handbooks were current, but where this was not the case, they were only dated by two or three years. Sixteen institutional policies were identified for analysis from fifteen institutions.

Units of analysis for the contents of the policies included:

- definition of plagiarism;
- description of plagiarism;
- classification of plagiarism into levels;
- penalties for plagiarism;
- types or examples of plagiarism;
- electronic detection;
- faculty responsibilities,
- sources of assistance; and
- statements of accountability.

The policies were examined individually for these components and the manner in which each institution presented each component was further analysed. The researcher also examined the location and length of the policies.

Content Analysis of Accreditation Policies and Guidelines

The researcher analysed accreditation policies and guidelines to see if there was evidence of the inclusion of academic integrity. She requested a list of accreditation agencies in the Caribbean from the University Council of Jamaica and received contact information for ten such agencies. The researcher then conducted an online search of their websites. In cases where documents were not available online, she contacted the agencies directly. She used the codes "academic integrity," "academic dishonesty," "academic misconduct" and "plagiarism" to search each policy and guideline. Where these did not yield any results, she read the policy to see if these ideas were presented in other terms.

Descriptive Survey

A descriptive survey was utilized to collect data from undergraduate students. The survey "examines a situation as it is [...] without changing or modifying the situation under investigation" (Leedy and Omrod 2019, 136). In order to accomplish this, the survey asked a large number of individuals the same questions, and the responses were later tabulated (Fraenkel and Wallen 2009, 431). Fowler advocates four main reasons for administering a survey: it captures information that is not available elsewhere; it uses probability sampling which can result in unbiased sampling; the instrument is standardized and this results in comparable information gathered from respondents; and it can be tailored to meet the needs of the researcher (2009, 3). These four reasons were considered relevant to this research.

Data Collection: Data were collected using a questionnaire which Leedy and Ormrod state "is more useful when a behaviour, attitude or other phenomenon of interest needs to be investigated" (2016, 143). The instrument, which was reused with permission (see Appendix 1), was developed by Mavrinac et al. in 2010 and was modified by Howard, Ehrich and Walton who subjected it to psychometric testing using the Rasch validation technique, among other traditional measures. The purpose of the psychometric testing was to ensure "confident quantification and measurement of its underlying constructs" (Howard, Ehrich and Walton 2014, 23). This should help to strengthen the measurement validity and answer the question of whether the instrument measures the concept that it was designed to. The instrument was modified for this study by the addition of items aimed at collecting demographic data which were variables under consideration.

In keeping with the best practice of making the survey "brief and simple to complete" (Hank, Jordan and Wildemuth 2009, 257), the modified questionnaire contained twenty-eight items and was divided into four sections (see Appendix 1). The first section contained six items which sought to collect demographic data, while sections 2–4 are subscales which collect data on the perceptions of students on factors which exacerbate plagiarism, justification for plagiarism and penalty for and severity of plagiarism. The instrument was designed as a five-point Likert Scale and students were required to tick the boxes that best reflect their opinions on each statement. Choemprayong and Wildemuth have established that rating scales are one of the most commonly used formats to measure psychological constructs such as perception (2009, 280), thus its use. The questionnaires were administered to intact class groups, and this resulted in low-cost and high response rate. It also provided the opportunity for the researcher to answer questions from the student about the research (2009, 281). The data collection lasted for three weeks during the 2018–2019 academic year.

Sampling: The sampling frame was the list of undergraduate students received from the University Office of Planning which reported that its undergraduate enrolment was 17,719 for the five faculties of interest for the 2015–2016 academic year. Using the SurveyMonkey sample calculator, with a population of this size, the sample needed was 1,007 with a confidence level of 95 per cent and a margin of error of 3 per cent. The researcher added thirty-three students to the sample to make it 1,040 in order to account for possible incomplete questionnaires.

Babbie is of the view that generalizing from the sample is the intent of survey research and notes that "careful probability sampling provides a group of respondents whose characteristics may be taken to reflect the larger population" (2013, 229). The researcher employed both cluster-based and random stratified sampling to select groups of students to participate in the research. Table 6.1 shows the distribution of the population across faculties and the sample size taken from each.

Students were drawn from five faculties, and based on the enrolment, the largest number of students (38 per cent) were from the faculty of social sciences followed by medical sciences (25 per cent). In keeping with the concept of "careful probability sampling," the researcher sought to ensure the sample size taken was representative of the enrolment in each faculty.

Table 6.1. Distribution of sample across faculties

Faculty	Population	Sample size	Percentage of sample
Humanities and Education	2,424	146	14
Law	550	31	3
Medical Science	4,510	260	25
Science and Technology	3,476	208	20
Social Sciences	6,759	395	38
Total	17,719	1,040	100

Statistical Analysis: The quantitative data were analysed using the Statistical Package for the Social Sciences version 23. The independent variable was correlated with the dependent variable to ascertain the strength and the direction of the impact one had on the other. The bivariate analysis determined the relationship between the dependent and independent variables. Chi-square test/Mann-Whitney U test was used to determine the existence of a relationship, and Phi tests were run to test the strength of these relationships. The data were analysed using the contingency table, which according to Babbie is "a format for presenting the relationship among variables as a percentage distribution" (2013, 415). In determining if a relationship exists, the researcher was willing to accept a 3 per cent level of significance. Analysis of Variance (ANOVA) and post-hoc tests were conducted in order to identify if there were significant differences in students' perception of plagiarism based on age and academic maturity. This provided the opportunity for the researcher to do a comparative analysis of the data.

Two variables, age and the number of years enrolled in school had more than two categories, and as such a one-way ANOVA was deemed appropriate to assess the mean differences in the scales as it relates to each variable. Post-hoc test was carried out in the ANOVA, using Bonferroni and Tukey B. In an attempt to determine the internal consistency of the data, a series of reliability tests were carried out on the overall plagiarism scale and subscales in the dataset. Those with a high Cronbach alpha (0.70 and above) were said to have good or acceptable internal consistency (Bland 1997, 272).

The intention of the study was to assess the mean differences in the plagiarism scale as it relates to gender and faculty. Considering that gender is a dichotomous variable, an independent samples t-test was utilized to assess the mean differences in the overall plagiarism scale and subscales, to assess whether there were differences in the perspectives of the males as opposed to the females.

Analysis of Qualitative Data: The qualitative data were analysed using Creswell's (2007) data analysis spiral which presents the following four steps for analysing qualitative data: data managing; reading and memoing; describing, classifying and interpreting; and representing and visualizing. In step 1, the data from each questionnaire were entered into a Microsoft word file. The entries were then organized according to themes based on the themes presented in the survey. The data were then presented and discussed.

Ethical Concerns

For the descriptive survey, the researcher sought an ethical review of the study by the Mona Campus Research Ethics Committee to ensure that it met the university's ethical standards. The researcher then obtained permission to collect data from the university's registrar. Informed consent is another ethical consideration for researchers. The researcher sought informed consent by requiring participants to complete consent forms prior to the collection of the data. In order to ensure anonymity and confidentiality (Cohen, Manion and Morrison 2000, 50), participants were instructed verbally and through the consent forms not to include their names on the questionnaires.

Secondary Data

The researcher used secondary data from four universities and from the Caribbean Examination Council. Secondary data is defined as "data that is collected routinely as part of the day-to-day operations of an organization, institution or agency" (Primary Data and Secondary Data 2015, 2). The data were collected by the institutions as part of their administrative activities, and not for the purposes of this research. The use of secondary data was considered appropriate in this context as the information was readily available, easy to obtain and covered a long period (Primary Data and Secondary Data 2015). The researcher sent requests to the registrars of the institutions for the number of cases of plagiarism for the period 2002–2017, which they supplied. Secondary data were analysed using Microsoft Excel and presented in charts and graphs.

Conclusion

This chapter outlined the methodology used to collect and analysed the data presented in the next eight chapters. Data were garnered from three content analyses and a survey which afforded students the opportunity to include qualitative data. Relevance sampling was used for the content analyses as the number of units identified was not large enough to warrant the use of any other sampling method. Stratified random and cluster-based sampling techniques were utilized for the survey to ensure that a representative sample was selected for participation. The sample of 1,040 was selected from the population of 17,719 undergraduate students enrolled at the University of the West Indies, Mona Campus, in Jamaica. Ethical considerations of informed consent, anonymity and confidentiality were observed, and the researcher obtained institutional approval to conduct research. Secondary data on the number of cases of plagiarism at the secondary and tertiary levels were also analysed.

Chapter 7

Snapshots of Plagiarism from across the Caribbean

Introduction

Given that schools are mirrors reflecting what happens in the wider society and vice versa, plagiarism in schools is likely to point to it within the society. In order to get a glimpse of rates and types of plagiarism in the Anglophone Caribbean, a content analysis was done of the reports of plagiarism in newspaper articles from the various English-speaking territories for the period 2002–2017. This chapter presents an analysis and discussion of the resulting data.

Background

Plagiarism is a worldwide phenomenon that threatens the integrity of institutions (Roka 2017, 2), and as such, it is one of the most researched topics in education. However, to date, only four studies have been done on plagiarism in the Caribbean by Walcott (2016), Porter (2016), Baker-Gardner and Smart (2017) and Welsh-Unwala (2019). There is therefore a need to conduct further investigations into plagiarism in order to get a better understanding of the extent to which this misconduct is being practised in the Caribbean.

Given that newspapers are a record of daily occurrences within a society, the researcher chose this as the starting point for this work. According to Tanacković, Krtalić and Lacović, newspapers are a valuable source of research data because they "reflect social and cultural values of a certain place and time and often contain unique information that cannot be found anywhere else" (2014, 2). The aim of this study was to determine the extent to which plagiarism was evident in Caribbean societies with the more specific objectives being to:

- identify cases of plagiarism in newspaper articles in the English-speaking Caribbean;

- examine the cases of plagiarism based on the types and the sectors in which they were found; and
- discuss the responses to plagiarism presented in these articles.

This was achieved through a content analysis of newspaper articles from CARICOM territories. This study will add a societal perspective to the issue of plagiarism, which is usually studied within the academic setting, and will also add to the emerging literature on plagiarism in the Caribbean.

Review of Literature

The dearth of research on the occurrence of plagiarism outside of academia was evident as there was little literature to be reviewed. Whereas there were anecdotal references to the many cases of plagiarism committed by well-known individuals, scholars tend to focus their efforts on researching plagiarism in academia. Due to the shortage of literature, some of the articles used are dated. Plagiarism in education will not be dealt with in this chapter but in a subsequent one.

Plagiarism in Politics: According to Wheeler and Anderson, "Politicians, more than anyone else, need to portray an image of integrity, honesty, and independent thought." They further state that the future of these politicians and their constituents depends on their level of honesty and plagiarism compromises honesty (2010, 166). On the contrary, Oransky and Marcus note that *Dissernet*, a network founded to protect the integrity of higher education qualifications in Russia, discovered approximately 5,600 cases of plagiarism among Russian politicians, as one out of every nine is believed to have plagiarized his dissertation (2016). Greenburg states that politicians who plagiarize inflict harm on their audience, the creator of the work and the opposition (2008).

Plagiarism in Journalism: Clarke notes that journalism courses in Australia do not emphasize plagiarism, although codes of ethics usually mention it. He notes that references to plagiarism by these codes are condemnatory, and often lack depth, and therefore concludes "plagiarism is rife, and only some of the most extreme cases are acted upon" (2006, 93). Chaney and Duncan further noted that a study of seventy-five journalism schools revealed seventeen of these had no written policies for plagiarism. In addition, no mention was made of plagiarism policies by educators (1985, 13). The findings of the analysis of fifty-eight written plagiarism policies in the United States by Chaney and Duncan (1985) would seem to support Clarke's findings of plagiarism among journalists which he attributed to the short turnaround time required to produce news stories, and the lack of opportunities for reflection because of the limited time (2006, 93). Moore and Murray identified another factor fuelling plagiarism among journalist and this was a lack of financial resources, which resulted in skeleton staff manning newsrooms (2008, 127).

In a recent survey of 953 journalists, Lewis and Zhong found that these professionals "were more likely to consider attribution optional if they were under pressure to produce, worked for a broadcast medium, were a content creator, were less experienced, or saw their principles as flexible" (2013, 148). Lack of instructions on plagiarism during training and a work environment with high pressure to produce, limited staff and limited turnaround time create the ideal conditions to exacerbate plagiarism.

Plagiarism in Entertainment: Clarke points out the difficulty of treating plagiarism in entertainment and music because of various practices which have become acceptable. He notes that the system whereby artistes learn from each other and the influences of technology combine to make deciphering acts of plagiarism difficult (2006, 94). Lee et al. developed computer software aimed at detecting plagiarism in music as they found that this had become a serious problem (2011, 828). The system works very much like text-matching software, except that it is aimed at detecting similarities in the melody. Lepera and Maneulin point out that plagiarism in music was also a cause for litigation (1999, 3).

Presentation and Analysis of Data

Eighteen territories were included in this search for articles. These are Anguilla, Antigua and Barbuda, Barbados, Belize, Bermuda, British Virgin Islands, Cayman Islands, Dominica, Grenada, Guyana, Jamaica, Montserrat, St Kitts and Nevis, St Lucia, St Vincent and the Grenadines, Trinidad and Tobago, and Turks and Caicos. Sixty-two articles which met the selection criteria were found in twenty-six newspapers from ten territories. The articles could be categorized as letters to the editor, commentaries, lead stories and editorials. Fifty-seven of the articles described actual cases of plagiarism in the Caribbean, both regionally and internationally, while the others were didactic in nature.

Number of Articles from Each Territory

The ten territories from which the newspaper reports emanate are shown in table 7.1 which provides a breakdown of the number of articles from each territory. Bates College states plagiarism is rampant in society generally

Table 7.1. Number of cases of plagiarism reported in online newspapers for the period 2002–2017

Territory	Number of newspapers	Number of articles	Percentage
Antigua and Barbuda	1	3	4.8
The Bahamas	4	8	12.9
Barbados	3	5	8.1
Bermuda	2	3	4.8
Dominica	3	5	8.1
Grenada	1	1	1.6
Guyana	5	10	16.1
Jamaica	3	18	29.0
St Kitts and Nevis	2	3	4.8
Trinidad and Tobago	2	6	9.7
Total	26	62	99.9*

*Figures rounded off.

(n.d.); however, although the number of articles found did not indicate this being the case in the Caribbean, it showed that plagiarism was present. The territories with the highest number of articles were Jamaica (29 per cent), followed by Guyana (16.1 per cent) and The Bahamas (12.9 per cent). The high number of articles from Jamaica can be explained from the perspective that it is the largest island in the English-speaking Caribbean and was the origin of a number of cases of plagiarism in CXC examinations. No cases of plagiarism were reported in newspapers from territories omitted from the table.

The literature on plagiarism reveals that there has been an increase in the number of cases of plagiarism globally with researchers such as McCabe (Bibliography – Academic Honesty 2006) and Jereb et al. (2018b, 1) ascribing this to the prevalence of the internet, while other researchers do not agree (Kayaoglu et al. 2015, 1; Ison 2015). Given the inconclusive findings from these various studies, it was important to determine if the number of reported cases of plagiarism in the Caribbean was increasing and so figure 7.1 presents a comparative view of the number of articles on plagiarism from 2002 to 2017. An increase in the number of articles would likely reflect a rise in the number of cases of plagiarism. From 2002 to

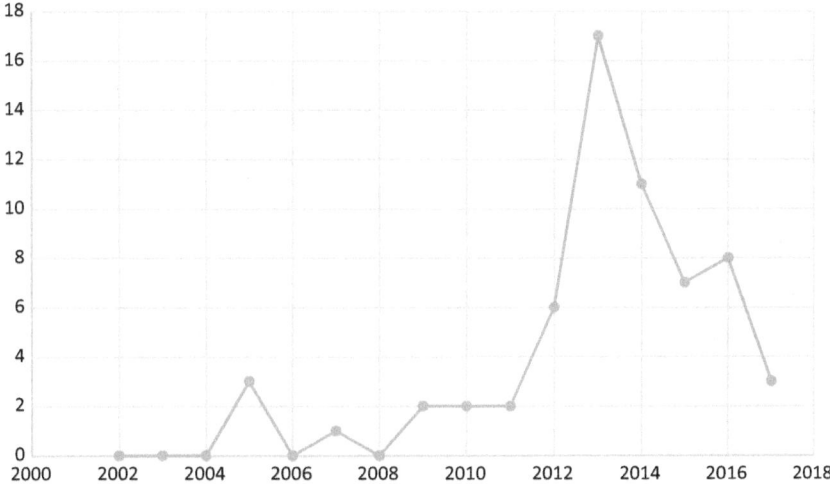

Figure 7.1. Number of articles on plagiarism published annually from 2002 to 2017.

2011, there were no more than three articles published on plagiarism in a given year; however, this changed in 2012 when the number of articles increased to six and then almost tripled in 2013 to 17 cases. This was the highest recorded number of articles in any given year during the period under study. The number of articles gradually fell over the next four years, reaching the starting figure of three by 2017.

The increase in 2013 resulted from the landmark case at Jamaica College which resulted in seventy students being penalized. It spawned a number of articles due to various persons weighing in on the issue. A detailed discussion of this is presented in Chapter 8. Whereas the number of cases of plagiarism increased generally, based on the literature, the number did not indicate a pattern of increase. Except for 2012–2016, the number of articles has remained relatively low over the period; however, this might not be reflective of the prevalence of plagiarism since most of the occurrences would not be reported as news except they were sensational or out of the ordinary. Furthermore, most institutions would tend to handle these as internal matters rather than making them public.

Articles by Sectors

Although plagiarism is categorized as academic misconduct, not all the cases of plagiarism reported in the articles occurred in education. The concept of the school as an open social system means there is a semi-permeable border between the school and the wider society. Therefore, what is present in one is likely to exist in the other as seen in table 7.2 when the plagiarism cases were classified according to the various sectors.

In keeping with the plethora of research literature on plagiarism in education, the highest number of articles (approximately 47 per cent) focused on education. The second-highest number of articles (29 per cent) was about plagiarism in politics, a reflection of international trends, and the website PlagiarismSearch.com states that plagiarism by Melania Trump was not an exception as it was a tradition among politicians (Plagiarism in Politics 2016). This would seem to be confirmed by Fawzy's list of ten world leaders who allegedly plagiarized (2016). Although plagiarism by politicians is so highly reported, there is little empirical data concerning its prevalence.

With regard to journalists, Rogers notes it is "jarring" when they are accused of plagiarism and states, "the first decade of the 21st century had no shortage of journalism-related scandals" (2019). While the percentage was not very high (4.8 per cent), it was still present and Uberti believes that the real challenge for journalism is deciding on a definition of plagiarism and how to respond to it (2014). The lack of a precise definition is also raised in the literature as one of the difficulties in finding solutions to plagiarism generally (Kokkinaki, Demoliou and Iakovidou 2015, 1; Louw 2017).

Types of Plagiarism

Due to the nature and purpose of the articles, it was difficult to neatly categorize the types of plagiarism into the various groupings advocated by organizations such as Turnitin, which seems mainly concerned with academia. Table 7.3 presents a broad classification of all the articles into five categories created by the author in an attempt to identify the types of plagiarism breaches.

The most prevalent type of plagiarism was unattributed borrowing, which accounted for 43.5 per cent of the articles and involved theft of academic content, political and academic speeches and newspaper articles. For the most part, the majority of or entire documents and speeches were plagiarized. Cheating on School-Based Assessments (SBAs) accounted for 24.2 per cent of the articles supporting the finding that there is a problem with plagiarism in education (Bretag 2013a, 1) and that secondary education has also been affected by this (Sisti 2007; Sureda-Negre, Comas-Forgas and Oliver-Trobat 2015). Of note was the series of articles published in Trinidad and Tobago aimed at educating the general populace about plagiarism. This accounted for 12.9 per cent of the total number of articles and demonstrated an awareness of the need for education on the topic in the region.

Table 7.2. Number of articles published by sector in each territory for the period 2002–2017

Countries	Education	Entertainment	Journalism	General	Politics	Religion	Total
Antigua and Barbuda	0	2	0	0	1	0	3
The Bahamas	8	0	0	0	0	0	8
Barbados	2	1	1	0	1	0	5
Bermuda	0	0	0	0	3	0	3
Dominica	4	0	0	0	1	0	5
Grenada	0	0	0	0	1	0	1
Guyana	3	0	2	3	2	0	10
Jamaica	10	2	0	0	5	1	18
St Kitts/Nevis	0	2	0	0	1	0	3
Trinidad and Tobago	2	1	0	3	0	0	6
Total	29	8	3	6	15	1	62
Percentage	46.8	12.9	4.8	9.7	29	1.6	100

Table 7.3. Types of plagiarism in articles

Description	Number	Percentage
Theft of musical lyrics/melody/dance moves	6	9.7
Cheating on School-Based Assessment	15	24.2
Unattributed borrowing (ideas, academic content, political speeches, academic speeches and so on)	27	43.5
General/Didactic	8	12.9
Other	6	9.7
Total	62	100

Responses to Plagiarism

Responses to plagiarism were mixed and seemed to correspond to the findings in the literature, as persons who shared similar political affiliations were tolerant of accusations of plagiarism brought against their colleagues. This concurred with Greenburg's statement that politicians who "borrowed" without giving due credit usually did not face any negative repercussions (2008). For example, in 2014, Roosevelt Skerritt, then prime minister of Dominica, was accused by the opposition party of plagiarizing political speeches, yet his political colleagues defended him (Walter Weighs in on Plagiarism Allegations 2014). On another occasion, a poll was conducted by *Dominica News Online* to get people's views on the importance of plagiarism in determining for whom to vote. This was after Lennox Lincoln, the leader of the United Workers' Party, was accused of plagiarizing. Though the results of the poll were not presented in the article, there were blog responses and social media posts. In these, people were of the view that "Dominica faced bigger problems that need to be addressed than that of plagiarism" (DNO Poll 2014).

In a somewhat similar manner, it was found that the response to plagiarism in education was treated with ambivalence in the articles. In the case of the College of the Bahamas (now the University of The Bahamas), the academic staff supported the president who confessed to plagiarism, much to the disdain of at least one newspaper which indicated its position in an editorial. Nevertheless, the president was subsequently re-appointed (Dames 2014). In cases of plagiarism in education, such as those involving SBAs, there was strong condemnation from the various stakeholder groups (Francis 2013; Gilpin 2013; Reid 2013a, c). However, there was also a desire for remediation as there were calls for education on plagiarism at the secondary and tertiary levels, which at least reflected an attempt to address the situation in a holistic manner. The newspapers did not call for sanctions for the students who plagiarized, but CXC applied the sanctions outlined in its guidelines.

Discussion of Findings

The data revealed plagiarism was being practised in the Caribbean, although based on the articles, there were no newspaper reports on the topic from some territories. The reporting of cases of plagiarism in newspapers is in line with international practices, as these publications capture daily happenings which are of interest to their audience. Another observation was that there seemed to be a relationship between the size of the territory and the number of articles. Jamaica, the largest territory in the English-speaking Caribbean, accounted for the highest number of articles. However, Trinidad and Tobago, which had almost twice the population of Guyana, recorded fewer cases of plagiarism. Although there is still discussion as to whether the number of cases of plagiarism is increasing in academia, based on the articles over the fifteen-year period, there was no significant increase in the number of reported cases. However, the cheating scandal at Jamaica College in 2013 resulted in a higher number of articles for that period.

In keeping with the categorization of plagiarism as academic misconduct, the number of cases in education far outnumbered those of any other sector. However, there was a significant number of articles on plagiarism in politics, and this also seems to be the case globally. Responses to plagiarism were different in various sectors, with education taking the most serious approach with suggestions for educating students to minimize a recurrence. The responses to plagiarism in politics were influenced by political affiliation with politicians supporting colleagues from their parties who plagiarized.

Overall, although the number of articles for the period was low, they are evidence that there is an awareness of plagiarism across the region. Generally, there seems to be a belief that plagiarism is wrong and ought not to be accepted although there is some level of ambivalence regarding it. Additionally, there seems to be the thinking that education can be beneficial in discouraging or deterring the practice.

Chapter 8

Maintaining Academic Integrity in Secondary Education in the Caribbean

Introduction

The implementation of systems and programmes for academic integrity in higher education will be strongly influenced by provisions for the development of academic integrity at the secondary level. It is, therefore, important to examine the practices and challenges in developing academic integrity at the secondary level in order to put into context what occurs in higher education. With this in mind, this chapter examines the processes used to ensure quality in secondary education in the Caribbean by presenting a background to the quality assurance process of Caribbean Examination Council (CXC). It discusses cases of academic misconduct at the secondary level as reported in newspapers in the Caribbean for the period 2002–2017 and examines the Council's responses to these. In addition, it presents and discusses data provided by the Council on the number of cases of suspected plagiarism in both Caribbean Secondary Examination Certificate (CSEC) and Caribbean Advanced Proficiency Examination (CAPE). It concludes with a discussion on the landmark case of plagiarism at Jamaica College in 2013.

Background

Like all examining boards, CXC has the responsibility of maintaining academic integrity in its examination processes and products, and it does so in collaboration with ministries of education and schools at the secondary level. One significant feature of CXC is the use of School-Based Assessments (SBAs), which affords students the opportunity to complete a part of their assessment and gain between 20 per cent and 60 per cent of the marks for a subject before the examination. The value assigned to the SBA component of the examination depends on the practical nature of the subject (Caribbean Examination Council 2015), and this therefore means the Council has to ensure the integrity of SBA as well as procedures and processes before, during and after examinations.

Griffith lauds the use of SBA as an excellent way of individualizing the curriculum by placing focus on individual students. CXC states it has been using SBAs since the inception of its examinations in 1979. According to the Council, SBA:

1. provides opportunities to gather data on student performance over time;
2. serves to motivate students by engaging them in meaningful activities that are relevant to them; and for teachers, it can reinforce curriculum aims and good teaching practices;
3. aligns assessment with curriculum and instruction;
4. provides students with multiple opportunities to demonstrate their competence;
5. allows students to be active participants in the assessment process;
6. gives credence and recognition to the teachers' informed judgements about students' performance; and
7. allows teachers to be critical leaders in the assessment process. (Caribbean Examinations Council 2016, 2)

The Council also notes that the SBA may take a variety of forms depending on the subjects and includes "portfolios, journals, dramatic presentations, research assignments, multimedia presentations, community projects, laboratory activities including investigations, site visits/field trips, orals, case studies, sporting activities and event planning, and designing/composing" for Technical and Vocational Education and Training subjects (Caribbean Examination Council 2016, 8–9). These SBAs are done at the schools, and thus each institution has a responsibility to ensure that policies, guidelines and systems are in place to provide adequate guidance to students so that they can complete these tasks with integrity. These should not only be applicable to students who are taking the CXC examinations, but schools should provide the environment to foster the development of academic integrity at all grades, thus making academic integrity a part of the institutional culture, a position which is further discussed in part 3.

Quality Assurance in Secondary Education: Griffith (2015) outlines several ways the Council carries out the process of quality assurance for external examinations. These include the use of specimen examination papers to guide teachers and students; the use of subject panels responsible for the development of specimen questions and mark schemes; the use of a chief examiner and two assistant chief examiners to form the examining committee for each subject; pre-testing of objective type items; the use of moderators for examination papers (29); a standardized examination administration and grading process (30); supervision of the marking of scripts; review of the marking by an independent technical advisory committee before grades are released; and the publication of a report for each subject to facilitate the opportunity for teachers to make adjustments in preparation of students (31).

The matter of academic integrity has implications for quality, and the Council has made provision for this in four documents. First, the manual titled, *Regulations for the Conduct of the Council's Examinations*, is aimed at ensuring that examinations are conducted so as to ensure integrity. In addition, the manual includes guidelines on how to report irregularities which occur during the course of the examination. Second, in its *Guidelines for Candidates Writing Examinations Offered by CXC*, the Council lists plagiarism as one of the many offences under penalties for misconduct. The Council does not provide a definition for plagiarism in this source but presents an example by stating, "Plagiarism, for example, in SBA assignments and artwork" (Caribbean Examination Council 2013a, 15). Third, the *SBA Handbook for Teachers* emphasizes the seriousness of plagiarism by stating it is "a universal intellectual offence and is taken very seriously" (Caribbean Examination Council 2013b, 24). Fourth, there is the *School Based Assessment Manual for Principals*, dated 2015. The Council also includes information on plagiarism in some of its syllabi.

The Council outlines the sanctions to be applied in the case of academic misconduct. It states cancellation of results in the subject is the punishment for plagiarism (Caribbean Examination Council 2013a, 17). In its handbook for teachers, the Council instructs that where plagiarism has been discovered in students' work "early," the class teacher should consult with the head of the department and the principal. The student should be given a warning and be required to do over the work (Caribbean Examination Council 2013b, 22).

In these documents, a passing mention is made of plagiarism, and this might have been in the interest of brevity. However, the literature does emphasize the importance of giving clear instructions on plagiarism (Tbilisi 2019, 2). In addition to the documents produced by CXC, the ministries of education in both Jamaica and Trinidad and Tobago have also developed national guidelines for ensuring integrity in the SBA process.

Within the region, there is no organized programme for education on academic integrity at the secondary level which could be due, in part, to a lack of a formal programme for the teaching of media and information literacy (MIL) in which academic integrity concepts are usually introduced. In other jurisdictions, the teaching of MIL is usually a responsibility assigned to the school librarian. However, the Caribbean lacks the capacity for undertaking this task due to the poor provision for school libraries and shortage of trained personnel in most countries, as generally school libraries are "relegated to the periphery of the curriculum" (Robinson 2007, 112).

Trinidad and Tobago and Jamaica have launched new curricula in primary and secondary schools during the last decade. An examination of both of these shows the inclusion of some elements of academic integrity instructions. Trinidad and Tobago makes mention of MIL in its curriculum, but the focus seems to be more on the media component than on information literacy. In Trinidad and Tobago, students are introduced to academic integrity, to include plagiarism, in the lower secondary school, and in alignment with Lai and Weeks' finding, this is embedded in the information communication technology curriculum (2009, 10). Elements of MIL are also evident throughout the Jamaican curriculum. Although Jamaica and Trinidad and Tobago represent approximately 70 per cent of the students who sit CXC annually, neither have a robust programme for the teaching of MIL to include academic integrity.

No matter how strong a system of quality assurance and accountability is, there will be individuals who will attempt to find ways to circumvent it. Heyneman believes an ethical academy can successfully handle a corrupt individual, with little damage to its reputation (2011, 13). This statement is based on the premise that checks and balances in the system are effective and efficient enough to identify and treat these breaches. This study therefore aimed to investigate the state of academic integrity in secondary education, viewed through the processes and practices of CXC. The researcher sought to:

- investigate the types of academic misconduct in CXC examinations as reported in newspaper articles for the period 2002–2017;
- discuss the treatment of these breaches by CXC; and
- discuss the prevalence of plagiarism among secondary students using data provided by CXC.

This study is important because, as the first of its kind, it opens discussion on a topic not yet investigated from this perspective in the Caribbean and so should add to the emerging literature on plagiarism in the Caribbean and to the literature on academic integrity in secondary education internationally. It should also stimulate discussion and could in the long-term lead to policy modifications and implementation.

Review of Literature

A blanket of silence surrounds the topic of plagiarism in the Caribbean, both at the secondary and tertiary levels, so much, so that even the literature reveals an absence of meaningful discussion on the topic. Occasional reports in the newspapers are usually the only indication that something has gone wrong; however, empirical data from other jurisdictions bear witness that plagiarism is in fact happening at the secondary level.

Sureda-Negre, Comas-Forgas and Oliver-Trobat note that plagiarism has not received the kind of attention at the secondary level that it has received in higher education (2015, 104), an observation supported by Lai and Weeks (2008, 2). Sureda-Negre and colleagues based their conclusion on responses from 2,794 Spanish students. The findings revealed plagiarism was "widespread" among secondary students with collage (called mashup by Turnitin) being the most popular infringement. Secondary students were more likely to engage in the least serious forms of plagiarism when compared to university students (2015, 108). Sisti (2007) agrees that plagiarism is rampant among secondary students. He concurs with Sureda-Negre, Comas-Forgas and Oliver-Trobat that secondary students were more likely to engage in the "least serious" forms of plagiarism. He mentions that they have a "list" of behaviours which they rank as acceptable and unacceptable (225). Students were, therefore, unwilling to engage in what they considered risky behaviours, such as purchasing papers from paper mills (Sureda-Negre, Comas-Forgas and Oliver-Trobat 2015, 108).

Plagiarism Facts and Stats also agreed that there is plagiarism at the secondary level. It reported data collected by the Josephson Institute Center for Youth Ethics which had one out of three secondary students saying that during the past year they used the internet to plagiarize material for an assignment. The conclusion by Josephson Institute Center for Youth Ethics was drawn from data collected from forty-three thousand students enroled in both public and private schools (Plagiarism Facts and Stats 2017). Plagiarism Facts and Stats also reported on research conducted by McCabe involving twenty-four thousand students at seventy high schools in the United States, which showed that 58 per cent of the students reported that they plagiarized (Plagiarism Facts and Stats 2017).

Lai and Weeks offer a possible explanation for plagiarism at the secondary level. They found that "the nature of plagiarism has not been clearly understood by students, and many schools considered it primarily as a copyright issue, with rules and regulations on plagiarism written as part of the Internet acceptable use policy" (2009, 13). This conclusion was drawn from a survey of incoming university students' understanding of plagiarism while they were in high school, combined with analysis of school rules and policies regarding e-plagiarism.

Tauginienė and Gaižauskaitė (2018) point out that poor practices regarding academic integrity at the secondary level are a causatory factor for academic misconduct in HEIs. They conducted a content analysis of policies of thirty-two high schools in Lithuania and concluded there was no systematic approach for dealing with academic integrity at the secondary levels. They posited that by the time students enter tertiary institutions, these poor practices have become entrenched and remediation becomes difficult (105). This lack of attention to plagiarism in secondary institutions is supported by the findings of Ukpebor and Ogbebor (2013) who surveyed one thousand students from fifty schools in Nigeria and found that the majority of students had never heard of plagiarism, while only a few could define the term (254). Kam, Hue and Cheung's (2018) findings from the sample of 257 grades 10 and 11 students concur with that of Ukpebor and Ogbebor (2013).

Data Presentation and Analysis

A total of twenty-six articles from five Caribbean countries were analysed and discussed. These include twenty-one articles on plagiarism that were used in Chapter 7, and five additional articles on academic integrity which did not qualify for inclusion in Chapter 7 based on its scope. Figure 8.1 shows the territories from which these articles originated.

Of the twenty-six articles analysed, the majority of these (54 per cent) originated from Jamaica with Barbados and Guyana each accounting for 15 per cent. Trinidad and Tobago (12 per cent) and St Vincent and the Grenadines (4 per cent) had the lowest percentage of articles. The high percentage of articles from Jamaica is a result of the case of plagiarism at Jamaica College in 2013, which attracted significant media attention due to its magnitude. From these

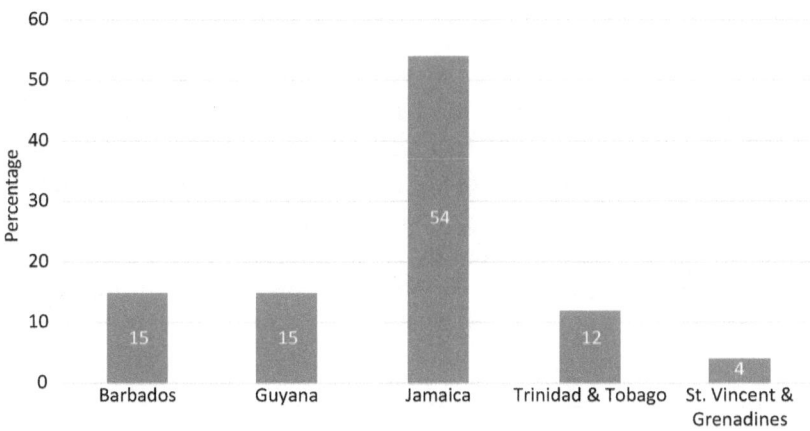

Figure 8.1. Number of articles on academic misconduct in secondary education by territories.

twenty-six newspaper articles, it was possible to glean information on types of academic misconduct at the secondary level and the contributory factors. The articles also provided information on the consequences meted out to those who breached integrity guidelines and the responses from education stakeholders and CXC to cases of academic misconduct. A discussion of the measures that were implemented by CXC to deal with academic misconduct follows, based on the information presented in these articles.

Types of Academic Dishonesty Practised by Secondary Students in the Caribbean

Hallak and Poisson state that academic fraud can occur at different points in the academic process (2007, 234). This was true of the types of academic misconduct practised in the region as will be evident from this discussion. Newspaper reports identified several types of academic dishonesty practised in the Caribbean by secondary students, teachers and others. These cases ranged from cheating in examinations to the submission of "fraudulent" SBA documents.

Cheating in the examination room was done in various ways. Students cheated in the examination room by bringing in the information written either on their bodies or on paper (Honore-Gopie and Rampersad 2009). In addition, some students tried to communicate with others in the examination room. Technology also posed a challenge as it was reported that 0.9 per cent or just over two thousand of the entrants for the 2011 examinations entered the examination room with cellular phones, a breach of the Council's guidelines, and were disqualified (CXC Aiming to Reduce Disqualification at Upcoming Exams 2012). This practice was described by one CXC official as a "recurring issue" (Wilson 2014). In St Vincent and the Grenadines, the results of thirty-one students were cancelled in 2011 because they took phones into the examination room. These rang and vibrated and were used to send text messages while the examination was in progress (Spence 2011). Susan Giles, assistant registrar of CXC, reported that there have been cases when students who have "photographic memories" have reproduced stories for the "English A" examination. Giles, also noted that in 98 per cent of these cases, the examiners were familiar with the reproduced stories (CXC Touts Introduction of Software to Arrest Plagiarism 2012).

Cheating in various forms also took place outside the examination room. One such was plagiarism with regard to the SBA. The *Kaieteur News Online* reported that Stephenson Grayson, assistant registrar, noted that plagiarism was usually detected "when dealing with SBA" (CXC Touts Introduction of Software to Arrest Plagiarism 2012). He explained detection was usually done by experts while assessing the projects. Sometimes, they were able to detect the act because the work was their own. Copying from the internet for SBA has also been identified as one of the ways the students cheat (Madden 2015).

Cheating is not always done by students as it was reported that there were cases where thieves stole and later sold examination papers for financial benefit (Cheating at Examinations 2015). Additionally, there were allegations of fraud resulting from a seventeen-year-old Trinidadian student "having prior knowledge of Mathematics and English" (Williams 2008). Another challenge encountered by CXC was the falsification of results. A case reported by *The Gleaner* stated that individuals were "selling doctored preliminary results slips on the streets" in Jamaica for as little as $12,000 Jamaican dollars (Reid 2012), less than US$100 at the time of writing. Further, in Trinidad, a principal and a physical education teacher were charged for forgery regarding CXC results (Secondary School Officials Charged with Fraud 2017), and in another reported case, persons were employed on the merit of "false" certification (Reid 2012).

A significant challenge with academic misconduct in the Caribbean was the prominent role played by educators in some of these alleged cases. Dianne Medford, assistant registrar of CXC, recounts a case of a teacher submitting SBAs on behalf of students. The SBAs contained work from a previous syllabus because no SBAs were done with the class (Morris 2013). In the landmark case at Jamaica College, which resulted in the rescinding of the grades of 70 sixth formers who did CAPE, teachers were found guilty of emailing SBAs to students for them to copy. Students were also instructed by teachers to copy from websites (Reid 2013b).

Cheating was not only evident in the public school system as private schools also had to grapple with the issue. Wilson (2014) made reference to one case of a teacher in a private institution in Jamaica doing SBA for a student for a cost (as reported by the student), an example of contract cheating. Another case of plagiarism in private school was also mentioned in *The Gleaner* in 2015 (Students Should Do SBAs under Exam Conditions 2015). It was not clear whether these two articles were referring to the same case. However, one could draw such a conclusion based on the similarities in the report.

Based on the articles, it was evident that there was a range of misconduct committed by various individuals. It was also evident, though from only one case, that contract cheating was among these. It is therefore expected that the council will remain vigilant in protecting the integrity of its examinations.

Causes of Academic Dishonesty

An analysis of the articles showed that there were several causative factors for academic misconduct which are in keeping with what the literature reports. Fernandes (2016), in a letter to the editor of the *Stabroek News* from Guyana, presented a strong case that there were too many SBAs which were hastily completed to meet submission deadlines. This supports the findings from the literature which states poor time management and too many assignments were definite factors that could lead to plagiarism (Vázquez-Recio et al. 2016, 2508; Sureda-Negre, Comas-Forgas and Oliver-Trobat 2015, 105). The need to hastily complete assignments could have resulted from having too many assignments to do (Sisti 2007, 221; Kayaoglu et al. 2015, 1), mental fatigue (Fernandes 2016) as well as procrastination (Hussein, Rushdi and Mohamad 2016, 639). Sureda-Negre, Comas-Forgas and Oliver-Trobat found the "greater the tendency to procrastinate, the greater the tendency to engage in plagiarism" (2015, 108). Fernandes (2016) opines that one of the issues that compound the time problem was the student's need to search in various places to locate the information needed to complete SBAs. Fernandes further states that students may be hindered in the process of finding information within the organizations in which they are conducting the research because the personnel is too busy to provide them with the required data.

An additional possible reason for plagiarism among Caribbean secondary students alluded to in the literature was the absence of detection systems as threat of detection worked in some cases to decrease cheating (Chapman et al. 2004). Hence, CXC's proposal to introduce the kind of software to identify plagiarism as a response to this. As reported by *Kaieteur News*, from as early as 2012, CXC reported that it would implement this strategy as being "in the near future" (CXC Touts Introduction of Software to Arrest Plagiarism 2012). Although there was no report in the articles of this being acquired, mention was made of it being used, possibly suggesting that the organization had actually acted upon its word (Morris 2013). However, based on the review of literature, the use of detection software to stem plagiarism has produced mixed results. Although it has been found to decrease the number of cases in high schools (Bailey 2013), students still continued to plagiarize in institutions which used it (Goh 2013, 307). Educating students about plagiarism is still regarded by many as the best way to help students develop academic integrity and so reduce their motivation to plagiarize (Hu and Sun 2017, 66; Saddiqui 2016, 12).

Plagiarism in the Caribbean might have been impacted by what Vázquez-Recio et al. refer to as "superficial monitoring" (2016, 5711). School administrators might not have been vigilant enough in ensuring that there was integrity in the process of completing SBAs. Principal Ruel Reid of Jamaica College admitted there had been "unethical and unprofessional conduct" by teachers when it was found that they sent labs that were previously completed to students so they could copy them (Reid 2013c). *The Gleaner* referred to these as "glaring lapses" and suggested that there was the need for "quality assurance measures" at all levels of the system (What If CSEC Cheating Widespread? 2013). The newspaper further reported that Hector Stephenson, executive director of the Overseas Examination Commission, identified the principal as the accountable officer tasked with ensuring academic integrity in the school (Reid 2013d), a statement supported by Campbell (2013) in her newspaper article on the same story.

Calls for secondary students to be taught about plagiarism from Jamaican educators (Gilpin 2013) seem to be based on the idea that students plagiarized due to a lack of understanding which has strong support in the literature (Vázquez-Recio et al. 2016, 5712; Gullifer and Tyson 2010, 22; Ismail 2018; Ali, Ismail and Cheat 2012, 610; Lai and Weeks 2009, 13). These calls came from two prominent Jamaican educators in response to the case of Jamaica College. Sharon Reid, president of the Jamaica Association of Secondary Principals, and Elaine Foster Allen, in her capacity as permanent secretary in the Ministry of Education, expressed the belief that education would be helpful in assisting students to avoid plagiarism (Gilpin 2013). In the rationale for its manual titled, *Guidelines for Managing School-Based Assessments (SBA)*, the Ministry of Education of Trinidad and Tobago acknowledged the need for education on academic integrity. It stated that there were many instances of "fraudulent and inexpert behaviours by candidates" including:

- plagiarism demonstrated through uncited or poorly cited quotations;
- unacceptable sources for research information;
- malpractice through collusion between students or overly extensive help provided by teachers; and
- fabrication and falsification of interview responses or experimental results (n.d., 4).

This too strengthens the case for instruction in academic integrity to include the proper use of source materials.

Based on the content analysis, the final reason for plagiarism in secondary education in the Caribbean would seem to be dishonest teachers (Reid 2013a; Wilson 2014; Madden 2015). In a commentary in *The Gleaner*, a writer lamented that "too many individuals of questionable background" were in the teaching profession (Campbell 2013). This statement was made as a result of the report on the number of cases of plagiarism facilitated by teachers, who offered to do SBAs for students (Wilson 2014) and others who encouraged students to copy previous SBAs (Reid 2013c). These professionals undoubtedly were guilty of inspiring the wrong behaviour in their students. This has impacted the number of cases of plagiarism at the secondary level and resulted in students facing penalties for cheating that could have been avoided. In an article titled, "Ban Them," the CXC's Hector Stephenson joined with the National Parent Teachers Association of Jamaica to advocate that teachers involved in academic misconduct should be punished by not being allowed to prepare students for future CXC examinations (Reid 2013a).

CXC's Response to Academic Dishonesty

A number of penalties were administered to students and others found guilty of academic dishonesty. With reference to CXC, Susan Giles stated, "[W]e live and die by our reputation" (CXC Lays Down the Law 2012). She reported that in cases where students reproduced short stories in English A, they would be given no marks for the stories. In addition, they would receive no marks for plagiarized SBAs (CXC Touts Introduction of Software to Arrest Plagiarism 2012). This was in keeping with the penalty outlined by CXC in its guidelines. Dianne Medford, assistant registrar in the Examinations Administration Division of CXC, also highlighted a case in which teachers did the SBAs for students and as a consequence they all received "ungraded" for these projects (Morris 2013). In the case of Jamaica College, the grades of the seventy CAPE students were rescinded (Francis 2013). Other penalties mentioned by the *Barbados Nation* for students who cheated were "disqualification from all exams for which the candidate has been registered, [. . .] or a two-year ban" (CXC Fraud Up 2012).

In cases of cheating, students were not the only ones who were penalised, nor were the penalties confined to reduction or rescinding of grades. According to Dianne Medford, there was a case where the same SBA was submitted under a different name resulting in the teacher, principal and the head of the department being suspended. In addition, the entire class did not receive a mark for that particular subject (Zero Tolerance for Cheaters, Cell Phones, 2012). There have also been court cases as the Council sought to protect its reputation. Hector Stephenson stated that CXC "had many cases where we have called in the police, people have been charged and a number of them thrashed out in the court, and people fined. There are always ongoing cases of fraudulent preliminary slips" (Reid 2013b). Court cases included a seventeen-year-old being charged with having prior knowledge of the contents of an examination (Williams 2008).

There was the reported case of a "hustler" who sold fraudulent CXC certificates. He promised an undercover news reporter that the information on the fraudulent certificate could be added to the CXC database. However, one CXC official noted this was impossible and explained that CXC utilizes a protected electronic system with a high degree of security (Reid 2013d). The Council also sought to put additional measures in place to deter cheating. Morris reported that there was a programme aimed at redesigning the submission of SBAs to reduce the level of cheating. She stated, "New systems are being analysed for SBA documents to be uploaded for analysis, which will identify plagiarism" (2013). If this was a reference to text matching software, then these do not identify plagiarism. Instead, they highlight matching text to facilitate further investigations. In commenting on the Jamaica College issue, Campbell (2013) explained that part of the challenge was the lack of an adequate history of quality assurance in the region. This suggests that CXC also depends on each territory having its own quality assurance system to ensure the integrity of its examinations.

From the analysis of the nature of academic misconduct that was practised, teachers, students and even persons outside of the education system are involved in these acts of dishonesty. These infractions included cheating in the examinations room, plagiarism in the SBA and the creation and sale of fraudulent certificates. Based on the various reports in the media and from CXC, several different penalties have been applied in the cases where individuals have been found guilty of behaviours that put the integrity of the CXC examinations at risk.

Prevalence of Plagiarism in CSEC and CAPE Examination

In light of the reports of cheating at CXC, an editorial in the *Stabroek News* in Guyana has raised pertinent questions across the region about the veracity of the SBA as a proficiency measuring tool (Cheating at Examination 2015). In commenting on the case of a man trying to enter the Jamaican police force with false qualifications from CXC, Stephenson said that this was not unusual, pointing out that three or four cases of the same kind had made it to the court during the last three years (Reid 2013b). Dianne Medford also indicated that the Council has seen a "steady flow" of cheating in examinations, with Jamaica having the largest number of cases of plagiarism due mainly to it having the most students sitting the examinations (Morris 2013).

Statistics from the Council were examined in an attempt to determine the prevalence of plagiarism. The data revealed there were 139 suspected cases for the period 2006–2018 of which ninety-seven were CSEC students, while the remaining forty-two were CAPE entrants. The data on the suspected cases of plagiarism in CSEC are presented in figure 8.2 by subjects.

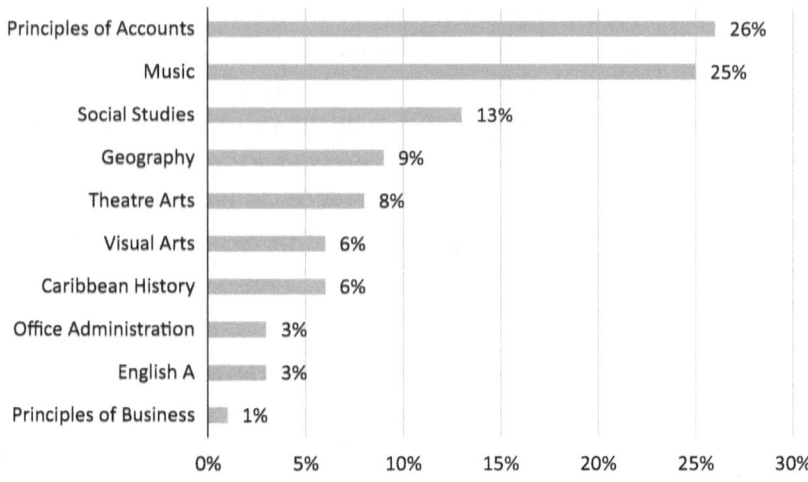

Figure 8.2. Cases of suspected plagiarism in CSEC subjects for the period 2006–2018.

Of the ninety-seven suspected cases of plagiarism for the CSEC subjects, the highest number (26 per cent) was for students registered for Principles of Accounts and this reflects McCabe's findings that business students cheated more than others (2011). The second-highest number of suspected cases was in Music (25 per cent) with English A (English Language) and Office Administration having a low number with only 3 per cent each. The suspected cases in Principles of Business (1 per cent) contrasted sharply with Principles of Accounts and deviated significantly from the finding that business students cheated more than other groups. One possible explanation for the low rates of plagiarism in English A, which is taken by a large percentage of the cohort of students, was that SBA for English A was only introduced in 2016 (Marchalleck 2015), and the majority of cases of plagiarism at CXC was evident in SBA. The 3 per cent would therefore represent data for only three (2016–2018) of the twelve years.

Suspected cases of plagiarism were found in nine of the thirty-three CSEC subjects offered by the Council and spanned nine of the sixteen territories, supporting the view of Giles that the number of cases was relatively low (Dottin 2013). Fifty per cent of the infractions were from one territory; however, due to confidentiality, the name of this territory was not provided by CXC for this paper, even though follow-up enquiries were made. Nevertheless, one might be tempted to assume that the territory with the highest number of cases might be Jamaica, based on Dianne Medford's admission in the press that it had the largest number of cases (Morris 2013).

Data for the number of suspected cases of plagiarism in CAPE subjects were provided for the period 2010–2016, and these are shown in figure 8.3. The number of cases adds up to 101 per cent due to rounding off.

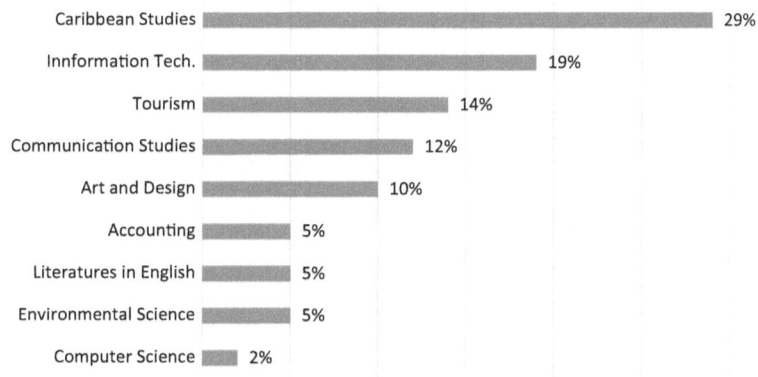

Figure 8.3. Cases of suspected plagiarism by CAPE subjects for the period 2010–2016.

Forty-two suspected cases were recorded for the period with Caribbean Studies (29 per cent) having the highest number followed by Information Technology (19 per cent), while Literatures in English and Environmental Science had 5 per cent each and Computer Science (2 per cent) recorded the fewest. The low number of business students who cheated in CAPE runs contrary to the findings in the CSEC data and also that of McCabe that business students cheated more than others (2011). The number of suspected cases in each subject seems to be relatively low and almost negligible given the large number of students registered for each subject. For example, in 2016, there were 30,859 students entered for CAPE (Pompey 2016).

Frequency of Suspected Cases of Plagiarism

One CXC official indicated that the number of cases of academic misconduct at CXC was not increasing (Morris 2013), although in 2012, Susan Giles, another senior assistant registrar, noted that fraud in CXC was on the increase, prompting a zero-tolerance approach by the Council (CXC Fraud Up 2012). Given that there has been so much debate in the literature as to whether the number of cases of plagiarism has increased since the emergence of the internet, a line graph was used to plot the annual data for cases relative to CSEC and CAPE. The results are shown in figure 8.4.

There were significant fluctuations in the data for CSEC subjects, which ranged from a low of zero cases to a high of thirty-two with the highest number of cases recorded in 2012 and 2015. CAPE also showed fluctuations ranging from a low of zero cases in 2011 to a high of eleven in 2012. The number of students who entered for CAPE subjects was significantly

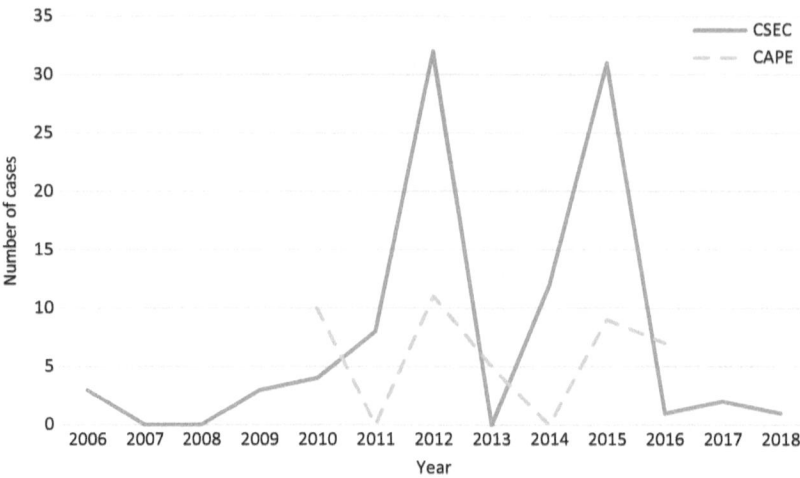

Figure 8.4. Number of suspected cases of plagiarism for the period 2006–2018.

lower than CSEC, hence the variations. Missing from this chart is the case of seventy Jamaica College CAPE students who were found guilty of plagiarism in 2013 (Francis 2013; Gilpin 2013; Reid 2013a).

Although there was anecdotal evidence that Caribbean secondary students were using the internet to plagiarize, as reported by officials of CXC (Madden 2015), there was no corresponding increase in the number of Caribbean secondary students who were caught plagiarizing given the increased access to the internet. Instead, for reasons not known to the researcher, some years recorded a higher number of cases than others. However, the fluctuations in the data also lead to questions as to how representative the numbers are of actual cases versus those detected and reported.

The Case of Jamaica College

In 2012, there was an admission from CXC officials that the Council was experiencing challenges with academic misconduct. This was borne out in articles titled, "CXC Touts Introduction of Software to Arrest Plagiarism" (2012), "Zero Tolerance for Cheaters, Cell Phones" (2012) and "CXC Aims to Reduce Disqualification at Upcoming Examination" (2012). However, one year later, the Council was faced with what could be described as its worse case of academic misconduct at Jamaica College. This was the most widely discussed and reported case of plagiarism in secondary education in the Anglophone Caribbean. It involved seventy students registered to sit the CAPE Physics examination in 2013. The registrar of CXC described it as a "sordid affair" (Reid 2013d). The facts of the case were pieced together based on information garnered from *The Gleaner* and the *Jamaica Observer*, the two most popular daily newspapers in Jamaica.

An investigation into plagiarism at Jamaica College was launched when a communication was sent to CXC headquarters in Barbados by a teacher who was dismissed from the school (Reid 2013c). Both the Overseas Examination Commission and the school launched investigations. A review committee examined coursework and statements regarding the matter and found there were both traditional and cyber plagiarism. In what *The Gleaner* described as a "dunce" move by a teacher, it was discovered that previously completed lab results were emailed to students by the teacher instructing them to rewrite these "in their own words" and submit them for assessment (Reid 2013c). Students were also instructed to copy from online sources. Although this was not plagiarism, it was also discovered that students were also allowed to mark the SBAs submitted by others without a rubric, practices not sanctioned by the Council (Reid 2013c).

The responses to this case were many, but there was general agreement among the respondents that the matter was wrong and could not be condoned. Francis (2013) captured the responses of Mark Nicely, president of the Jamaica Teachers Association, the union representing the majority of government teachers at the primary and secondary levels in Jamaica. He labelled plagiarism, "thievery" (Francis 2013), in keeping with the perspective in the literature. He claimed plagiarism robbed children of the opportunity to develop and practice research skills, another position supported by the literature (Foust 2016). Nicely decried the teachers who helped the students to plagiarize, suggesting that these teachers should not be allowed to continue to prepare students for CXC. This position was supported by the National Parent Teacher Association of Jamaica (Reid 2013a). The Jamaica Teachers' Association president expressed the view that the decision of whether or not to employ teachers involved in this misconduct in other schools should be made on a case-by-case basis, and the severity of the offences should be a deciding factor. He indicated that the union would not support any member involved in this behaviour and stated the teachers should be disciplined. The union president then encouraged CXC to "consider employing more vigorous strategies to monitor and investigate the SBA process" (Francis 2013).

In a situation such as this, the failure of the system should not only be blamed on the teacher and so Jamaica College accepted responsibility and launched a multi-pronged response to the matter. Both Reid (2013c) and Francis (2013) reported on the actions taken by the school to remedy the effects of this case of plagiarism. It was reported that the school implemented an honour code, an action supported by McCabe and Trevino (1993) and a practice used in universities in the United States. However, honour codes are usually implemented as part of an honour system, and by themselves, they have little impact on cheating (Mason, Gavrilovska and Joyner 2019, 1009). In addition, even within the honour system, the conclusion drawn from research on the effectiveness of honour codes is mixed (Barnard-Brak, Schmidt and Wei 2013, 231). Jamaica College apologized to its stakeholders and accepted financial responsibility for the misconduct by agreeing to pay for the subject for students who wanted to resit it in the following year. A letter of "condemnation" was sent to the teacher who encouraged the students to plagiarize. The school opted not to appeal the outcome of the case, and this could be understandable, given that Dianne Medford stated no appeal had ever been successful (Morris 2013).

CXC responded to the matter by revoking the grades of the seventy students who were involved, applying the penalty outlined in the guidelines. Students were, however, given the opportunity to resit the examination during the 2014 sitting. The Ministry of Education in Jamaica expressed satisfaction at the outcome of the incident but did not let the matter rest there (Reid 2013c). Two years later, the *Jamaica Observer* reported that the Ministry of Education had implemented stricter measures aimed at eliminating academic dishonesty. These included schools complying with the following six criteria under the monitoring of the Ministry: internal quality assurance, accountability, communication, monitoring, teacher support and school readiness. In addition, schools were to be assessed during the SBA season to "determine how well their administrative systems comply with the required standards" (Education Ministry Implements Stricter Measures for CXC SBAs 2015).

Discussion of Findings

Like other jurisdictions worldwide, the Caribbean has to manage issues of academic integrity that occur in spite of the systems put in place to reduce and eliminate these. In keeping with Hallak and Poisson, academic misconduct in secondary education in the Caribbean had many manifestations and occurred both inside and outside the examination room (2007). Within the examination room, students cheated by copying from the information they brought in, sometimes written on their bodies, rewriting sample stories they had memorized and using cellular phones to communicate with each other. Outside the examination room, academic integrity breaches included falsification of examination results, plagiarism in SBAs and theft and resale of examination papers. Teachers were involved in some cases of academic misconduct. The causes of academic dishonesty were in keeping with the findings in the literature.

In keeping with the practices which exist elsewhere, CXC and the ministries of education have put policies in place. Like most other institutions worldwide, the Council has taken a punitive approach to academic misconduct and it is not sure how effective this has been in curbing these cheating behaviours. There are still no programmes in place in the Caribbean to teach students about academic integrity in a holistic manner. When compared with the number of students registering for CSEC and CAPE, the number of cases of plagiarism seems minuscule and did not show any substantial increase over the period. What is worrisome is that the seventy cases of plagiarism at Jamaica College would have gone unnoticed had not a disgruntled teacher decided to report it, suggesting that cases of plagiarism could go undetected, a challenge with plagiarism management internationally. Overall, the data reveals that there is an urgent need to continue to strengthen the systems of academic integrity at all levels of the secondary system and by all stakeholders.

If academic integrity is to be maintained, it will take all parties working together. Schools have to do their part in ensuring that they teach students about academic integrity while maintaining robust administrative processes. These would make it more difficult for teachers to facilitate the kinds of cheating behaviours reported in the newspaper articles. Furthermore, lessons on academic integrity should be embedded in the curriculum and taught and practised at every level of the secondary system. This would at least ensure that students entering higher education already have some basic knowledge in this area which they can use to guide their actions. The HEIs could then build on this knowledge. As the institution in the Caribbean vested with the responsibility to oversee external examinations, CXC has been carrying out its mandate even as it responds to breaches by applying the stipulated sanctions; however, a more regional approach in the form of policies at the CARICOM level would be beneficial in ensuring the education systems embrace academic integrity in a more holistic manner.

Chapter 9

Academic Integrity and Plagiarism Policies of Caribbean Higher Education Institutions

Introduction

This chapter presents a content analysis of the plagiarism policies of fifteen HEIs native to the Caribbean to arrive at an understanding of their perspectives on plagiarism. Using five of the eight codes adapted from Hu and Sun (2017) and adding three additional ones, the researcher examines the contents of the plagiarism policies. This is done by describing the elements present in the policies, discussing how they are manifested and comparing them to what obtains in plagiarism policies elsewhere as presented in the review of the literature.

Background

Merriam-Webster defines a policy as a "definite course or method of action selected (by government, institution, group or individual) from among alternatives and in the light of given conditions to guide and, usually, determine present and future decisions." In education, policies are important because, according to Forstall, "they are the most effective way to create safe and supportive learning environments" (2019), but in order to accomplish this goal they must be clear and purposeful. Danielson (2006) insists that faculty contribute to the school culture by being responsible for interpreting the policies for students in their classes and ensuring this is done in a coherent manner.

An academic integrity policy is one of the many deemed necessary by most HEIs worldwide to support student learning while developing and maintaining integrity within the institution, and the majority of HEIs in the Caribbean have implemented this. The researcher felt it was important to conduct an analysis of these policies to get a better understanding of the state of academic integrity in the Caribbean. For the most part, this might be the only document in these institutions which focuses on academic integrity in the absence of a system that takes an integrated approach to the matter. Therefore, the objectives of this study were to:

- identify HEIs in the Caribbean with plagiarism policies or guidelines;
- examine the contents of the policies
- determine the approach taken to plagiarism based on the policies.

By analysing these policies, this current work will make an important contribution to the existing body of knowledge by creating an awareness of the HEIs' approach to academic integrity which could result in the following benefits: provide institutions the opportunity to be informed about what others are doing; reveal gaps that need to be addressed and possible best practices that can be adapted and adopted; and open an avenue for discussion of a topic that previously received little attention in the region. It will also break the silence on a topic that is of great concern in academia but has not featured significantly on the Caribbean's research agenda.

Review of Literature

The study of plagiarism policies is not new, although it has not received the attention accorded to the other aspects of the topic. Outstanding examples of plagiarism policy analysis include that done by Hu and Sun (2017) who studied the plagiarism policies of eight Chinese universities and by Kokkinaki, Demoliou and Iakovidou (2015) from Cyprus who examined students' perception of plagiarism and relevant policies. Another very comprehensive study, *Impact of Policies for Plagiarism in Higher Education Across Europe (IPPHEAE)*, was reported on by Glendinning (2014) and involved HEIs from twenty-seven European countries. The aim was to compare and evaluate the different approaches to plagiarism and academic misconduct, specifically focusing on:

- strategies for countering plagiarism (awareness, prevention, detection);
- any policies and procedures implemented at institutional and national levels, and how visible and effective they are; and
- e-tools in use for detecting plagiarism and how they are deployed (Glendinning 2014).

The findings from this project indicated the existence of poorly defined policies for the assurance of academic integrity in many parts of Europe. Additionally, when policies were present, these were not being monitored or reviewed (Glendinning 2014, 17). Based on the reach of these studies, one can conclude that the study of plagiarism policies was considered important for devising strategies for making its management more effective.

McGrail and McGrail examined the policies of twenty research-based institutions in the United States and concluded that although individual university policies on plagiarism have always existed; little analysis has been done on what they contain or should contain, and there was no overall guide to what policies on plagiarism were in place anywhere (2015, 15). Sutherland-Smith studied plagiarism policies available on the websites of twenty top universities in Australia, Canada, the United Kingdom and the United States and observed that plagiarism management was important to these institutions as it helped them to maintain their ranking and prestige (2011, 130). This links the possession of such policies with the rank and prestige of the academic institution and should serve as a strong motivator, along with other factors, for putting them in place.

Gilbert et al. described the process used to develop a culture of academic integrity for California Community Colleges. With regard to the state of the academic integrity policies, the team reported the following scenario: "While catalog statements concerning academic integrity exist throughout California's Community College System, they vary widely in terms of length, tone, content, and specificity. Some statements reflect the minimal bureaucratic language of a board policy . . . other colleges have created fully fleshed out policies and explanations that represent an ongoing, college-wide discourse on academic integrity" (2007, 5). Institutions have plagiarism policies, but for the most part, there are several variations in these. What is also evident is that when institutions desire to make their academic integrity systems more effective, they begin by examining current policies.

Data Presentation and Analysis

Fifteen institutions were identified, and these had a variety of policies online including those for plagiarism and academic integrity. Some institutions had statements on academic integrity and plagiarism that were so brief, that to call them policies would be a misnomer; however, since only these were available, they were analysed. Table 9.1 shows the institutions from which the policies were selected.

Jamaica, with seven institutions, and Trinidad and Tobago, with three, accounted for the majority of HEIs which had plagiarism and academic integrity policies. Policies were also identified for one institution in The Bahamas, another from Guyana and two from the mainland territory of Belize. The UWI, a regional institution with five campuses, had two policies – one for undergraduate and another for those pursuing graduate

Table 9.1. Institutions with online academic integrity and plagiarism policies

Territory	Number of institutions	Name of institutions
Jamaica	7	Northern Caribbean University (NCU)
		University of the Commonwealth Caribbean (UCC)
		Edna Manley College of Visual and Performing Arts (EMCPVA)
		University of Technology, Jamaica (UTECH)
		The Mico University College (MUC)
		Caribbean Maritime University (CMU)
		Jamaica Theological Seminary (JTS)
Trinidad and Tobago	3	University of the Southern Caribbean (USC)
		College of Science, Technology and Applied Arts of Trinidad and Tobago (COSTAATT)
		The University of Trinidad and Tobago (UTT)
Belize	2	Galen University (GU)
		University of Belize (UB)
Guyana	1	The University of Guyana (UG)
Bahamas	1	The University of The Bahamas (UBa)
Region	1	The University of the West Indies (the UWI)

programmes; therefore, sixteen policies from fifteen institutions were analysed. The majority of institutions (eleven out of fifteen) from which policies were obtained were universities which tended to be well known and were likely to have their documents online.

The policies of the various institutions were found in the three locations as displayed in figure 9.1.

Of the fifteen institutions, four (27 per cent) had "stand-alone" policies which could be located on the internet as independent documents (including undergraduate and graduate policies from the UWI), or as web pages for Jamaica Theological Seminary (JTS) and College of Science, Technology and Applied Arts of Trinidad and Tobago (COSTAATT). The policies of nine institutions (60 per cent) were contained in handbooks. The location of the policies concurs with Kokkinaki and colleagues who noted that the

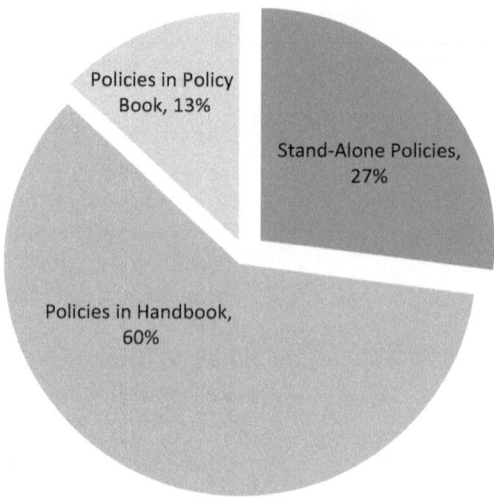

Figure 9.1. Location of academic integrity and plagiarism policies.

most frequently cited source from which students got information about plagiarism were the web, course booklets, student guides and handbooks (2015, 4). Galen University (GU) and the University of Belize (UB), which represented 13 per cent of the sample, had their academic integrity policies contained in documents specifically devoted to policies. The placement of these policies also concurred with the findings of McGrail and McGrail (2015, 19) and Hu and Sun (2015, 60). Having policies online was an indication of the importance attributed to them by the institutions (Hu and Sun 2017, 63).

In their analysis of plagiarism policies, McGrail and McGrail noted that the name of the policy "can communicate either a positive or negative tone" (2015, 19) and that policies in the United States tend to have a positive, negative or neutral wording. Hu and Sun went further by stating that the naming of the policy can also be evidence of whether the institution took a punitive or regulatory approach to academic integrity (2015, 63). Using McGrail and McGrail categories, the majority of the Caribbean policies had either a positive or neutral label. Examples of positive labels include "Academic Responsibilities and Rights of Students" (Galen University) and "Academic Honesty" (University of Belize and University of the Commonwealth Caribbean (UCC)). Some policies were a part of the student Code of Conduct document and thus bore this neutral label. This was the case of COSTAATT which named its policy "Students Code of Conduct." The universities of Trinidad and Tobago and Guyana named their policies in the negative with the former choosing the title "Academic Dishonesty" and the latter "Academic Misconduct." Overall, neutral and positive terms outnumbered the negative terms. McGrail and McGrail postulate that positive wording of the labels for the policies "drew attention to behaviours that uphold honourable conduct." On the other hand, negative wording highlighted the "act of violation or breach of desired behaviours and ethical standards" (2015, 20).

The extent of a policy is an indicator of its comprehensiveness and might reflect the importance attributed to the subject by the organization. Extent, in this context, has to do with the length of the policies in terms of the number of paragraphs and pages. Five policies representing 33 per cent of the sample had statements and guidelines on academic integrity or plagiarism that were one page or less. These included the University of The Bahamas, COSTAATT and the University of the Southern Caribbean (USC). The Interactive Students Handbook from the University of The Bahamas had three sentences on plagiarism (2018, 22), and this scant treatment was telling, given the high-profile case of plagiarism at the College of The Bahamas (later renamed the University of The Bahamas) in 2005 (Dames 2014; Turnquest 2014; Johnson 2014). This case accounted for eight articles in four online newspapers which are included in the analysis in chapter 7. Edna Manley College for the Visual and Performing Arts (EMCVPA) had one page, while Northern Caribbean University (NCU) had a short paragraph consisting of four lines in the 2016–2018 graduate bulletin.

Five other institutions (33 per cent) had policies on integrity that were two or three pages long, namely, GU, UCC, and the Universities of Guyana, Trinidad and Tobago and Belize. The remaining six policies ranged from four pages (the UWI Undergraduate Regulations on Plagiarism 2011) to eleven pages (University of Technology 2019).

Academic integrity and plagiarism were treated differently by the various institutions. Some had academic integrity policies to include plagiarism, while others had policies for plagiarism separately. Some gave extensive treatment to academic integrity, setting out examples of academic misconduct and the process for treating these while others were cursory. Sutherland-Smith also found that policies in the world's top universities "vary greatly in extent of details given about the act of plagiarism" (2011, 131). The difference between one short paragraph, as in the case of NCU, and eight pages (the UWI graduate policy) could be described as a great variation. Therefore, the majority of the institutions gave coverage to the topic of plagiarism, but in vastly different ways even as McGrail and McGrail (2015, 21) observed.

It was also seen that some institutions identified plagiarism as a form of academic misconduct, defined it and presented sanctions and procedures for treating all types of academic misconduct collectively. These included EMCVPA, The University of Trinidad and Tobago (UTT), GU, the Mico University College (MUC) and the University of Technology (UTECH). Other institutions, such as the UCC, included details on plagiarism in their academic integrity policies and set out procedures and penalties for plagiarism, separate and apart from other types of misconduct. Of the sixteen policies previously identified, four did not have sufficient content to make further analysis viable. These were from NCU, COSTAATT, the University of the Southern Caribbean and the University of Trinidad and Tobago.

A modified version of the approach to the analysis of plagiarism policies used by Hu and Sun (2017) was utilized in this research. Figure 9.2 contrasts the codes used by Hu and Sun with those utilized in this work. The researcher used five of Hu and Sun's eight codes shown by the overlapping areas of the Venn diagram and made minor modifications to three of these. The term "teacher responsibilities" was replaced by "faculty responsibilities" for this analysis in keeping with the general approach of the author throughout this work. Hu and Sun discussed procedures and sanctions as one code, but they were separated for this discussion. The

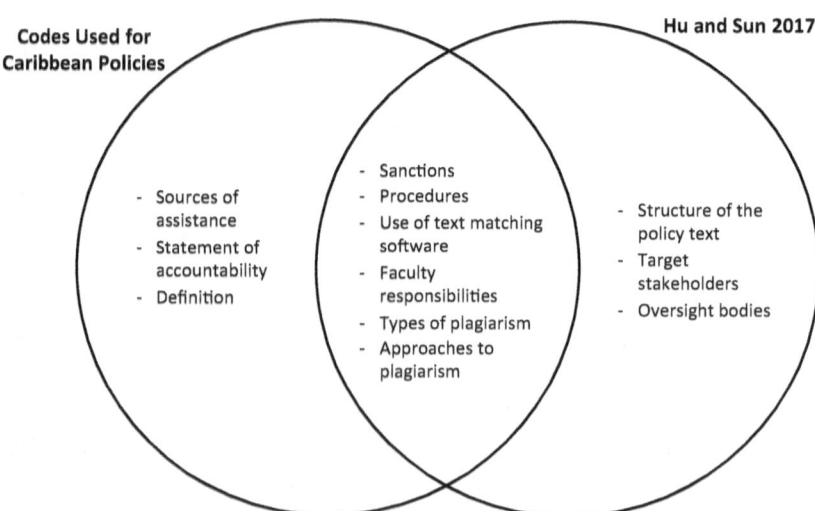

Figure 9.2. Comparison of codes used for analysis of Caribbean policies with Hu and Sun's codes.

code "prevailing approaches and discourse" was modified to "approaches to plagiarism." Three additional codes (sources of assistance, statement of accountability and definition) were added to those adapted from Hu and Sun, while three codes used by them were not applied in this work. The brevity of some of the policies did not make it expedient for analysis of these other elements feasible. The codes are referred to as elements of the policies in the discussion which follows. Table 9.2 provides a summary of the elements present in the twelve policies which were analysed. A discussion of the presence of these various elements follows.

The most popular element of the policies was a definition of plagiarism, and as is shown in table 9.2, it was evident in eleven of the twelve policies. In keeping with the punitive nature of policies in the region, "sanctions" was the second most popular element. Other popular elements included sources of assistance, faculty responsibilities and types and examples of plagiarism. Electronic detection and levels of plagiarism were the least popular elements. Each of these will be further discussed in the following sections.

Definitions of Plagiarism

All the policies examined, except for the University of The Bahamas, provided a definition of plagiarism, but there were significant differences among them, concurring with McGrail and McGrail who found a "plethora" of definitions (2015, 21). This was also in keeping with Pincus and Schmelkin's observation of the difficulty of defining plagiarism and identifying the behaviours associated with it (2003, 196). This lack of a precise definition has implications for students who transfer from one university to another, for those entering HEIs without an understanding of plagiarism, and for the development of academic integrity programmes (McGrail and McGrail 2015, 33).

Nushi and Firoozkohi (quoting Pecorari), identified six common elements of a definition for plagiarism. These were "(1) an object (i.e., language, words, text), (2) which has been taken (borrowed, stolen, and so on.)[,] (3) from a particular source (books, journals, Internet), (4) by an agent (student, person, academic), (5) without (adequate) acknowledgement and (6) with or without intention to deceive" (2017, 2). The analysis of regional policies showed that the majority of the policies had four or more of the six elements presented by these researchers.

Most institutions adopted the generic definition, presenting it in varying forms. One such institution was the UB which defined plagiarism as "presenting another person's idea or work and claiming it as your own (i.e., without properly acknowledging the source)" (University of Belize 2018, 5). Other institutions presented more compact definitions, and there

Table 9.2. Elements present in Caribbean plagiarism policies and guidelines

Components of policy	UWIG	UWI UG	EMPVA	MUC	UTECH	GU	UB	UCC	CMU	UG	U of Ba	JTS
Definition	✓	✓	✓	✓	✓	✓	✓	✓	✓	✓		✓
Levels	✓	✓										
Types/Examples	✓		✓	✓		✓	✓				✓	
Procedures	✓	✓			✓		✓	✓				✓
Sanctions	✓	✓	✓	✓		✓	✓	✓				✓
Electronic detection	✓	✓										
Faculty Responsibilities	✓	✓		✓	✓	✓	✓	✓				
Sources of assistance			✓	✓					✓		✓	
Statement of accountability	✓	✓										

were nuances in these definitions that were worth discussing. The most comprehensive definition came from the CMU. It states, "Plagiarism is the unauthorized and/or unacknowledged use of another person's intellectual efforts and creations however recorded, including whether formally published or in manuscript or in typescript or other printed or electronically presented form and includes taking passages, ideas or structures from another work or author without proper and unequivocal attribution of such source(s), using the conventions for attributions or citing used by the Caribbean Maritime University" (Caribbean Maritime University Student Handbook 2018, 72).

This detailed definition embodies several elements worth pointing out. Firstly, it states failure to give credit is plagiarism. Secondly, it speaks to format by stating, "however recorded," and this is critical in this technological era as the internet is seen by some as the driving force behind plagiarism (Jereb et al. 2018a, 1). However, it incorrectly suggested that only what was recorded can be plagiarized with the use of the term "however recorded." The definition by CMU also speaks to what can be plagiarized: "passages, ideas or structures" (2018, 72). These are referred to as the objects of plagiarism (Nushi and Firoozkohi, 2017, 2, quoting Pecorari). It must be noted however, that the word "ideas" does not always suggest a fixed format as is denoted by the words "however recorded."

Sutherland-Smith notes that in cases where the object to be plagiarized can be broadly interpreted, decision-makers could give a narrow or broad interpretation. This is "because there is room for subjectivity." She notes, however, that this breadth is sometimes the university's desire to make provision for the emerging technology which has the potential to create new objects (2011, 131). The last element of the definition from CMU implies that there is an accepted format in which credit should be given (Caribbean Maritime University 2018). This is important as it addresses the fact that citations must be correctly done, a practice with which students struggle (Anney and Mosha 2015, 213; Clearly 2017).

The definition from the University of Guyana (UG) introduced the concept of intent, as it states, "[P]lagiarism is using the words, idea, data, illustrative material, statement or works of others without due acknowledgement, *deliberately or inadvertently*" (emphasis mine, 2016, 2). The matter of ignorance or intent within the region, which goes to the heart of the definition of plagiarism, was investigated by Baker-Gardner and Smart. They discovered both graduate and undergraduate Caribbean students were plagiarizing due to ignorance (2017, 199). The MUC in its definition introduced a moral element by stating that plagiarism is "a dishonest act" and adding the most widely used definition. The UCC acknowledged unintentional plagiarism by stating that students had plagiarized if they "intentionally or unintentionally appropriate the works of others as their own" (University of the Commonwealth Caribbean 2018, 60).

Levels of Plagiarism

McGrail and McGrail noted the existence of two levels of plagiarism in the policies they analysed. They also presented the case of the University of South Florida, Tampa, which differed from the norm, in that it outlined four levels of plagiarism (2015, 31). This distinction, though popular in the American policies is not as evident in the Caribbean. The UWI in both its undergraduate and graduate policies clearly established that some acts of plagiarism were more serious than others by categorizing the less serious ones as Level 1, while the more extreme occurrences as Level 2. The UWI defines Level 1 plagiarism as, "plagiarism which does not meet the definition of Level 2 plagiarism." It defines Level 2 plagiarism as, "plagiarism undertaken with the intention of passing off as original work by the plagiariser work done by another person or persons" (The University of the West Indies 2013, 1). The matter of intent becomes critical for applying sanctions, and while some policies specify levels of plagiarism, this is implied in others which often treated unintentional plagiarism by assigning less severe sanctions.

Types and Examples of Plagiarism

Hu and Sun discovered that some universities provided a range of types and examples of plagiarism in their policies (2017, 63), and this was also evident in the regional policies. However, the researchers also found that the majority of policies did not provide adequate information on the "more subtle forms of transgressive intertextuality such as improper attribution and insufficient paraphrasing with attribution" (2017, 63), and this was also true in the Caribbean. The challenges of defining plagiarism (Kokkinaki, Demoliou and Iakovidou 2015, 10) and the lack of instruction at the secondary level (Baker-Gardner and Smart 2017, 199) make it expedient for HEIs to list examples as a means of helping students to avoid plagiaristic behaviours.

The most comprehensive listing of objects that can be plagiarized was obtained from UTECH which states "articles, essays, journals, diagrams, graphs, tables, computer software, GIS files, photographs, digital images, designs, models, maps, dissertations, reports, projects, lectures, music or other works of art" (University of Technology 2019, 187). Providing students with this kind of information is a practice of many universities in the United States (McGrail and McGrail 2015, 21), while for the Caribbean, only six of the twelve policies reflected these features.

There were commonalities in terms of some practices such as copying and pasting and the lack of use of quotations where required. Other practices such as collusion, multiple submissions and contract cheating were classified differently by these institutions. UTECH, the UB and EMCVPA spoke of multiple submissions of assignments in their policies. However, they did not consider this a sub-category of plagiarism. On the contrary, other institutions such as the MUC and CMU treated multiple submissions as plagiarism. McGrail and McGrail found this uncertainty in university policies in their study (2015, 25), and it is evidence of the challenges inherent in understanding and explaining plagiarism and could possibly point to limited knowledge of those who craft these policies (Hu and Sun 2017, 65). Additionally, the UCC and UB considered incorrect citation and negligence in citing as plagiarism but this was not explicitly stated in the other policies.

One form of academic dishonesty which institutions incorrectly categorized was contract cheating. The MUC (The Mico University College 2017, 58) and UCC (University of the Commonwealth Caribbean 2017, 60) considered the submission of a paper written by someone else as plagiarism. However Bretag (2018b) convincingly argues that it is contract cheating and not plagiarism. These differences indicate the need for a general consensus across the region as to a definition of plagiarism and a detailed listing of what behaviours constitute such. Such an understanding must be informed by international perspectives and could be developed by Council of Human and Social Development, the "organ" of Caribbean Community with responsibility for education Caribbean Community Secretariat 2001, 23.

As important as this listing of examples of plagiarism is, McGrail and McGrail found that universities did not have a common set of examples of what should be classified as plagiarism (2015, 5), a finding supported by Hu and Sun (2017, 63), and the same situation pertains in the Caribbean. Sutherland-Smith contends that varying lists from HEIs could result in what is deemed plagiarism in one institution, appearing acceptable in another. She explains that this anomaly becomes more critical in an environment with a transient student population (2011, 132), such as the Caribbean. Identifying objects is also important as students might be aware of the breach in taking another person's words based on the most popular definitions. However, they might not know that taking ideas or structures or some of the other objects identified previously is equally wrong.

Procedures for Treating Plagiarism

Whereas the majority of policies analysed by Sutherland-Smith detailed the procedures and processes for treating allegations of plagiarism (2011, 134), this was clearly not the case in the region where the policies were more in line with Hu and Sun's findings from Chinese universities that "[s]ome were backed up by robust and transparent procedures for detecting and handling plagiarism, while others only gave general descriptions" (2017, 64). Five of the policies contained procedures for treating plagiarism, with The UWI being very detailed about the process for handling both Levels 1 and 2. UTECH also had a detailed document which dealt with academic misconduct in general, including plagiarism.

McGrail and McGrail found that plagiarism policies of universities in the United States, which constituted their sample, usually had a multilevel process beginning with the faculty member, and preliminary investigations aimed at determining whether to proceed with the allegations (2015, 27). This was also the case with the Caribbean policies that included detailed information on the process for managing allegations of plagiarism. The instructor at Jamaica Theological Seminary (JTS) was required to have a preliminary discussion with the student, described as the "initial step" in dealing with allegations of plagiarism (McGrail and McGrail 2015, 27). The instructor then completed a form which was submitted to the dean's office, and an entry was made in the institution's "Student Plagiarism Database," to ascertain if the student had a previous infraction (Jamaica Theological Seminary 2020). This policy introduces the Student Plagiarism Database, suggesting an organized system for tracking infractions. The plagiarism discovery form should also make reporting of instances of plagiarism easier for faculty.

Based on the review of the policies, cases of alleged plagiarism were heard by various committees. At the UWI, they were heard by the Campus Committee (The University of the West Indies 2013, 3). McGrail and McGrail found that similarly, universities in the United States utilized an academic review body which included faculty, administrative officers and students. They noted that students were involved in the process to varying degrees, especially where there were honour systems (2015, 30). In such universities, students were allowed to preside over the "cases" of plagiarism and recommend sanctions. The University of Mary Washington was one such institution which utlised the honour system and placed the outcomes of its hearings on its website. The absence of the honour system model in the Caribbean means limited participation by students. Based on the information contained in the policies, student representatives were allowed to attend hearings at the UWI and UTECH. The UWI graduate policy allowed for a graduate student representative to sit on the Committee of Inquiry. Other members of the committee were the chair of the board or his nominee and one academic board representative from each campus.

Glendinning found that universities from various countries in the European Union (EU) also used institutional panels to determine the application of sanctions for plagiarism (2013, 11).

Part of the procedure in investigating matters such as plagiarism is giving the students who were facing allegations the opportunity to have their voices heard, as well as having the chance to seek redress in the event they were not satisfied with the outcome of an allegation. Sutherland-Smith believes the student does not have to be physically present to have a voice as this can be done by gathering as much evidence as possible before making a decision (2011, 134). The majority of institutional policies were silent on this matter. The UWI provided students with the option to appeal to the Senate (2013, 8). Students at the JTS could appeal to the academic affairs committee, but this had to be done no later than fourteen days after being informed of the decision. If the students were not satisfied with the outcome of the appeal, they could make an appeal to the academic dean (Jamaica Theological Seminary 2020). Both graduate and undergraduate policies at the UWI outlined the procedure for appeals.

The UB outlines a very simple process for treating allegations of plagiarism which included a timeline for dealing with each step in the process. Attaching a timeline to the process was important, as it ensured it was conducted in a timely manner while decreasing the uncertainty and undue anxiety on the part of the student arising from a lack of information or clear guidelines on the process. UTECH outlined a timeline for the process, and a timeline was also provided in the UWI's graduate policy for each step in the process.

Sanctions

In keeping with the punitive nature of the policies in the Caribbean, ten of the twelve policies prescribed sanctions for plagiarism. The University of The Bahamas seemed to capture the general position of the regional institutions regarding sanctions. It states, "Intellectual integrity is the foundation on which The University rests. Intellectual dishonesty, for example, cheating, using another person's work without acknowledging the source, submitting work done by another, and so on, is not tolerated. Acts of academic dishonesty could result in an 'F' for the assignment/examination; an 'F' for the course; and suspension or expulsion from The University" (University of The Bahamas 2018, 22).

This statement represents the sum of the university's information provided to undergraduate students on academic integrity in this handbook. Whereas it does not use the term "plagiarism," this can be inferred from the phrase "using another person's work without acknowledging the source." However, the question arises as to how plagiarism is treated in this context, given the vagueness which this statement conveys. The prevalence of sanctions in regional policies reflects Saddiqui's statement that the majority of plagiarism policies in HEIs have sanctions (2016, 3).

The common sanctions for plagiarism were warning or reprimand, reduction in marks for the assignment, reduction of grade for the course, requiring students to resubmit the assignment, a grade of zero, suspension, exclusion from all future examinations for a period to be determined by the university and expulsion. Some of these findings were in keeping with the conclusions of McGrail and McGrail (2015, 30–31), Kokkinaki, Demoliou and Iakovidou (2015, 8) and Hu and Sun (2017, 64). Based on the policies, the decision as to what sanctions should be applied for plagiarism was largely dependent on the contextual factors included in some policies.

The UB stated that the sanction to be applied depends on "the gravity of the violation" (University of Belize 2018, 6) and indicated that it could assign both an academic and/or a disciplinary sanction when students were in breach of its academic honesty rules, a finding similar to that of McGrail and McGrail (2015, 30). This was also in keeping with Berlinck's proposal that the extent of plagiarism, the level of the students and their knowledge of institutional policies and disciplinary rules of the institutions should all be considered (2011, 369 citing McDonald and Carrol 2006). In concurring with international practices, the UWI based its decision of the sanctions to be applied for plagiarism at the undergraduate level on "the circumstances of the particular case; the seniority of the student; and whether this is the first or a repeated incidence of Level 2 plagiarism" (The University of the West Indies 2011, 3).

There were differences in some of the sanctions in the policies examined when compared with those presented in the literature. For Level 1 plagiarism, McGrail and McGrail found that the American universities had the following sanctions: assignment of a research project on a relevant topic; make-up assignment at a more difficult level; and required attendance in a non-credit workshop or seminar on ethics or related subject (2015, 31) which were not evident in the regional policies. Community service was not a prescribed sanction for plagiarism in the Caribbean; however, Berlinck (citing Maurer, Kappe and Zaka 2006) identified this as a sanction applied at Stanford University and the University of California at Berkley. Berlinck noted there was little consensus on how and when to apply the sanctions (2011, 368), and a similar situation seemed to exist in the Caribbean.

At the UWI, allegations of plagiarism were treated differently among graduates and undergraduate students. The differences in the UWI's perception of the seriousness of plagiarism by graduate students were evidenced not just by variations in the length of the policies but also by the clear distinctions made between plagiarism in coursework and thesis writing. The graduate policy was approximately twice the length of the undergraduate one being more detailed. Graduate students who plagiarized in work other than theses or major project reports (Level 1 plagiarism) were given reduced marks, and it was required that a report be made to the examinations section. If the plagiarism occurred in either a thesis or a major project, the work had to be returned for revision and resubmission (The University of the West Indies 2013, 4). Level 2 plagiarism at the undergraduate level at the UWI may result in failure and exclusion from all future examinations for a period to be determined, or expulsion (The University of the West Indies 2011, 4).

The more proactive approach of attendance at non-credit workshops or seminars which was used in some institutions in the United States was not practiced in the Caribbean. GU came closest to this practice. According to its policy, support was provided for students who plagiarized so that the behaviour did not recur (Galen University 2017). This approach was usually practised in universities which take a constructive, instead of a punitive approach to academic integrity, such as the University of Mary, Washington (2020). A student found guilty of plagiarism for the first time at GU received an "F" in that component of the course and was required to attend mandatory counselling sessions with the university counsellor. The aim of this was to assist students to understand "the lifelong consequences of plagiarism" (2017, 26). An intervention plan was also created to assist the student to develop and practise academic integrity. The sessions were logged and a report was made to the student's academic advisor when the stated objectives were achieved. Students who committed a second offence were given a failing grade for the course, had to sign a contract that they will not cheat again and went back to counselling. A third offence resulted in expulsion (Galen University 2017, 29). This seemed like a more effective approach that considered not only the need to discourage plagiarism by applying sanctions, but also the responsibility to support the student who hopefully will develop a greater appreciation for academic integrity.

Electronic Detection Systems

There was limited evidence of the use of electronic detection systems in the regional policies, although these were evident in seven of the eight Chinese universities studied by Hu and Sun (2017, 43). The two policies on plagiarism from the UWI made reference to the use of these systems by stating that a student's work suspected of being plagiarized may be "subjected to further electronic scrutiny in order to verify its freedom from plagiarism" (University Regulations on Plagiarism Graduate Diplomas and Degrees 2013, 3), referring to its use of Turnitin. Based on its policy, UCC used Turnitin in a more positive way where students were encouraged to use it to check their work prior to submission in order to identify problems with referencing so they could correct them, suggesting that plagiarism was limited to referencing. The policy from the UCC also advised students that Turnitin should be "used as part of the marking process as a means of checking the originality of submitted work" (University of the Commonwealth Caribbean 2018, 63). Based on information contained in the policies in the Caribbean, the electronic system was being used both as part of the procedure after students had completed their work and also as a tool to guide students in their writing (Charubusp 2015, 78)' however, based on the policies analysed its use was not very popular. Based on knowledge of the HEI landscape in the Caribbean the researcher believes text matching software was more widely used than indicated in the policies.

Faculty Responsibilities

Five of the twelve policies outlined the responsibilities of faculty and administrators, especially as it related to the procedure to be followed after students were suspected of plagiarism. However, the MUC departed from this practice, requiring lecturers to include information on plagiarism in the course outlines and to provide clarification for students on the topic. The practice of embedding information on plagiarism in course outlines is supported by Nushi and Firoozdohi who found that 16.6 per cent of the course outlines of the 207 Iranian university faculty contained information on plagiarism (2017, 8). Andrews et al. noted that students received information on cheating from course syllabi, orientation programmes, honour council participation and investigations of cheating episodes (2007, 1032). Glendinning also found varying practices regarding the involvement of lecturers in treating plagiarism in the EU. She discovered that whereas 47 per cent of EU teachers "take decisions about whether a student has plagiarised," only 34 per cent of those in Austria reported that plagiarism was monitored at the faculty or subject level. This compares to 55 per cent of respondents in the United Kingdom who stated that it was monitored by an institutional quality manager (2014, 10).

UB clearly outlined the responsibility of faculty by stating, "Lecturers and academic department chairpersons are *primarily responsible* for academic discipline. Lecturers are expected to consult with academic department chairpersons to prevent and respond to incidences of unauthorized duplication of academic work for more than one course, plagiarism and cheating, while ensuring that students' right to due process are upheld and that sanctions are appropriate to infractions" (emphasis mine, 2018, 5).

Requiring lecturers and academic departments to be "primarily responsible" for academic discipline contravenes the suggestions provided in the literature which presents academic integrity as an institutional responsibility to be shared among the students, faculty and administrators (Saddiqui 2016, 4; Gallant and Goodchild 2011, 8). McGrail and McGrail speak to the faculty's need for administrative support in dealing with plagiarism because they believe in cases where this does not exist, the faculty will not carry out this mandate (2015, 40).

The UWI required mandatory reporting by faculty as it stated that where "an examiner has evidence of Level 2 plagiarism in the material being examined, that examiner *must* report it to the Head of Department or to the Dean" (emphasis mine, 2011, 3). While reporting was mandatory for the examiner, other persons were given an option to report as the policy stated, where "any other person who in the course of duty sees material being examined that has evidence of Level 2 plagiarism that other person *may* report it to the Head of Department or Dean" (emphasis mine, 2011, 3). The UB required reporting by faculty, but the language of its policy was not as strident as that used by the UWI as seen by the former's use of the word "should" in detailing faculty's responsibility to report plagiarism. Based on these policies, faculty in some institutions may also be required to attend hearings for allegations of plagiarism.

Aside from the faculty involved in teaching the courses in which suspected cheating occurs, the policies stipulated the roles of other faculty who have administrative roles. Heads of departments and deans were usually given defined roles in the procedures for dealing with allegations. The lecturers first dialogued with the heads of departments when plagiarism was suspected, and the latter were tasked with the responsibility of ensuring the validity of the claims. In some cases, as in the UB (University of Belize 2018), heads of departments were vested with the responsibility of passing the suspected cases to the deans.

Reference to Sources of Assistance

Seven of the twelve policies contained information designed to help students avoid plagiarism, and these took a variety of forms including information on acceptable writing and citation practices. Examples of information provided to students from these policies were noted as follows: "Students must give written credit and acknowledgement to the sources of thoughts, ideas, and/ or words quoted directly, paraphrased or used with reference to a general idea. In cases where words are used which were written by someone else the student must enclose the cited portion with quotation marks and provide an appropriate citation (e.g. footnote, endnote, bibliographical reference)" (Caribbean Maritime University 2018, 72).

The MUC provides similar instructions: "For words quoted which are written by someone else, enclose the cited portion with quotation marks and provide an appropriate citation (e.g. footnote, endnote, bibliographical reference)" (The Mico University College 2017, 58). The similarity between the preceeding instructions from MUC and CMU is difficult to overlook. Galen University provides information regarding term papers and individual and group work. It states, "Students should avoid plagiarism by using footnotes and quotations to give credit to all sources of information. They should also reference all scholarly sources they use and keep all working notes as proof of their work until they have received a grade and decided not to appeal that grade" (2017, 26).

The UCC included a statement informing students that they should speak to the librarians or the lecturers if they needed assistance or were having challenges completing a paper on time (University of the Commonwealth Caribbean 2019, 60). Librarians have long been identified as valuable partners in academic integrity development (Wood 2004; Lampert 2008; Lampert 2006). A link was also provided to a tutorial on how to use American Psychological Association style manual. The webpage of JTS, which contained the policy on plagiarism, provided a link to a PowerPoint presentation which gave students additional explanations on plagiarism and detailed the process in cases where there were allegations. The web page also provided students with scenarios aimed at helping them to identify plagiarism and gave them pointers as to how to avoid it (Jamaica Theological Seminary 2020).

What was noticeable throughout this analysis was the responsibility placed on students to ensure that they practised academic integrity, but there was no similar emphasis placed on the role of the institution in the process. The literature records the likely failure of any attempt to ensure academic integrity which does not include active student engagement (Saddiqui 2016, 12). Targeted assistance was definitely needed, and this required committed institutional support. Students required more assistance than was identified by the policies.

Statements of Accountability

Both policies at the UWI and that for the EMCVPA were the only three that made reference to accountability which took the form of statements completed and signed by students to the effect that the work they submitted was their own original work and they had not plagiarized. The purpose of this was to get students to reflect on the work done and ensure that it met the ethical guidelines of the institution. However, in their research with Caribbean students, Baker-Gardner and Smart found that students thought these statements of accountability were actually the University's plagiarism policy, a document they had never read (2017, 194). It must be noted that students in Gullifer and Tyson's study made the same critical error (2014, 1202), which leaves one to conclude that students lacked the basic knowledge regarding institutional perspectives on plagiarism, and the structures in place to prevent it.

Approaches to Plagiarism

Having examined the contents of the policies, there were other considerations that warranted discussion. One such was the approach to plagiarism adopted by regional HEIs. The most glaring issue was the superficial treatment given to the matter by some institutions which relegated it to only a few lines leading one to wonder how serious they were about the issue.

Another challenge was the language used in the policies which was a reflection of policies elsewhere. Sutherland-Smith expressed concern about the language used in plagiarism policies and found that the majority of the policies from the United States used legal language. She posited that this was aimed at maintaining the status quo of the powerful and the powerless. She noted the perpetrator was usually framed as an "offender," and the outcomes of an investigation into allegations of plagiarism were "framed linguistically as a range of penalties" (2011, 133). She further stated that, in keeping with the tenets of the law, there was the overarching view in the policies that the outcome would result in a winner and a loser as "the allegations will be proven or not and the student punished or not" (2011, 133).

The JTS and the UWI's policies used legal language; however, it was not possible to determine if this was meant to keep the status quo as suggested by Sutherland-Smith (2011, 133). The JTS stated that plagiarism could be a "costly crime," before outlining the procedures for treating allegations (Jamaica Theological Seminary 2020). The UWI's legalistic leaning was obvious by the use of terms such as "appeal" and "evidence." It went on to say, "The Committee of Inquiry is not a court of law, but the hearing shall be conducted in the rules of natural justice." At the hearing, the "case" was heard and the student could "be represented by a friend or attorney-at-law." During the hearing, the student had the opportunity to call a "witness" (The University of the West Indies 2013, 6).

UTECH's policy used less legalistic language than the UWI's; nevertheless, the legal tone could not be missed. The section of the handbook that spoke about academic misconduct made reference to the word "statute" in the heading. Within the body of the policy were examples of words, such as "offences" used to label instances of misconduct. Additional words reflecting the legal language were "witnesses", "penalty", "appeal" and "hearing". These conveyed the legal tone that Sutherland-Smith found in her analysis. UTECH's policy stated that the university could have legal representation at the plagiarism hearing; however, the cost would be borne by the student if the appeal was dismissed (University of Technology 2019, 203). The use of legal language by these institutions was also reflected in the policies of Chinese universities (Hu and Sun 2017, 65).

McGrail and McGrail found that some policies presented plagiarism as unprofessional, morally or ethically suspect and also described it as an action that cheated persons of intellectual growth (2015, 34). Sutherland-Smith agreed and stated that the majority of universities took an ethical approach in detailing students' responsibilities in completing academic tasks, thereby passing the responsibility to the students (2011, 133). The JTS adopted the moral tone in considering plagiarism as "tantamount to stealing" (Jamaica Theological Seminary 2020), a stance that was understandable given the emphasis of their programmes on religious training, while EMCVPA described it as unethical (Edna Manley College of the Visual and Performing Arts 2017, 57).

The approach to plagiarism presented in these policies was what the literature described as punitive (Sutherland-Smith 2011, 127). Although seven of the twelve policies had information to guide the students, or referred them to other sources for further assistance, this was not enough. The punitive approach, as the term suggests, focused more on punishment rather than presenting students with the opportunity to develop critical skills and learn from their mistakes. Additionally, the language of some of the policies was likely to pose some challenges to the students, especially those just entering a tertiary institution; however, the institutions did not seem to give much consideration to this.

Discussion of Findings

Caribbean HEIs have demonstrated an awareness of plagiarism, but for the most part, the institutions were at the rudimentary stage where the focus was on having a policy that addressed academic misconduct. These policies had a variety of names and reflected different emphases and understandings of plagiarism by the institutions. Some were disciplinary policies which outlined various forms of misconduct and how these were to be treated.

These policies might list plagiarism as a disciplinary breach, among several others, and deal with penalties and procedures for such breaches without specifically giving attention to plagiarism. Other misconduct policies had sections devoted to the treatment of plagiarism, while some institutions had policies dedicated to it. The analysis of the sixteen policies from fifteen institutions revealed that some gave in-depth treatment to academic integrity and plagiarism, while others made only a passing mention. These policies were located in handbooks and on institutions' websites as was the case globally (McGrail and McGrail 2015, 17).

The analysis of nine elements contained in the policies using the method employed by Hu and Sun (2017) revealed practices that conformed to findings elsewhere in the literature. The majority of the policies provided a generic definition of plagiarism (McGrail and McGrail 2015, 21) stating that it involved the use of the work of others without giving credit. Further, while they differed somewhat in the contents of what constituted the act, the majority contained most of the elements identified by Pecorari (as quoted by Nush and Firoozkohi 2017, 2). Additionally, in some cases, the legal, and sometimes not easily fathomed, nature of the language of the policies could be an impediment to the students' understanding of them.

Sanctions featured predominantly in the policies (Hu and Sun 2017, 64), and these were dependent on the severity of the case and usually ranged from the re-submission of the assignment for the milder cases to expulsion for the most severe ones. Sutherland-Smith, in observing the failure of focusing on sanctions to address the issue of academic misconduct, stated that "[s]ystematic focus on deterrence and punishment is addressing only part of the issue and the educative value of those approaches alone is questionable. Academic research suggests plagiarism is multi-layered and requires a variety of strategies within an overall framework of ethical sustainability" (2010, 13).

The distinction between plagiarism committed by undergraduate and graduate students seemed unrealistic, seeing there was no mention of providing formal instructions on plagiarism in the policies to make students better equipped for the demands of graduate work. There was therefore the expectation that students would learn by doing in their undergraduate programmes. Hu and Sun found that plagiarism in graduate work was given serious scrutiny, whereas it received scant treatment for undergraduates (2017, 64) somewhat reflecting the current practice in the Caribbean. This seems to be an anomaly given students' need to develop and practice academic integrity at all levels and findings from the literature which indicated that students continued to follow practices learnt previously (Tauginienė et al, 2018).

Overall, the policies took a punitive approach with students bearing the responsibility to act ethically within the context of having a policy online which provided few resources or other support systems. Berlinck notes that when this approach is used, everybody loses due to a lack of intellectual, moral and ethical growth (2011, 370). In addition, this approach deprived students of the assistance required to develop the knowledge and skills needed to act ethically and absolved the institution of its responsibility to create a culture of academic integrity. It was also observed that procedures for treating plagiarism seemed similar across institutions; however, what differed was the level of details included in the policies with just over half of them mentioning any sources of assistance for students in understanding plagiarism. Therefore, the absence of sources of assistance for students rendered the policies incomplete as the strategies presented only partially addressed the issues by applying sanctions after the fact. The policies did not outline systems and strategies to help students learn about plagiarism.

Some good practices were evident in the policies. For instance, in one institution, Turnitin was presented as a tool to assist students during the writing phase so they could make adjustments to assignments prior to submission. In addition, one university kept a database of students who plagiarized. Another commendable practice was the provision of assistance in the form of counselling and an intervention plan for students who plagiarized. Despite these measures, there was a need for HEIs in the Caribbean to provide a systematic and targeted programme for developing academic integrity among the students. Victoria University in Melbourne, Australia, states that a culture of integrity includes emphasis on shared responsibility, a strong education focus reflected in guides for students, the inclusion of information and guidance on individual units, and a range of learning activities to support them (Eckersley, Borland and Henderson n.d.).

The commonalities between the education systems of the various territories and the regional institutions, such as the UWI and Caribbean Examination Council, provide an excellent opportunity for the start of a regional discussion on academic integrity. This should help HEIs arrive at a shared understanding of plagiarism and adopt a common definition that would serve their constituents and the administrative processes. There also needs to be a common understanding of the behaviours that constitute plagiarism and the need to develop a common approach to developing and maintaining academic integrity generally.

Chapter 10

Academic Integrity, Accreditation and Plagiarism in Higher Education

Introduction

This chapter explores the relationship between accreditation and academic integrity and investigates the inclusion of standards for academic integrity in the quality assurance processes of Caribbean territories through a content analysis of accreditation policies. It then investigates the strategies in place in universities to educate students on academic integrity and ends with an analysis and discussion of data from four Caribbean universities on the number of cases of plagiarism for the period 2004–2017.

Background

Institutional accreditation is a benchmark of quality valued by academic institutions, and the University Council of Jamaica (UCJ) defines accreditation as "the status granted to a programme or institution that has been found, through self-study and peer review, to meet or exceed established standards for educational quality" (2021). The Commission on Dental Accreditation identifies the following eight functions of accreditation which are germane to others:

1. certifying that an institution or programme has met established standards;
2. assisting prospective students in identifying acceptable institutions;
3. assisting institutions in determining the acceptability of transfer credits;
4. helping to identify institutions and programmes for the investment of public and private funds;
5. protecting an institution against harmful internal and external pressure;
6. creating goals for self-improvement of weaker programmes and stimulating a general raising of standards among educational institutions;

7. involving the faculty and staff comprehensively in situational evaluation and planning; and
8. establishing criteria for professional certification and licensure and for upgrading federal assistance (2021).

Except for number eight, all the functions listed are relevant to this discussion on accreditation in the Caribbean.

From as early as 2012, the US Council for Higher Education Accreditation (USCHEA) took the initiative to explore the relationship between academic integrity and accreditation by inviting International Center for Academic Integrity to make a presentation titled, "Accreditation and Academic Integrity" at its conference. The relationship between accreditation and academic integrity was further strengthened in 2017 when a "group of global experts" conducted research on the role of accreditation bodies in tackling academic corruption. This project had the backing of the internationally recognized UNESCO International Institute for Educational Planning (O'Malley 2017).

At a conference on academic integrity in Montenegro, Europe, it was decided that "the issue of having a national or institutional code of ethics in higher education should be subject of a wide debate. The new national quality assurance body should be awarded with responsibility to monitor implementation of ethical principles as a requirement in the accreditation process" (European Union and the Council of Europe 2017, 7) Furthermore, Judith Eaton, president of the USCHEA, views academic integrity as integral to the accreditation process. She believes evidence of an institution's attempts at fighting corruption can be determined by examining its academic integrity processes, although the impact of corruption on programmes and institutions is not yet ascertained (Eaton 2018, 8). It is generally accepted that without attention to integrity, the system loses its credibility, and the qualifications obtained by graduates will be held in doubt (Hallak and Poisson 2007, 234).

HEIs in the Caribbean are guided by both internal and external quality assurance processes. External quality assurance agencies in the Caribbean are mandated to provide quality assurance for programmes at the tertiary level, and based on the emerging discussion, part of their responsibility includes ensuring that these institutions develop and practise academic integrity (Daniel 2016, 2). The UCJ identifies data on plagiarism as one of the evidence that the institution seeking accreditation is adhering to ethical standards in teaching, research and administration (2019, 23). Further, Berlinck said that keeping data on academic misconduct was important in assisting the institution to evaluate the extent of plagiarism and find solutions (2011, 370). Universities in the Caribbean have been keeping data on academic misconduct although it is uncertain if they were being used. This study, therefore, sought to investigate the inclusion of academic integrity in accreditation policies and guidelines of Caribbean countries and examine the prevalence of plagiarism in four universities in the Caribbean. These institutions combined had close to fifty thousand students at the time of writing and offered a variety of programmes from certificates to doctoral degrees. Within this context, the study set out to:

- investigate the presentation of academic integrity in the policies and standards of accreditation agencies in the Caribbean;
- explore ways in which HEIs provide education to students on academic integrity;
- determine the prevalence of plagiarism in the selected institutions; and
- evaluate whether gender impacts the number of students who plagiarize.

To date, there has been no study which investigated the link between accreditation and academic integrity and examined the prevalence of plagiarism in the Caribbean; therefore, this study will begin to fill this gap. In addition, it will remove the "blanket of silence" about plagiarism which exists in the Caribbean, stimulate discussion and help institutions to examine the structures in place to manage plagiarism. It will also add to the international literature as the Caribbean's voice on plagiarism needs to be heard.

Review of Literature

In 2016, the Council for Higher Education Accreditation or Council for International Quality Group (CHEA/CIQG) released the *Advisory Statement for Effective International Practice*. It described this advisory as "a wake-up call to higher education worldwide – particularly to quality assurance agencies . . . [It notes] HEIs, governments, employers and societies generally, in both developed and developing countries, are far too complacent about the growth of corrupt practices" (Daniel 2016, 2). By making specific mention to developing countries, which include those in the Caribbean, and using the term "worldwide," Daniel is emphasizing a shared responsibility to ensure academic integrity that all countries need to recognize. The policy listed the following examples of corruption:

- sale of examination papers or exam-related materials and use of essay mills;
- bribery of invigilators, proctors or markers;
- impersonation of candidates and ghostwriting of assignments;
- plagiarism and cheating in continuous assessment, assignments and exams; and
- inconsistence and favouritism in marking. (Daniel 2016, 7)

To combat these, the following preventative actions were presented:

- adopt, publicise and implement codes of conduct for the behaviour of staff and students;
- inform students of the sanctions for plagiarism/cheating.

In the advisory statement, CHEA/CIQG issued a call to action, stating that "[g]overnments, quality assurance agencies and HEIs worldwide must become more aware of the threat that corruption poses to the credibility, effectiveness and quality of higher education" (Daniel 2016, 9). It suggests a collaborative approach to treating academic corruption by national governments, quality assurance agencies, HEIs, faculty and staff, students, the press/civil society, employers and professional bodies. Some of the suggestions include publishing and implementing ethical codes for researchers; checking research theses with anti-plagiarism software; encouraging faculty to write about corrupt practices in the local, regional and international press and publishing the rankings of HEIs on the criterion of academic integrity (Daniel 2016, 15–16). There is therefore no doubt that quality assurance agencies have become involved with the matter of academic integrity.

Bretag emphasizes the importance of HEIs conforming to the requirements of quality assurance agencies by warning that "advice has been provided by national quality assurance agencies with the expectation that it will be followed – those higher education institutions that naively or willfully ignore these guidelines may risk future registration and/or accreditation" (2018b, 20). The relationship between accreditation and academic integrity is now solidly forged, and although these are still early days, the likelihood is that this will strengthen, given the common focus and contribution to quality education.

Accreditation in the Caribbean

Accreditation is an integral component of the quality mandate of the Caribbean education system with the objective of serving as a vanguard for the region, ensuring that the programmes delivered at the post-secondary and tertiary levels meet or exceed the minimum level standards agreed on by the stakeholders. Roberts (2007) reports that this search for quality is not new to the Caribbean. She explains that from as early as 1875, Codrington College in Barbados sought to validate its programmes through affiliation with an overseas university. She further states that when the University College of the West Indies (now the UWI) was established in 1948, it followed suit. Roberts credits Trinidad and Tobago for introducing formal accreditation to the region in the 1970s (46).

The accreditation structures within the Caribbean have since become more formalized. Article 35 of the Revised Treaty of Chaguaramas establishes the mandate for accreditation by stating:

1. Council for Human and Social Development, in consultation with the competent organ, shall establish common standards and measures for accreditation or when necessary for the mutual recognition of diplomas, certificates and other evidence of qualifications of the nationals of the member states in order to facilitate access to, and engagement in, employment and non-wage-earning activities in the Community.
2. The member states shall establish or employ, as the case may be, appropriate mechanisms to establish common standards to determine equivalency or accord accreditation to diplomas, certificates and other evidence of qualifications secured by nationals of other member states. (Caribbean Community Secretariat 2001, 28)

To further the accreditation mandate, the Caribbean Area Network for Quality Assurance in Tertiary Education (CANQATE), which is a member of the International Network for Quality Assurance Agencies in Higher Education, was incorporated in 2009. Alleyne noted that there is a legislative framework for the establishment of national accreditation agencies in eleven territories – Antigua and Barbuda, Barbados, Belize, Dominica, Grenada, Guyana, Jamaica, St Christopher and Nevis, St Vincent and the Grenadines, Suriname, and Trinidad and Tobago. Although the legislation for Belize was passed in 2004, to date there is no accreditation agency (2015, 90) as the National Accreditation Council for Belize is still awaiting final approval (Accreditation Agencies and Quality Assurance in Belize 2021). Alleyne reports that the functions of national accreditation bodies in the region include "developing systems for institutional accreditation, assessment/recognition of qualifications earned outside national boundaries; and facilitation of free movement by qualified nationals in the CSME" (2015, 89–93). Academic integrity would be given due consideration as the agencies develop systems for institutional accreditation.

Although the CANQATE constitution does not make explicit reference to academic integrity, three of its purposes are relevant to this discussion. These are to:

1. promote the theory and practice of the improvement of quality in tertiary education;
2. promote and assist in the implementation of best practices in quality assurance in tertiary education; and
3. encourage and support research in the field of quality assurance and accreditation. (Caribbean Area Network for Quality Assurance in Tertiary Education n.d.)

These are relevant as the development of a culture of academic integrity is a best practice that is likely to lead to improvement in the quality of education. A culture of academic integrity could also be considered best practice. Of importance is the impact of academic integrity on quality assurance, and there are many other aspects of academic integrity and accreditation that can become the subject of research.

According to Perkins, ethics in academic pursuits in the Caribbean is embodied in the standards of the national accrediting bodies. The ethical mandate of accreditation makes it compulsory that academic integrity is given a significant place in any standards or programmes for accreditation. Perkins postulates, "There is no quality without ethics and ethical practice redounds to educational quality" (2015, 111). Academic integrity should, therefore, be specified in the accreditation guidelines, and Caribbean HEIs should be prepared to demonstrate proof of having established the required systems, strategies and processes for developing and maintaining academic integrity during the accreditation process.

Data Presentation and Analysis

Primary data collected from the content analysis of the accreditation policies and an informal survey plus secondary data on the number of cases of plagiarism in four universities were analysed and presented in this section.

Academic Integrity in Accreditation Policies

Accreditation standards were obtained for analysis from six of the nine English-speaking territories which were members of CANQATE in order to determine the extent to which academic integrity was included. An additional set of standards was located for The Bahamas which is not currently a member. Some guidelines were publicly available on the websites of these institutions, and where this was not the case, the researcher requested them. Of the ten countries under discussion, no standards were received for Dominica, Antigua and Barbuda, and Grenada. There was no evidence of the inclusion of academic integrity in the guidelines for The Bahamas, Trinidad and Tobago and St Kitts and Nevis. The absence of the requirement for the inclusion of academic integrity as a part of the accreditation process might lead institutions to give scant attention to this vital area of academic life.

Elements of academic integrity were included in the accreditation guidelines for Jamaica, Guyana, Barbados, and St Vincent and the Grenadines. The guidelines for programme and institutional accreditation in Barbados stated that the Barbados Accreditation Council "perceives quality in institutions as . . . a culture which embraces integrity and ethical conduct" (n.d., 4). This statement, though not specific to academic integrity, could include the same; however, there was no further evidence of reference to academic integrity in the five standards presented in the documents.

St Vincent and the Grenadines, Jamaica and Guyana stipulated that institutional accreditation was dependent on the applicant's ability to provide evidence of the measures aimed at ensuring academic integrity. St Vincent and the Grenadines focused on the need for a policy, stating that in order for the institution to obtain accreditation, it must have and enforce "policies on ethical behavior, conflict of interest, academic honesty and integrity" (National Accreditation Board SVG n.d.). In addition, it spoke to the integrity of research by faculty, staff and students, placing the emphasis not only on the students but also on the faculty. This inclusion of faculty as a target group for academic integrity was also evident in the standard from Jamaica which also focused on research, presumably including that of faculty. The focus on only a policy for academic honesty and integrity might indicate a misunderstanding of the multi-layered nature of academic integrity (Sutherland-Smith 2010, 13).

The National Accreditation Council of Guyana stated that it would "refuse to approve the grant of a certificate of accreditation to the applicant if the Council has reasonable grounds to believe that the applicant – cannot assure . . . overall academic integrity" (n.d., 140). This should also be evident in what the Council refers to as "network delivery" interpreted by the researcher as online teaching. There was no indication in the standards of the evidence institutions had to produce to provide "assurance" to the accrediting body. This lack of specificity might lead to differing interpretations by the institutions.

The Jamaican policy was the most comprehensive, covering both institutional and programme accreditation in detail with respect to academic integrity. This is understandable given the complexity and diversity of the higher education landscape in Jamaica when compared to the other territories. It presented academic integrity as a criterion for both programme and institutional accreditation, listed the indicators which would verify its presence and outlined the evidence that institutions needed to present as proof of its existence.

The manual for institutional accreditation included academic integrity in two of its ten standards which needed to be met for the accreditation to be granted. Institutions were required to have "policies on student rights and responsibilities, including those related to academic dishonesty and procedural rights," and these were to be "clearly stated, well publicized, readily available and implemented in a fair and consistent manner" (University Council of Jamaica 2017, 59). However the focus on academic dishonesty goes against what is now trending in academic integrity practices (International Center for Academic Integrity 2014). By emphasizing the need for clarity, accessibility and availability, the UCJ was embodying some of the suggestions presented by Bretag et al. (2011). Additionally, the UCJ required that the institution "demonstrates that it has in place properly documented procedures and regulations covering . . . academic integrity – including safeguards to combat academic corruption and misconduct" (University Council of Jamaica 2018, 41).

With reference to intellectual property, UCJ required the institution to uphold "sound ethical practices and respect for individuals through its teaching, scholarship/research, service and administrative practice; this includes demonstrating its commitment to principles of protecting intellectual property rights." It further detailed the evidence of this as "Feedback from stakeholders on the extent of the institution's adherence to ethical standards in teaching, research and administration, published codes of ethical practice, academic misconduct regulations, signed agreements regarding plagiarism, case reports" (University Council of Jamaica 2018, 41). For programme accreditation, the *Manual for the Visiting Team* treats academic integrity as an issue related to assessment. The UCJ required institutions to have "clearly documented policies, including sanctions, on academic fraud." It stated that assessors were to look for policies on academic fraud and plagiarism in addition to logs of cases of plagiarism and analyses of the effectiveness of the policies (2019, 23). UCJ's attempt to focus attention on academic integrity during accreditation suggests some thought has gone into its importance as a part of the quality mandate.

Based on the prevailing practices in the Caribbean, the approach to academic integrity taken by these accreditation agencies was punitive with the focus being on ensuring that institutions had policies a policy, evidence that students observed the guidelines in the policies and where they failed to do so, evidence that institutions were applying sanctions. Berlinck states that "by adopting this approach to identify and punish plagiarism, pure and simply, everybody loses, because there is no intellectual, moral and ethical growth" (2011, 370). Given that the accreditation agencies aim to "promote the theory and practice of the improvement of quality in tertiary education" and to "promote and assist in the implementation of best practices in quality assurance in tertiary education" (Caribbean Area Network for Quality Assurance in Tertiary Education n.d.), they occupy an influential place in the education hierarchy of the Caribbean with regard to policy development and implementation. They are in a key position to contribute to the implementation of a culture of academic integrity at the institutional level and help to ensure that institutions maintain this. Hence, there is a need for greater stringency in adherence to their measures and an openness to the adoption of more positive and effective methods, besides the punitive ones, for achieving and maintaining academic integrity.

Academic Integrity Education in the Caribbean

Three institutions provided data on the strategies used to educate students about academic integrity. Two of these were from Jamaica, and the third was from Trinidad and Tobago. Based on the responses, education on academic integrity was embedded in foundational courses usually taken by all students and in information literacy sessions provided by the library. In these courses, students were introduced to plagiarism and taught the dynamics of preparing references and writing in-text citations. In addition to these, undergraduate students were required to take research courses which should help to hone their research skills to include the practice of academic integrity. However, one finding from the qualitative data reported in chapter 12 was that students in the institution where the research was done, which also taught academic integrity as part of a unit in a course, did not think sufficient emphasis was placed on ensuring they understood plagiarism. Based on this limited data, it can be concluded that some level of education was being provided on academic integrity. Seeing that an in-depth investigation was not carried out and that information was received from only a few institutions due to the challenges of Covid-19, this requires further research.

Rates of Plagiarism in Four Caribbean HEIs

HEIs, including those in the Caribbean, tend to keep track of the number of academic integrity infringements in order to satisfy accreditation agencies,

Table 10.1. Population and number of cases of plagiarism for the period 2004–2017

Institution	Enrolment (2016–2017)	Number of cases
Institution 1	18,469	142
Institution 2	18,222	44
Institution 3	6,702	20
Institution 4	5,769	14
Total	49,162	220

track students' behaviour with reference to academic integrity as in the case of Jamaica Theological Seminary and detect trends. Table 10.1 presents the data for enrolment and the number of cases of plagiarism garnered from four institutions for the period 2004–2017.

The total enrolment for the four institutions for the 2016–2017 academic year was just below fifty thousand students. Institutions 1 and 2 had almost the same number of students and accounted for approximately 75 per cent of the total enrolment for the four institutions. Based on table 10.1, there were 220 cases of plagiarism at these 4 institutions. Although Institutions 1 and 2 had approximately the same number of students, the number of cases at Institution 1 more than tripled that at Institution 2. The website Check for Plagiarism reports that the true incidence of plagiarism among students is "higher than one in six" (Cyber Plagiarism and Statistics 2020), a sharp contrast with the data in table 10.1. There might have been some students who plagiarized but were not caught, and others who were caught, but not reported by lecturers. In addition, 220 cases from the region did not include cases which were not considered "serious," as these were usually dealt with at course and departmental levels.

In order to determine whether the number of cases of plagiarism had increased over the period under investigation, the data for the period 2010–2016 were examined. This period was chosen because it represented the most complete set of data available. Only three of the four institutions provided data for the number of cases of plagiarism by year. No annual data was provided for Institution 3 which was subsequently left out of this section of the analysis. The average number of reported cases per year is presented in figure 10.1.

The data showed fluctuations during the period with an overall increase by 2015–2016. The number of cases for the period ranged from a low of eight in 2010-2011 to a high of twenty-nine in 2014-2015. Although, generally, an increase can be seen in the number of cases over the period, from eight in 2010-2011 to nineteen in 2015-2016, it is difficult to establish

Academic Integrity, Accreditation and Plagiarism in Higher Education | 145

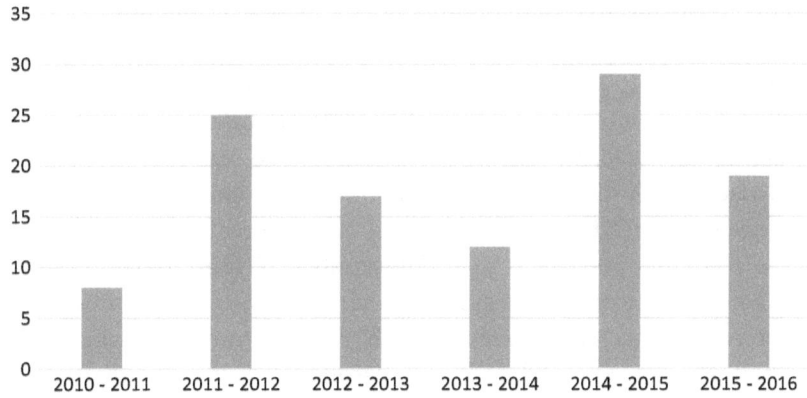

Figure 10.1. Average number of reported cases of plagiarism for three institutions for the period 2010–2016.

whether this trend is likely to be sustained based on the fluctuations in the data. Again, noting the limitations mentioned previously, one can only tentatively conclude that in keeping with the literature on plagiarism (Sureda-Negre, Comas-Forgas and Oliver-Trobat 2015, 105), the number of cases in the region seemed to be increasing.

A comparison between the number of cases of plagiarism annually (as presented in Figure 10.1) with data from other universities revealed that cases in the Caribbean were significantly less than those recorded elsewhere. The University of Mary Washington (2021b) posts summaries of cases of plagiarism online for each academic year. For the 2015-2016 academic year, a total of twenty cases were recorded. The institution had a population of 4,727 students and ranked number 16 in Regional Universities South in the 2020 Best Colleges listing (Overview of University of Mary Washington 2021a). It had a vibrant honour system, and allegations of misconduct were managed by the Honour Council. Reports of academic misconduct can be made online, and support is provided for students who violate the honour code. McCabe and Trevino note that colleges with honour codes usually record fewer academic misconduct cases (1993, 525).

The number of cases of plagiarism recorded by the University of Mary Washington for the academic year in consideration was eight less than the highest average figure of twenty-nine cases reported in the Caribbean from the four HEIs for 2014–2015. These four Caribbean universities had a total enrolment of nearly ten times than that of the University of Mary Washington. These figures show great disparity, as the latter institution which had an established programme for academic integrity, had an incidence rate of approximately 1:236 compared to the three Caribbean institutions with 1:1,500. These figures are based on calculations using the total enrolment and the highest annual number of cases of plagiarism.

Data from Oxford University also provided another source for comparison. With its current population of almost twenty-four thousand, the University of Oxford recorded a total of fifty-three cases of plagiarism for the academic year 2017–2018 (University of Oxford 2021), a ratio of 1:453, compared to only three cases of other types of academic misconduct (Roller 2018). This was in keeping with the literature that plagiarism is the most prevalent form of academic misconduct. This was described as a "record number of cases" and came amidst reports of 40 per cent increase in the number of cases of academic misconduct at twenty-four leading HEIs in the United Kingdom, including Oxford. The total number of cases from these twenty-four universities increased from 2,640 to 3,721 in one academic year (Marsh 2018). From a cursory examination of the figures, it could be deduced that the rates of plagiarism in the Caribbean seem significantly lower than those existing elsewhere. The statement held true even when figures for these regional universities were compared with other high-ranking institutions which had robust systems of academic integrity. The reasons for these differences certainly require further research.

Figure 10.1 shows fluctuations in the number of cases of plagiarism when the data of three universities were examined collectively, and so further analysis was done on individual institutions. The literature is inconclusive about whether cases of plagiarism were on the rise even though Curtis and Vardenega reported that the rate of plagiarism was trending down based on the results from their ten-year time-lag study of Australian university students. They found that "both students' understanding of plagiarism and the extent to which they consider plagiarism to be a serious issue trended upward over the decade" (2016, 20) and combined with technological initiatives were helping to counteract the possible negative impacts of plagiarism from the internet (2016, 2). Other studies point to an increase in the rates of plagiarism due to the influence of the internet (Carpenter et al. 2006, 184). In a bid to establish whether the number of reported cases of plagiarism was increasing in the Caribbean, the data from Institutions 1, 2 and 4 were examined and the results are shown in a line graph in figure 10.2.

Fluctuations in the number of reported cases were evident from all three institutions when the data were examined for an extended period, mirroring the findings reported in figure 10.1. However, over the thirteen-year period,

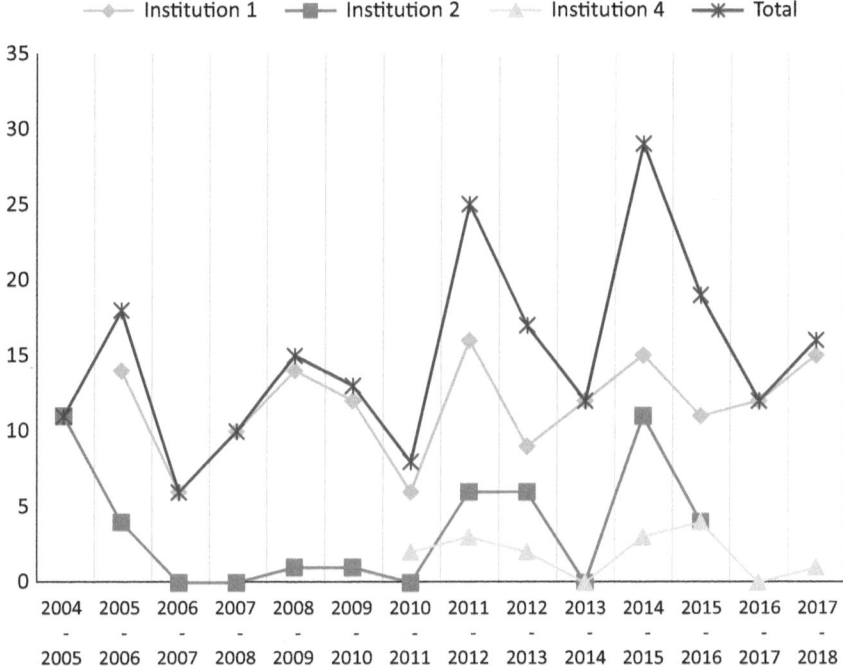

Figure 10.2. Comparison of reported cases of plagiarism for three institutions for the period 2004–2018.

the number of cases showed only a marginal increase, the causes for which could not be ascertained based on the lack of research in the Caribbean. Even with the pervasive use of the internet, which was believed to be a major contributor to plagiarism (Sureda-Negre, Comas-Forgas and Oliver-Trobat 2015, 105), there was no substantial increase recorded at these institutions over the period.

The literature points out that academic maturity is one of the variables that was likely to impact levels of plagiarism (Goh 2013, 307), so this was investigated in the current research. Figure 10.3 presents the number of reported cases of plagiarism by academic year groups for students enroled in Years 1–4.

Based on the data, Year 3 students, the majority of whom were likely to be in their final year of studies, had more reported cases of plagiarism (73 per cent) than the other year groups combined. This is opposite to Goh's findings that rates of cheating were lowest among Year 3 students (2013, 307). This high rate of plagiarism could arise out of the need to ensure that they completed their programmes as well as because lecturers were less tolerant of plagiarism

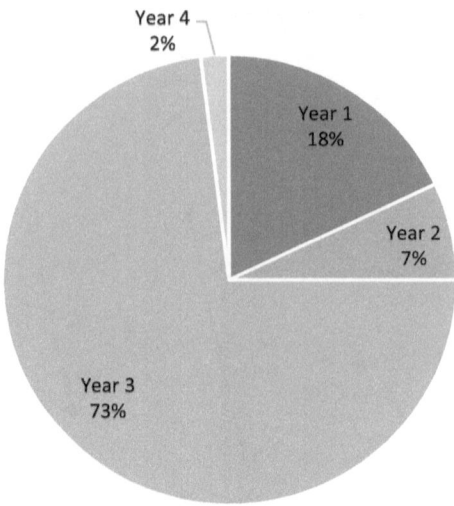

Figure 10.3. The number of cases of plagiarism by year groups at Institution 2.

at this level and so did more reporting. Walker and White reported that some faculty "admitted that they refrained from reporting plagiarism when they perceived that an investigation might negatively influence the student's advancement, especially at the upper level" (2014, 8). Walker and White's finding did not concur with the findings in this study.

Wilkinson found that participants who did not possess the requisite knowledge and skills to cope with the demands of academic work were more likely to plagiarize (2009, 101) a statement that might be true of students just entering HEIs. However, in this analysis, only 18 per cent of the cases of plagiarism involved Year 1 students, and the small percentage of Year 4 students who plagiarized was reflective of the low enrolment in that year group given that the majority of degree programmes in these institutions lasted for three years.

The literature on the impact of gender on plagiarism is inconclusive, but evidence leans towards males being more likely to plagiarize (Ismail 2018, 12; Sheets and Waddil 2009, 4). In order to decide if gender was a significant variable in plagiarism in the Caribbean, the data were analysed based on this variable. Only Institution 2 provided data by gender, and so based on this limitation, caution is encouraged when making generalizations from this data.

The data showed that there were more reported plagiarism infractions by males (55 per cent) than females (45 per cent) at Institution 2 at which the population consisted of approximately 63 per cent females and 37 per cent males. It was evident that although the ratio of females to males in the population was almost 2:1, the ratio of reported cases for males to females was almost 1:1. This means that in this institution males were cheating significantly more. This finding was similar to that of Sureda-Negre, Oliver-Trobat and Comas-Forgas (2015, 103) and others. However, in a meta-analysis of the eighteen studies on the impact of gender on cheating, Bretag found that for the majority, gender was not a significant variable in cheating although nearly one-third showed this as a factor (Bretag, 2018a, 7–8). Therefore, based on the literature it would appear that while gender did have some impact upon students' cheating, it was not a significant one. Nevertheless, the findings of this research indicate that in at least one Caribbean institution, males were plagiarizing twice as much as females, a variable which needs further research.

Discussion of Findings

An analysis of accreditation policies and guidelines showed variation in the treatment of academic integrity and plagiarism. Whereas some territories made no mention of these, others included the importance of HEIs having a policy for programme and institutional accreditation. The Jamaican policy was the most detailed, outlining the evidence that institutions had to present to signify their commitment to academic integrity. However, the insistence of the accreditation agency on policies and not on structures to educate students about plagiarism indicated a punitive approach to plagiarism which is symptomatic of the region. Accreditation agencies are instrumental in ensuring quality in higher education and so the approach they take to academic integrity is likely to impact academic integrity practices in each institution.

The data from four HEIs indicated that Caribbean tertiary students, like those in other parts of the world, were plagiarizing. Over the period under investigation, 220 major cases were recorded and this number seemed insignificant when compared to overall enrolment. However, the real extent of this practice in HEIs in the Caribbean could not be determined from the data provided for various reasons, including a general absence of information overall; the lack of consensus on a definition and the type of behaviours that constitute plagiarism and commonality in its treatment; and missing data on the "less severe" cases of plagiarism which were usually treated at a course or departmental level.

Based on the available data, the number of cases of plagiarism fluctuated over the period which stood in direct contrast to the findings from the University of Berkley in California which showed a 126 per cent increase between the period 1998 and 2001 (Berlinck 2011, 369) and Oxford University. This might have been due to various factors not present in the Caribbean situation, and so only a marginal increase in the number of cases was observed for the period under discussion.

It was also difficult to make a reasonable comparison of plagiarism data from the region with that obtained elsewhere, due to each institution managing infringements differently. Additionally, other factors which could impact the comparison of cases across institutions and geographic boundaries were the definitions adopted by institutions, the rate of reporting and whether or not there was an established culture of academic integrity. In spite of the challenges inherent in making a comparison between the number of cases of plagiarism in the region and those at universities elsewhere, the data available from other institutions provided a useful reference point for HEIs in the region.

Of interest, was the fact that the plagiarism data from other universities were readily available online which differed significantly from what were obtained in the region where data on the subject were usually not shared with others outside of the administrative structure within the institutions. The data revealed that males and final year students were more likely to cheat than others and that the rate of plagiarism among Year 3 students was substantially higher than for the other groups. These findings were in direct contradiction to those of Goh which showed that Year 3 students cheated less than those in other years (2013, 307).

An examination of the policies for academic integrity and plagiarism in HEIs in the region revealed that faculty bore most of the responsibility for managing plagiarism allegations and that these institutions did not have a culture of academic integrity. The low incidence of plagiarism in the region might have been a result of low levels of reporting by faculty for the following reasons: lack of institutional support (McGrail and McGrail 2015; Thomas 2017), the stress of dealing with students cheating behaviours (Coren 2011, 291; Keith-Spiegel et al. 1998, 215) and limited evidence or lack of courage to report infractions (Keith-Spiegel et al. 1998, 215). In addition, reporting plagiarism required extensive time and effort (Keith-Spiegel et al. 1998, 215; Stowe 2017); there were concerns about retaliation or a legal challenge; the belief that cheating students failed and the worse cheats did not get caught (Keith-Spiegel et al. 1998, 215). Coaltar, Lim and Wanorie pointed out that faculty's responses to academic dishonesty were impacted by a lack of agreement on the judicial process and the difficulty of compiling evidence or proof of misconduct (2007), and Andrews et al. noted that these might be interpreted by the student as a lack of commitment to academic honesty on the part of faculty (2007, 1033). Given these various factors, it is possible that faculty might under-report suspected cases of plagiarism so the number of actual cases is likely to be more than the reported cases.

For these reasons, the data from the four universities might not necessarily reflect the actual number of cases and further investigation would be necessary to determine this as well as if the number of cases was increasing. Given that these institutions use text-matching software, it would also be instructive to determine the impact, if any, of the software on the detection and deterrence of plagiarism. Students in the Caribbean were plagiarizing, but for a number of reasons already mentioned, it was difficult to determine its prevalence. Therefore, although the numbers recorded were low, this should not be a reason for complacency. There is still the need to develop a culture of academic integrity which would ensure a systematic approach to educating students and faculty on plagiarism. There is also the need to collect and analyse data from the various HEIs in the Caribbean that can present a true reflection of academic misconduct practices within them.

Chapter 11

Undergraduate Students' Perceptions of Plagiarism

Analysis of Quantitative Data

Introduction

This chapter begins with a brief review of the literature on students' perceptions of the factors which contribute to plagiarism, justifications for plagiarizing and their perceptions of the severity of and the penalty for the act. It then presents an analysis and discussion of the quantitative data on the perceptions of plagiarism of 1,039 undergraduates enrolled in five faculties at a leading university in the Caribbean.

Background

The prevalence of plagiarism and the difficulty in collecting empirical data due to the sensitive nature of the topic have led many researchers to investigate students' perceptions, with the hope of gaining a better understanding of the subject to inform the development of programmes aimed at helping to stem it. Nushi and Firoozkoho (2017, 5) cite Pecorari who claimed there was no need for additional research on this aspect of the topic; however, a dearth of information on it in the Caribbean speaks to a need for regional research. Walcott investigated the attitudes of second-year computer students using the Attitude Towards Plagiarism Survey. He discovered they had a "moderate, positive attitude towards plagiarism." He also found many of these Caribbean students "believed that self-plagiarism is not harmful and therefore should not be punished" (2016, 63). The findings of this small-scale study indicated a need for further investigation.

Based on the foregoing, the objectives for this study were to:

1. explore students' perceptions of the factors that exacerbate plagiarism;
2. examine students' perceptions of justification for plagiarism; and
3. investigate students' perceptions of the severity of and penalty for plagiarism.

This study is significant because it fills a gap in empirical works on plagiarism in the English-speaking Caribbean while adding to the emerging research on the topic regionally and internationally. It should also send a message to the international higher education community that the Caribbean has a vested interest in academic integrity, and this might help to inspire greater confidence in regional institutions.

Review of Literature

This review focuses on students' perceptions of the factors which fuel plagiarism, arguments that students are likely to use to justify plagiarism and their perceptions of the severity of and penalty for plagiarism. The majority of the studies reviewed were conducted between 2005 and 2017, and they are mainly from North America, Europe and Australia, with smatterings from other geographic locations.

Ramzan, Asif and Adeeb discovered that students believed that the tolerance of universities and the leniency of faculty towards plagiarism were causative factors (2018, 77). Students generally believed that the faculty's concerns about plagiarism are much ado about nothing; therefore, they exhibit what Power described as a "curious sense of separation" from the topic. They view plagiarism as something that is imposed on them by others (2009, 657), and although they know it is unethical (Carpenter et al. 2006, 192), they have found ways to justify the action (Howard, Ehrich and Walton 2014, 386). It was also discovered that students were more likely to commit various types of plagiarism if they believed their peers were plagiarizing (Fish and Hura 2013, 33).

Sisti attributes students' justification for plagiarism to a lack of confidence in their ability to adequately complete academic tasks, confusion, necessity, paraphrasing, incompetence, ease and peer pressure. He explains that students in search of a justification for plagiarizing usually present a reason that could fit into one of these categories (2007, 222). Andrews et al. found that students justified cheating by evaluating the importance of the task they were assigned and plagiarized if they did not consider it relevant (2007, 1033). These researchers also discovered that students justified plagiarism based on the instructor's attitude and instructions, peer pressure or whether they felt cheating made the work easier (2007, 1033). Carpenter et al. in agreeing with Andrews et al. (2007) note that students use "instructor-based neutralizations" rather than course-related "excuses." Students cited too much work given by the instructor as justification for cheating. They deflected responsibility for acting honestly from themselves and placed it on the faculty and the institution (Carpenter et al. 2006, 192). This further supports Power's finding of a lack of student engagement with plagiarism (2007, 657). Self-plagiarism was justified by students who advocated that they cannot steal from themselves (Howard, Ehrich and Walton 2014, 386).

One of the findings from the review of literature is the difference in perceptions of plagiarism held by faculty and students, with the former viewing it as a serious academic breach, while the latter did not (Gullifer and Tyson 2010, 17; Lynch et al. 2017). Students' perception of the severity of the act of plagiarism was also likely to impact their perception of the sanctions that should be applied when there are breaches. As shown from studies done by Sisti (2007) and Andrews et al. (2007, 1032), the decision to practise academic integrity can stem from a desire to avoid the consequences of academic misconduct. However, some students were aware of the penalty but still chose to act dishonestly (Goh 2013, 318; Lynch et al. 2017, 2862). Generally, students demonstrated an ambivalence towards the severity of and the penalty for plagiarism.

In an examination of the perceptions of plagiarism held by students, Charubusp discovered that 31.7 per cent of the sixty students sampled were undecided as to the severity of the punishment meted out for plagiarism and believed it was an exaggeration of the seriousness of the issue. On the other hand, 36.7 per cent agreed that plagiarism was a serious matter (2015, 70). Furthermore, in a mixed-methods study conducted by Gullifer, these sentiments were echoed by participants in the focus groups who "believed that sanctions for plagiarism were too draconian and harsh" (2013, 265), a finding supported by Yeo (2007, 199).

This lack of understanding of the severity of plagiarism might be due to the punitive sanctions or lack thereof (Andrews et al. 2007; Gullifer 2013). Andrews et al. stated that participants in their study reported that when students were caught plagiarizing they were not punished. These students felt it was "due to fear of developing a negative school image, fear of litigation, or 'connections' by parents" (2007, 1032). Gullifer, on the other hand, found that participants in her research were so nonchalant about plagiarism that they ranked it among "the least serious of all behaviours" (2013, 267). They perceived that "academics were too pedantic about attribution and citation practices, to the point of being too exacting about grammatical correctness of the citation outputs" (Gullifer 2013, 268). This indicates a lack of knowledge and understanding of the ramifications of plagiarism and also a misunderstanding of their roles and responsibilities as student researchers.

Data Presentation and Analysis

Questionnaires were administered to 1,040 students in years 1–4 from the faculties of Medical Sciences, Social Sciences, Humanities and Education,

Law, and Science and Technology. (See chapter 6 for a breakdown of the sample). The researcher analysed 1,039 of these questionnaires and discarded the one that was incomplete. The questionnaire, comprised mainly of a Likert scale, contained twenty-eight items. The first six items collected demographic data, while the remaining twenty-two items were placed on three subscales aimed at measuring students' perceptions of factors of plagiarism, justification for plagiarism and the severity of and penalty for plagiarism. The data in this study were compared with that of Howard, Ehrich and Walton (2014) who modified the questionnaire and used it to study the perceptions of Australian students, and Walcott (2016) who used a similar instrument with computer science students in the Caribbean.

Perceptions of Factors Which Exacerbate Plagiarism

Eight questions on the first subscale examined the factors that exacerbate plagiarism, and the responses are reported as percentages in table 11.1. Numbers were rounded off and so may not add up to 100 per cent.

Based on the percentage of students who agreed and strongly agreed, they were most likely to plagiarize when their friends permitted them to copy (40.3 per cent). The friend factor (Sisti 2007) was not as prominent in Walcott's (2016) study as only 22 per cent agreed with the statement. However, the students in Walcott's sample were thrice as likely to be influenced by this factor as those studied by Howard, Ehrich and Walton as only 7.7 per cent of the respondents in the latter study agreed. The second factor most likely to influence students to plagiarize was having more important obligations (38.6 per cent), a factor which was not significant for the students studied by Howard, Ehrich and Walton as only 5.7 per cent agree with this statement. Whereas short deadlines and a heavy workload were influential for 24.4 per cent of the sample in this research, it was not so for Howard and colleagues as only 2.3 per cent of their sample agreed. When compared to the results obtained by Howard, Ehrich and Walton, the percentage of students agreeing to each statement on this subscale were higher for every item in this study, suggesting that these respondents were more likely to be influenced by these factors.

The majority of participants (62.4 per cent) believed that plagiarism was commonly practised and agreed with the statement in item 9 that "Those who say they have never plagiarised are lying." According to Chapman et al., students who cheated frequently tend to overestimate the cheating behaviours of other students and this was likely to lead to further cheating (2004, 246). This finding deviated significantly from that of Howard, Ehrich and Walton (2014) who reported that only 22.7 per cent of their sample agreed with this statement, less than half of that obtained in this

Table 11.1. Perception of the factors which exacerbate plagiarism

Factors that exacerbate plagiarism	SA (in %)	A (in %)	U (in %)	D (in %)	SD (in %)	NR (in %)*
7. Short deadlines or a heavy workload give me the right to plagiarize a bit.	8.0	16.4	12.9	31.1	31.3	0.4
8. A plagiarized paper does no harm to the value of a university degree.	4.3	11.6	14.1	33.1	36.4	0.5
9. Those who say they have never plagiarized are lying.	33.9	28.5	21.1	10.1	6.0	0.5
10. Plagiarism can be justified if I currently have more important obligations or tasks to do.	2.9	7.9	15.0	43.5	29.9	0.8
11. Sometimes, it is necessary to plagiarize	7.0	26.1	17.1	27.5	20.6	1.6
12. I am tempted to plagiarize if I have permission from a friend to copy his or her work	10.8	29.5	11.0	28.1	20.5	0.1
13. I am tempted to plagiarize if I currently have more important obligations or tasks to do.	8.6	30.0	10.6	31.3	19.0	0.6
14. I am tempted to plagiarize because, even if caught, the punishment will be light (the reward outweighs the risk).	1.2	4.2	7.9	38.3	48.2	0.2

study. Walcott also reported findings that deviated from those obtained in this study. Only 41 per cent agreed with this statement, and approximately an equal number (40 per cent) were undecided (2016, 74). The responses to the statement "Sometimes it is necessary to plagiarise" were instructive as 33.1 per cent of the respondents in this study agreed, a figure which is comparable to the 30 per cent in Walcott's study. This figure far surpassed the 3.6 per cent in Howard, Ehrich and Walton's study (2014, 386).

The factor least likely to influence students to plagiarize was the light penalty, as agreed to by 6.4 per cent of the participants, and it had the highest percentage of disagreement (86.5 per cent) on this scale. This high level of disagreement is significant and might be due to either fear created by the emphasis on sanctions as suggested by the qualitative data, or a belief that they will not be caught. Other factors with a high percentage of disagreement were justifying plagiarism as a result of having more important obligations (73.4 per cent) and the belief that plagiarism does no harm to a degree (69.5 per cent). Howard, Ehrich and Walton did not report on the level of disagreement to these factors, but based on the fact that levels of agreement for the three items were lower than 10 per cent, it could be concluded that they recorded high levels of disagreement.

The percentage of responses for "Undecided" and "No Response" were worth considering, as they provided additional insights. The highest percentage of "Undecided" responses on this subscale was 21.1 per cent for item 9, followed by 17.1 per cent for item 11 which stated, "Sometimes it is necessary to plagiarise." Item 11 also had the highest percentage of "No Responses" (1.6 per cent). This ambivalence towards plagiarism cannot be ignored as it suggested students have not taken a position on some of the important issues, or they did not want to commit themselves to responses that they believed would present them in a negative light.

Perceptions of Justification for Plagiarism

Six questions were asked to gauge students' justification for plagiarism, and the responses are displayed in table 11.2.

Items on this subscale attracted the highest number of responses, and these were largely clustered around "Agree" and "Strongly Agree" suggesting that students used a number of justifications for plagiarism. Item 15 was the only one on the entire scale which had 100 per cent responses, indicating that this was important to the students. As many as 77.7 per cent would justify plagiarism with the statement, "You cannot avoid using other people's words." In this research, the second-highest percentage of "Strongly Agree" responses in this subscale (35.2 per cent) was for this statement. This response concurred with Walcott's findings of 80 per cent agreement (2016, 73), while for Howard, Ehrich and Walton only 44 per cent agreed (2014, 36). Other likely justifications for plagiarism in this research were the arguments that undergraduate students were just learning and should be given some leniency (51.7 per cent) and that previous descriptions can be used since they do not change (65 per cent). The argument that was least likely to be used as justification was that plagiarism should not be considered serious since it does not involve taking tangible assets, and 61 per cent of the sample disagreed.

The items on self-plagiarism attracted high levels of agreement. Three quarters of the respondents agreed that self-plagiarism should not be punishable as it was not harmful, and this was only 9 per cent higher than the findings of Walcott (2016). Although only 58.7 per cent of Howard,

Table 11.2. Students' responses for justification for plagiarism

Statements	SA (in %)	A (in %)	U (in %)	D (in %)	SD (in %)	NR (in %)
15. Sometimes you cannot avoid using other people's words, because there are only so many ways to describe something.	35.2	42.5	8.2	9.9	4.1	0.0
16. It is justified to use previous descriptions of a concept or theory, because they remain the same.	23.0	42.0	19.6	12.5	2.3	0.7
17. Undergraduate students, because they are just learning the ropes, should receive milder punishment for plagiarism.	18.8	32.9	19.5	19.2	9.0	0.7
18. Self-plagiarism is not punishable because it is not harmful (you cannot steal from yourself).	45.8	29.2	13.1	7.8	3.0	1.2
19. It is justified to use your own previous work, without providing citation, in order to complete the current work.	21.7	27.1	21.9	22.5	6.4	0.4
20. Since plagiarism is taking other people's words rather than tangible assets, it should not be considered a serious offence.	4.7	11.5	21.6	38.3	22.8	1.1

*SA – Strongly Agree; A – Agree; U – Undecided; D – Disagree; SD – Strongly Disagree

Ehrich and Walton's (2014) sample agreed that self-plagiarism should not be punishable, this was one of the few items that had a level of agreement that was comparable to that of this study and the findings of Walcott (2016). Item 18 which checked whether students would justify self-plagiarism with the statement that it is not harmful attracted the most "Strongly Agree" responses (45.8 per cent) in this subscale and the overall scale.

Based on the data, possible justifications for plagiarism would be the necessity of using the words of others as there were limited ways of describing a concept, the thinking that previous descriptions of a concept or theory do not change and undergraduates were just learning so they should be shown leniency. Students would justify self-plagiarism on the grounds that it is not harmful so it should not be punishable as one cannot steal from oneself. It was interesting to note that for the most part, the responses in this study mirrored those of Walcott, whose sample was drawn from a population similar to that of this research. However, they differed significantly from those of Howard, Ehrich and Walton (2014) who worked in academic contexts with a strong culture of academic integrity in higher education.

Perceptions of the Severity of and Penalty for Plagiarism

The literature often points to differing perceptions of the severity of and the penalty for plagiarism between staff and students, with some students believing that it is not as serious as faculty claimed (Gullifer 2013, 208). Eight questions were asked to gather students' perceptions on the severity of and penalty for plagiarism, and the responses are shown in Table 11.3.

The majority of students (67.2 per cent) disagreed with the statement "Plagiarism is not a big deal" with another 55.9 per cent also disagreeing that it should not be considered a serious offence, and 57.4 per cent disagreeing that it was justified to copy parts of a published paper. Although more than half of the sample seemed to believe that plagiarism was a serious matter, if these responses were to be taken at face value, these numbers were still low given the importance of academic integrity in higher education, and the emphasis placed on not plagiarizing. Howard, Ehrich and Walton reported levels of agreement for these items between 1.6 per cent and 7.3 per cent. Again, noting that their research did not report on levels of disagreement, it would then lead one to conclude that these low levels of agreement would signal high levels of disagreement with these statements when compared to the responses for this study.

Twenty-three point six per cent of the respondents believed it was acceptable to ignore plagiarism in a high-quality paper, a figure which was much higher than the 9 per cent in Walcott's study (2016, 73). However, these both surpassed the 4.4 per cent found by Howard, Ehrich and Walton (2014, 386). The respondents believed plagiarism undermined independent thought (68.1 per cent), and interestingly, this item had the highest percentage of "No Response" (3.3 per cent) for the entire scale. Only 43 per cent of Walcott's sample agreed that "Plagiarism improvises the investigative spirit," a statement that is similar to item 26. The 78.2 per cent who believed self-plagiarism should not be punished in the same manner as plagiarism concurred with the 70 per cent in Walcott's study who shared this belief (2016, 73).

The highest number of "Undecided" responses was on this subscale. Almost a quarter of the sample was undecided as to whether plagiarism

Table 11.3. Responses for the severity of and penalty for plagiarism

Severity and penalty	SA (in %)	A (in %)	U (in %)	D (in %)	SD (in %)	NR (in %)*
21. Plagiarised parts of a student's paper should be ignored if the paper is otherwise of high quality.	6.7	16.9	22.3	37.0	16.7	0.3
22. Self-plagiarism should not be punishable in the same way as plagiarism is	41.5	36.7	11.8	6.0	3.4	0.7
23. If you cannot write well because of unfamiliarity with the topic area, it is justified to copy parts of a paper already published in that area in order to accurately represent those ideas.	4.1	18.4	19.7	38.2	19.2	0.3
24. Given a commonly perceived decline in moral and ethical standards, it is important to discuss issues like plagiarism and self-plagiarism.	35.8	43.1	12.5	3.4	2.6	2.6
25. Plagiarism is as bad as stealing an exam.	17.9	31.0	15.9	21.7	11.9	1.6
26. Plagiarism undermines independent thought.	28.7	40.1	13.4	11.1	3.5	3.3
27. Since plagiarism is taking other people's words rather than tangible assets, it should not be considered a serious offence.	5.5	14.2	23.6	37.0	18.9	0.9
28. Plagiarism is not a big deal.	4.9	10.1	17.1	39.2	28.0	0.7

SA – Strongly Agree; A – Agree; U – Undecided; D – Disagree; SD – Strongly Disagree.

should be considered a serious offence. In addition, 22.3 per cent were undecided as to whether plagiarized parts of a paper should be ignored if the paper was of high quality. Another 17.1 per cent were undecided as to whether or not plagiarism was a big deal. When the "Undecided" and the "No Responses" on this scale were totalled for each item, the responses showed that although the majority of students were indicating an understanding of the seriousness of plagiarism, there was still a significant sector of the sample that either believed differently or the students had not made up their minds about the matter. Whereas students believed plagiarism undermined independent thought and was a "big deal," they did not think it should be considered as bad as stealing an exam, and just more than half of them (53.7 per cent) disagreed with the statement that it should be ignored in a high-quality paper. This ambivalence towards plagiarism was also evident in the qualitative data where students expressed the belief that plagiarism, though wrong, could be justified for a variety of reasons including the need to graduate and a desire to help a friend.

The item with the highest percentage of agreement (78.9 per cent) on this subscale had to do with the respondents believing that it was important to discuss plagiarism and self-plagiarism. This compares favourably with 71 per cent from Walcott's sample (2016, 74), and 69 per cent from Howard, Ehrich and Walton's (2016, 36). This is the item that has the highest level of similarity in perception when the responses are examined across the three studies. The need for education on plagiarism is supported by the qualitative data which is presented and analysed in the following chapter.

Discussion of Findings

Students' perception of the factors which influenced plagiarism corresponded to the research findings discussed in the review of literature in chapter 3. For this group of students, the most influential factors were likely to be the friend factor (Sisti 2007), having more important obligations, and the belief that others were plagiarizing. There were high levels of agreement with the arguments that were likely to be used to justify plagiarism. Of the six items on this scale, five scored between 48 per cent and 78 per cent in terms of agreement. The high levels of agreement is telling leading one to wonder whether students were actually using these justifications.

In terms of the responses for the severity of and penalty for plagiarism, it was clear that students believed that plagiarism undermined independent thought, and the majority thought that it was a big deal. However, marginal disagreement with ignoring plagiarised parts of a high quality paper, and the seriousness of taking words which were not tangible asset signals a significant number of students who did not believe plagiarism was all that serious. What is evident is that overall they agree that plagiarism was wrong, however, when it came to identifying specific behaviours they were not convinced that these practices were inappropriate. The students' ambivalence on the penalty and severity of plagiarism revealed the differences between faculty and students' perception of plagiarism (Yeo 2007; Gullifer and Tyson 2010). The majority believed self-plagiarism should be treated differently from other forms of plagiarism.

Although on the surface students' perceptions of plagiarism might seem to be "correct," an examination of the areas of disagreement, the "Undecided" and the "No Responses," indicated that there was a level of ambivalence towards the topic that cannot be ignored. The belief that others were plagiarizing which was evident by the responses of these students is believed to be one of the motivating factors for students to plagiarize (Broeckelman-Post 2008, 206; Carpenter, Harding and Fineli 2006), and this should not be disregarded. In addition, high levels of disagreement and indecision about whether or not plagiarism was a serious matter indicated a wrong perception that could possibly lead to unacceptable behaviours. Another finding that signalled a need for intervention was the belief that plagiarism should be ignored if the paper was of high quality. Here students were not discerning enough to realize that the quality of the paper was questionable if it contained plagiarized material. The high responses for the justification of plagiarism was another indicator that students were not convinced about the seriousness of plagiarism, hence their desire to "explain it away."

When the responses of the participants in this study were compared to those of Howard, Ehrich and Walton's study (2014), the results showed a great disparity in the majority of areas. The participants in the Australian study believed that plagiarism was a serious matter, and their responses differed from those in this study on every subscale. It must be noted that these Australian participants were from universities which had strong academic integrity cultures. As a matter of fact, academic integrity is an integral part of the national higher education landscape in Australia. It was therefore possible that their perceptions had been shaped by this environment. This conclusion could be supported by the fact the findings from Walcott's (2016) study, which was done at a university in the Caribbean, shared striking similarities with the findings in this research.

Students perceived there was a need for education on plagiarism, a finding supported by the data from the qualitative research, and also from the findings of Howard, Ehrich and Walton (2014) and Walcott (2016). Education as a means of decreasing the incidence of plagiaristic behaviours was often included among the recommendations made by those who study plagiarism. In addition, empirical data exists to indicate that education on plagiarism significantly increases students' knowledge of the topic and decreases dishonest behaviours.

Chapter 12

In Their Own Words – Undergraduates' Perception of Plagiarism

Introduction

The survey yielded qualitative data from three lines on the questionnaire which invited students to provide additional comments. This chapter presents an analysis and discussion of the responses garnered from 267 students. The data are organized and discussed according to the themes which emerged from the review of the literature.

Background

Education administrators must have a fulsome understanding of students' perception of plagiarism in order to develop effective programmes and activities to stem this form of academic misconduct. To gather qualitative data to paint a fulsome picture, the researcher provided three lines on the survey and invited students to add their comments. This gave students the opportunity to express their beliefs and proved to be valuable supplementary information to the data collected by the Likert scale.

Data Presentation and Analysis

Data were provided by students from the five academic faculties who took part in the survey. Two hundred and sixty-seven students (26 per cent of the sample who participated in the survey) provided comments. Of the 267 students, 33 per cent were males and 67 per cent were females. This gender compliment was almost representative of the ratio of males to females in the university population. The Faculty of Social Sciences had the highest number of students responding to the questionnaire and the highest number of participants providing qualitative data (52 per cent), while very few respondents (2 per cent) were from the Faculty of Law. The Faculty of Medical Sciences (20 per cent), Science and Technology (18 per cent) and Humanities and Education (8 per cent) accounted for the remainder of the respondents.

The demographic data for the participants who provided qualitative responses were also examined to determine the spread of the responses over the year group, seeing that academic maturity was a variable in this study. Figure 12.1 shows the percentage of students from each year group who provided qualitative data.

The majority of respondents (36 per cent) were in Year 1, and Year 3 followed with 32 per cent. Year 4 students from the Faculty of Medical Sciences represented only 3 per cent of the respondents, and this when added to the 32 per cent of students in Year 3 means that 35 per cent of the students were in their final year of study. Except for Year 4, the participants were almost equaly divided among year groups, so the data should present a balanced perspective.

The data were coded into seven themes, based on the issues presented in the review of literature, and the responses were tabulated to determine which themes were most dominant as this might reveal the importance of the issues for the students. Some students produced extended responses which reflected more than one of the themes, and these were tallied and calculated as percentages of the 267 participants. Figure 12.2 shows how the responses were distributed under each theme and when added up, this amounts to more than 100 per cent to reflect the fact that some students provided more than one response.

The majority of the comments (36 per cent) related to the severity of and penalty for plagiarism, which was no doubt a response to the emphasis

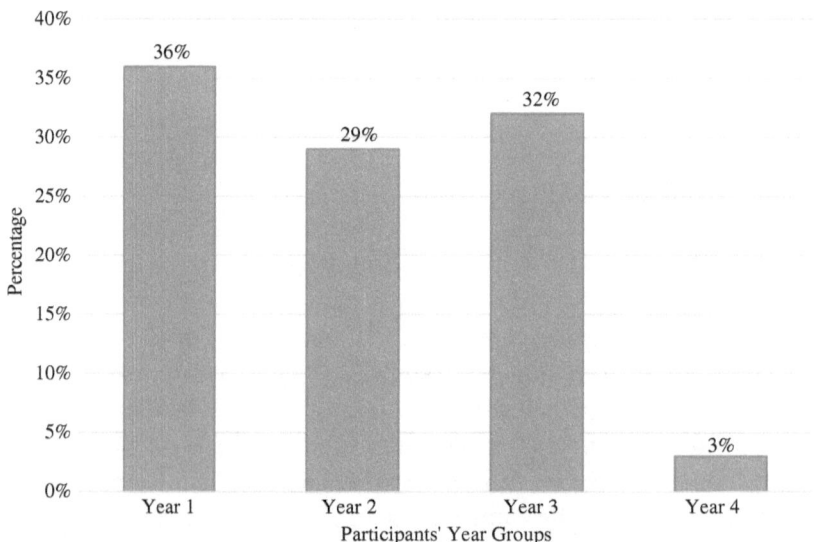

Figure 12.1. Qualitative data respondents by year groups.

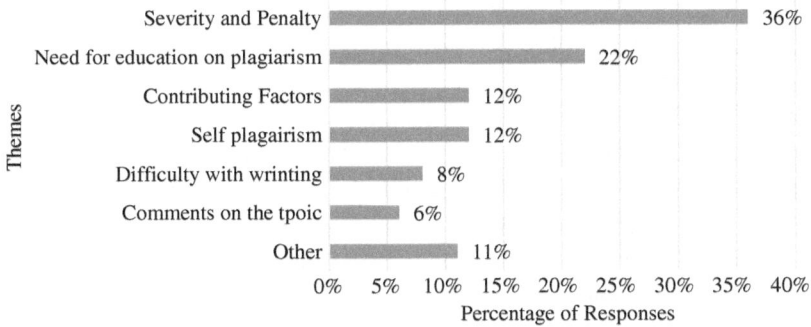

Figure 12.2. Qualitative responses by themes.

placed on penalties by Caribbean institutions as seen by the fact that ten of the twelve policies from regional HEIs previously analysed included information on penalties. Further, a focus on sanctions is characteristic of the punitive approach to plagiarism (Saddiqui 2016, 3) which was largely practised in the Caribbean. Twenty-two per cent of the students wrote about the need for education on plagiarism, which was in keeping with the literature as education is viewed as one of the most effective strategies for developing academic integrity and thereby reducing rates of plagiarism (Welsh-Unwala 2019, 33). The fewest responses related to students' comments on the topic (6 per cent) and a range of issues related to challenges in writing (8 per cent). These categories will be examined in further detail in the following sections.

The Severity of and Penalty for Plagiarism

The ninety-six responses for the severity of and penalty for plagiarism were further categorized. Fifty-five per cent of these responses stated that plagiarism was wrong or was "a serious ethical issue," while 33 per cent stated that it was not right, but these students believed it was justifiable and 10 per cent agreed it was acceptable. The remaining 2 per cent of the responses were general comments about the severity of and penalty for plagiarism which did not fit into any of the previous categories. Overall, 43 per cent of the respondents felt that it was either acceptable or justifiable, and this kind of thinking by this significant number of students was a serious matter. This might explain Gullifer's observation that students who felt that plagiarism was acceptable tended to adopt a dismissive tone and seemed to have detached themselves from the ethical aspects of the issue (2013, 267).

The minority of students who believed plagiarism was acceptable were very firm in their positions, perceiving that plagiarism was either harmless or necessary and either way should not be given the kind of emphasis it was getting from the institution. One student who felt that plagiarism was acceptable expressed her position using the Jamaican vernacular, "Unuh too extra!" This suggested that individuals insisting on the avoidance of plagiarism (presumably faculty in this context) were overemphasizing what was not important. Another student conveyed the same idea, though in a milder tone, by stating that plagiarism was not as bad as people made it seem. The terms "unuh" (another word for "you" plural) and "people" suggested a level of detachment from the subject and conveyed the idea of "we" versus "them" (Power 2009, 657). Another student expressed her impatience with the topic by stating, "Plagiarism is not that serious. Thank you, next?" This extreme position did not find much support from the majority of students. The quantitative data also supported these findings indicating that there was a small but significant segment of the sample who believed plagiarism was acceptable and that penalties were overbearing. This was evident from their perceptions that plagiarism in a paper that was of otherwise high quality should be ignored (23.6 per cent), plagiarism should not be considered a serious offence (19.7 per cent) and plagiarism was not a big deal (15 per cent).

Almost a third (33 per cent) of the respondents in this category considered plagiarism wrong but justifiable, a finding supported by the high number of responses on the *Justification for Plagiarism* subscale presented in chapter 11. This desire to justify plagiarism was supported by arguments used in the literature such as the necessity of plagiarizing to pass courses (Power 2009, 649), the difficulty inherent in expressing themselves and using proper citations (Anney and Mosha 2015, 213), and the amount of a work plagiarized and the consequences (Andrews et al. 2007, 1036). Their justifications were not always valid as one student stated, "Students should be allowed slight leniency when it comes to plagiarism as there is only so much information about a subject." In this information age, this limitation no longer applies, given the rate at which information was being produced daily. Over "2.5 quintillion bytes of data are created every single day" (Ahmad 2018), and a cache of information on any topic can be found online.

The strident tones and plausible reasons given by the 55 per cent of the students who felt plagiarism was wrong showed an understanding of the impact of plagiarism on the individual as well as the institution. Some students pointed to the harmful nature of the practice, and one noted plagiarism "[r]educes the ability to apply self-thought," while another stated,

"Individuals should always try to think for themselves instead of depending on the ideas of others." One second-year student was very expressive and provided a well-thought-out response: "Plagiarism is a serious matter not just because of the stealing aspect, but also because it handicaps students' thinking and application." Some students demonstrated an understanding of the role of education in preparing them for the world of work and how plagiarism defeated that purpose. One felt it was likely to have a negative impact on the performance in the world of work in which, "We need our own independent thought."

The responses of some students showed they were aware of their roles and responsibilities within the teaching and learning context, and they were also cognizant of the detrimental effects of plagiarism. One student looked beyond the individual to the qualifications being sought and opined, "A plagiarised degree means that you have not acquired the degree fairly." This reference to fairness alludes to the six fundamental principles of academic integrity postulated by the International Center for Academic Integrity (2014). Plagiarism is a breach of the concept of fairness as students would have acquired a degree without expending the expected effort and in doing so, put other students who did what was required at a disadvantage.

Another student referred to the wider university context and the skills to be acquired and noted that plagiarism should be punished as it opposed those ideals. However, this differed from the presentation of plagiarism in the regional policies of HEIs which predominantly focussed on how plagiarism deprived the creator of the work of credit but did not focus on how it robbed the plagiarist of valuable learning opportunities. One respondent, concerned about the reputational damage that could accrue from plagiarism, stated, "The university should do something about the matter so it is not viewed bad[ly] by the public." Another respondent succinctly summed up the reason students ought not to plagiarize by explaining: "The university is a place where students are told to read for their degrees. It is also a place for independent thinking, use of understanding and thorough presentation of the material learnt. This means plagiarism should be less among the student population as skills like this should have been learnt well. They should be punished." This level of understanding is what institutions ought to seek to develop in students; however, based on the data, it seems more the exception than the norm.

Some respondents felt plagiarism was wrong as it was unfair to the creator of the work, which largely echoed the sentiments of the most often quoted definition of the topic. One student proffered the idea that "Since people put a lot of work into published material, it is not okay to steal another's work and make it your own without giving credit to them." Others focused on the moral aspects of plagiarism, noting that it was unethical and that it could be equated to cheating on a test. One student indicated the possible lifelong negative repercussion of plagiarism by stating, "These habits may seem harmful at low levels but it eventually becomes habitual and a lifestyle in adulthood." Research has shown that persons who cheated in school were likely to cheat in the workplace and to be unfaithful to their spouses (Josephson Institute of Ethics 2009), although Harding et al. did not corroborate this in their study (2003, n.p.). The students did not seem to grasp the global impact of plagiarism as mentioned by Hallak and Poisson (2007, 243), but their responses demonstrated a good understanding of some of the personal and institutional ramifications.

The participants' thoughts on the penalty for plagiarism seemed to be aligned with their perception of the seriousness of the act. Those who felt that plagiarism was acceptable also believed it should not attract any penalties, with one student stating, "I honestly believe universities have a lot more things to worry about than plagiarism." Another set of respondents felt that plagiarists ought to be punished, but this should be dependent on the severity of the offence in terms of the amount of content that was plagiarized, the level of the students and the reasons for plagiarizing. This practice of treating cases of plagiarism based on contextual factors was evident in some regional policies and supported by McGrail and McGrail (2015, 30). One student's response sums up the thinking of this group. She states, "I think each case is different and one needs to consider all the possible reasons and thought processes leading up to plagiarism."

The respondents who felt that plagiarism was wrong for the most part believed that it ought to be punished. One student stated, "If plagiarism is a problem have harsher punishment for it," inferring that punishment would act as a deterrence, a finding by Glendinning (2014, 13), and deemed to be ineffective by Saddiqui (2016, 3). One student who believed plagiarism was wrong but disagreed with the penalties stated, "I believe plagiarism is not right, however some of the penalties could be less." Another respondent felt that the punishment for plagiarism at the secondary level should be harsher, and another stated that the absence of penalties would hinder students from becoming critical thinkers. There was also the sentiment expressed that at the higher levels, such as from Year 2 to postgraduate, "heavy stringent measures" should be applied to those who plagiarized. Several students believed that undergraduate students should be given lighter penalties for plagiarism, seeing that they were just learning about the topic, concurring with practices at the University of the West Indies (2013).

The thinking that sanctions will deter plagiarism ignores the multifaceted nature of the problem. It is based on the thinking that plagiarism is either a moral or ethical problem. It opposes the finding which is so prevalent in the literature that poor writing skills (Kayaoglu et al. 2015; Dias and Bostos 2014; Charubusp 2015) and lack of knowledge of plagiarism (Husain, Al-Shaibani and Mahfoodh 2017; Gullifer and Tyson 2010; Ismail 2018; Ukpebor and Ogbebor 2013) are significant contributory factors among others.

Need for Education on Plagiarism

One of the overarching themes in the literature is the need for targeted education on plagiarism (Berlinck 2011, 358; McGrail and McGrail 2015, 38; Sutherland-Smith 2011, 136). Students also recognized this need and made suggestions as to how this could be done. Almost 25 per cent of those who provided comments felt there was a need for education on plagiarism, and they went on to identify the challenges they faced (Charubusp 2015, 77). The students cited a lack of instruction on plagiarism at the secondary level, agreeing with Baker-Gardner and Smart (2017, 201). In keeping with the literature, they cited additional challenges such as poor writing skills, an inability to correctly complete citations, a lack of awareness of what constituted plagiarism (Ukpebor and Ogbebor 2013, 265) and poor paraphrasing skills (Charubusp 2015, 78).

Students also admitted to a lack of understanding of how "not to plagiarise," in addition to inadequate education on the topic. This need for education on how to avoid plagiarism was also noted by Thompsett and Ahluwalia (2010). One example of the inadequacy of education on plagiarism was provided by a student who wrote, "While learning about plagiarism one was taught to just switch up a word or two, or a sentence just to avoid plagiarising. This is stupid to me because it is still the same concept you are trying to bring across."

The researcher also surmised there was a need for education on plagiarism based on some of the wrong ideas presented in the responses. For example, one student wrote, "Plagiarism should be pardoned, given the writer (you) states the sources from which ideas were taken." However, once the credit is given to the source using a standardized citation style, it was not considered plagiarism.

Some students used the lines provided for comments to list their questions on the topic. Two examples of these were "How do we not plagiarise?" and "Yes, we have common knowledge but when we get research we use other people's sources to write our own, so should we quote that?" Other factors listed by the students to support the need for plagiarism education included the fact that plagiarism was committed sometimes due to a lack of knowledge, and this too is supported by Ali, Ismail and Cheat (2012, 610), Berlinck (2011, 367) and Vázquez-Recio et al. (2016, 5707). The difficulties involved in defining and understanding plagiarism were heard in the various comments of the students. One stated that there were "different perceptions and explanations as to what the topic is." Another added, "I honestly do not even understand completely what it is and why it is such a big deal. We need to be more informed about it."

Words used to describe plagiarism included "current and complex," "unclear," "scary" and "obscured." One student stated that plagiarism "baffled" her, while another complained that sometimes plagiarism "is not even completely understood." Therefore, their desire for education on plagiarism seemed necessary and reasonable. There was obviously a disconnect between administrators who created plagiarism policies, put these online and expected students not to plagiarize and the students who were confused about plagiarism and were asking to be educated about it.

Hu and Sun believed that the institution that failed to "provide useful information and educate students about what constitutes plagiarism missed a valuable opportunity to foster students' understanding of plagiaristic behaviours and facilitate their efforts to learn and use sources in responsible and effective ways" (2017, 65). Walcott (2016) and Howard, Ehrich and Walton (2014) reported a high percentage of students who agreed with the need for education in plagiarism in their research that utilized similar instruments as used by this researcher. Porter (2016) and Walcott (2016) recommended education as a means to assist students in the Caribbean to learn about plagiarism. Welsh-Unwala (2019) found that Caribbean students in her action research benefitted from education on plagiarism. Therefore, the students' desire to be educated about plagiarism has significant support from the literature and ought to be given due consideration by educational institutions.

In keeping with suggestions from Ismail (2018) and Kayaoglu et al. (2015), students suggested that instruction on plagiarism could take the form of courses, workshops or seminars. References were made to using the university librarians and lecturers as the means of delivering this instruction and for it to be embedded in the foundation courses, like English, for freshmen. The students seemed convinced that education on plagiarism was the most effective way to ensure that they did not plagiarize. One student concluded, "Plagiarism is a topic that is not taught well in our society. Undergraduate students are placed in a position to learn this lifelong lesson in a few semesters." Their sentiments seem to indicate that whereas the institution has a structured approach to teaching the course content, it lacked a systematic approach to educating students about plagiarism.

Factors Contributing to Plagiarism

There were many factors given as contributing to plagiarism and these aligned with the literature. They included difficulty completing references accurately (Cleary 2017), a heavy workload (Vázquez-Recio et al. 2016, 5711), a lack of time and a limited understanding of the topic (Sisti 2007, 222). Other factors were a lack of knowledge of plagiarism, limited resources, the ease with which they could plagiarize (Power 2009, 649), lack of punishment, poor instructions on plagiarism at the secondary level (Baker-Gardner and Smart 2017), poor monitoring by staff and short deadlines that attracted penalties when students did not submit assignments on time.

Justifications for Plagiarism

Participants found ways to justify plagiarizing, and the majority of these concurred with the literature. There was the thought that everybody was doing it and there was no way to use words that no one has used before. One student stated, "Whilst plagiarism is considered so bad, it is not harmful to anyone because people do learn from other people's thoughts and theory which might not be plagiarism but was just not cited." From reading this statement one can conclude that this student's justification shows a misunderstanding of plagiarism.

One observation made by students that led to a rationalization of plagiarism was that lecturers used notes and PowerPoint slides without giving credit to the sources from which the information was taken. This practice of deflecting responsibility from themselves to the faculty is termed "instructor-based neutralization" (Carpenter et al. 2006, 192). Further justification for plagiarism included the desire to help a friend and the drive to achieve high grades. One student felt that plagiarism was a lesser evil than failing to graduate and stated, "Some students who are struggling in classes require some sort of help either from a friend or somewhat a small minority of plagiarism. It's not a big deal. They are trying to help themselves."

Bretag found that students with a lower grade point average were more predisposed to cheat; however, high-performing students also cheated (2018a). This was borne out by one "committed plagiarist" (McGrail and McGrail 2015, citing Beasely) who felt plagiarizing was not about passing, but more so about obtaining the best grades: "I don't believe plagiarism is right, but sometimes it is a necessary evil as I have to do what it takes to ensure I graduate with the best of grades." Describing plagiarism as "a necessary evil" supports the perception that it is inevitable, and another student concured stating, "Plagiarism is bad but it cannot be stopped," while another felt it could not be controlled. Some respondents also believed that plagiarism was permissible, as long as the amount plagiarized was not too much. One student limited the amount that was permissible to "a line or two," while another opined: "To reproduce another person's work (the entire work) is entirely wrong. However, if the level of plagiarism is 25 percent or less, I don't think it is much of an issue." Students were aware that plagiarism was wrong, but in some cases, their sense of helplessness might be driven by the lack of knowledge on the topic and the lack of structured opportunities to acquire knowledge that might empower them to act otherwise.

Difficulty with Writing

From some comments, it could be deduced that whereas some students were conversant with the requirements of responsible authorship, others were experiencing difficulties with writing. These responses can be divided into two main categories – a lack of knowledge of good writing practices and the need for improved writing skills. Other students had a misunderstanding of their roles as student researchers. One respondent who showed that she did not possess the required knowledge of the conventions of writing and properly incorporating sources into her work stated, "Nothing is wrong with copying and pasting and then giving reference." Another expressed a similar sentiment by stating, "I believe once we cite where we copied the info from even if we just copy and paste it is just good because we are giving credit to the writer." This response showed little motivation on the part of the student to engage with the content and arrive at an understanding that would be beneficial to her academic growth.

The matter of paraphrasing, which is an important skill in avoiding plagiarism, was highlighted by the participants. One respondent stated, "I do believe paraphrasing is a necessary part of completing an assignment or any work." Another student clearly expressed the importance of the skills of summarizing and paraphrasing for effective writing stating, "To avoid plagiarism it is important that students are taught how to summarise and paraphrase so that they can use their own words effectively, without running the risk of plagiarism. Students should also note that paraphrasing and neglecting to provide citations properly is considered plagiarism." This response shows a student with a mature and knowledgeable attitude towards plagiarism and, hopefully, one who did not participate in the act because of this knowledge.

Other students noted the difficulty in expressing their ideas. One obviously frustrated student summed up the situation by writing, "Plagiarism isn't absence of independent thought. If I did the research but struggle to express myself why can't I be allowed to "steal other people's work" in order to get a better grade? If I don't I'll be marked down because my explanation is unclear. School is utter foolishness at times."

The statement showed that coupled with writing challenges, this student was experiencing some level of frustration and a misunderstanding of the role of school in helping her to better develop the expressive ability which she lacked.

One recurring theme was that if you came up with a thought that someone also had already expressed, you can claim the thought as your own and do not need to cite a source for it. One student asked in relation to this idea, "As academics when we write it sounds like plagiarism, however it is our unique thoughts. However, because we conceive it how do we go about validating it when there is no printed evidence of it? We know that we must have heard it somewhere before but cannot recall or find a specified source." This quotation demonstrated a misunderstanding of writing conventions regarding the use of the works of others and might also be lacking the information literacy skills which are critical to locating information resources to address an information need. Another student, struggling with her identity as an emerging researcher noted, "Sometimes the paper that one may plagiarise sounds way better than that person could put in their own words."

Some students seemed oblivious to the fact that lecturers do not expect undergraduate students to sound like experts but instead required them to synthesize what they had read and integrate it into their own work using paraphrasing and summarizing skills, and adding quotations where appropriate, while ensuring that they provide the correct references. This was a part of the learning process, and when this was done, it reflected that the students understood and have internalized and integrated the information within their own knowledge system. The students' struggle as described in their own words further strengthened the case for HEIs to offer education on plagiarism.

Self-Plagiarism and Unintentional Plagiarism

Self-plagiarism not only generated the most questions in the comment section, but it also provided the largest window to reveal the students' lack of knowledge of plagiarism. Two students noted the need for additional information on the topic, with one stating, "More information should be provided on self-plagiarism because I was unclear about the definition of such a concept." Another, noting the lack of discussion on self-plagiarism, stated, "Students should be informed more about self-plagiarism to understand whether or not they have done so. Where plagiarism is discussed it is always in relation to other people's work." Other students were incredulous and for the most part dismissed the idea. One stated, "I believe that self-plagiarism makes no sense and it should not exist," while another strongly argued, "I don't believe self-plagiarism is a thing especially unpublished work cause 'a oofa work, nuh mine?'" In essence, the student was asking, "Isn't it my work?" The majority of these students had never heard the term self-plagiarism, and one student simply stated, "Did not know self-plagiarism was a concept."

Another theme that emerged which might support the need for education on plagiarism was unintentional plagiarism. The main reason cited for unintentional plagiarism was the students' challenges with referencing and citation requirements. One student stated, "Sometimes it is not a deliberate attempt to plagiarise/steal people's work but a failure to cite sources as a result of forgetfulness and so on. Sometimes a source is simply overlooked." This concurs with the findings of Cleary (2017). Another reason produced for unintentional plagiarism was that students sometimes reproduced knowledge from memory without giving proper attribution.

Relevance of the Topic

The responses regarding the relevance or importance of the topic in the academic setting were coded in the "Other" category and were the largest number of responses under this theme. Although these responses were not significant in terms of their numbers when compared to the others, the researcher felt it was important to discuss them as they provided additional insights into students' thoughts on the topic. The majority of the responses about the topic were positive. One student stated that the topic was "important to bring across the awareness of plagiarism and the seriousness of the consequences involved." Students felt that this research was likely to have a lasting impact on the way plagiarism is viewed by various members of the academy. One student stated that the study was "[a] good step towards eradicating the issue," while another stated, "It would be very important and helpful with our projects."

In support of the conclusion that the study would result in some benefits for them, another stated, "Good topic to research as many undergraduate students like myself have a challenge in avoiding plagiarism." In addition to "good" and "important," the adjective "necessary" was also used by some students to describe the study. One student, who thought it was a great topic, felt that the findings should be shared. A respondent explained that she had mixed feelings about plagiarism, while another felt that the survey was too philosophical, possibly suggesting that it did not substantially meet her needs.

Student's engagement with the topic was also evidenced by the questions they asked the researcher during the data collection phase. In addition, the research generated discussion from the majority of groups while the students were completing the questionnaire, and lecturers also joined in asking and answering questions. Overall, these responses confirmed the researcher's belief that plagiarism was a timely, relevant topic to investigate to give it greater prominence in the discussions and policies concerning academic integrity, especially at the higher education level.

Discussion of Findings

Students expressed an interest in the subject of plagiarism evidenced by the high number of respondents who provided qualitative data and those who made positive comments regarding the study. For the most part, their concerns revolved around themes that were present in the literature. Their beliefs about plagiarism fell into three broad categories, with the majority of students indicating that plagiarism was wrong and a significant number believing it is wrong but justifiable. However, a handful of students expressed the belief that plagiarism was acceptable. Despite seemingly high regard for the ethics of plagiarism, this might not deter students from plagiarizing (Hosny and Fatima 2014, 748).

Justifications for plagiarism were many as students also used what Carpenter and colleagues referred to as "instructor-based neutralizations," noting their lack of use of sources when making presentations and giving lecture notes (2006, 192). Another justification was the friend factor as reported by Sisti (2007, 1033), and some students thought that plagiarism could not be avoided, and it was permissible if it was minimal. These justifications were also in concert with the findings of the quantitative data which showed that students believed that one of the factors most likely to influence plagiarism is permission from friends to copy their work.

Students were open about their lack of and limited competence in academic writing as contributory factors to plagiarism. There was also a limited understanding of their roles as student researchers and how to use the works of others responsibly, and a challenge with citing and referencing (Kayaoglu et al. 2015, 11; Cleary 2017). Given these weaknesses, it was understandable that students articulated a need for education on plagiarism which concurred with the recommendations arising from the majority of studies on plagiarism. The students' responses to the concept of self-plagiarism also revealed a further need for education as many of them had never previously heard the term. Apart from these challenges, the students indicated that one of the causes of unintentional plagiarism was a lack of knowledge, a conclusion also arrived at by Baker-Gardner and Smart (2017, 198). In their study, Caribbean Library and Information Studies students cited a lack of instructions at the secondary level, and their questions during the focus group discussion indicated a lack of understanding of some of the ways persons plagiarize.

The responses of students indicated a range of issues that needed to be considered in developing a system for academic integrity. Their interest in the subject and the call for education on plagiarism made by students should not be ignored, as this could be to the detriment of higher education in the region. HEIs, therefore, need to begin to seek strategies to develop academic integrity in their students, thus meeting the students' needs while simultaneously protecting the reputation of institutions.

Chapter 13

Perceptions of Plagiarism by Academic Discipline and Gender

Introduction

Academic discipline and gender have emerged as independent variables in the study of plagiarism, and so, the perceptions of students were examined based on these variables. This chapter begins by presenting a brief review of the literature on students' perceptions of plagiarism by gender and academic faculty. It then includes a detailed presentation and analysis of the data collected from 1,039 undergraduate students and concludes with a discussion of the findings.

Background

Academic discipline and gender are two of the variables to consider in the study of plagiarism. Moskovitz states "conventions and ethics associated with using text vary across academic domains and genres" (2016, 5), which suggests that what might be viewed as plagiarism in one discipline might not be viewed the same in another. There is also the fluidity between disciplines as students enroled in one faculty might pursue courses in another based on their personal interests and the demands of their programmes. Hu and Lei state that "empirical inconsistency exists with regard to whether there are disciplinary influences on students' perceptions of plagiarism" (2015, 6).

The impact of gender on various aspects of academic life has been well documented, and the study of plagiarism is no exception. Researchers such as Jereb et al. (2018a), Bilić-Zulle et al. (2005) and Hussein, Rusdi and Mohamad (2016) have studied the impact of gender on perceptions and practices with regard to plagiarism. Based on these considerations, this researcher felt it was necessary to investigate students' perception of plagiarism from both gender and academic discipline perspectives to see if these variables were impacting the perceptions of students in the Caribbean. The aim of this study was to determine if there were differences in perception of plagiarism based on students' gender and academic discipline. The researcher therefore proposed a null hypothesis which states gender and academic discipline do not impact students' perceptions of plagiarism. The objectives of the study were to:

- investigate the impact of gender and academic discipline on students' perceptions of the factors which exacerbate plagiarism;
- assess the impact of gender and academic discipline on students' perception of the justification for plagiarism; and
- determine whether gender and academic discipline impact students' perception of the severity of and penalty for plagiarism

This study, like the others in this work, seeks to investigate a phenomenon that has previously not been studied in any depth in the Caribbean, thereby adding to the regional literature while contributing a regional perspective to the international literature on the topic of academic integrity.

Review of the Literature

The literature reviewed in this section was drawn from studies conducted globally. As noted before, due to a dearth of literature on plagiarism in the Caribbean, only one regional study could be found for the review. This review focuses on perceptions of plagiarism based on gender and the academic disciplines present at the institutions in which the data were collected, namely, medical sciences, social sciences, law, humanities and science and technology.

Plagiarism by Gender: Gender has emerged as one of the variables given due consideration in the discussion of factors which impact plagiarism, and to date the results of the research on the impact of gender on plagiarism are mixed, leading Bilić-Zulle to conclude that it was not a determinant in plagiarism (2005, 199). Similarly, Jereb et al. also found that there were no significant differences in cheating when gender was considered among his sample of 485 German and Slovene students (2018a, 12). A nearly similar conclusion was arrived at by Ismail (2018) who investigated the perceptions of plagiarism of Iraqi medical and nursing students. He found that, although the incidence of plagiarism among males was slightly higher than among females, there was no significant difference between them (2018, e197). Bretag's meta-analysis of eighteen studies also revealed that gender was not a significant variable in the majority of these (2018a, 7–8).

On the contrary, Sureda-Negre, Comas-Forgas and Oliver-Trobat (2015) reported that cheating was more prevalent among males at the secondary level, a finding which concurs with Bavaharji et al. (2016, 115), and Hussein, Rusdi and Mohamad (2016) who investigated plagiarism at the undergraduate level. Sheets and Waddil also found that males cheated more on assignments, while both males and females cheated equally on tests (2009, 11). Hu and Lei cited two significant studies that pointed to the higher likelihood of cheating among males than females. The first was done by Whitely in 1998 who examined a sample of 107 studies (2015, 5). The second was conducted by Whitley, Nelson, and Jones a year later and involved the analysis of 44 studies done in the United States and the United Kingdom (2015, 5).

Becker and Ulsted believe the differences in plagiaristic behaviour between males and females can be partially explained by the observation that males might be more prone to risk taking than females (2007, 78). In their examination of cheating by American and Indian Master of Business Administration students, Taylor-Bianca and Deeter-Schmelz found that in the former group, males were more likely to cheat than females, but that Indian males and females cheated equally (2007, 81).

The findings on the perception of both genders in carrying out plagiarism favour females as plagiarizing less, even as an investigation into student ethics, conducted by Becker and Ulstad found that, generally, females were perceived to be more ethical than males (2007, 77). In support of this, Jereb and colleagues (2018a) advance the view, based on an analysis of research findings, that females have a more negative attitude to plagiarism than males, and thus females were less likely to plagiarize. Ismail found a connection between the perception and the level of plagiarism of male students, as those who plagiarized were likely to have a positive perception of plagiarism (2018, 199), meaning they view it as less harmful. The research on the impact of gender on plagiarism, although not conclusive, suggests that males are more likely to cheat than females.

Plagiarism Across Academic Disciplines: No current comparative data could be found on plagiarism across disciplines. Instead, what was identified were data on academic misconduct that were almost twenty years old at the time of writing; nevertheless, they will be included here. Despite the datedness, the data were considered relevant to this discussion, given that plagiarism is the most widely practised form of academic dishonesty. The information in table 13.1 was garnered from a PowerPoint presentation created by Don McCabe, founder of the International Center for Academic Integrity, and made at the University of Florida's Ethics Symposium in 2011. The data were collected from over five thousand graduate students from thirty-two colleges and universities in the United States and Canada between 2002 and 2004 (McCabe, Butterfield and Trevino 2006, 294).

Table 13.1. Relative levels of cheating among graduate students in the United States and Canada

Academic disciplines	Number of students	Per cent
Business	429	56
Engineering	237	54
Science	376	50
Health professionals	393	49
Education	498	48
Law	104	45
Social science/humanities	562	39

Based on the table, the highest relative level of cheating was found among business students (56 per cent) with the lowest among social sciences and humanities students (39 per cent each). Engineering (54 per cent) and science (50 per cent) were the other faculties with relatively high levels of cheating. The health professions also recorded a high level of cheating (49 per cent), and this marginally surpassed the percentage for law (48 per cent) and education (45 per cent). Based on the data, it would seem there are differences in the prevalence of cheating among students based on the discipline, with some disciplines having significantly more instances of cheating than others. Further discussion of cheating in each discipline follows with more current data.

Social Sciences: In discussing academic integrity in the social sciences, Löfström indicates there were considerable differences between the sub-disciplines which needed to be taken into consideration (2016). Although McCabe presents business as an academic discipline separate from social sciences in table 13.1, in the context in which the researcher conducted the study, business studies was considered a sub-discipline of social sciences, and so it will be treated as such in this review. Other sub-disciplines are hotel and tourism management, economics, government, sociology, psychology and social work.

Rosentiel (2006) notes that 56 per cent of graduate students pursuing a Master of Business Administration acknowledged that they cheated, compared to 47 per cent of the respondents in other disciplines. This supports McCabe's findings that business students were identified as the most frequent cheaters among American students. However, this was not confined to the United States as, in their study of Malaysian undergraduate business students, Hussein, Rusdi and Mohamad found that although students had a high awareness of plagiarism, this did not deter them from engaging in the practice, which was facilitated by the use of the internet and compounded by procrastination (2016, 639). Chapman et al. found that marketing students, one subset of business, were guilty of cheating more than other groups of business students (2004, 236). Data on contract cheating presented by Lancaster and Clarke support the findings that business students engaged in cheating more often than others. Lancaster and Clarke further noted the concern raised by Stevens et al. that business schools might not be emphasizing moral responsibilities enough as they reported rates of cheating by business students ranged from 13 per cent to 91 per cent (2016, 3–4). The literature on academic integrity in the social sciences focuses heavily on business students, who, based on the literature, were cheating possibly more so than other groups. It was possible that high rates of cheating in this sub-discipline have led to an increased interest among researchers.

Collins and Amodeo (2005) commented that although the literature on social work has addressed plagiarism, this was not done in an extensive manner. Lofstrom also stated that social work students may be exposed to moral content and language in their programmes of study (2016, 4). He, therefore, believed this has had a positive impact on the rates of cheating among social work students.

Medicine: The high incidence of academic misconduct among health professionals uncovered by McCabe has been borne out by recent research. In a review of twenty studies in nursing, Lynch et al. found that "plagiarism is common among nursing students," they inadvertently and intentionally plagiarized and the structures to address the behaviours were not effective (2017, 2845). These were not the only set of medical students who plagiarized, as Bilić-Zulle et al. found that plagiarism among doctors in training in Croatia was also high. They found that only 9 per cent of the students indicated that they had never plagiarized, while the remaining 91 per cent copied between 1 per cent and 95 per cent of the text for assignments (2005, 129). Epidemiology students in Peru were also involved in plagiarism (Carnero et al. 2017, 1183), and elsewhere, warnings issued to student doctors were found ineffective in deterring the practice (Bilić-Zulle et al. 2005, 126). In a survey of medical and nursing students in Iraq, Ismail found a 54 per cent prevalence of plagiarism in the overall sample, with a higher incidence among the medical students (2018, 197).

In investigating pharmacy and medical technology students' attitudes towards plagiarism, Pupovac et al. found that although 90 per cent of the sample believed that plagiarism retarded the development of an "investigative spirit," 58 per cent felt that plagiarism was not harmful to science. Only

19 per cent agreed that plagiarism was bad and 34 per cent was undecided, while the remaining disagreed (2010, 308). On the contrary, Thompsett and Ahluwalia (2010) in their investigations of final year pharmacology students found that the majority of students believed that plagiarism was cheating and thought it was ethically and morally wrong. The majority of students (57 per cent) in the foregoing research also indicated that they were having challenges differentiating between plagiarism and collusion, and almost 50 per cent stated that plagiarism helped them to learn the content better (Thompsett and Ahluwalia 2010), so it is possible that perception might not be impacting practice. Plagiarism is practised by the various subgroups of medical students who hold varying perspectives on the issue. The prevalence varies from study to study, and it seems that strategies in place to reduce plagiarism among them have not been effective.

Law: There was little data available for plagiarism among law students. Hansen and Anderson contend that "[a]ttribution expectations are thus different in legal practice from those in academia" (2015, 421). In spite of these differences, these authors put forward three reasons it was necessary to ensure that law students did not plagiarize. First, when law students plagiarize, this means that they are not learning by doing their law school assignments and thus this will undermine the law school's pedagogical function. Second, the students are unfairly competing for grades among their peers, and by so doing, they are working against key university values such as honesty and merit. Third, such students are not fulfilling in good faith their responsibilities as members of the university community, and this brings into question their ability to later serve the public in good faith as lawyers with professional responsibility (2015, 421). James cites the requirement of some courts in Australia for the disclosure of past cases of academic misconduct prior to candidates being admitted to law practice (2016, 4). He therefore recommends that in these jurisdictions, it would be advisable for law schools to incorporate academic integrity in the curriculum (2016, 7). This recommendation should be applicable to all educational institutions and disciplines.

Humanities: Stenmark and Winn describe the humanities as "overlooked" in the study of ethics compared to business, medicine, engineering and other sciences (2016, 1). They further argue that this has resulted in little empirical data on research ethics in the discipline (2016, 2). Rosentiel also found in his investigation among graduate students, based on self-reporting, that the prevalence of academic dishonesty was lowest among social sciences and humanities students (2006). This was in keeping with the findings of McCabe shown in table 13.1. It is apparent that more research needs to be done on plagiarism in the humanities.

Science and Technology: Sentleng and King found that 58 per cent of the students pursuing a degree in applied science at an African university admitted to summarizing "frequently" or "sometimes" without providing the source (2012, 62). In addition, over 50 per cent of the students admitted to paraphrasing without providing the required citation (61). Seventy-one point nine per cent of the sample admitted to plagiarizing from the internet (57), and 40 per cent reportedly invented data (51). An overwhelming majority (75 per cent) indicated that they had never submitted the work of another person, leaving the reader to assume that the remaining 25% did. Walcott studied a group of Caribbean students pursuing a programme in computer science and found they had a "moderately positive attitude towards plagarisim [sic] (which is not desirable)" (2016, 63). However, Simon (2016) pointed out that the very nature of the non-text-based disciplines makes it difficult to compare it with text-based ones.

The obvious conclusion to be drawn from the discussion of the literature is that there is cheating in all academic disciplines. One can also conclude that cheating seems to be more prevalent in some disciplines than others. However, at best, these latter conclusion cannot be stated definitively as there are likely to be many other variables that need to be examined in order to draw such a conclusion.

Data Presentation and Analysis

The sample consisted of 1,039 students distributed across five faculties. Table 6.1 presents the enrolment in each faculty and the size of the sample chosen.

The total undergraduate enrolment in the faculties that were of interest in this research was 17,719. The faculty of social sciences had the highest enrolment of 6,759 students (38 per cent) while the faculty of law had the lowest. Although a representative sample was taken from each faculty, (see table 6.1) there is likely to be a social sciences bias in the findings based on the size of that faculty; however, this is indicative of the composition of the student population. The researcher collected demographic data on gender in order to investigate whether it had an impact on students' perceptions. Females were the more numerous making up 69.7 per cent of the sample. These figures compared favourably with the institution's five-year average of 67 per cent

Table 13.2. Gender difference as it relates to the overall plagiarism scale

	Group statistics				
	Gender	N	Mean	Std. deviation	Std. error mean
Plagiarism scale	Female	724	80.42	8.10	.30
	Male	315	78.52	8.52	.48

females and 33 per cent males for the period 2012–2017 which was calculated by the researcher.

Perception of Plagiarism by Gender

An investigation of the perception of plagiarism by academic gender showed overall differences between genders and significant differences in each subscale. Table 13.2 presents the data for the overall scale for the 1,039 respondents.

The mean for females (80.42) was approximately 2 per cent points higher than the mean for males. In keeping with this trend, the standard deviation and standard error of mean were higher for males than for females. An independent samples test was performed on the data by gender in order to get a more fulsome understanding of the overall differences in perception between both groups. The results are displayed in table 13.3.

As can be seen in table 13.3, the mean scores were significantly different from each other ($t = 3.42, p = 0.001$) with the perception of females showing a higher score ($M = 80.42$) as opposed to males ($M = 78.52$). The finding suggested that females were more likely to have a stronger opposition to plagiarism than males, a finding supported by Jereb et al. (2018a) who found that females had a more negative attitude towards plagiarism which should make them less likely to plagiarize. Although the impact of gender on plagiarism is inconclusive in the literature reviewed, the finding in this study supports the view that males at this university had a more positive perception of plagiarism and therefore might be more likely to plagiarize. This was supported by empirical data in chapter 10 which showed that the incidence of plagiarism among males when compared to females in the population was significantly higher.

In order to get a deeper understanding of the differences in perception between both genders, there was an analysis of the perception of plagiarism based on the three subscales. Tables 13.4 and 13.5 show the differences as it relates to the factors of the plagiarism subscale.

On the factors of plagiarism subscale, the mean for females (29.43) was higher than the mean for males (27.80). Males recorded higher scores for the standard deviation and standard error of mean. This was a reflection

Table 13.3. Independent samples test for the entire plagiarism scale

		Independent samples test							
		Levene's test for equality of variances		t-Test for equality of means					
								95% confidence interval of the difference	
		F	Sig.	t	df	Sig. (two-tailed)	Mean difference	Std. error difference	Lower	Upper
Plagiarism scale	Equal variances assumed	1.06	.303	3.42	1,037	.001	1.90	.56	.81	2.30
	Equal variances not assumed			3.36	571.40	.001	1.90	.57	.79	3.01

Table 13.4. Gender difference as it relates to the factors of plagiarism subscale

		Group statistics			
	Gender	N	Mean	Std. deviation	Std. error mean
Factors of plagiarism	Female	724	29.43	5.12	.19
	Male	315	27.80	5.34	.30

of the trend on the overall plagiarism scale in figure 13.3 suggesting that there was a gender difference in the perception of the items on the factors of plagiarism subscale. Further analysis of the factors of the plagiarism subscale was done. This took the form of an independent samples test. The results are shown in table 13.5.

As can be seen in table 13.5, the mean scores were significantly different from each other ($t = 4.65$, $p = 0.000$) with the perception of females showing a higher score ($M = 29.43$, $SD = 5.12$) as opposed to males ($M = 27.80$, $SD = 5.34$) in relation to their perspective on factors of plagiarism. The finding would suggest that the females had a stronger opposition to these factors when compared to their male counterparts, a pattern in keeping with the findings from the overall data in table 13.3 and previous studies (Jereb et al. 2018a; Ismail 2018).

Becker and Ulsted found that there were differences in the ways males and females justified plagiarism in their research (2007, 89), and this finding suggested a need for analysis of this variable in this research. The results for the gender differences for justification for plagiarism in this research are displayed in table 13.6.

The results of the independent samples t-test for the justification for plagiarism subscale is displayed in table 13.7.

As can be seen in table 13.7, the mean scores were significantly different from each other ($t = 2.44$, $p = 015$) with the perception of males showing a higher score ($M = 22.35$, $SD = 3.61$) as opposed to females ($M = 21.74$, $SD = 3.76$) as it related to their perspective on the justification for plagiarism. The findings would suggest that males were less likely to justify their reasons for plagiarism as opposed to their female counterparts. Becker and Ulsted observed that females may be "more prone to obey societal rules as long as they have no special reason or justification for acting unethically" (2007, 89). Justification for them might therefore be an important issue in the decision to act unethically.

Findings from the qualitative research showed students were concerned about the penalties for plagiarism and that, whereas, some did not think plagiarism was a serious matter, the majority disagreed. It was, therefore, necessary to investigate the differences in perceptions by gender. The

Table 13.5. Independent samples sub-test for the factors of plagiarism subscale

		Independent samples test							
		Levene's test for equality of variances		t-Test for equality of means					
								95% confidence interval of the difference	
		F	Sig.	t	df	Sig. (two-tailed)	Mean difference	Std. error difference	Lower	Upper
Factors of plagiarism	Equal variances assumed	.74	.39	4.65	1,037	.000	1.63	.35	.94	2.31
	Equal variances not assumed			4.57	575.13	.000	1.63	.36	.93	2.33

Table 13.6. Gender difference as it relates to justification for plagiarism subscale

	Group statistics				
	Gender	N	Mean	Std. deviation	Std. error mean
Justification for plagiarism	Male	315	22.35	3.61	.20
	Female	724	21.74	3.76	.14

results of gender differences as it relates to the severity of and penalty for plagiarism are displayed in table 13.8.

On this subscale, the mean for females (14.32) was higher than that for males (13.55), and both the standard deviation and the standard error of mean were higher for males than for females.

An independent samples test was conducted for the severity and penalty subscale in order to get additional information. The results of this test are presented in table 13.9.

As can be seen in table 13.9, the mean scores were significantly different from each other ($t = 3.43$, $p = 0.001$) with the perception of females showing a higher score ($M = 14.32$, $SD = 3.26$) as opposed to males ($M = 13.55$, $SD = 3.43$) as it related to the perspectives of severity and penalty. The females were more likely to oppose the views expressed when compared to their male counterparts. Based on the responses, females perceived plagiarism as being a more severe offence than males, in keeping with the findings displayed in table 13.9, and this would suggest that since they believed it was a more serious offence, they were less likely to plagiarize. Ismail's finding that students who plagiarized were more likely to have a positive perception of plagiarism (2018, 199) was applicable here. The finding that males were more inclined to take risks (Becker and Ulsted 2007, 78) could be one of the possible explanations for their less severe view of plagiarism. At least, in this one institution in the Caribbean, more males were plagiarizing than females and they showed less agreement with the items on severity and penalty.

Perception of Plagiarism by Academic Discipline

Although a review of the literature shows that plagiarism is evident in all academic disciplines, Hu and Lei postulate that there is a difference in knowledge of plagiarism and its causes among students based on their discipline. They found that discipline "not only consistently and reliably predicted the likelihood of detecting plagiarism . . ., but it also emerged as the most important predictor in each case" (2012, 840). A difference in knowledge might also be an indicator that there is a difference in perceptions

Table 13.7. Gender difference as it relates to independent samples t-test for justification for plagiarism subscale

		Independent samples test							
		Levene's test for equality of variances		t-Test for equality of means					
								95% confidence interval of the difference	
		F	Sig.	t	df	Sig. (two-tailed)	Mean difference	Std. error difference	Lower	Upper
Justification for plagiarism	Equal variances assumed	.562	.454	2.44	1,037	.015	.61	.25	.12	1.10
	Equal variances not assumed			2.48	619.71	.014	.61	.25	.13	1.10

Table 13.8. Gender difference as it relates to severity of and penalty for plagiarism subscale

		Group statistics			
	Gender	N	Mean	Std. deviation	Std. error mean
Severity and penalty	Female	724	14.32	3.26	.12
	Male	315	13.55	3.43	.19

(Welsh-Unwala 2019, 33). In addition, Simon points out differences between text and non-text disciplines and indicates that traditional means of defining and identifying plagiarism in text-based disciplines are not applicable in non-text-based disciplines (2016, 13).

An analysis of variance test was performed to see if there were significant differences in the perception of plagiarism among the students from the five academic faculties. Table 13.10 displays the results of the test.

Based on the overall perspective on plagiarism and the severity and penalty, there were no statistically significant differences in the students' perception based on their faculties. However, there were statistically significant differences based on the subscales of the factors causing plagiarism, $F(4) = 6.37, p < .001$, and the justification for doing it, $F(4) = 6.18, p < .001$.

To further explore the differences between groups, a post hoc was done and it indicated that for the factors causing plagiarism, students from the faculty of social sciences were 1.30 times more likely to disagree with these perspectives than those in science and technology. However, social sciences students were 1.75 times least likely to disagree than those students of the faculty of humanities and education. Additionally, students of humanities and education were 3.06 times more likely to disagree to the factors of plagiarism as opposed to those of science and technology, and 1.85 times more likely to disagree than those of medical sciences. In relation to the justification for plagiarism, students of the social sciences are 1.10 times least likely to disagree with the justification for plagiarism as opposed to those of science and technology. While, on the contrary, students from science and technology were 2.04 times more likely to disagree with the justification for plagiarism than those from humanities and education.

The results for the factor of plagiarism scale were presented on a line graph to give the reader a visual picture of how the data were compared. This is shown in figure 13.1.

Table 13.9. Independent samples test for severity and penalty subscale

		Levene's test for equality of variances		Independent samples test					
				t-Test for equality of means				95% confidence interval of the difference	
		F	Sig.	t	df	Sig. (two-tailed)	Mean difference	Std. error difference	
									Lower	Upper
Severity and penalty	Equal variances assumed	1.57	.211	3.43	1,037	.001	.77	.22	.33	1.20
	Equal variances not assumed			3.37	571.20	.001	.77	.23	.32	1.21

Table 13.10. Mean differences on the plagiarism scale as it relates to faculty

		Analysis of Variance test				
		Sum of squares	df	Mean square	F	Sig.
Plagiarism scale	Between groups	377.92	4	94.48	1.38	.238
	Within groups	70,682.20	1,034	68.36		
	Total	71,060.11	1,038			
Factors of plagiarism	Between groups	684.35	4	171.09	6.37	.000
	Within groups	27,768.58	1,034	26.86		
	Total	28,452.93	1,038			
Justification for plagiarism	Between groups	335.32	4	83.83	6.18	.000
	Within groups	14,037.13	1,034	13.58		
	Total	14,372.44	1,038			
Severity and penalty	Between groups	104.06	4	26.02	2.36	.052
	Within groups	11,402.48	1,034	11.03		
	Total	11,506.55	1,038			

The mean for factors of plagiarism was lowest for students from the faculty of science and technology, and highest for students from humanities and education, suggesting that students from the faculty of humanities and education were most likely to agree with these factors. Other faculties fell between these two extremes.

The results for the justification for plagiarism subscale are displayed on the line graph in figure 13.2.

The results on this subscale are the opposite of what was obtained on the line graph in figure 13.2. Students in the faculty of science and technology scored the highest mean on the justification for plagiarism subscale meaning that they are most likely to use the arguments presented to justify plagiarism, while students from the faculty of humanities and education scored the lowest, suggesting that they were least likely to justify plagiarism. All other faculties fell between these two extremes.

The results of the means of severity of plagiarism are displayed in figure 13.3.

Perceptions of Plagiarism by Academic Discipline and Gender | 193

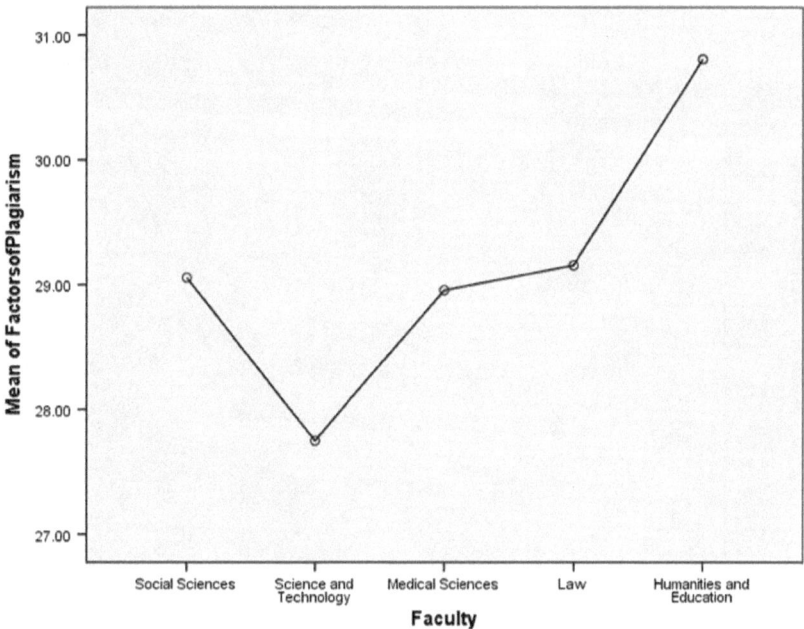

Figure 13.1. Line graph showing mean of factors of plagiarism subscale.

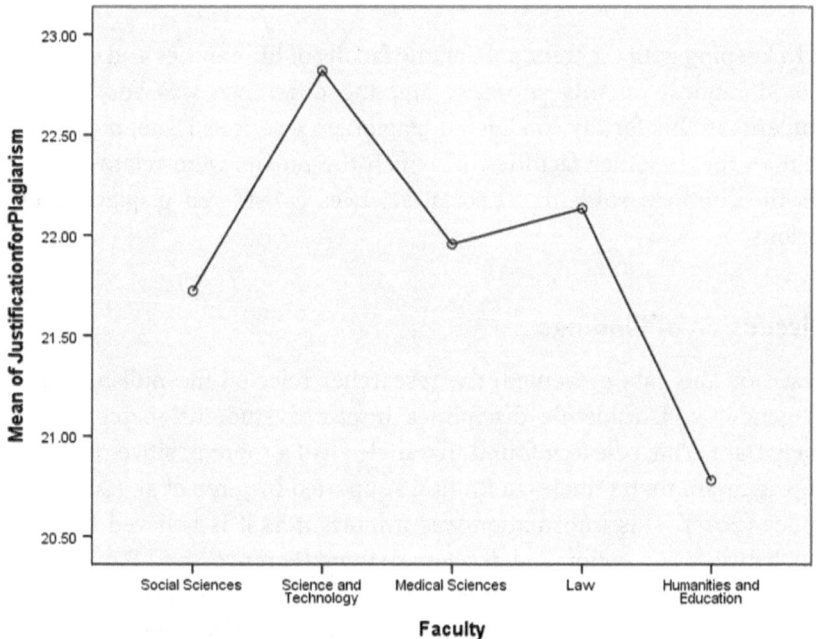

Figure 13.2. Line graph showing mean of justification for plagiarism subscale.

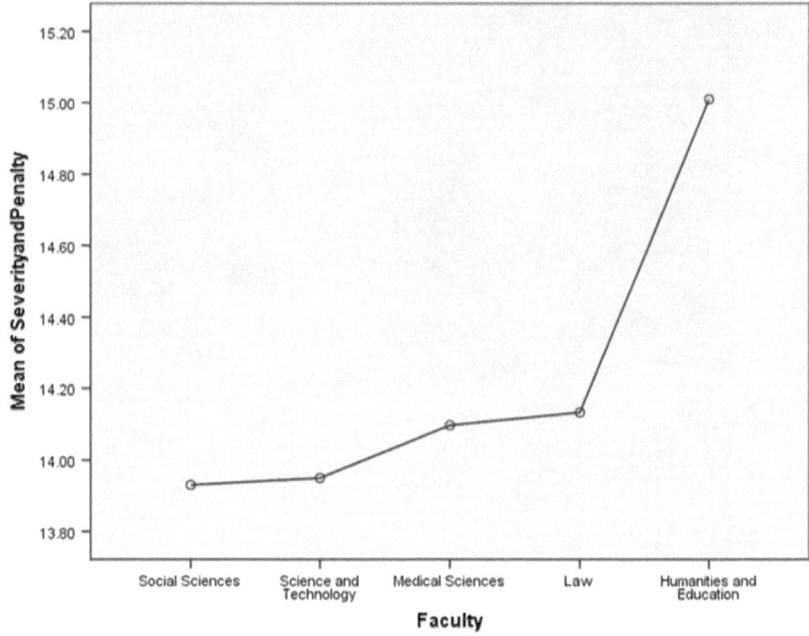

Figure 13.3. Line graph showing mean of severity of and penalty for plagiarism subscale.

In keeping with the trends so far, the faculty of humanities and education scored highest on this subscale, and the difference was very marked. Students in this faculty considered plagiarism a serious issue, much more so than for the other faculties, in which the means were relatively close. On the contrary, students in social sciences considered plagiarism least serious.

Discussion of Findings

Based on the data presented, the researcher rejected the null hypothesis as gender and academic disciplines impacted students' perceptions of plagiarism. This research found that males had a more positive perception of plagiarism than females, a finding supported by Jereb et al. (2018a) and Bailey (2015). This information was important as it is believed there is a link between perception and decision making (Ferguson and Bargh 2004). This suggested that males in this particular institution were more likely to plagiarize than females based on their perception. This was borne out by the data presented which showed that in an institution where the male-to-female ratio was approximately 1:2, the ratio of plagiarism cases by gender was almost equal. Although the male-to-female ratio in this research of approximately 1:2 was somewhat representative of the university's population, Howard, Ehrich and Walton made an observation that was also relevant to this research. They noted that the restricted sample of males in their research might have impacted the results as it might have "prevented detection of differential item functioning" (2014, 22).

With regard to perceptions of plagiarism based on academic disciplines, the findings of this research indicated no statistically significant difference between the students' perceptions, irrespective of the faculties from which they came. This differed from the findings of Chrysler-Fox which revealed that academic discipline impacted the rate of plagiarism as students with a business management background were more likely to cheat than students enroled in the humanities (2017, 662). However, based on academic discipline, there were significant differences in the students' perception of the factors which led to plagiarism. Students enroled in humanities and education at the university from which the data was collected were most strident in their disagreement with the factors that caused plagiarism, and those registered in science and technology had the lowest level of disagreement with the list of perceived factors.

Based on the findings from this chapter, any programme implemented to develop academic integrity in the Caribbean will have to take academic discipline and gender into consideration. Ignoring these nuances might result in programmes geared to the entire university population, but which do not meet the particular needs of unique groups within the population. Further investigation is necessary to determine the extent of these differences, and the ways that institutions can best cater to the needs of each group.

Chapter 14

Perception of Plagiarism by Age and Academic Maturity

Introduction

This chapter examines the differences in perceptions of plagiarism among undergraduate students by age and academic maturity. In order to accomplish this, it presents an analysis and discussion of data collected through the administration of a survey which involved the use of a Likert scale to register participants' responses.

Background

The literature highlights age and academic maturity as two variables that impact students' knowledge and perception of plagiarism. It must be stated that students do not progress through higher education in the Caribbean based on age, as is the case with early childhood, primary and secondary education. Therefore, there is no parallel between age and academic maturity. In this research, academic maturity refers to the year of study in which the student is currently enroled. This carries the understanding that students in the first year would be generally considered less mature than those in the final year of their programmes.

There is an expectation that the longer students have been exposed to higher education the more knowledgeable they will be about academic integrity (Kayaoglu et al. 2015, 21). However, the literature points to an anomaly in this regard as it was discovered that some students who were expected to be more academically mature were cheating more than those who just entered the academy (Walker 2010, 11), a finding supported by the analysis of data presented in chapter 10. Bretag (2018a) presents age as a determining factor in plagiarism; however, Thompsett and Ahluwalia (2010) found that although older students were more knowledgeable about plagiarism, this did not impact their perceptions. The researcher therefore wanted to explore whether Caribbean students' perceptions of plagiarism were impacted by age and academic maturity and therefore proposed a null hypothesis that age and academic maturity did not influence students' perception of academic maturity. In this study the researcher set out to:

- investigate the impact of age and academic maturity on students' perceptions of the factors which exacerbate plagiarism;
- assess the impact of age and academic maturity on students' perception of the justification for plagiarism; and
- determine whether age and academic maturity impacted students' perception of the severity of and penalty for plagiarism.

This study will add to the sparse body of literature on plagiarism in the Caribbean, form a background for future investigations into the topic and add a regional voice to the international discussion on academic integrity.

Review of Literature

Age and academic maturity are two of the factors often considered when researchers examine the variables which impact plagiarism. However, these variables have not been given the same kind of attention as academic disciplines, gender and geographical location. This section provides a brief review of the available literature which delves into students' perceptions and practice of plagiarism based on their age and academic maturity. The researcher focused on practice too given the dearth of information on perceptions based on age and academic maturity. It is expected that practice might provide some insights into perceptions.

Perception and Practice of Plagiarism by Age: The impact of age on plagiarism has been the subject of several studies; however, the findings are inconclusive. Olson and Shaw investigated plagiarism among children of seven, nine and eleven years old. They found that students had a negative perception of their peers who copied the pictures of others compared with those who created original drawings. Students explained their negative evaluation by expressing concerns about copying (2010, 431). This suggests that although students might not know the word plagiarism at that age, they are able to recognize at least one blatantly plagiaristic behaviour.

Bretag cites Crown and Spiller (1998) and Brimble (2016) who concluded that age was one of the key factors which impacted students' cheating behaviour (Bretag 2018a, 7). According to Whitely, cheating was "negatively correlated with age" (1998, 242). He therefore concluded that age, and not academic maturity, impacted students' cheating behaviour. Chrysler-Fox found that age was a significant variable in his research and that older students were more likely to cheat (2017, 662). When Chrysler-Fox compared his four groups of students, he found statistically small differences between the groups. Those below twenty-four years had the smallest amount of similarity in their writing when compared to the twenty-five- to twenty-nine-year-olds and the thirty-five and older group. There was no statistical difference in cheating between the twenty-five to twenty-nine age group and those twenty-five and below (2017, 665). On the other hand, Walker found that students in the twenty-one to thirty age group had higher levels of plagiarism compared to those below twenty years. This meant that older students were plagiarizing more than the younger ones (2010, 10). Therefore, both Chrysler-Fox and Walker found that younger students were less likely to cheat when compared to their older peers.

Kremmer, Brimble and Stevenson-Clarke also found age to be a factor in students' propensity to cheat (2007, 1). Their research findings contradicted those presented previously as they found that cheating behaviours decreased with an increase in age (2007, 10). Another interesting finding from their research was that younger students tended to engage in collaborative cheating more than older students (2007, 10). Bretag noted that the research results on the impact of age on cheating were "not without ambiguity" (2018a, 7), and this position is shared by this researcher. One feature noted in the review of literature that was likely to impact the results was the differences in age bands used by the researchers which made it somewhat difficult to get a more specific and realistic picture of the impact of age on the prevalence of plagiarism.

In an examination of students' perception of plagiarism by age, Thompsett and Ahluwalia (2010) found that students' perceptions did not differ except in regard to their perceived understanding of plagiarism and the effectiveness of Turnitin. More mature students perceived they had a higher understanding of plagiarism than their younger counterparts. On the other hand, a higher number of younger students (4.18 out of 5) believed Turnitin (United Kingdom) "does not tell students how to avoid plagiarism" when compared to the mean of 3.33 out of 5 for more mature students (Thompsett and Ahluwalia 2010). The response to this item showed younger students possess more knowledge than older students at least in one area.

Perceptions and Practice of Plagiarism by Academic Maturity: It is expected that the longer the students are exposed to higher education, the more likely it is that they will develop a better understanding of academic integrity (Kayaoglu et al. 2015, 21). This thinking is evident in institutions such as the University of the West Indies which assigns stricter penalties to graduate students who plagiarize. However, this is not necessarily so, as Murray, Henslee and Ludlow found (2014, 10). Wilkinson's (2009) study provides some insight into the issue as she examined the students' and staff's perceptions of plagiarism, and separated the students' responses by year groups in a three-year programme. When asked about their ability to correctly reference and cite, the second-year group rated the highest (13 per cent) in the "very confident" category. The year one students had the highest response (36 per cent) in the "not confident" category, compared with 17 per cent of the third-year students (2009, 101).

Walker found that students who had just enroled in the higher education institutions (HEIs) from among whom the sample was drawn plagiarized less than those enroled for longer periods, and the rate of plagiarism increased between Years 2 and 4 (2010, 11). The frequency of plagiarism was also high among graduate students (Walker 2010), but McCabe pointed to lower rates among graduates when compared to undergraduates (Plagiarism Facts and Stats 2017). Based on the limited number of studies available for review, it is clear that the findings on the impact of age on students' perception of plagiarism is inconclusive.

Data Presentation and Analysis

A representative sample of students was sought from each year group. Table 14.1 shows the number of students from each year group who participated in the survey. Data were analysed using tables and charts generated by SPSS version 23 and Excel.

The number of students in Years 1–3 was almost equal, with Year 2 having the smallest number ($n = 322$), and Year 1 the largest ($n = 339$). The range between the highest and the lowest number was seventeen students, and the researcher did not think this was significant enough to skew the results. The fifty-one students in Year 4 were from the faculty of medical sciences, and the decision was taken to include them. Although they were fewer in numbers than the other year groups, in the interest of representativeness, it was considered important that they be included. They comprised only 4.9 per cent of the overall sample.

On the questionnaire, age was an independent variable that was presented in four ranges: twenty-five years and below, twenty-six to thirty-five, thirty-

Table 14.1. Number of participants by year group

Year	Frequency	Percentage
1	339	32.6
2	322	31.0
3	327	31.5
4	51	4.9
Total	1,039	100

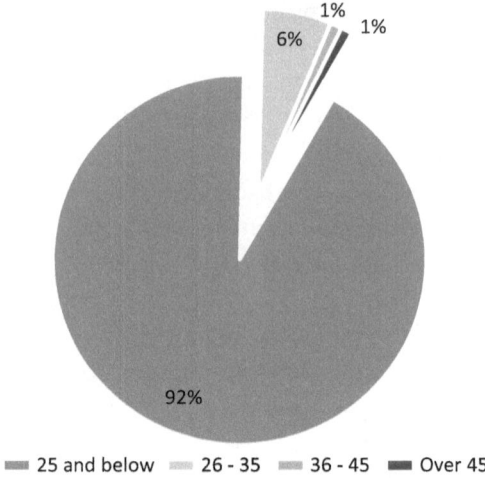

Figure 14.1. Age of participants.

six to forty-five and above forty-five. Figure 14.1 shows the ages of the participants. The majority of the participants (92 per cent) were twenty-five years and below, 6 per cent were in the twenty-six to thirty-five age group and the remaining 2 per cent were above thirty-six years old. This speaks to a generally young population, many of whom were likely to be entering university directly from high school. The ages of the respondents did not reflect that of the general university population because, based on data obtained for the 2016–2017 academic year, 72 per cent of the population enroled at the university were in the twenty-four and under age group. Seventeen point eight per cent was in the twenty-five to thirty-four age group. Nine per cent of the enrolment for that period was in the forty-five and above age group. These data were taken from the university's statistics which were available online. The variations in age can be attributable to the inclusion of graduate students in the university data, but not in the sample used for this study. The average age of graduate students was likely to be higher than that of undergraduates.

Perception of Plagiarism by Age

Given the inconclusive nature of the impact of age on perceptions of plagiarism, the researcher sought to discover if the age factor impacted Caribbean students' perception of plagiarism. Given that the majority of students were in the twenty-five years and below age group, this might impact the data. An analysis of the data on the perception of plagiarism by age is displayed in table 14.2.

Table 14.2. Mean differences in age as it relates to the four scales

		Analysis of Variance test				
		Sum of squares	df	Mean square	F	Sig.
Plagiarism scale	Between groups	123.292	3	41.10	.599	.616
	Within groups	70,932.16	1,034	68.60		
	Total	71,055.45	1,037			
Factors of plagiarism	Between groups	308.46	3	102.82	3.78	.010
	Within groups	28,143.35	1,034	27.22		
	Total	28,451.80	1,037			
Justification for Plagiarism	Between groups	831.96	3	277.32	21.18	.000
	Within groups	13,536.18	1,034	13.10		
	Total	14,368.14	1,037			
Severity and Penalty	Between groups	37.51	3	12.51	1.13	.337
	Within groups	11,467.86	1,034	11.10		
	Total	11,505.37	1,037			

There was a statistically significant difference between the ages of students based on their perspectives on the factors of plagiarism ($F(3) = 3.78$, $p = .011$). There was also a statistically significant difference between the ages of students based on their perspectives on the justification for plagiarism ($F(3) = 21.18$, $p < .001$). However, there were no significant differences in age as it related to students' perspectives on the overall plagiarism scale and the severity and penalty subscale.

In identifying the specific age groups where the differences existed, post hoc tests were conducted. Given that the plagiarism scale and the severity and penalty subscale showed no significant differences and there was no evidence of such in the post hoc, the discussion will focus on the findings regarding the factors of plagiarism and justification for plagiarism subscales. The post hoc analysis showed that there were significant differences between the perspectives of students aged twenty-five and below and those twenty-six to thirty-five years. Both tests indicated that students twenty-five and below were 1.83 times least likely to disagree with the factors of plagiarism, as opposed to those within twenty-six to thirty-five years. The results are displayed in figure 14.2.

Based on figure 14.2, younger students were more likely to agree about the factors that caused plagiarism. This was followed by students over forty-

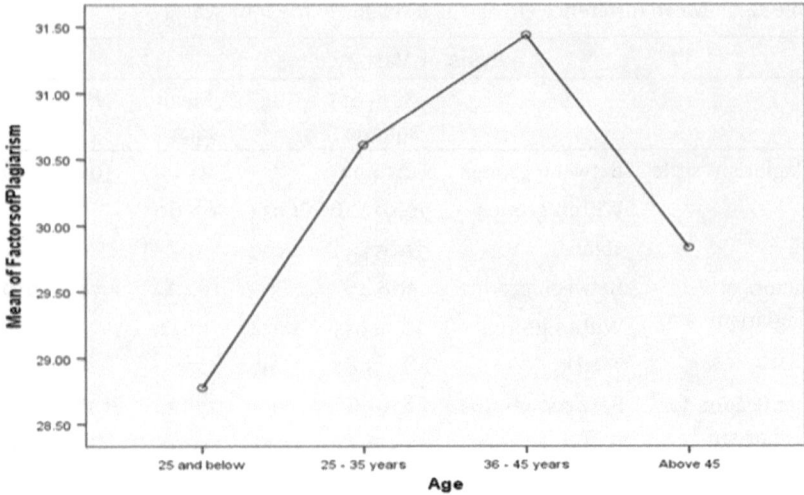

Figure 14.2. Perception of factors of plagiarism by age groups.

five with those in the thirty-six to forty-five age group being most likely to disagree with the list of factors on this subscale.

For justification for plagiarism, there were significant differences between the age groups of twenty-five and below and the other groups. The findings suggest that students twenty-five and below are 2.85 times more likely to disagree with the justification for plagiarism than those twenty-six to thirty-five, 4.13 times more likely than those thirty-six to forty-five years and 4.36 times more likely than those above forty-five years. The mean justification for plagiarism by subscale is shown in figure 14.3. Compared to the twenty-five and below group, the level of agreement seemed to decrease as the students got older, with the highest level of agreement among students thirty six to forty-five.

Perceptions of Plagiarism Based on Academic Maturity

As noted previously, academic maturity has been identified as a variable in the study of plagiarism, with many researchers analysing the data by year group. This was done to try and determine if the number of years students were enrolled in university had an impact on their perception of plagiarism. This research sought to examine the impact of the "academic maturity" variable. The results of the Analysis of Variance test to determine the perception of undergraduate students by academic years are presented on table 14.3.

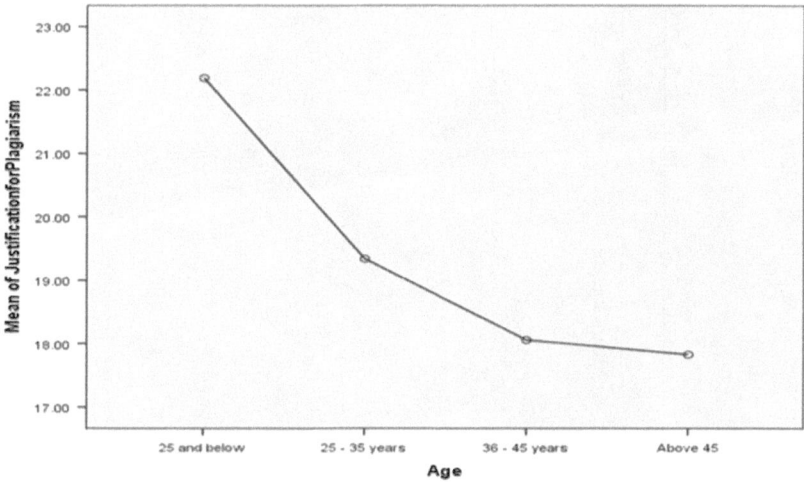

Figure 14.3. Mean of justification for plagiarism subscale by age.

There were no statistically significant differences in the overall perspective of plagiarism based on the number of years' students were enroled in the university. However, as it related to the subscales, there were statistical differences. On perspectives relating to the factors of plagiarism, there were significant differences in perspectives of students based on the number of years in school ($F(3) = 3.79, p = .010$). With regard to justification for plagiarism, there were also statistically significant differences based on year ($F(3) = 3.65, p = .012$). Additionally, for severity and punishment, there were statistically significant differences based on the students' year ($F(3) = 5.94, p < .001$).

Looking at the data in more detail using the post hoc test, the findings suggested that for factors of plagiarism, students in Year 3 were 1.29 times more likely to disagree with the factors of plagiarism than students in Year 1. However, those from Year 3 were .95 times more likely to justify plagiarism than students in Year 1. Consequently, students in Year 1 were .67 more likely to support the perspectives on the severity and penalty than those of Year 2 and .99 more likely than those of Year 3 as is shown in figure 14.4.

Whereas Year 1 students showed the lowest level of disagreement with the severity of and penalty for plagiarism, Year 4 students showed the highest level of agreement. Given the implications that the penalty for plagiarism was likely to have for the completion of programmes, the level of disagreement was understandable. Students in Years 3 and 4 were likely to be most affected if caught plagiarizing.

Table 14.3. Mean differences as it relates to years in school

		Analysis of Variance test				
		Sum of squares	df	Mean square	F	Sig.
Plagiarism scale	Between groups	363.16	3	121.06	1.77	.151
	Within groups	70,696.95	1,035	68.31		
	Total	71,060.114	1,038			
Factors of plagiarism	Between groups	309.20	3	103.07	3.79	.010
	Within groups	28,143.73	1,035	27.19		
	Total	28,452.93	1,038			
Justification for plagiarism	Between groups	150.51	3	50.17	3.65	.012
	Within groups	14,221.93	1,035	13.74		
	Total	14,372.44	1,038			
Severity and penalty	Between groups	194.64	3	64.88	5.94	.001
	Within groups	11,311.91	1,035	11.93		
	Total	11,506.55	1,038			

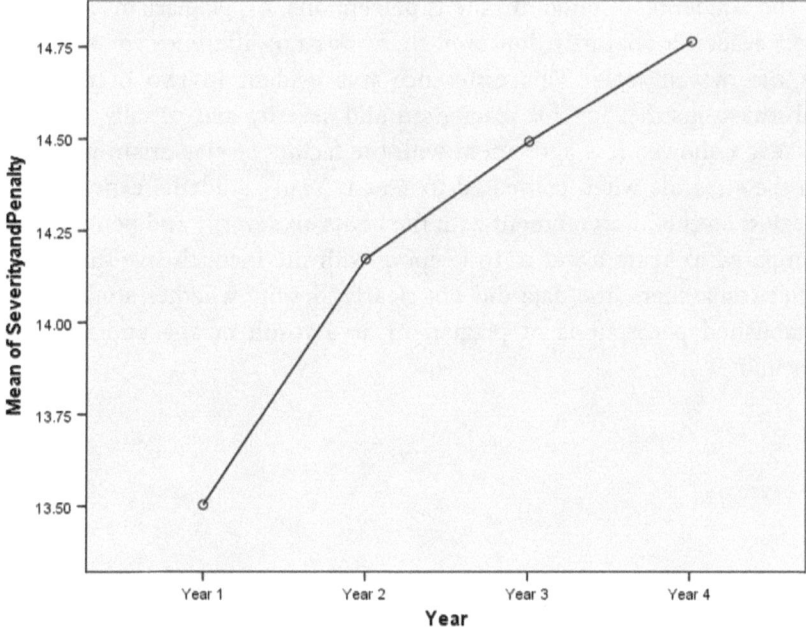

Figure 14.4. Line graph showing the mean of the severity of and penalty for plagiarism by year group.

Discussion of the Findings

The chapter explored undergraduates' perception of plagiarism by age and academic maturity. These results concurred with the findings of Thompsett and Ahluwalia (2010) where the students' perception scores on the various subscales of the plagiarism scale differed. This made it difficult to identify the overall impact of age on the perception of plagiarism. However, based on the data, younger students seemed to disagree more with the factors that influenced plagiarism when compared with the twenty-six to thirty-five age group. The differences between the twenty-five and below group were more pronounced on the justification for plagiarism subscale. The views of the twenty-five years and below group differed more from those of the other groups as the age of the respondents rose. If the belief that perceptions impact behaviours applied in this context, then based on the justification for plagiarism subscale, the older the students, the more likely it was that they would plagiarize and justify plagiarism using the range of arguments presented on the subscale.

The students differed in their perceptions of plagiarism based on their academic maturity; however, there was no difference in perception on the overall scale. This difference was evident in two of the three subscales: justification for plagiarism and severity and penalty. Students in Year 3 showed less agreement with the factors of plagiarism presented on the subscale when compared to Year 1. Year 3 students expressed the greatest level of disagreement with the items on severity and penalty when compared to Years 1 and 2. In keeping with the inconclusive findings of other researchers, the data did not clearly identify whether students had established perceptions of plagiarism as a result of age and academic discipline.

Chapter 15

Conclusions Drawn from the Research

The aim of the research was to gain an understanding of the state of academic integrity in the Caribbean, with a particular focus on plagiarism. This chapter presents the main conclusions drawn from the research which was guided by the following objectives:

- determine the prevalence of plagiarism in various sectors of Caribbean societies and responses to its manifestation;
- investigate the prevalence of academic integrity in secondary and tertiary education in the Caribbean;
- evaluate HEIs presentation and treatment of plagiarism in their policies;
- determine undergraduate students' perceptions of the causative factors and penalties for plagiarism;
- examine undergraduate students' perceptions of the justifications for plagiarism;
- investigate the inclusion of academic integrity in accreditation policies and guidelines of member territories; and
- propose strategies aimed at assisting institutions to develop a culture of academic integrity.

Using triangulation, the researcher gathered primary data from the following sources: newspaper articles; plagiarism policies; accreditation policies and guidelines; and undergraduate students. Secondary data were obtained from the Caribbean Examination Council (CXC) and four regional universities. These were analysed and discussed to meet the research objectives.

Prevalence of Plagiarism in Education in the Caribbean

A review of the literature on plagiarism globally revealed its presence both in the wider society and in secondary and tertiary education (Hallak and Poisson 2007), and in all academic disciplines even though some seemed more prone to this malady than others (McCabe 2011). The research on plagiarism in the Caribbean was currently in its infancy stage, so very few empirical studies were found. Data collected from newspaper articles point to instances of plagiarism in the Caribbean and that it is most prevalent in education and politics, and evident to a lesser extent in entertainment, and journalism. The Caribbean, with its emerging academic integrity structures, had recorded a number of cases of academic misconduct, including plagiarism, at both the secondary and tertiary levels based on newspaper reports.

Based on the content analysis of twenty-six newspaper articles, academic misconduct at the secondary level included offences committed both inside and outside the examination room. Chief among these was cheating in examination, which was manifested in several ways including copying from information brought into the examination, sometimes written on body parts; attempting to communicate with other students; bringing mobile phones into the examination room; and rewriting CXC sample stories for English A (language) from memory. Cheating outside the examination room took several forms including plagiarism of SBAs; falsification of examination results; and students having prior knowledge of the contents of examination papers. Of note was the involvement of educators in helping students to cheat with some of these educators being implicated in scandals, for example the 2013 incident at Jamaica College.

Secondary students cheated for a variety of reasons, and these were in keeping with the literature on academic integrity. One letter to the editor advocated that there were too many school-based assessments (Fernandes 2016), an opinion supported by empirical data (Vázquez-Recio et al. 2016, 2508). Added to this was difficulty in obtaining information to complete assignments and mental fatigue. The absence of text-matching software to detect possible cases of plagiarism was another causative factor. This was likely compounded by the lack of instructions at the secondary level on academic integrity, a factor which university students identified in the qualitative data and which was supported by the findings of Baker-Gardner and Smart's (2017) study of the topic among students in a university in Jamaica. Superficial monitoring of the preparation of SBA was another factor contributing to plagiarism.

The newspaper reports of cases of academic misconduct in CXC were corroborated by data on the number of cases of suspected plagiarism provided by the council which was low when compared to the number of students sitting the examinations. There were fluctuations in the number of cases even with the increase in the use of technology, a trend contrary to the findings from the literature (Carpenter et al. 2006, 184; McCabe

2011). In addition, cheating was more evident in some subjects than others, with those with the highest number of cases being Music and Principles of Business at the CSEC level and Caribbean Studies at the CAPE level.

CXC responded to cases of academic misconduct based on the severity of each case. For example, in cases where students plagiarized SBAs and reproduced the stories of others in the examination, they were given no marks. For more severe cases such as fraud, legal redress was pursued as the council sought to protect its reputation. The case of plagiarism at Jamaica College drew regional attention in 2013, but to date, no clear system or structure for educating students on plagiarism has been established, which was identified as a critical need at the time.

New curricula in Trinidad and Tobago and Jamaica have recently been launched at both the primary and secondary levels. The curriculum of Trinidad and Tobago had lessons on academic integrity, but these were not in depth enough and were not evident throughout the entire curriculum. These lessons did not provide students with the foundational knowledge needed for them to respond appropriately to situations which presented opportunities to act unethically. The Jamaican national curriculum gave scant attention to academic integrity. Elements of academic integrity were scattered throughout the curriculum, but in most cases, there was an expectation that students will apply these skills and little evidence of a strategic focus on the teaching of these.

The findings from the data on plagiarism from the four universities in the Caribbean revealed that final-year students and males were more likely to plagiarize than other groups. Although the findings on the impact of gender on plagiarism were mixed in the literature reviewed, there was a leaning towards higher rates of plagiarism among males when compared to females. This was also true in the Caribbean where perceptions and practice favoured males as more likely to plagiarize than females. Higher rates of plagiarism among Year 3 students, when compared to other years, was evident in the Caribbean. The literature revealed that Year 1 students who were just entering tertiary institutions tended to have a higher rate of plagiarism than students in other years, and this was due mainly to the fact that they were just learning the demands of the academic environment (Wilkinson 2009, 101).

The rate of plagiarism among institutions differed significantly. Although two institutions had roughly the same enrolment, the rate of plagiarism showed marked differences with one institution having more than thrice as many cases as another. Overall, the number of cases was significantly lower than that at elite universities such as Oxford. At the tertiary level, the number of cases of plagiarism fluctuated annually just like at the secondary level. However, the low number of cases of plagiarism should not be construed as representing the number of infringements committed by students.

The literature points to many factors which could account for the difference in the actual versus reported cases. The faculty's preference for dealing with cases of plagiarism at the course level and not making formal reports which they believe can be damaging to the students' future is one reason for not reporting (Walker and White 2014, 8). Another factor that was likely to deter faculty from reporting suspected cases was the amount of time to be committed to the process (Marsden 2014). Faculty might also be limited by insufficient evidence, and there was always the possibility of a legal challenge to the institution (Marsden 2014). Since only half the students who got caught plagiarizing were reported (Boyle, Boyle and Carpenter 2006, 39), a lack of reporting tended to lead to further plagiarism and the cycle continued. Therefore, the low number of cases of plagiarism reported was not necessarily a cause for comfort, but was likely an indication that more research was needed to investigate the actual level of plagiarism among students at both the secondary and tertiary levels.

HEIs Presentation and Treatment of Plagiarism in Their Policies

The majority of HEIs in the Caribbean had a plagiarism or academic integrity policy online, and these varied based on scope, depth and where policies were located. Some institutions had an academic integrity policy which included plagiarism, while some had a separate plagiarism policy. Others embedded their plagiarism guidelines in the disciplinary policies. An analysis of the elements contained in the policies of fifteen institutions showed that policies varied greatly. The most popular elements were the definition of plagiarism and the accompanying sanctions. The least popular elements were electronic detection and statements of accountability.

Institutions adopted a variety of definitions of plagiarism, with the most popular being the generic definition of "using the works of others without giving credit." The majority of the policies contained four or more of the six elements deemed necessary in the definition of plagiarism as cited by Nushi and Firoozkohi (2017, 2). What was obviously lacking was a common understanding of plagiarism based on the definitions. Some institutions separated acts of plagiarism based on severity, using the labels "Level 1" to refer to milder cases and "Level 2" to refer to more serious cases. Less than half the policies analysed presented procedures for dealing with plagiarism, and some of these were not clear enough for students to gain a perspective on the entire process. Clarity was also affected by the language of the policy, missing timelines and steps in the process.

For the most part, the sanctions for plagiarism presented in the policies reflected those present in institutions globally. These ranged from giving students the opportunity to resubmit assignments to expulsion from the institutions. The heavy emphasis on sanctions, which was also evident in the qualitative data, spoke to a punitive approach to plagiarism. However, there was minimal focus on helping students develop the knowledge and skills necessary to act with integrity. Students were fearful of plagiarizing due to the threats of sanctions and the lack of knowledge of how to avoid plagiarism. Only one institution provided students with the opportunity to get counselling, and assistance with developing skills although much details was not provided on the latter. Some of the policies referred students to sources of assistance including the institution's library, but given the complexity of plagiarism, this was not adequate to deal with the challenges.

Based on the policies, faculty was involved in different ways in ensuring that students practised academic integrity and in managing allegations of academic misconduct. Some institutions required lecturers to provide information on plagiarism in their course outlines, but this was more the exception than the norm. Others placed the responsibility for academic integrity on the lecturers but did not detail the administrative support available to assist them to carry out this mandate. Based on the wording of the policies, only one institution required mandatory reporting of plagiarism, but it could not be determined from the policy if this was enforced. The lack of mandatory reporting and the placing of responsibility for academic integrity on lecturers would likely lead to the underreporting of cases of plagiarism as lecturers were likely to find it onerous (Kieth-Spiegel et al. 1998; Coren 2011; Thomas 2017; McGrail and McGrail 2015). There was evidence of the use of "statements of accountability" in the policies which students were required to complete and submit as evidence that they had not plagiarized. However, the effectiveness of this could be questioned as research findings showed that students in one of the institutions where the accountability statement was used thought it was the plagiarism policy (Baker-Gardner and Smart 2017, 194).

Although these institutions had an awareness of the need for policies on plagiarism, the effectiveness of these policies in stemming the act needs to be carefully considered. The great disparity in the contents of these policies also had implications for students who transferred from one tertiary institution to another whether to complete a degree or pursue further studies. The fact that policies were online did not guarantee students will read them (Baker-Gardner and Smart 2017, 194; Gullifer and Tyson 2014, 11), so emphasis needed to be placed on educating students about the contents of these. A consensus on the definition of plagiarism is needed to limit confusion on the part of students, and the role of faculty needs to be given careful attention so they are actively involved in the education and practice of academic integrity and willing to report infringements. If these are not accomplished, the struggle to achieve academic integrity will be fruitless.

Undergraduates' Perception of Plagiarism

Students' behaviour is likely to be influenced by their perception of an issue. The data from 1,039 undergraduate students on perceptions of plagiarism examined how they perceived the factors most likely to cause them to plagiarize, the arguments most likely to be used to justify plagiarism and their perceptions of the penalty for and severity of plagiarism. The findings which were in keeping with the literature revealed that the friend factor (Sisti 2007), whether students had more important obligations, the belief that others were plagiarizing (Howard, Ehrich and Walton 2014), and the thinking that sometimes it was necessary to plagiarize were perceived as the factors most likely to influence students to plagiarize. There were many arguments that students were likely to use to justify plagiarism: the difficulty in avoiding the use of the words of others; the use of descriptions of a concept or theory since these do not change; and the thinking that undergraduate students were just learning. Students were therefore not making the connection between learning and certification. Based on their perception, the degree was valued, but the learning did not appear to be given equal value. Institutions with limited monitoring systems were likely to have high cases of plagiarism seeing that the low possibility of being caught incentivized students to take the risk. The literature cites this as a factor in the decision to plagiarize (Vázquez-Recio et al.2016, 5711; Bahadori, Izadi and Hoseinpourfard, 2012; Sisti 2007, 222; Howard, Ehrich and Walton 2014, 31).

The majority of students had never heard about self-plagiarism and many did not believe it was harmful, a finding reflected in Walcott's study of Caribbean computer science students (2016). This ignorance points to a need for education on plagiarism. The students' perceptions of the factors which caused plagiarism aligned with findings of other studies, and so did for justification of plagiarism (Howard, Ehrich and Walton 2014; Lee 2016; Fish and Hura 2013).

The qualitative data provided additional insights into the students' perceptions. While some students believed the faculty's concerns with plagiarism were "much ado about nothing," others believed the study of plagiarism was relevant and expressed the hope that it would somehow benefit them in the future. The majority of students believed plagiarism was wrong, and this number accounted for just a little more than 50 per cent of the responses for the qualitative data. More than 40 per cent of the students believed that plagiarism was acceptable, or that it was wrong, but could be justified. Students in the latter groups seemed to detach themselves from the issue, choosing instead to focus on the need to complete their studies or help each other out. This high percentage of students who did not hold a negative view of plagiarism is worrisome and should serve as an indicator to HEIs that there is a need for immediate intervention.

The qualitative responses also provided data regarding students' challenges which resulted in plagiarism. Students were challenged by a lack of understanding of good writing practices and needed assistance to improve their writing skills, and students also indicated a need for education on plagiarism. Additionally, students had a misunderstanding of their roles as emerging researchers, believing they were expected at their level to present writing of the quality of the articles which appeared in academic journals. The students' ability to identify their challenges, which directly aligned with the literature (Ukpebor and Ogbebor 2013; Charubusp 2015; Kayaoglu et al. 2015), showed an awareness on their part which HEIs need to further investigate in order to gather data to inform their programme development.

The research also examined the impact of four independent variables on the students' perceptions of plagiarism. These variables were gender, academic discipline, year in which students were currently enrolled (academic maturity) and age. It was discovered that males were more agreeable to the statements about plagiarism than females, a finding that might account for the fact that they plagiarized more based on the findings of the empirical data presented in this research. Whereas academic discipline did not significantly impact students' overall perception of plagiarism, the statistics revealed significant differences in their perception of the factors which led to plagiarism. Students from the faculty of humanities and education were least likely to agree with the many named factors. In contrast, students from the faculty of science and technology were least likely to disagree. The students' perceptions of plagiarism were also impacted by age as younger students tended to disagree more with the factors which led to plagiarism. Older students were more likely to agree with the factors which led to plagiarism and also seemed more likely to use the justifications. The data on the impact of academic maturity on the students' perceptions of plagiarism can best be described as inconclusive.

There was a difference in the perception of the factors that caused plagiarism when the data from Years 1 and 3 were examined, with the latter being less likely to agree with the factors. On the contrary, Years 1 and 2 students showed more agreement with the severity and penalty of plagiarism than Year 3. This finding was supported by the findings from the analysis of plagiarism data that showed that Year 3 students cheated more. It therefore seemed possible that higher levels of disagreement with the severity and penalty were a reflection of practice among that group.

Academic Integrity and Accreditation

The content analysis of accreditation policies and guidelines revealed a significant disparity in the way accreditation agencies treated academic integrity. Some territories made no mention of it in the accreditation guidelines, while others considered it a criterion for programme and institutional accreditation. Even among those territories that did, there were glaring differences. Some territories alluded to academic integrity in their policies, and others gave it a passing mention, while Jamaica included standards related to academic integrity and detailed the evidence that had to be presented to determine if the standards were met. Accreditation agencies occupy a very important place in the higher education structure, and their role in ensuring quality is critical to advancing the academic integrity mandate.

From the analysis of data, conclusions have been drawn that concur with those from other jurisdictions as reported in the review of literature. However, there were important nuances that captured the Caribbean perspective. It is imperative for the Caribbean to begin to develop a robust system of academic integrity, which among other strategies, focuses on strengthening students' knowledge and competencies, thereby decreasing the need to practise academic misconduct. This will require regional, national and institutional systems and interventions. Failure to do so will result in the Caribbean education system being vulnerable as the technology provides additional opportunities for cheating, and contract cheating tests the strength of even the most robust academic integrity systems currently in place worldwide.

Part 3

Developing a Culture of Academic Integrity

Overview

Based on the foregoing analysis and discussion of the data, this part presents a summary of the findings and recommendations for the implementation of a system of academic integrity in the region and a culture of integrity in each institution. Chapter 16 presents nine major findings, the majority of which are in keeping with those of the studies from other geographical locations. The research also revealed the weaknesses in the provision for students to learn academic integrity that were not unique to the Caribbean. Chapter 16 also discusses the need for both a regional and a national framework for academic integrity by describing the practices elsewhere and making suggestions for the implementation of some of these practices in the Caribbean.

Chapter 17 presents a detailed discussion of what should be included in an institutional context aimed at developing a culture of academic integrity and introduces the Triad for Academic Integrity which outlines the stakeholders that are important in the establishment of such culture. The chapter also discusses the institutional framework that is required. It examines why regional institutions need to consider a centralized system for academic integrity and explains the roles of administrators within this framework. It concludes with a discussion of the role of the academic library in helping to create a culture of academic integrity.

Faculty and students are critical to the success of any programme to develop academic integrity, and Chapter 18 examines their roles and responsibilities. Using two sets of principles advocated by Pavela, McCabe and Mcduff (2017) and Chickering and Gamson (1987), the chapter presents tangible ways faculty can advance the ethical academy through their daily activities and interactions with students. The chapter then focuses on four responsibilities of students with regard to involvement in programmes of academic integrity, and closes by examining barriers to the engagement of faculty and students in academic integrity programmes and activities.

Chapter 19 examines the four elements and sub-elements of an academic integrity programme. These elements form what is called the PACT (Prevention, Mitigation, Assessment and Curation of Academic Integrity Based on Values and Taxonomy) model (Siaputra 2019). Each element with the accompanying sub-elements is discussed in detail in the chapter. Chapter 20 examines strategies for providing education and training for the development of academic integrity in students. It begins by examining the need for education and training within the region, making a case based on the findings and recommendations at the beginning of chapter 16. It briefly examines academic integrity education at the pre-university level and then probes content and methodology that can be used in the development of academic integrity in HEIs. It also presents examples of academic integrity programmes that have been implemented elsewhere. Chapter 21 summarizes the findings and outlines the strategies that can be implemented to chart the way forward and make the shift from a punitive approach to academic integrity to a culture of integrity which is beneficial to students, institutions and the region as a whole.

Chapter 16

Regional and National Framework for Academic Integrity

If students avoid cheating because they fear the consequences, I can live with that. But I would rather students avoided cheating because they realized that, in the long run, they were hurting themselves, too.
— Pettigrew (2010)

Introduction

The major findings and recommendations from the investigations to determine the state of academic integrity in the Caribbean open this chapter. It then explores the need and reasons for a shift from mere policies on academic integrity to a culture of academic integrity. It outlines the necessity of an academic integrity policy at the regional level, and academic integrity systems at the national level, citing examples from the European Union (EU). It later presents a discussion as to whether academic integrity is an ethical issue, moral dilemma or educational challenge.

The State of Academic Integrity in the Caribbean: Findings and Recommendations

The overall aim of the research was to describe the state of academic integrity in the English-speaking Caribbean. In order to do so, the author utilized triangulation of sources and methods to provide a fulsome description. Data sources included content analyses of newspaper articles, plagiarism policies and accreditation standards; the analysis of secondary data on the number of cases of plagiarism at both the secondary and tertiary levels; and the collection, via survey, of qualitative and quantitative data on the students' perception of plagiarism. The major findings can be summed up as follows:

1. Newspaper reports showed plagiarism in the Caribbean was present in many sectors, but it was more prevalent in education than in other sectors.
2. Plagiarism was evident at both the secondary and tertiary levels in the region. However, due to a variety of factors, it was difficult to determine the extent to which regional students were plagiarizing.

3. Policies and guidelines on plagiarism and academic integrity were available in HEIs. For the most part, these presented a punitive approach to plagiarism, holding students responsible for their behaviour and allocating little responsibility to the institutions.
4. Accreditation standards for some territories included academic integrity, but these also presented a punitive approach to academic integrity and plagiarism.
5. There were significant variations among policies on plagiarism and academic integrity, indicating a lack of agreement on various aspects of plagiarism, including definitions and types of behaviours which could be categorized as such.
6. Students had varying perceptions of plagiarism, with the majority believing that it was harmful to their academic growth as well as the institution and should not be tolerated. However, there was a significant segment of the sample that believed that plagiarism was not wrong, or that it was wrong but could be justified.
7. Males and final year students were more likely to plagiarize than other groups.
8. The majority of students felt there was a need for education on plagiarism.
9. There was a need for regional and national policies on academic integrity and plagiarism which should lead to improved knowledge of and attention to plagiarism at the institutional level.

These findings point to a need for the establishment of systems within the region geared at developing a system of academic integrity.

Gallant and Kalichman argue the need for improvement in HEIs and within education systems generally with regard to the management of plagiarism, and the Caribbean is no exception. They articulate that failure to do so strategically and intentionally will create an environment which is conducive to corruption (2011, 27). The findings from this research present evidence that academic misconduct, specifically plagiarism, is evident in both secondary and tertiary educational institutions. Therefore, improvements are needed to ensure this does not foster an environment conducive to corruption. Based on the findings, the following recommendations are being made:

1. The main recommendation is the need for the region to implement a policy for the development of academic integrity. The regional policy must include definitions of plagiarism and a glossary defining the behaviours which constitute plagiarism, an approach used in Europe (Tauginienė et al. 2018). This regional approach is necessary due to the interrelatedness of the education systems across territories.

From this regional policy, each territory will then need to develop a national policy for academic integrity which would outline the general approach to be used by institutions to develop academic integrity and manage the allegations of misconduct.
2. HEIs need to develop institutional systems for academic integrity which reflect the elements of the national policies, but which take into consideration the uniqueness of each.
3. There needs to be the development and implementation of introductory programmes on academic integrity at the secondary level. These would provide students with a basic understanding of academic integrity to be further developed at the tertiary level.

From Plagiarism Policies to a Culture of Academic Integrity

Developing and maintaining academic integrity is the responsibility of various stakeholders at the regional, national and individual levels (Drinan 2011). Policies for academic integrity and plagiarism are not sufficient to ensure that students practice academic integrity as some Caribbean students had never seen the policy (Baker-Gardner and Smart 2017, 194). To further compound this problem, Gullifer and Tyson found that even in HEIs where academic integrity is emphasized, only 50 per cent of the students actually read the policy (2014, 11). In addition, some Caribbean students have limited or incorrect knowledge and understanding of plagiarism, which is likely to negatively impact the interpretation of the policies, even if they decided to read them.

As recommended, changes are needed at the regional, national and institutional levels to move from the current practices of providing policies and guidelines to achieving a culture of academic integrity in the region. Sutherland-Smith maintains that adopting an ethical discourse about the relationship among academics, universities and students provides the opportunity to begin the discussion about the implementation of sustainable plagiarism management in universities (2010, 13). Glendinning is of the view that a "lack of consensus on what constitutes plagiarism" is possibly the greatest hindrance to developing academic integrity in the EU (2014, 7). This lack of consensus is evident in the Caribbean, so steps must be taken to develop a regional policy.

Aside from the issues raised previously, there are three compelling reasons for Caribbean HEIs to change their approach to managing academic integrity, namely: trends in HEIs; the need for institutional accreditation which will soon begin to require a constructive approach to academic integrity; and the global nature of the education system which is dependent on the quality of the education system in each country. Trends in higher education are leaning towards the use of constructive approaches to managing academic integrity. One example of the commitment to developing a culture of academic integrity was the Impact of Policies for Plagiarism in Higher Education Across Europe project launched in twenty-seven countries in the EU between 2010 and 2013. The overall goal of the project was to determine the practices that existed so as to develop interventions (Glendinning 2014, 1).

Another influential project aimed at developing academic integrity was the Academic Integrity Standards Project launched in Australia between 2010 and 2012 which resulted in the development of exemplars for academic integrity. Australian universities were encouraged to adapt these standards "to their own contexts to facilitate consistent academic standards" (Academic Integrity Standards 2013, 11). These projects, aimed at gathering empirical data to inform strategies to promote academic integrity, demonstrate that countries are seeking alternatives to the current practices that do not work. As student-centred institutions, universities need to execute the societal mandate to assist students to develop into ethical human beings. Consequently, there must be a shift from plagiarism and academic integrity policies to programmes for the development of academic integrity.

Caribbean universities, like those internationally, place a high premium on programme and institutional accreditation as a stamp of approval for the quality of education being offered in an increasingly competitive environment. The expectation is that national accreditation agencies in the Caribbean will align their practices to those of the international community as collectively all accreditation agencies are integral in the global attempt to ensure quality education. International associations such as Council for Higher Education Accreditation and International Network for Quality Assurance Agencies in Higher Education have embraced academic integrity as part of their mandate. The former, in association with the Council for International Quality Group, issued a call for national associations to implement this practice. Guyana, Jamaica, and St Vincent and the Grenadines have already done so, even though this focus needs to be strengthened. The other territories will be expected to follow suit so as to keep up with the prevailing practices.

Globalization makes regional academic integrity an imperative due to the migration of Caribbean nationals, regional students' participation in online education, and the enrolment of international students in Caribbean institutions. One feature of globalization is international migration, and according to the International Organization for Migration, the "Caribbean region has one of the highest net emigration rates in the world" (Responding to Migration Challenges in the Caribbean 2009). In 2007, the rate of migration from the Caribbean was four times higher than that of Latin America (Migration in the Caribbean: Current Trends, Opportunities and Challenges 2017, 7). Given this constant movement, Bakhtiari and Shajar stress the importance of developing a national qualification for participation in the global economy (2006, 98). The Caribbean has already achieved this milestone, so protecting the integrity of its qualifications becomes paramount. Developing systems to accomplish this is also a vital issue in the transnational education market.

Another feature of globalization is online learning which Bakhtiari and Shajar describe as a "powerful tool for developing countries" (2006, 98). It provides Caribbean nationals with the opportunity to access education from anywhere in the world, thus categorizing them among what is called "international students" by first world universities. However, this is not without problems. According to Evans-Tokaryk, the globalization of education has "contributed to competing and contradictory understanding of plagiarism in contemporary western academic culture" (2014, 7). This results in international students sometimes possessing a different understanding of plagiarism than that of the institutions in which they enrol (Bamford and Sergiou 2004, 17). This is another factor which signals the need for a direct focus on academic integrity within the region.

Another effect of globalization is that many Caribbean nationals are leaving the region to study overseas with the preferred destination being the United States, home to 64.7 per cent of the Caribbean migrants (International Organisation on Migration 2017, 12). Other popular destinations are the United Kingdom and Canada. At one of the many US Embassy's College Fairs held in Kingston Jamaica, Don Cunningham, a recruiter for Lincoln College of Technology, said, "The world is a smaller place today, and being that Jamaicans are everywhere, it is important to do overseas study" (Harris 2014). Additionally, the *Jamaica Observer* noted a growing demand for Canadian education by Jamaicans citing that the number had increased from 400 in 2010 to 3,500 in 2019 (Francis 2019). This supports Marklein's (2018) view that international universities are now looking to Latin America and the Caribbean in a bid to stem enrolment shortfalls. The destination countries for Caribbean nationals already have or are developing systems for academic integrity.

An increasingly mobile student population would be at a distinct disadvantage in countries and institutions with a strong culture of academic integrity if they have no previous exposure to this. In addition, Caribbean institutions such as the University of the West Indies (UWI) are marketing their products to an international audience. Consequently, if students who are familiar with such a culture of academic integrity study in Caribbean institutions which do not place emphasis on academic integrity, they might believe academic misconduct is tolerated.

Change is necessary as the current practice of providing a policy for plagiarism and academic integrity has not been successful in decreasing instances of this misconduct because it does not address some of the pertinent issues (Craig and Dalton 2013, 108). To further exacerbate the situation, educating students on academic integrity and providing punishment where rules are breached has not been effective for the past two decades (Gallant and Kalichman 2011, 36). This, therefore, means a new approach is needed if HEIs are going to successfully develop students who practise academic integrity. Curbing Corruption, an organization established in 2018 to help businesses, academia and multilateral organizations fight corruption, presents eight approaches to change. Although these are not specific to the education sector, they are worth considering in the context of this discussion. The six approaches that are relevant are:

1. people-centred approaches: working directly with affected communities; building networks and coalitions of supporters;
2. monitoring approaches: strengthen oversight groups and their independence;
3. justice and rule of law approaches: prosecuting, raising confidence, improving laws;
4. transparency approaches: making visible what others wish to keep hidden;
5. integrity approaches: motivating, instiling pride and commitment; and
6. whistleblowing approaches: finding safe ways for people to speak up. (Reform Approaches and Experience 2019)

No single approach will be adequate in successfully helping to create a culture of integrity, but a combination of these might prove useful. The strategies discussed in this section embody these approaches. It must be emphasized here that as was the case in the EU and Australia, change must be based on in-depth research, as this work can only be considered a preliminary investigation. Gallant and Kalichman noted that developing a healthy, ethical environment will demand a clear grasp of the problems which need to be solved in addition to being "clear about the environment that is desired" (2011, 35). This can only be achieved by studying the issue from multiple angles and through multiple lenses.

In order to build a culture of integrity, institutions have to be purposeful and willing to embrace and follow the four stages in this process, namely:

1. recognition and commitment;
2. response generation;
3. implementation; and
4. institutionalization (Gallant and Drinan 2008).

At the initial stage, there is a recognition that academic integrity is a desired institutional goal and academic misconduct is a problem. This must be accompanied by a commitment to finding solutions. Commitment should lead to action as solutions are developed and implemented to create the desired environment and simultaneously manage the challenges. Over time institutionalization should result as strategies are repeatedly implemented.

The extent to which there is recognition of problem in the Caribbean is not clear; however, as stated previously, the aim of this work is to generate interest and discussion so that further investigation may follow. This should help educators in the region to begin to examine the issue in a critical and holistic manner.

Regional Approach to Academic Integrity

Heyneman states that Latin America and the Caribbean has the second most corrupt education system globally (2011, 15), indicating a need for a regional approach to the development of academic integrity. This can be facilitated through the Council for Human and Social Development one of the four ministerial councils of CARICOM "responsible for the promotion of human and social development in the Community," and in particular the "promotion and development of education at all levels" (Caribbean Community Secretariat 2001, 13). This regional approach is possible and necessary, given the integrated nature of the education systems of the Caribbean as evidenced by the two regional education institutions, CXC and the UWI. In addition, CARICOM already has a mandate for accreditation, and so advancing the topic of academic integrity as part of the mandate could be considered.

There is precedence for a regional approach when one examines the European Network for Academic Integrity project which was aimed at raising "awareness in the matters of plagiarism, academic ethics, scholarly values and academic integrity" (Tauginienė et al. 2018). The focus was on students and the various stakeholders in the academic community. The project included: "A toolkit for cross-sector cooperation [...] and Handbook for improvements in academic integrity [...]. The latter output consists of seven sub-outputs, such as general guidelines for academic integrity, glossary of terms related to academic integrity, self-evaluation tools for students, teaching and research, self-assessment tool for institutions/faculties/departments and briefs" (2018, 2).

This policy document is very comprehensive and speaks to all aspects of academic integrity. In addition, it provides a glossary aimed at ensuring common understanding in the interpretation and implementation of the policy. A glossary of this kind serves to limit the confusion which is evident in the definitions, types and examples of plagiarism presented in the Caribbean academic integrity and plagiarism policies. Finally, the project facilitates each country in the EU to develop its own systems within the framework of this larger context, thereby catering to its circumstances. This is an example that can be assessed in order to obtain ideas for the implementation of a regional policy in the Caribbean.

CANQATE had an early presence in the discussions of the need to integrate academic integrity into the accreditation process. In 2012, the network invited Trecia Bertram Gallant, the director of the academic integrity office at the University of California, San Diego, to be the speaker for the plenary session at its annual conference. She addressed the conference on "Ethics and Academic Integrity in Tertiary Education." This seems to have borne some fruits since Jamaica, Guyana, and St Vincent and the Grenadines currently include academic integrity in their accreditation standards for programme and institutional accreditation. Other agencies need to adopt this approach, and all territories need to push beyond the punitive approach to a more holistic focus.

National Academic Integrity Programmes

In order to move the region forward in developing a culture of academic integrity, there has to be a commitment to it at the national level. There are several advantages to this approach as it: creates a context within which institutions will develop their cultures of academic integrity; gives the issue importance by placing it on the national agenda; and provides support for students who advance from one level to another, or move from one institution to another. The concept of a national policy on academic integrity or plagiarism is alien to the Caribbean, but Sarlauskiene and Stabingis advocate for a national definition of plagiarism (2014, 639) and the most likely place to have this is within a national policy. Tomas and Glendinning (2015) identified some countries in Europe which have national policies, with the United Kingdom, Austria and Sweden named as the top three ranking countries in terms of their "Academic Integrity Maturity" and these have national policies. The United Kingdom and Sweden also ranked highly on the 2020 list of countries with the best education systems (Education Rankings by Country 2020). Various agencies rated the countries differently, but for the most part, they were ranked in the top ten by the majority of agencies. The following is a combined list of academic integrity activities at the national level within these countries:

- research into plagiarism by academics and dissemination of the results nationally;
- national quality auditing systems;
- use of software to detect possible cases of plagiarism;
- public management of students' complaints of unfair practices;
- collecting national statistics on the number of cases of academic misconduct;
- requirements for academic integrity policies in research;
- high awareness and understanding of both plagiarism and academic writing;
- training and development of students at various levels;
- working groups exploring policy issues; and
- publication of the report on academic misconduct cases.
(Glendinning 2013)

Such a commitment to academic integrity at the national level reveals the seriousness with which it is viewed in other education systems when compared to the Caribbean.

Despite the effective practices of these countries, Glendinning found that very few EU countries had implemented "national policies and procedures for monitoring aspects of academic integrity at the bachelors and masters level" (2014, 8). This shows that although there are exemplary practices, the focus on academic integrity at the national level is still emerging. However, Gallant and Kalichman's assertion that factors at all levels of the education system are influential in shaping individual and institutional ethical responses (2011, 40) suggests the need for a national approach to the academic integrity.

The recommendation for the Caribbean is an adaptation of some of the practices in the United Kingdom, Austria and Sweden after research is done to examine their feasibility for implementation. Regional ministries of education have tertiary units, and so the responsibility for overseeing the national programme for academic integrity could be assigned to them. The particular practices that could be adopted from the countries in the EU are:

- stimulation of research on academic integrity and plagiarism in each territory. Funding could be provided for this research by ministries of education that are constantly on a path to improvement. Findings could be disseminated as papers and guidance notes, as in the case of the United Kingdom;
- implementation of several working groups at the national level to explore academic integrity policy issues;
- design of pre-university activities for teaching good academic practice.
- development of a national system for collecting data annually from HEIs about academic misconduct cases. Reports could be published at agreed intervals. This data could also be used as part of the evaluation for the academic integrity programme nationally;
- inclusion of training in aspects of academic conduct and integrity in bachelor's and master's programmes. This could be a phased approach depending on the needs of the students at each institution.
- implementation of a nationally prescribed policy for managing allegations of academic misconduct, involving an institutional panel to oversee this.

These should prove beneficial as they would serve to create a national awareness of academic integrity and send a signal to students that they are expected to abide by guidelines set by the individual institutions. They would also create the framework necessary to ensure students are provided with the support needed in order to act with integrity.

From a Punitive Approach to a Culture of Integrity

A study of the literature reveals a variety of approaches to academic integrity with the majority of writers agreeing that there are two main approaches although they are called by different terms. Gallant (2011) and Lampert (2006) adopt the categorizations rule compliance and integrity. Rule compliance, which is a judicial or legalistic process, focuses on following rules and involves punitive or reactive responses. Blum (2009) uses the term "law and enforcement" to describe this approach. She notes that students are likely to either ignore the "laws" or follow them reluctantly. The integrity approach focuses on values, honour and ethics, is student-oriented and has a less rigid process.

In keeping with the integrity approach, Walker and White found that some faculty held the erroneous belief that students were primarily responsible for plagiarism (2014, 8), and Berlinck (2011) concurs with this finding. Walker and White also discovered that faculty felt their main role was to review institutional policies with the students and to detect plagiarism (2014, 5). They further contended that this traditional approach to treating plagiarism is individualistic, as it focuses on either the student or the teacher. On the one hand, teachers are expected to structure learning activities and conduct an assessment in ways that make it difficult to cheat. On the other hand, is the belief that students who cheat have not adhered to the expected and acceptable standards (2014, 3).

Saddiqui describes the focus on students as central to the problem of academic misconduct as a "deficit model of education" and claims it represents a punitive approach with the main goal being deterrence. Other features of this punitive approach are warnings, monitoring and policing, and applying penalties (2016, 3). While the literature supports some elements of the punitive approach (Berlinck 2011, 367), critics argue that it does not take into consideration the variety of issues surrounding the students' cheating behaviours (Power 2009, 659). Saddiqui points out that sanctions and threats are usually promoted, but institutions fail to articulate the positive aspects of academic integrity. She also contends that the emphasis on sanctions fails to address the root causes of academic misconduct found in the literature (2016, 3). This seems to be the current position in the Caribbean.

In agreeing that there are two general approaches to academic integrity, Garrett uses the concept of a continuum. However, unlike Walker and White who utilize the continuum to discuss the levels of intentionality to engage in plagiarism, Garrett (2011) uses it to describe approaches to plagiarism. She notes that at one end of the continuum there is the decentralized approach which is haphazard, opaque and inconsistent. At the other extreme is the highly centralized approach where breaches of academic integrity are reported to an academic integrity office. She contends that most institutions fall in the middle of this continuum where reports are made to a divisional head, such as a head of department, who then reports to the dean as is evident in the Caribbean.

Garrett is critical of both the rule compliance and integrity approaches. She agrees with Berlinck (2011) and Walker and White (2014) that the student is usually seen as the problem in both the integrity and punitive approaches and pointedly explains: "[they] attribute the cause of the problem to the character of the individual student, who is assumed to be dysfunctional or acting in dysfunctional ways. The vernacular is morally laden and generally characterizes the student and his or her conduct as honest or dishonest, honorable or dishonorable, moral or immoral, good or bad" (2011). Based on these arguments, it is clear that there is a need to explore another approach that is more adequate in meeting the challenges of academic integrity from the perspective of students and faculty.

Hu and Sun, on the other hand, insist that along with these two, there is also a third approach to academic integrity. Firstly, there is the punitive approach, which is the most predominant and equals Gallant's rule compliance and lends itself to the use of text-matching software like Turnitin. Secondly, there is the self-regulatory approach which espouses ethics education and the use of honour codes, in keeping with what Gallant (2011) refers to as the integrity approach. Thirdly, there is the educative approach, also called the educational or instructional approach, which focuses on the overall development of the students by the institution (Hu and Sun 2017, 56). Saddiqui states that this approach aims to help students acquire knowledge of "conventions and expectations, thereby providing them with less impetus to commit an academic integrity breach as a result of ignorance regarding the rules or a lack of skill" (2016, 4).

The International Center for Academic Integrity (ICAI) currently focuses on the holistic approach which combines the self-regulatory or integrity approach with more robust institutional support for developing academic integrity (Fishman and Chu 2017). This includes moving from compliance to integrity, including academic integrity and ethics in the curricula, developing academic integrity specialists and examining the role of institutions in developing academic integrity. The ICAI's approach reflects the thinking of Saddiqui who contends that "standalone, ad hoc academic integrity interventions in higher education are unlikely to engender lasting and meaningful change at institutions" (2016, 1).

Effective approaches to dealing with academic misconduct, such as plagiarism, rest largely with faculty and institutions. The former interact with the students on a daily basis and know their weaknesses, needs and challenges, and they also implement the policies of the institutions. The institutions, on the other hand, are the agents responsible for establishing policies and programmes to guide the actions of both faculty and students. Therefore, any system for developing academic integrity, which aims to be constructive and not punitive, needs to be holistic, taking into consideration all parties involved and should embody mitigation, prevention and a process for managing allegations of misconduct and the rehabilitation of those who have breached guidelines (Siaputra 2019).

Ethical Issue, Moral Dilemma or Educational Challenge?

An ongoing debate exists as to whether academic misconduct is a matter of ethics, morality or lack of education, and the perspective institutions take on the issue will determine the approach they take to remediation. According to Blum (2009), those who believe academic misconduct is a matter of morality tend to emphasize the use of honour codes aimed at encouraging students to "do the right thing." She instead proposes that academic misconduct is an academic issue and as such, "[t]reating academic integrity as a constellation of skills, taught largely through the long apprenticeship of higher education, is the most promising approach."

Gallant and Goodchild take the ethics approach (2011, 4), a position supported by Heyneman (2011, 23). These writers are of the view that although there is an expectation that ethics will be a part of the organization, it is often not addressed at the institution-wide level. Heyneman, therefore, calls for institutions to make ethics a strategic institutional priority (2011, 13) and Gallant and Kalichman advocate for the ethical academy, an institution in which faculty, staff and students operate in an ethically healthy environment. This increases the likelihood that members will choose to do the right even when there are competing interests. They believe this ethical academy should be characterized by individual responsibility and institutional integrity (2011, 32).

Research has shown that students also believe that institutions of learning should actively seek to instil ethical values in them as part of the educational process. For example, surveys conducted by the Josephson Institute of Ethics to establish if students supported the need for a positive approach to dealing with academic integrity found that approximately 90 per cent of the respondents strongly supported the view that "schools should be more active in seeking to instill core ethical values like honesty, responsibility, and respect, and in developing good character in children" (Josephson Institute of Ethics 2009). Findings like these strengthen the view that plagiarism is an ethical issue which can be remedied by ethics education (Gallant and Kalichman 2011, 29).

Former academic Stanley Fish (2010) caused much debate when, in his blog post, *Plagiarism Is Not a Big Moral Deal*, he opined that essays about plagiarism tend to be "philosophically and morally inflated." According to him, plagiarism is more a breach of "disciplinary decorum" and should not be viewed as a matter of morals. Fish's article was widely read and commented on with academics agreeing and disagreeing. Beyerstein and others presented counter-arguments explaining why plagiarism is a moral issue. Beyerstein contended that the morality of plagiarism is "rooted in honesty and fairness." She further argued that plagiarists set out to deceive as they present work done by someone else as their own, thus benefitting from this deception by obtaining grades, honours and jobs (2010). Perry (2010) also weighed in on the argument, supporting Beyerstein's position that plagiarism is a moral issue. She noted the decreased value of academic qualifications if plagiarism were to be considered an acceptable practice. The conclusion to be drawn from this discussion and the available literature is that there is no consensus about whether plagiarism is an ethical or moral issue.

The focus on plagiarism as an ethical, moral or educational issue exclusively might be narrowing the scope of the problem with which HEIs have to contend as a misdiagnosis of the problem might also render useless any attempt to resolve the issue. This might explain why East and Donnoley believe plagiarism can result from a combination of factors. They state that "breaches of academic integrity can be described as ethical issues and or issues of convention and practice. The ethical issues relate to dishonesty and cheating, while conventions of practice are concerned with the pedagogical specifics of acknowledgment, referencing and how knowledge is discussed" (2012, 3).

In this work, plagiarism is considered to be a combination of the preceding issues in keeping with East and Donnoley's (2012) conclusion. This is supported by McGrail and McGrail (quoting Beasley 2004) who identify three kinds of student plagiarists:

1. the accidental plagiarist who carries out the act due to ignorance;
2. the opportunistic, due to the low chances of being caught; and
3. the committed plagiarist who will engage in cheating behaviour regardless of the systems and structures in place to deter it (2015, 11).

The accidental plagiarist does not have either an ethical or a moral problem; his is educational and can be remedied through teaching and practice. Both the opportunistic and committed plagiarists might have ethical and moral weaknesses and might be able to benefit from ethics education to varying degrees. The call for education as a means of limiting academic misconduct is focused on equipping students with the necessary writing skills, knowledge about the purpose and use of citations, and an understanding of plagiarism.

Beale also believes that based on the research, students can be divided into the following three groups with respect to their approach to academic integrity, and there are similarities to those of Beasley quoted above: "(1) law-abiding and aren't much affected by their institutional culture. They will fastidiously follow all the rules; (2) intent upon pursuing loopholes, and where the loopholes aren't big enough, they just kind of evade the rules; and (3) greatly affected by the institutional culture and represents the majority of students" (2003, 408). Beale's categorization includes all students, which was not the case with the previous list which focused on only those who plagiarized. Any intervention to develop honest students and decrease the instances of plagiarism will need to give consideration to these categories advocated by McGrail and McGrail and Beale. Based on Beale's categorization, academic integrity programmes are important as they will also likely impact the third set of students which is the largest group.

There are likely to be many challenges to the development of a system of academic integrity in the region, and it is expected that this will have to involve a multisectoral approach, to include governments and institutions from various territories. However, given the need to maintain quality education in the region, the benefits that accrue to the region should be worth the efforts expended. In addition, the region has practices from elsewhere that it can look to in order to determine how to proceed, and the existing structures on which this system can be built.

Conclusion

In order for the Caribbean to advance the cause for academic integrity, it needs to move from academic integrity and plagiarism policies to developing a culture for academic integrity. Push factors for the implementation of a culture of academic integrity are changes in accreditation requirements, international trends in academic integrity and opportunities for online education. Through the The Council for Human and Social Development, the region should begin to consider the development and implementation of a regional policy for academic integrity at both the secondary and tertiary levels. This regional policy should inform national policies in each territory, reflecting its particular need. The national policies should present an educational approach to academic integrity, and this should include both education in ethics and the intricacies of good writing and proper citing. Regional and national policies should form the framework within which institutional policies are developed.

Chapter 17

Institutional Context for Academic Integrity

Introduction

Both a national and regional framework for academic integrity build the foundation for the development and implementation of institutional academic integrity programmes. This chapter details the roles and responsibilities of the institution for achieving this, with reference to the triad for the development of academic integrity. It presents the centralized approach to academic integrity as the suggested way for organizing the programme and uses Caldwell's Ten Steps for Academic Integrity (2010) as a practical guide in developing the programme. It concludes by examining the role of the academic library in helping to develop, implement and promote a culture of academic integrity.

Triad for Developing Academic Integrity within Higher Education Institutions (HEIs)

Society believes that schools are responsible not just for providing content and skills but also for the development of moral graduates (Meng et al. 2014, 134). Hence, schools should ensure that students leave with not just the requisite skills but also the moral education to be suitable agents who can be charged with the future direction of the society. According to Bretag (2018a), "A genuinely holistic approach [to academic integrity] involves promoting integrity in every aspect of the academic enterprise. This includes university's mission statements and marketing, admissions processes, nuanced and carefully articulated policy (with the resources to promote the policy and the 'teeth' to enact it), assessment practices, and curriculum design." These activities take place at the institutional level; therefore, regional and national policies for academic integrity create the context within which institutions can develop and implement their programmes. The institution is a critical stakeholder in developing academic integrity. Regardless of the structures which exist at the regional or national levels, it is the place where the programme will be developed and implemented.

Approaches to academic integrity usually reflect an institution's perspective on the issue. Sadiqqui uses the term "academic integrity community" to emphasize the shared nature of the responsibility for academic integrity within institutions (2016, 4). To convey this same notion, Sutherland-Smith uses the term "web of ethical relationships" (2010, 13) and Gallant and Kalichman go further by precisely identifying the three main actors – teachers, students and administrators. They view the institutions as a web of interdependent relationships in which teachers teach or fail to teach, students learn or fail to learn in relation to each other and to the faculty, and administrators lead or fail to lead in relation to the school and within the political and economic environment (2011, 39) alluding to the concept of the school as a social system (Hoy and Miskel 2005). To further emphasize the importance of the institutional environment, Gallant and Kalichman state that "people are profoundly affected by the institution in which they operate" (2011, 39). Kezar and Sam sum up the importance of taking an institutional approach to academic integrity by stating that the "establishment of an ethical culture in an institution is a necessary component in building an ethical academy, and should be foremost in the minds of leaders of the institution" (2011, 153).

Sadiqqui suggests that shifting the view away from students to institutions requires identifying stakeholders and their roles within systems for academic integrity. She believes, "identifying the groups within academic stakeholder communities serve to emphasize the interconnected nature of academic integrity management" (2016, 4). Sadiqqui cites Nayak, whose survey found that 84 per cent of 5,538 Australian students believed academic integrity was the responsibility of the university but felt that students were more responsible than the academic and administrative staff (2016, 5). Sadiqqui opines that where there is "responsibility for providing the guiding framework, rules, conventions, and policing of academic integrity; and responsibility of abiding by those rules and conventions" (2016, 5), this division is likely to suggest students are perpetrators and faculty enforcers. She further advocates that care has to be taken with how to operationalize the responsibilities of staff and students.

Berlinck agrees with shared responsibility by stating that the parties involved should be students, teachers and the institutions (2011, 370). Pavela, McCabe and McDuff support this triadic approach to developing academic integrity. One of their Ten Principles of Academic Integrity for Faculty is the need to "[r]ecognize that promoting and protecting academic integrity is a collaborative endeavor involving shared leadership by students, faculty members and administrators" (2017).

The emphasis on a triadic approach to academic integrity is supported by this writer, and, as a consequence, the triad for developing academic integrity is the reference point for the discussion of the roles and responsibilities

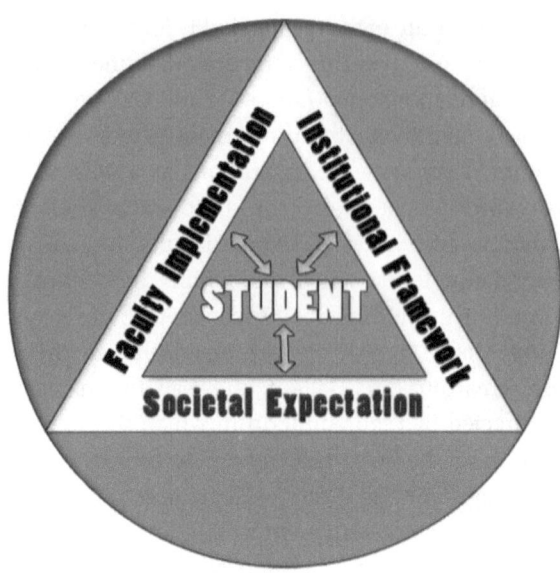

Figure 17.1. Triad for academic integrity.

of the various stakeholder groups. The triad, shown in figure 17.1, has three major elements: institutional framework, faculty implementation and societal expectations. It places the student at the heart of the process, embedded within the processes and structures and actively involved in the tasks aimed at developing integrity. In the discourse found in the regional policies analysed previously, the student is viewed as the primary agent of academic misconduct. In this triadic approach, at the heart of the academic integrity process is the student, who, provided with the necessary support, should aim to act with integrity.

HEIs are expected to provide the institutional framework which facilitates the impartation of education and the development of morals, ethics and other desired characteristics which will benefit the students who are central to the process. In so doing, it is expected that institutions will put in place adequate structures and processes to ensure that students develop and practise academic integrity. Faculty is important, seeing that they are the ones who are likely to interact with the students and identify and report breaches of academic integrity. Students, at the heart of the triad, are impacted by societal expectation, the institutional framework and faculty implementation, even as these also impact each other.

The combination of the elements in the triad should provide the right context within which students can develop academic integrity. The triad is relevant, as Gallant and Kalichman view individual misconduct as "a system issue, shaped by the individual, organisational, educational and societal factors." They conclude that structures, procedures and cultures are shaped by forces within each system (2011, 36). Therefore, attempting to develop academic integrity without identifying the stakeholders and having a grasp of their roles and responsibilities will likely result in failure

Societal expectations act as the impetus for the development of academic integrity; hence, it forms the base of the triad. HEIs operate within a society with systems for accreditation, mechanisms for moving from one level of education to another and legislative frameworks. Whereas societal expectations can have a positive effect on academic integrity, these same factors can also impede the process. Gallant and Kalichman identify the following societal factors which influence HEIs: competition for scarce resources; lack of political and societal efforts to control, prevent and punish corruption; and the increasing sophistication and proliferation of technology (2011, 41). In situations where these factors exert considerable control, they might compromise the institutions' attempts to implement successful academic integrity programmes.

Institutional Framework

Gallant and Kalichman propose three expectations of institutional integrity that signal the need for an institutional framework. They believe institutions

1. must do what they promise to do – an obligation to society;
2. must respond to problems by fixing ineffective and inefficient systems to mitigate factors which cause the problems; and
3. are not perfect but must implement structures and processes, creating and sustaining a culture that supports ethical conduct (2011, 34).

Gallant and Goodchild also agree that higher education does not have to be perfect; however, due to the impact of the graduates, activities and research, HEIs should constantly seek the ethical high ground (2011, 4). The most effective way of achieving this is to approach academic integrity from an institutional perspective. Bretag and Mahmud, reporting on presentations done by senior academic representatives from Australian universities with exemplary academic integrity policies, observed, "All five representatives [...] reiterated the importance of an institutional commitment to a culture of integrity, as both an aspiration and as a tangible practice" (2016, 3). Gallant and Goodchild warn that failure to treat misconduct as a "systematic issue that will likely result in ethical corruption" (2011, 81) is detrimental to institutions.

Bretag believes instead of focusing on students, responsible institutions should aim for "a holistic and multi-stakeholder approach encompassing educational policymakers, senior managers, teaching academics and advisors, students at all levels, researchers, editors, and reviewers" (2013, 2). She also believes that students should be provided with academic integrity information during orientation and this should be supplemented with "embedded and targeted support in courses and at every stage" and visual reminders on campus. She advocates that this is only possible in the context of partnership with students and professional development for staff. Bretag also advocates for the use of new technologies to help students while they complete assignments, and as a tool for detecting plagiarism (2013, 2). The approach advocated by Bretag should impact the culture of the institution, especially if the strategies are implemented over the long term, thus resulting in the development of a culture of academic integrity.

A combination of strategies can have a significant positive impact on developing academic integrity while simultaneously deterring academic misconduct. As is suggested by Carnero and colleagues, an institutional approach is definitely needed if success is to be achieved. These researchers successfully used: an intensified research integrity and scientific writing education; a stepwise, cumulative writing process; honour codes; an active search for plagiarism in all academic products; and a "zero-tolerance" policy in response to documented cases in a master's programme in Peru (2017, 1183). This resulted in no cases of plagiarism for that year.

Similarly, Kokkinaki, Demoliou and Iakovidou recommended that universities in Cyprus implement the following measures to treat or develop academic integrity: teach students about plagiarism, academic dishonesty and the idea of giving credit to the rightful owner of the original work; implement this consistently through faculty and by auditing institutions' policies and procedures for the prevention of plagiarism; the employment of sanctions against plagiarism; and the use of plagiarism detection software to deter plagiarism and to enable students to accomplish proper academic writing (2015, 10). An institutional approach to academic integrity is critical for HEIs which are seeking a solution to academic misconduct, or for those who just want to bolster their academic integrity profile.

Aside from the implementation of initiatives such as those described previously, academic integrity needs to be seen and heard on campus. One example of the visibility of academic integrity was shared by Adelphi University in New York. In branding academic integrity as an institutional venture, Adelphi University (n.d.) holds an annual Academic Honesty Awareness Week which is launched at a critical point in the semester, before the period when the highest numbers of academic violations are committed. Activities geared towards both students and faculty during this period was one way in which the institution helped to create and promote a culture of academic integrity. This is another example of the institutional approach to academic integrity as it involved the entire campus.

Centralized System for Academic Integrity: A centralised system for academic integrity is a vital part of the institutional framework. Eriksson and McGee (2015) are of the view that students are more likely to engage in cheating behaviours if they believe that there is a culture of cheating in their institutions. This suggests that just having a culture of honesty helps to curb the rate of academic misconduct. Floyd, Taylor and Queen (2019) mentioned three ways institutions can support and promote academic integrity: to recognize the importance of academic integrity; dedicate time and resources to the programmes and processes; and have a centralized approach to academic integrity through the establishment of a central office, or an individual dedicated to academic integrity. The identification of the centralized approach by these authors lends credence to the position that this approach is important to the development of a culture of academic integrity,

Garrett believes that a university's approach to dealing with academic misconduct is influenced by how centralized the process is and opines that in universities "with highly decentralized responses, faculty members handle cheating as they see fit" (2011). This ad hoc approach is not likely to be effective. Administrators are key players in creating and implementing a centralized system in which:

- there is clear commitment from the highest levels of universities;
- there are clearly defined duties and responsibilities;
- there is clear and proper system regulation and decision making;
- there is possibility to get sponsorship and help from specialists; and
- there is access to support and specialist advice (Carroll and Appleton 2001, 36).

These allude to the importance of the institutional framework in achieving success. The acknowledgement of the need for access to support and specialist advice suggests faculty and administrators might not have the required knowledge to implement a system of academic integrity, and so additional training might be needed.

Based on the review of literature and attendance at conference presentations, the author was able to identify six versions of this centralized approach practised in universities worldwide. These are:

1. appointing a dedicated academic integrity officer who operates out of a unit dedicated to academic integrity;

2. assigning the responsibility for academic integrity to the person responsible for students' conduct;
3. assigning duties for academic integrity to full-time faculty who has reduced teaching responsibilities;
4. assigning responsibilities for academic integrity to a member of the administrative staff;
5. combining the responsibilities for academic integrity with the duties of the research officer; and
6. the use of an academic integrity committee.

The use of a dedicated integrity officer as part of the centralized approach is evidenced by an online search which revealed this position was present in some universities. However, it was referred to by different terms, such as academic integrity officer, academic integrity and conduct officer, plagiarism officer, integrity officer or academic misconduct officer. Some institutions, such as the University of Central Florida (n.d.), have a position called Student Conduct Coordinator, with academic integrity as one of the areas of responsibility assigned to that person. The officials in charge of centres for academic integrity usually report directly to the Provost office.

Some universities, such as the University of Maryland (2019), had a research integrity officer who was responsible for the academic integrity in that institution. The research integrity office was also staffed by other individuals including compliance specialists, a conflict of interest officer and a chief accountability officer. In other institutions, academic integrity officers were full-time faculty who were assigned the additional responsibility of ensuring that academic integrity policies and procedures were implemented in their institutions. The University of Wollongong used the preceding model and stated that it had two academic coordinators per school who were responsible for "providing advice to Subject Coordinators on how to conduct investigations, making determinations on the findings and outcomes of investigations and for actioning low-level outcomes arising from findings of academic misconduct, where appropriate, within their Faculty" (n.d.). These examples give a sense of the seriousness with which academic integrity is viewed outside the Caribbean.

In other institutions, individuals who were responsible for academic integrity were members of the administrative staff, tasked solely with the responsibility for academic integrity. Usually in these institutions, these individuals operate out of a central office. In one model, academic misconduct was seen as a disciplinary matter and was managed by the person or office responsible for student discipline. At the University of Maryland (2019), academic integrity is managed by the Office of Student Conduct.

Regardless of which model is used, integrity officers and an integrity centre are tangible expressions of an institution's commitment to developing academic integrity and simultaneously dealing with academic dishonesty in a constructive manner. On the one hand, they send a message to students and others that unethical behaviours within the academy are not acceptable. On the other, they signal the willingness of the institution to offer assistance to students in developing their skills so that they will practise academic integrity.

The person who performs the roles and duties of an academic integrity officer has many responsibilities. The University of Leeds in the United Kingdom outlined the following duties for its academic integrity officer, who is also a member of the academic staff:

- overseeing the investigation of suspected cases of plagiarism;
- ensuring consistent procedures and practice across the school;
- working with tutors to raise awareness of plagiarism issues;
- actively promoting the use of Turnitin within the school/faculty and developing standard practices in consultation with colleagues;
- promoting good practice in academic writing and sharing best practice with other schools;
- ensuring that all students in the school/faculty complete the online plagiarism tutorial; and
- providing discipline-specific content for the generic online tutorial, if required (Role Description: Academic Integrity Officer 2011).

The duties support the use of a multipronged approach to academic integrity with a strong emphasis on education for students on both plagiarism and writing. There is also evidence of the acknowledgment of the differences across disciplines which are likely to require different strategies for academic integrity.

Another variation was the academic integrity or academic honesty committee used by universities such as Fordham, the University of Nebraska and Auburn University. This committee was usually comprised of faculty, administrative staff and students tasked with the responsibility to: receive reports of allegations of plagiarism, investigate the allegations, schedule the case review, report violations to the dean, provide annual reports on its activities and plan workshops for educating students (Fordam University n.d.). Whatever model is adopted, what was evident was that an institution's commitment to academic integrity was expressed through the creation of a system that supported students' academic growth. This is best achieved through a centralized system for academic integrity which offered students expert advice and dedicated support so they do not plagiarize. In cases where students do engage in academic misconduct, this centralized system must also afford them the remediation they need even after the stipulated penalties were applied.

Having established that a centralized institutional approach to academic integrity is the desired approach, the matter of how it can be done needs to be examined. One example of how to implement a programme is Cam Caldwell's Ten Step Model which follows:

1. articulation of a clear purpose and mission;
2. orientation and training of faculty;
3. explanation and clarification of current policies;
4. implementation of a realistic process for addressing violations;
5. attainment of student ownership;
6. empowerment of students in education and enforcement;
7. maintenance of dialogue with stakeholders;
8. refinement of the ethics curriculum;
9. monitored enforcement and documentation of results; and
10. evaluation of outcomes and communication of results (2010).

This model was chosen because it embodies some recommended practices in education and is very clear, and the detailed steps should make it easy for institutions to implement. These steps include stakeholder involvement, ownership and monitoring. It approaches academic integrity from both an ethical and educational perspective and includes instruction in ethics and empowerment of students through education (Gallant and Kalichman 2011, 36). It also emphasizes training for staff, a significant stakeholder group in the process of academic integrity development and promotion. This is a feature of a systems approach to academic integrity supported by Carboon (2013) and East (2016, 8).

Another set of recommendations which could prove useful in crafting a programme at the institutional level was advocated by Blum. These can be given consideration within the ten steps presented previously. They are:

- Organize conferences with faculty and students. Put the issues out in public; spell them out so everyone knows what we are talking about. Allow students a voice in framing the issue.
- Admit that the rules are rather arbitrary. Intellectual property is not an eternal value.
- Demonstrate and admit the lack of agreement between students and faculty or administrators.

- Raise the problem of intellectual property as a theoretical and historical issue.
- Separate intellectual, legal and bureaucratic dimensions of academic citation.
- Compare students' quotation and inter-textual practices with academic citation practices. Be explicit about the similarities and differences in citing and quoting, paraphrasing and borrowing. Show there are different norms in different contexts – for instance, quoting from movies versus books, in papers – all legitimate in their own way.
- Sort out the various sorts of plagiarism. (Blum 2009)

These suggestions from Blum are insightful as she promotes education as a means of developing academic integrity and targets areas identified in the research as problematic, such as the differences in perception of staff and students. She also highlights the grey areas that are likely to lead to confusion, such as the arbitrariness of rules. These recommendations, if implemented, should help to decrease frustration and confusion among students.

Benson and colleagues sum up the need for institutional support by outlining the reasons the various stakeholder groups are important. They state that:

> At the immediate level, a buy-in is required from faculty members, as they constitute the frontline interface between students and the University. At the next level comes the necessary endorsement from department chairs and deans, and beyond this, engagement by university-wide support departments, such as academic integrity offices and technical support from the staff responsible for maintaining Learning Management Systems, such as Blackboard. In addition, institutional champions are needed to take on the important role of communication and dissemination of project status and progress and, most importantly, to develop a realistic work plan with distinct goals and objectives (2019, 14).

Attention to the inclusion of various groups and outlining the contributions they can make will ensure that the programme is more likely to succeed.

The Role of the Library in Promoting Academic Integrity

Librarians are natural partners on the journey to accomplishing academic integrity in any institution. Two countries that integrated the library into their attempts to develop academic integrity are Cyprus and Hungary (Glendinning 2013). Lynn Lampert (2006) of California State University makes a case for the inclusion of librarians noting that they are usually exposed to students' cheating when they sit on committees dealing with cases of academic misconduct and are sometimes required to search for plagiarized sources, a role described as "anti-plagiarism enforcer" by Wood (2004, 237). This, therefore, gives them an insight into plagiaristic practices within the academy. Gail Wood, director of libraries at SUNY Cortland in New York, is a librarian who served as chair of the Academic Grievance Tribunal, which hears cases of academic misconduct. Based on her experience she states that "librarians could assume a strong, active role in the process of modeling academic integrity within the institution." She further states: "A librarian's understanding of the Internet and the flow of scholarly information would be helpful in not only avoiding academic dishonesty, but also in developing a strong expressive voice in the student-scholar, one who uses information wisely and appropriately in support of original ideas" (2004, 237).

Lampert advocates some ways that librarians can advance academic integrity in their institutions. These include conducting investigations into plagiarism and unethical use of information from a disciplinary perspective; familiarizing themselves with preferred styles of formatting and code of ethics for the disciplines; investigating the standards needed for accreditation based on each discipline; and identifying resources geared towards the study of the ethical use of information in each discipline (2006, 9). This list presents a very passive role for librarians, confining them to the traditional role of resource providers, a view too often held by institutions and library users.

Wood provides a six-point strategy for librarians to use to assist students to develop academic integrity and, hence, avoid plagiarism in which the librarian is an active partner. The librarian should:

1. Become a champion for the intelligent, ethical uses of information by knowing the definitions of academic integrity and dishonesty, incorporating values into reference and instructional services, as well as by participating in the campus-wide and interdisciplinary debates on academic integrity.
2. Teach the complexities of the web-based resources, which include the searching of proprietary databases that are not reached by web search engines, and by moving beyond plagiarism detection to teach the critical thinking skills needed to intelligently evaluate information resources of all kinds.
3. Develop partnerships with many other departments and disciplines in order to model and teach the complex role that information has in our lives.

4. Disseminate information through websites, tutorials, and other instructional materials that reflect on the relationship between the ethical use of information and academic integrity.
5. Work with faculty to develop assignments that emphasize active learning and interactions with scholarly materials and class exercises that emphasize the research process, good study skills and sound time management.
6. Balance the use of detection software with preventative behaviours, such as honest discussions during instructional sessions and during reference encounters (2004, 240).

As part of their training, Caribbean librarians are usually equipped with some skills to execute the strategies identified above. They possess specialist knowledge in resource management that might not be in the repertoire of academic staff. They are also knowledgeable about issues of intellectual property rights and the ethics of information use and management. Given their broad knowledge as information professionals, they should therefore be actively engaged in the drive to develop programmes and policies for academic integrity. However, if academic librarians in the Caribbean are required to function in the roles outlined above, consideration would need to be given to the levels of involvement and the amount and type of additional training needed. An additional consideration would be how to assign duties to librarians who already might be executing a variety of job functions. Institutions would need to decide if there is a need to employ additional staff or reassign the current staff.

One of the avenue through which librarians can positively contribute to the institution's attempt to develop academic integrity is through the teaching of information literacy. Participating in various committees concerned with academic integrity gives the librarian knowledge that can be used in the design and implementation of education programmes. This is recommended since librarians are charged with the responsibility to "coordinate and deliver information and digital literacy sessions to students, researchers and staff" ("Academic Librarian" 2020). The teaching of information literacy in HEIs is guided by the Association of College and Research Libraries' (ACRL) Information Literacy Standards for Higher Education, and Lampert suggests the integration of information literacy into academic integrity.

ACRL (2016) advocates that information literacy promotes the concept that information has value because it is a commodity. Therefore, students should respect the creative work of others and give credit to the creators of knowledge. They should also see themselves as contributors of knowledge and not just consumers. ACRL further states that students should see research as inquiry and scholarship and also as conversation. In this context, they follow established legal and ethical guidelines in gathering and using information. They are also expected to seek multiple perspectives in the information-gathering process and request help when needed. Information literate students also see information seeking as strategic exploration and seek guidance from experts, such as librarians and faculty (Association of College and Research Libraries 2016). ACRL presents the teaching librarian as a multiskilled person who carries out many roles as shown in figure 17.2.

All these roles are important to the academic integrity programme. As an instructional designer, the librarian is able to help develop the education component of the programme and conduct lessons as the teacher and teaching partner. As an advocate, she can speak out on behalf of the students, ensuring they get the assistance they need. If librarians are to support the development of academic integrity, they also have to be lifelong learners as a result of the rapid changes in the way knowledge is shared, created, distributed and stored.

Information literacy sessions are aimed at helping students to achieve maturity in their use of information. Wood (2004) presents a graphic illustration of the integration of academic integrity into information literacy through its Information Literacy and Integrity Model presented in figure 17.3.

This model clearly shows that the student at the heart of the model is expected to acquire a variety of skills in order to use information effectively and ethically. These skills range from locating and selecting the resources from which to extract information to citing the sources used. Academic integrity would be incorporated into the various tasks on the model.

There are several models for the integration of the library in the academic integrity programme. The Rochester Institute of Technology presents an example of an academic library that houses the academic integrity team which has developed online modules for the teaching of academic integrity. It focuses on both traditional and non-traditional forms of plagiarism in its online teaching modules and has sample lessons for faculty on teaching academic integrity. The library also hosts an annual academic integrity fair and developed a podcast series for teaching academic integrity (Nicosia 2019). Librarians were also important stakeholders in the development of the collaborative teaching and learning design implemented by Latrobe University (2021).

The University of South Florida is another example of an academic library that is actively involved in academic integrity. It designed and implemented an online series of three games for STEM graduate students. This was a collaborative project between the University of Florida Marston Science

Figure 17.2. Roles of teaching librarians.

Librarians and the University of Florida Digital Worlds Institute (Leonard et al. 2013). Schrier and Gibson developed a set of recommendations for persons and institutions interested in designing games to teach ethics education, by drawing on interdisciplinary research (2011, 1372). Librarians can use these as guides to design games for the academic integrity programmes.

The library of the University of Notre Dame in Australia has a web page called *Checklist: Library Information Skills Toolkit* which includes videos, tutorials and quizzes on academic integrity. These are organized by academic disciplines and include American Psychological Association and Chicago citation guides. The academic library, therefore, seems to be a good place to host the resources for the academic integrity programme, a practice in some Australian libraries (East and Donnelly 2012, 9). Academic librarians in some institutions such as the UWI are involved in academic integrity activities including checking of curricula vitae for academic staff to verify publications, checking of theses for graduate students and conducting

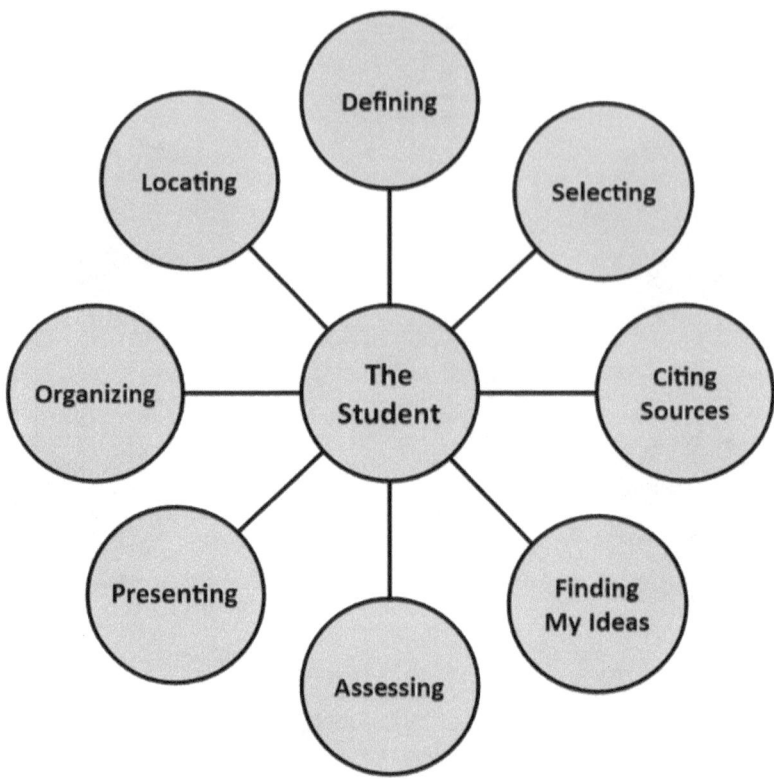

Figure 17.3. Information Literacy and Integrity Model.

information literacy sessions. With some adjustments in their current operations, academic libraries in the Caribbean should be able to become actively involved in the development, implemetation and maintenance of academic integrity programmes in their institutions.

Academic libraries serve faculty as well as students, and therefore the library's focus on academic integrity should include both groups as seen in the previous examples. Mansoor and Ameen conducted a survey of ninety-nine university libraries and interviewed nine librarians in Pakistan to determine their roles in preventing plagiarism among researchers. These libraries offered theses checking services for graduate students and provided training to faculty in the use of text-matching software. The researchers found that library staff was willing to assist in preventing plagiarism. They believed that support from the university administration and effective policies would help libraries to be more effective in discharging this duty (2018, 241).

Gilbert outlines that library staff can assist with the programme in the following ways:

Resources for faculty can be provided by librarians for accessing the most recent information about academic dishonesty and plagiarism. Classroom faculty can usually rely on their library colleagues for information regarding commercial term paper mills, research paper archives, web sites with archived student papers, access to electronic versions of journals that are not likely to appear in typical web searches, tools for differentiating purposeful from unintentional academic dishonesty, the omission of data in order to slant an argument, detecting plagiarism, access to online classroom lecture notes, and more valuable resources. Librarians can demonstrate both helpful faculty resources and Internet cheating web sites at faculty workshops conducted during flex day, department meetings, and other professional development activities (2007, 11).

This is a very detailed listing and encompasses the many ways librarians serve faculty. It would therefore be helpful if at least some of these were combined in the formal programme for academic integrity within the Caribbean institution.

The academic integrity programme at each institution is likely to be different based on the uniqueness and needs of the organization; however, ensuring that each programme is built on a good foundation and guided by effective principles is important as this will determine success or failure. Institutions will therefore be required to carry out institutional assessments such as strengths, weaknesses, opportunities and threats (SWOT) analysis in order to ensure that the programmes that are developed are fit for the intended purpose.

Conclusion

A national framework for academic integrity provides the context within which institutions can design and develop their programmes based on the triad for academic integrity which consists of societal expectation, faculty implementation and institutional framework. Embedded within the triad is the student for whom the academic integrity programme was implemented. Caldwell's (2010) ten-step process for the establishment of academic integrity programmes is suggested as a model that can be used to guide the development of institutional policies. Within this process, consideration needs to be given to Blum's (2009) recommendations. Academic libraries are valuable partners in the establishment of academic integrity as librarians are equipped with the knowledge and skills to assist both staff and students to develop and practice integrity. Institutions would do well to include librarians on committees and teams working to create and implement programmes for academic integrity. The resources for academic integrity can also be housed in the academic library and on its website since this is a central place used by both staff and students.

Chapter 18

Roles and Responsibilities of Faculty and Students

Introduction

With reference to the triad for academic integrity, this chapter discusses the roles and responsibilities of faculty and students. First, it examines the importance of faculty as critical partners in developing and maintaining academic integrity based on the literature. Then it utilizes Pavela, McCabe and McDuff's *Principles of Academic Integrity for Faculty* and Chickering and Gamson's *Seven Principles for Good Practice in Undergraduate Education*, to describe ways faculty can ensure the development of a culture of academic integrity. The chapter then discusses the roles and responsibilities of students in developing and practising personal and institutional integrity. It also briefly examines barriers inhibiting the engagement of faculty and students in academic integrity activities.

Faculty as Critical Partners

Lee (2019) believes that academic integrity is a part of the fabric of an institution's reputation whether this reputation is positive or negative, and that a positive institutional reputation comes from faculty and culture that promote academic integrity; however, a negative reputation can be a result of cheating scandals. Academic misconduct does not only impact an institution's reputation as Fish and Hura believe students benefit from doing their own work as they learn research skills, writing skills and content , an opportunity that is missed when they cheat. Therefore when they operate in an environment where academic integrity and learning are emphasized, they reap long-term benefits (2013, 42). Faculty is critical to achieving this goal, and Morris and Carroll believe that any focus on academic integrity which aims to be holistic must focus on what staff is doing (2016, 1). They identify several categories of staff as critical, including senior, professional, teaching and academic support staff and quality assurance specialists (2015, 3). The discussion in this chapter focuses on faculty. Other staff members who work with the programme would be a part of the institutional framework.

Faculty Implementation: Faculty implementation of the programmes for academic integrity forms one side of the triad as their actions must be considered within the framework of an institution's commitment to academic integrity. A focus on faculty is integral to the development and maintenance of a culture of academic integrity as they are the persons who directly influence students' perception and understanding of academic integrity (Dant 1986, 83). Benson et al. call faculty the "frontline interface between the university and the student" (2019, 14). Morris agrees and explains that faculty's perception of plagiarism will likely influence their approach, in that, on the one hand, faculty may believe it is the students' responsibility to educate themselves on plagiarism; thus, any infringement of the institution's policy could be seen as intentional. This is the "transmissive" approach. On the other hand, there is the transformative approach where the educators acknowledge the complexity of plagiarism, believe that it is an organizational issue and take a developmental approach which is likely to include academic writing (Morris 2016, 5).

Faculty are influential, so much so that informing "students that instructors look for plagiarism in assignments and that there are consequences if it is discovered can help to deter students from plagiarizing and create an environment where it is clear that ethical behavior is valued" (Fish and Hura 2013, 42). Thus, faculty are an important element in the triad for the following reasons:

- Individualized faculty responses to plagiarism are cited as one of the main factors which undermine institutions' attempts to successfully develop academic integrity (Walker and White 2014, 4).
- Faculty "bear the initial burden of a decision on how and whether to respond when violations are discovered" (Stowe 2017).
- In examining the reasons students plagiarized, Vázquez-Recio et al. noted that some of these were due to teachers and the teaching models and methodology they employed (2016, 5711), a finding supported by Berlinck (2011, 368). Students from Slovenia voted teaching methods the second most influential factor fuelling plagiaristic behaviours (Jereb et al. 2018b, 11).
- Students are more likely to plagiarize when there is a low possibility of being caught (Power 2009, 649), and also if the lecturer does not explicitly warn against the behaviours (Sisti 2007, 221). So faculty serve both an educative and preventative role.
- Staff have "highly personalized definitions of plagiarism," which may differ from that of students and the institution. This may impact the policy implementation phase of the programme (Flint, Clegg and Macdonald 2006, 152). Common ground is needed if the academic integrity programme is to achieve success.

Any attempt to develop a culture of academic integrity in HEIs must give priority to faculty as an important stakeholder and should seek to minimize or eliminate the teacher-related factors that mitigate against achieving this goal. They are unable to carry out their roles effectively if they do not possess the requisite knowledge of academic integrity and understand the processes in place to educate students and manage infractions. This focus on faculty is likely to help to ensure a common institutional understanding of academic integrity and result in a more even implementation of such a programme.

According to Wilkinson, students were confused by the different approaches of staff members to plagiarism. To further compound the problem, 78 per cent of staff felt they gave adequate information on plagiarism to students compared to the 43 per cent of students who felt they were receiving adequate information. In addition, staff did not commit to checking for plagiarism and "students were receiving mixed messages about expectations and penalties and this may be contributing to students' failure to understand the rules of referencing and how to avoid plagiarism" (Wilkinson 2009, 103–4). Therefore, as a major stakeholder in the development and practice of academic integrity, the faculty's role must be given careful consideration.

Support for Faculty: Floyd, Taylor and Queen (2019) advocate that institutions which are serious about developing a culture of academic integrity need to dedicate time and resources to the programme. On the contrary, Parnther (2016) identified limited resources of time and money as challenges to the provision of opportunities for academic integrity education by some institutions, and these are real problems that Caribbean HEIs are likely to face. Given the importance of the role of faculty in the implementation of a programme of academic integrity, some amount of time and resources will need to be expended to provide both administrative and moral support (Gamage, de Silva and Gunawardhana 2020, 2). This will ensure that institutions have structures in place to make teaching students about academic integrity and reporting infractions as seamless as possible, given that part of the challenge of dealing with academic misconduct is the time that it demands from faculty who are already performing several other roles (Marsden 2014).

Faculty will need to be sensitized about the need for academic integrity education, and their knowledge and skills in the area of academic integrity may need to be strengthened. Given that faculty sometimes have differing knowledge and perceptions on the topic (Louw 2017, 125–26); professional development will be required (Saddiqui 2016, 10). Within the Caribbean this can be accomplished through workshops and seminars as professional development for staff is expected to be part of the offerings of all HEIs. This should prove to be cost-effective as existing structures would be used. Another faculty related challenge identified by Parnther (2016) is the lack of engagement of part-time faculty who have commitment elsewhere, and she suggests providing them with increased opportunities to share and disseminate ideas. This could be facilitated in the many research forums that are part of the daily activities of HEIs. Another activity that could be used to combat the impact on students due to the inability of part-time faculty to engage with academic integrity activities is to have some departmental sessions on academic integrity for students. This would ensure that they are provided with support in the event the part-time lecturers are not able to do so.

Strategies for Developing and Practising Integrity

There are a variety of strategies that staff can implement to support the goal of institutional integrity, and they can be guided by the *Principles of Academic Integrity for Faculty* developed by Pavela, McCabe and McDuff (2017), and the *Seven Principles for Good Practice in Undergraduate Education* postulated by Chickering and Gamson (1987). The combination of these two was successfully used by Craig and Dalton to develop a communications programme at an engineering university in the United Arab Emirates. It resulted in decreasing plagiarism and improving students' critical thinking skills (2014, 64). These principles find support from the literature as will be evident in the discussion.

Eight of Pavela, McCabe and McDuff's ten principles of academic integrity for faculty will be presented in this section as actions faculty can take to assist students to develop and practise academic integrity. The remaining two were already discussed under the role of the institution. The common elements in their list and that of Chickering and Gamson have been aligned in table 18.1 and will be discussed together.

Based on the overlaps between the two lists, it seems plausible to consider that developing academic integrity is one of the "good practices" in undergraduate education, and rightly so. Further discussion of the strategies faculty can employ in order to transition from policies to academic integrity culture is presented in the following sections. It must be noted that not all the strategies are applicable in every situation.

Affirm Academic Integrity as a Core Institutional Value: In order to ensure that academic integrity is treated as a core value of the institution,

Table 18.1. Comparison of principles of academic integrity and principles for good practice

Pavela, McCabe and McDuff *Principles of Academic Integrity for Faculty* (Updated 2017)	Chickering and Gamson *Seven Principles for Good Practice in Undergraduate Education* (2019)
Affirm academic integrity as a core institutional value	
Provide clear expectations for academic integrity and assess how well students understand them	Communicate high expectations
Reduce opportunities and temptations to engage in academic dishonesty	
Respond to academic dishonesty when it occurs	Give prompt feedback
Know your students and encourage their capacity for learning, self-management and trust	Encourage active learning Respect diverse talents and ways of learning
Develop creative forms of assessment that enhance student learning	Emphasize time on task
Affirm the role of teachers as guides and mentors	Encourage contact between students and faculty
Foster a lifelong commitment to the pursuit of knowledge	
	Develop reciprocity and cooperation among students

Bretag's suggestion to ensure that academic integrity is visibly displayed in the university's mission statements, marketing, admission processes, academic integrity policies, assessment practices and curriculum design (2013a, 2) is very pertinent. In institutions where academic integrity is a core value: stakeholders are clearly identified and their roles established; students know about academic integrity; stakeholders are able to identify physical evidence of its presence such as an office or a person; and students know where they can get needed help on the topic if they so desire. In order for Caribbean institutions to achieve this desired state, there will need to be substantial policy changes.

Whereas the institution is the leader in ensuring academic integrity is a core value, faculty is integral to the implementation of the strategies and policies within the courses they teach, and Parnther (2016) found they were the most influential persons in the institution when it came to academic integrity. Students are more likely to cheat in courses where lecturers do not explicitly discuss plagiarism nor warn against it (Sisti 2007, 221; Broeckelman-Post 2008, 206). Faculty, therefore, need to become "academic integrity champions" (Bretag and Mahmud 2016, 1), helping to educate students about institutional policies and requirements and ensuring these are followed. One way this can be done is by inclusion in course outlines (Nushi and Firoozdohi 2017, 1). In reinforcing academic integrity as a core value, faculty also need to ensure that they engage students in discussions about academic integrity at the beginning of the semester. In Caribbean institutions where accountability statements are used, the purpose of these should be clearly stated. It should not be assumed that students, especially those new to the academy, understand the purpose of the accountability statements. This should be followed up with additional discussions prior to the submission of assignments. Discussion of plagiarism is also important after assignments have been marked if there is evidence of an academic breach.

Provide Clear Expectations and Assess Students' Understanding: One of the challenges with academic integrity is the differences in understanding of what it means to both faculty and students. This stems not only from the difficulty in defining aspects of academic integrity, such as plagiarism, but also from the difficulty of trying to categorize the various expressions of academic misconduct. It would be unreasonable to expect students to embrace and practise academic integrity without ensuring they have the requisite knowledge base; therefore, it is incumbent on institutions to educate students.

According to Pavela, McCabe and McDuff, there should be a formative assessment of this knowledge to provide opportunities for the implementation of remedial actions, where necessary. Pavela, McCabe and McDuff (2017) also state that students should be provided with guidelines for academic integrity in advance including the behaviours that are not acceptable when they do collaborative work, the penalties for failing to abide by the guidelines and information on how academic integrity enhances students' learning. These are best provided by the faculty who interface with students daily. Finally, students should have an opportunity to discuss these expectations with the faculty. In addition, Gullifer and Tyson believe HEIs should provide opportunities for active engagement with the policy in ways that will not contribute to the information overload usually experienced by students (2014, 1214).

High Expectations: Chickering and Gamson (1987) believe if faculty expect more in terms of learning, they will get more from students at all levels of the system. Certainly, if faculty hold the bar high for academic integrity and provide students with the skills and tools needed, they will rise to the occasion. Academic integrity is an important element of the learning process, and if students understand this, it is expected they will strive to act with integrity. Faculty is critical to the buiding of this knowledge.

Reduce Opportunities and Temptations: Pavela, McCabe and McDuff (2011) suggest faculty can reduce these by enhanced security and better classroom practices. To accomplish this, Bailey suggests teachers can adopt some of the following strategies to reduce possible misconduct: choose plagiarism-proof topics, require multiple drafts, request handwritten portions, use in-class portions, and require a combination of paper and online sources (2011a). Assignments and instructions should be clear (Pavela, McCabe and McDuff, 2017), and faculty should avoid recycling assignments from year to year so as to decrease the temptation for students to cheat (Walker and White 2014, 8). High-quality assessment which limits opportunities for plagiarism can be accomplished by having another faculty member, possibly a second marker, review tasks before they are given to students. HEIs in the Caribbean already have the practice of assigning a second marker to their courses, so this should not be too difficult to implement.

Faculty also need to maintain vigilance throughout the semester, for example students are more likely to cheat in courses where there is little possibility that they will be reported (McCabe 2011), or where there is scarce or superficial monitoring (Vázquez-Recio et al. 2016, 5711). This was borne out by one respondent who provided some of the qualitative data on the questionnaire. She commented that the lab technician "does not really check if we plagiarise, so we are tempted to reword." Faculty, therefore, need to be vigilant and capitalize on the opportunities that have the potential to be teachable moments and use them as such.

Provide Feedback and Respond to Academic Dishonesty When It Occurs: Feedback is critical to student learning. Wees (2010 citing research conducted by Choy, McNickle and Clayton 2009) notes that students regarded timely feedback from teachers as very important to their performance and the opposite is also true. Feedback helps students who are learning about academic integrity to understand which behaviours conform to acceptable practices and so strengthen the likelihood of them being repeated, as well as highlight unacceptable behaviours, thus reducing their occurrence. According to Chickering and Gamson, "No feedback can occur without assessment, but assessment without timely feedback contributes little to learning" (1987).

Where students choose to cheat in spite of the many structures in place to help them, faculty need to act in ways prescribed by the institution as this is feedback. It would also be helpful if faculty share outcomes of cases of plagiarism with students (Berlinck 2011, 370) in order to help them understand the institution's commitment to treating breaches of policies and guidelines. This will send a signal to students that misconduct will not be tolerated and should therefore serve to decrease its occurrence. Further, it should also dispel the notion that there are no consequences for cheating, thereby deterring future occurrences (Fish and Hura 2013; Broeckelman-Post 2008).

Know and Encourage Students: Pavela, McCabe and McDuff advocate that one principle of academic integrity for faculty is, "know your students and encourage their capacity for learning, self-management and trust" (2017). Where there are small classes and tutorial systems that facilitate knowing the students, institutions should encourage this and the faculty should seek to practise it. In large university systems, it might seem more like an ideal that might not be feasible, a challenge noted by Barrett et al., who reported that classes in their institution had approximately 250 students (2004, 52) which made establishing personal contact challenging. Within the higher education structures of the Caribbean, large lectures, "short" semesters and high numbers of adjunct lecturers might mitigate this, but it should be encouraged where possible.

Respect Diverse Talents and Ways of Learning: Howard Gardner's theory of multiple intelligences is well known to educators and should be reflected in classrooms at all levels. To do otherwise would be to expect learners to learn in ways that are unnatural to them which might encourage cheating. The essence of this theory is that human beings learn in different ways, and instructions should be varied, catering to the eight general ways (intelligences) in which individuals learn (Cherry and Morin 2019). In keeping with Gardner's theory, Chickering and Gamson (1987) advocate that while students are expected to learn in new ways, they should also be allowed to learn in ways that come naturally to them. They postulate that whereas teachers and students have responsibility for the quality of education, HEIs and the education administrators have to lead the charge in this by shaping an environment that is favourable to good practice, one of which is academic integrity.

Encourage Active Learning and Creative Assessment: Active learning, recommended by Chickering and Gamson (2019), is defined as "a broad range of teaching strategies which engage students as active participants in their learning during class time with their instructor." This involves students working together during class, and also doing individual work and reflection. Creative assessment which is a natural outcome of active learning, is one sure way to decrease plagiarism. Creative assessment should help to decrease the incidence of assignments that are not clear or are too theoretical, both of which are likely reasons for students to plagiarize (Vázquez-Recio et al. 2016, 5710). This challenge was noted by Caribbean students in the analysis of qualitative data collected by this researcher. They believed that assignments that were too challenging would influence them to plagiarize.

According to Brigham Young University (2019), alternative assessment, also known as performance tests or authentic assessment, is an assessment method aimed at measuring proficiency rather than knowledge. Although it can be costlier and the rating process more subjective than traditional assessment, Brigham Young University (2019) promotes it because, when compared to traditional assessment, it has the advantage of facilitating the assessment of valuable skills. In addition, it is usually done in a more realistic setting, focuses on student performance and quality of work and can be easily aligned with established learning outcomes. By its very nature, alternative assessment limits the opportunities for students to cheat and creates more opportunities for the application and development of higher-order thinking skills.

Pavela, McCabe and McDuff (2017) advocate for a shift in the role of assessment from assigning grades to evaluating if learning has taken place. They, therefore, advise that peer and self-assessment should be encouraged. This is in keeping with a recommendation from the University of Waterloo. In its report on the findings of the academic integrity survey, the University of Waterloo found that there was a need to adjust the methods used for student evaluation in order to inhibit cheating (Office of Research Integrity, University of Waterloo 2013).

In supporting the effectiveness of authentic assessment, the University of Tasmania contends that "the most effective approach to reducing or eliminating cheating and plagiarism in your unit is through a combination of teaching about academic integrity, and designing assessment that minimizes the opportunities" (2018). Some universities globally provide guidance to faculty, similar to that given by the University of Tasmania, aimed at reducing plagiarism in assignments. These include the University of Surrey (United Kingdom), Oxford Brooks University (England), Carleton University (Canada) and the University of West Florida (United States). In his *Practical Assessment Strategies to Prevent Students from Plagiarising*, Hendry (n.d.) suggests faculty could also require students to complete a reflection as part of the assignment. There is a need for additional training in assessment techniques for faculty (Gamage, de Silva and Gunawardhana 2020, 21), so they will be better able to design effective alternative assessments.

Emphasize Time on Task: Students need strategies for managing time so adequate attention can be given to academic pursuits. Time management is critical given the short semesters, which in the Caribbean last approximately thirteen to fifteen weeks, the number of assignments to be completed for each course, and the fact that many students manage multiple roles such as parenting, work, spousal responsibilities and so on. In addition, there is the students' propensity for procrastination (Sureda-Negre, Comas-Forgas and Oliver-Trobat 2015, 103), in addition to a lack of organization, and poor time management skills (Vázquez-Recio et al. 2016, 5711). These are some of the most significant factors fuelling plagiarism. Addressing the challenge of academic misconduct means helping students to develop strategies to cope with the factors that are likely to exacerbate the practice.

HEIs use varying strategies to help students manage their time so as to decrease the need to plagiarize. SUNY Empire State College (2021) in New York takes an exceptional approach by utilizing an assignment calculator which allows students to enter the assignment due date, the date they are going to start and the type of assignment. The calculator then provides a breakdown of the activities involved in completing the assignment and an estimate of how long it will take to complete each, thereby helping students to plan effectively to meet deadlines. Within other contexts such as the Caribbean, faculty can help students to manage their time by breaking assignments into smaller blocks, with timelines added. Whatever system the institutions and faculty choose to use, what is imperative is that the time factor is a significant contributor to plagiarism, and some attention needs to be given to how to lessen its effects.

Teachers as Guides and Mentors: Learning is a journey and faculty need to be seen as the guides helping students to develop the required knowledge, skills and competencies. Pavela, McCabe and McDuff (2017) suggest an affirmation of the role of teachers as guides and mentors. Mentoring represents an important element of the relationship as teachers are able to use scaffolding and models of their own work to help learners. Chickering and Gamson (1987) are not as specific as Pavela and colleagues regarding the role of faculty as guides. Without specifying the type of interaction, they advise that contact between students and faculty should be encouraged. They further state that when students have contact with faculty, both inside and outside the classrooms, it is likely to increase the students' motivation and involvement. Both Chickering and Gamson, and Pavela and colleagues stress the significant influence teachers have on their students. They believe that this can assist students to act ethically. Eriksson and McGee insisted on the importance of linking students to support systems in order to mitigate the need to cheat (2015, 12). Unavoidably, faculty is a part of that support system.

Lifelong Commitment to the Pursuit of Knowledge: A desire for learning will decrease the temptation to participate in academic misconduct because these are opposing activities, and Pavela, McCabe and McDuff (2017) believe teachers can help students develop a commitment to lifelong learning. This will shift the emphasis from the acquisition of qualifications, a factor which strongly contributes to plagiarism (Heyneman 2011, 17), to the acquisition of knowledge and skills which will be necessary for future academic pursuits.

Develop Reciprocity and Cooperation: This concerns maximizing the social nature of the human being so that learning becomes a cooperative and coordinated effort (Chickering and Gamson 1987), thus decreasing the need for the competition which sometimes leads to dishonesty. This collaborative approach has the added benefit of sharpening students' thinking and deepening their understanding as they share ideas and respond to the comments and views of others. The assumption is that these students will know the difference between collaboration and collusion as the academic integrity systems in place within the institutions would have provided them with opportunities to learn.

Graduate Education on Academic Integrity

The literature points to plagiarism among graduate students (Rosentiel 2006; ASBPE Staff 2014; Ramzan et al. 2012), and although the incidence appears to be lower than for undergraduate students, it is still considered high (Plagiarism Facts and Stats 2017). Caribbean graduate students are plagiarizing and to some extent, this is due to ignorance (Baker-Gardner and Smart 2017), and this concurs with the findings of the Integrity Standards Project (Mahmud and Bretag 2013) that one in five graduate students report they have never heard about academic integrity. Based on these findings, it is expected that education in academic integrity will continue at the graduate level, as there is a need for graduate students to get a basic understanding of academic integrity and develop competencies such as knowledge of the "more subtle forms of transgressive intertextuality such as improper attribution and insufficient paraphrasing with attribution" (Hu and Sun 2017, 63).

Some institutions provide dedicated support for graduate students. The University of Waterloo in Ontario, Canada offers a compulsory graduate version of its plagiarism module. It also provides a link to the undergraduate package should graduate students require a refresher course (University of Waterloo n.d.). Many other institutions such as Penn State College of Earth and Mineral Sciences also have a webpage dedicated to academic integrity for graduate students. Some of these web pages such as that of the University of Northern Carolina contain extensive information particularly suited to the needs of graduate students, including information on the process for obtaining ethical approval for research. The approach taken by the University of Waterloo to provide basic as well as advanced material on academic integrity, and to make this available so graduate students can pursue it at their own leisure is beneficial, as it provides options based on convenience and skill level. Such an approach could be adopted for the Caribbean.

Discipline-Specific Approach to Plagiarism

The discussion of academic integrity generally does not capture the nuances of the many academic disciplines in HEIs. To ignore these differences would be to devise programmes that take a uniformed approach to plagiarism which might not be effective in practice. In analysing strategies to combat plagiarism Barrett et al. found that many were not relevant to computer science, engineering and mathematics. An additional finding of importance was that collusion was more evident than plagiarism in computer science. Barrett et al. concluded that plagiarism prevention needs to have a disciplinary focus as styles, content and assignments differ among disciplines (2004, 49–51). Simon also suggests the importance of adopting an approach to academic integrity that takes into consideration the peculiarities of non-text-based disciplines (2016, 13). This makes the roles of faculty more important as they are required to interpret institutional academic integrity guidelines and make them applicable within each discipline. The University of Leeds is one of the few institutions which provides training based on academic discipline (Role Description: Academic Integrity Officer 2011).

In examining the differences between text and non-text-based disciplines, Simon concludes that the amount of literature on plagiarism in non-text-based disciplines was significantly less. She enumerates the differences between academic integrity in these two types of disciplines, namely: what constitutes breaches of academic integrity; means and usefulness of detecting similarities; differences in professional practices; lack of recognized ways of referencing work from external sources; and differences in reasons for colluding and plagiarizing. She concludes the discussion by stating that disciplines that required non-text-based assignments need to come to an agreement on what would constitute academic misconduct but was not hopeful that this will happen anytime soon (2016, 13).

Role of the Student

Academic misconduct is likely to have a devastating impact on students, whether done out of ignorance or with intent. Considering that systems of academic integrity are developed for students, they were not considered a stakeholder in the triad but are at the centre of the process and the programme. In summing up their importance, Gallant and Kalichman state that "it is ultimately the student who comprises the academy and not the faculty" (2011, 36). They noted that students faced with an ethical challenge will respond based on their knowledge, skills and attitudes and that students normally have these four challenges:

- interpreting the situation as involving an ethical dilemma that has multiple possibilities of action, which impacts others differently (ethical sensitivity);
- determining which action is the most ethically justifiable (ethical judgement);
- giving greater value or weight to the most ethically justifiable action over self-interest (ethical motivation); and
- having the courage, conviction and determination to choose the right course of action, despite hardships, challenges and frustrations (ethical character)

They propose the latter three actions become invalid if students do not possess the basic knowledge about plagiarism and academic integrity and are not able to evaluate the situation they are in so as to exercise an ethical judgement (Gallant and Kalichman 2011, 38). This seems to be the case in students who unintentionally plagiarize. Hence, equipping students with the requisite knowledge of the topic becomes critical to developing this ethical sensitivity.

Responsibility of Students: Students have two main responsibilities in that they are expected to acquire knowledge of academic integrity and use that knowledge to inform their behaviour. Most institutions enshrine students' responsibility in their academic policies. On the contrary, rather than just being the subject of the academic integrity policy, students are expected to participate in the development and modification of the programmes (James 2016, 9). It is, therefore, expected that their ideas and input will be sought and that they will also serve as facilitators of the interventions (Saddiqui 2016, 4).

A search of the websites of several universities indicates that some outlined the responsibilities of students with regard to academic integrity. The American University of Washington DC sums up students' roles and responsibilities in a typical list with six points. They believe students are responsible for:

- pursuing conscientiously the academic objectives which they have set;

- conforming to the regulations of the university and the school or college in which they are enrolled, and of the classes in which they are registered;
- knowing the requirements for their particular courses, regarding such issues as collaborative work, use of study aids, or take home examinations;
- completing all examinations, tests, written papers and other assignments according to the standards set forth in the Academic Integrity Code;
- learning the conventions of documentation and acknowledgement of sources required in academic discourse; and
- reporting suspected violations through the faculty member, in whose course the alleged violation occurred, if the student wishes to bring forth a charge (American University of Washington DC 2019).

The responsibilities outlined by the American University of Washington DC are suitable in a context where there is an established culture of academic integrity. However, that is not the case in the Caribbean; therefore, some rudimentary work will need to be done to arrive at this point. The following five main responsibilities which encapsulate those of the American University are being suggested for the Caribbean setting. Caribbean students are responsible to: educate themselves on opportunities within the academy to get information on academic integrity; participate in programmes and activities aimed at developing and maintaining academic integrity; practise academic integrity; seek assistance when needed; seek out opportunities to reinforce existing knowledge and skills and acquire new ones; and pass on the message about academic integrity.

Get Information on Academic Integrity: The students' first responsibility is to educate themselves on all the resources and opportunities available for developing academic integrity. The understanding, based on the previous discussion, is that the institutions would have already put these in place and provided opportunities for students to be informed; therefore, within this framework, the student has to act. Caribbean HEIs have multiple ways of imparting information to students, including the use of physical notice boards, through lecturers or course representatives (where these exist), online through student portals and on the institutions' websites and via its handbooks. The literature also suggests that the information can also be made available in course outlines (Andrews et al. 2007, 1032).

Whatever the means by which the information on academic integrity is disseminated, students should make every effort to get it. Too often, students are bogged down with the university experience and sometimes with extra-curricular activities, so they tend to overlook valuable information. In addition, Gullifer and Tyson point to the challenge of information overload which might affect new students during orientation (2014, 1214); therefore, providing them with too much information on academic integrity during this period might not be very effective. Having the information accessible to students after the orientation period is advised. Academic integrity is important, and Caribbean institutions need to ensure this information is placed in the hands of the students.

Participate in Programmes and Activities: Students are also expected to take the initiative to participate in the development and implementation of programmes and activities aimed at helping them to develop academic integrity whether or not these are mandatory. No system for developing and maintaining academic integrity can be effective without the input of students in the development and implementation of the programme (James 2016, 9). Students, therefore, must make themselves available to participate in this process as their needs, expectations and feedback are integral to its outcomes. The model from Latrobe University is an example of how students can be involved in shaping the programme. East and Donnelly noted that students formed the pilot groups for the referencing tool and provided feedback which resulted in adjustments to the referencing module. In addition, 1,006 students responded to the survey to collect preliminary data about the programme (2012, 6). Caribbean HEIs have student governments upon whom administrators should be able to draw to get student participation.

The honour system which is used in some institutions in the United States shows students' involvement in academic integrity programmes by listening to cases and assigning sanctions. Caribbean students need to make themselves available to assist in developing the programme, becoming involved in its implementation by sitting on committees, giving feedback and providing assessment data to inform the development of the programme. They are also important advocates who can pass on the message of academic integrity. Students also have responsibility for helping to ensure that the reputation of the institution is kept intact, as this has implications for the value, real and perceived, of the qualifications they obtain. One way this can be done is by reporting acts of misconduct, a requirement of students at Roanoke College (Roanoke College 2012). However, it is incumbent on the institution to ensure that systems are in place where students can make these reports anonymously, so there are no repercussions. Some universities have an online reporting system that affords students anonymity.

Practise Academic Integrity: This is the most important responsibility of students. They must be willing to act with integrity, as this is the heart of the programme. This includes completing their own work, following acceptable standards for citation and referencing and ensuring group work is done following established and accepted guidelines. Regardless of the programmes and activities that are in place, they will fail if students do not choose to practise integrity. In addition, students put their academic careers at risk by failing to practise integrity.

Reinforce Existing Knowledge and Skills and Acquire New Ones: Academic integrity needs to be treated by institutions as a developmental issue and seen by students as such, and so they should be actively engaged in the process of seeking opportunities to reinforce existing knowledge and skills and also acquire new ones. Plagiarism is a complex phenomenon (Morris 2016, 5; Sutherland-Smith 2008, 3), an issue identified in the analysis and discussion of the qualitative data; therefore, the skills will need to be developed and practised over time. Students will therefore need to take the initiative to pursue their own learning through the use of resources provided by the institution.

Seek Assistance When Needed: Students also have a responsibility to conduct a realistic assessment of their strengths and weaknesses. They should then utilize the support systems provided to access whatever help is needed. Cornell University (2018) refers students to additional resources, should they need further assistance. Flinders University advises students to take "advantage of the education opportunities provided for education on academic integrity, and seek additional assistance, if required" (2021). Penn State University (2021) suggests students can seek assistance from a learning centre, counsellor, adviser or instructor if they feel overwhelmed. There was evidence of attempts to include some forms of assistance in regional policies, but some of the sources identified would not be very helpful to students as a result of their limited knowledge. Caribbean HEIs need to ensure that they provide adequate support systems for students so they know where to obtain assistance.

Barriers to Engagement of Faculty and Students

The institution needs to be aware of the barriers to faculty and students' engagement and take steps to minimize these. Some barriers preventing faculty's engagement in an academic integrity programme are inconsistent knowledge and skills, ignoring breaches, lack of institutional support, workload and stress (Saddiqui 2016, 6–7). Administrators can remedy these by appointing an academic integrity officer; providing resources for adaptation and use in the classroom; treating academic integrity as a teaching and learning issue, and providing opportunities for this to be embedded into the curriculum; and for faculty to be involved in professional development in the area of academic integrity (Saddiqui 2016, 10).

Another likely barrier to student and faculty's engagement is the challenge of finding time and space in the curriculum for academic integrity activities. As noted previously, the academic integrity toolkit could be considered as it has resources that require structured time while providing opportunities for students to pursue their own learning at their own pace. Some academic integrity activities are already embedded in the information literacy sessions being conducted by academic libraries, in addition to the content covered in foundational courses offered in some Caribbean HEIs. What would therefore be needed is auditing of these activities to see what already exists (Gilbert et al. 2007), and including these as elements in the programme so that time and manpower are maximized. Some elements of the programme could be completed by students at their own leisure, for example during the semester breaks.

The culture of the individual institution must be given due consideration as it can either facilitate or impede the implementation of a culture of academic integrity. Organization culture can be defined as "the set of values beliefs and norms together with symbols like dramatised events and personalities that represent the unique character of an organisation" (Archie P.). Understanding organizational culture is important because:

- every organization has its own personality;
- the personality of the organization defines its environment;
- it differentiates an organization from others;
- it is relatively enduring or stable over time;
- it is perceived by the members and the outsiders; and
- it exercises a significant influence on the attitudes, behaviour and performance of organizational members (Archie P.)

The discussion of the implementation of a culture of academic integrity in the Caribbean has to take into consideration the culture of the organizations in which change is to be introduced, as some institutions might be more responsive to change than others.

The concept of academic integrity as it is being promoted in this work is new to the Caribbean and so there would need to be sensitization of staff and students in order to get buy-in. Gilbert et al. suggest, "As the institution commits to a culture of academic integrity, attitudes, policies, and procedures may need to be adjusted or reviewed, but this should involve a healthy discussion among all constituents" (2007, 6). Some amount of interest in academic integrity already exists on the part of the students as seen by the level of participation in the data collection for the survey, the many questions asked by the students and the discussions generated by the questionnaire. Gilbert et al. suggest that students could assume advisory roles in institution-wide discussions, a strategy that is applicable in the Caribbean. This inclusion would also be helpful in getting buy-in and perspectives on the programme from the persons for whom the programme is being designed.

Students do not become engaged in matters of academic integrity in HEIs for a number of reasons. Some of the barriers to students' engagement include the lack of a programme for academic integrity and ignorance of policies; unfamiliar policy language; limited knowledge and awareness of academic integrity; and limited opportunities for participation. Many institutions, such as those in the region, do not have programmes for academic integrity, and it is not possible for students to be engaged if there is no avenue for engagement. Students may have access to the policy, but this makes little difference. According to the literature, the policy may be written in legal language that is foreign to students (Sutherland-Smith 2010). They may therefore not read the policy, or if they do, they might experience challenges understanding it. This makes it difficult for them to share their knowledge with others.

Another factor that might impact the students' ability to understand the policy is their limited knowledge of academic integrity, as evidenced by the findings from the qualitative data. This might be made worse by the assumptions of the writer of the policy that the audience understands the use of certain terms and concepts. In systems where there might be activities aimed at promoting academic integrity, they might offer few opportunities for students' involvement, as in some cases these are created by the university administration and handed down to students.

Given the harsh financial reality of the Caribbean and the downturn in national economies, funding academic integrity projects is likely to be a substantial challenge. While there might be existing structures in place to facilitate activities such as professional development, additional expenditure will still be required for the launch and continuity of the programme. Given the importance of academic integrity and the fact that research has found a correlation between academic misconduct in schools and dishonest practices in the workplace (Nonis and Swift 2010), institutions could seek partnerships with entities in the private sector that have an interest in the topic so that they could provide funding. Seeking grants from non-governmental organizations might also be an option that institutions can explore. Another alternative would be to develop the programme and phase it in beginning with the existing structures such as professional development for staff and gradually adding other components of the programme when financial resources are available.

Conclusion

All elements of academic integrity coalesce in the classroom with faculty and students. Faculty are an important element in the academic integrity triad as they are responsible for ensuring that the policies of the university regarding academic integrity are implemented. They do so not just by providing instructions on academic integrity but also by designing lessons and assessments which limit the students' opportunities to cheat and modelling appropriate behaviours. Students could be considered the principal actors in academic integrity, and so they occupy pride of place at the centre of the triad. They are responsible for acting ethically within the frameworks developed by the institutions and as such they will require knowledge of academic integrity as well as the writing conventions that will make it possible for them to complete tasks ethically. There are barriers to the engagement of faculty and students that need to be considered prior to the implementation of the programme.

Chapter 19

Elements of the Academic Integrity Programme

Introduction

With reference to the Prevention, Mitigation, Assessment and Curation of Academic Integrity Based on Values and Taxonomy (PACT) model, this chapter explores the elements that are vital to implementing a successful culture of academic integrity. It examines the importance of developing the capacity of both faculty and students so that they practice integrity and the resources and assessment that are important to the prevention of academic misconduct. Details are presented on reporting procedures, investigations and recommendations when there are allegations of misconduct. Advocacy for the academic integrity programme is looked at along with the role of mitigation in developing academic integrity. The honour system used in some HEIs in the United States is examined as well as its viability for application within the Caribbean. The chapter concludes with a discussion of the importance of programme evaluation.

Elements of a Programme Designed to Develop a Culture of Integrity

Having identified the roles and responsibilities of the various stakeholders in creating a culture of academic integrity, it is now important to focus on the elements that are vital to its development and maintenance. The PACT model (see figure 19.1), developed by Siaputra (2019), is used in this section to identify the elements of the programme because of its comprehensive listing of the key elements. Its graphical presentation also provides the opportunity to get an overall picture of the elements and sub-elements of academic integrity at a glance, including the way they relate to each other.

Based on the model, the four major elements essential to any programme aimed at developing a culture of integrity are mitigation, prevention, managing the allegations of misconduct, and rehabilitation. They are further divided into thirteen sub-elements, each of which will be discussed in the following paragraphs.

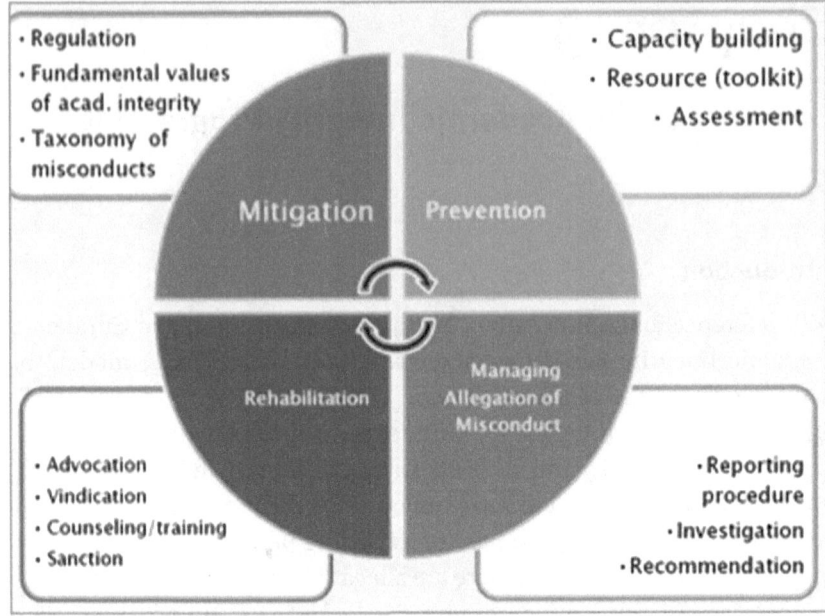

Figure 19.1. PACT model showing elements of an academic integrity programme.

Mitigation

In keeping with the view that no singular approach to developing academic integrity will be effective, Siaputra (2019) posits the need for mitigation strategies that include regulations, fundamental values for academic integrity and a taxonomy of misconducts. Students should be aware of these as knowledge of them not only helps to create an awareness of the seriousness with which deviant behaviours are treated, but their presence also indicates to students that the institution has a mandate and established procedures to treat academic misconduct. It also signals that academic misconduct will not be tolerated and removes the excuse of ignorance. More importantly, it also signals the institution's willingness to work with students to develop their capacity and help them practice integrity.

Regulation: Berlinck advocates that the "establishment, implementation and dissemination of well-defined regulations are essential to good academic conduct" (2011, 371). Hall-Hertel, Davis and Birkett (2018) agree, and in their PowerPoint presentation to the 100th Annual Conference of the National Association of Student Personnel Administrators, remarked that policies serve as the moral code of academia at an institution; promote fundamental values of honesty, originality and precision in coursework and research; outline institutional expectations; and direct the attention of individual and collective accountability in maintaining ethical standards of academic behaviour.

Most regional HEIs already have a policy for plagiarism or academic integrity. The ideal place to begin discussions on how to develop a culture of academic integrity is with this policy. Many suggestions exist in the literature as to how a policy should be written and what it should contain. A good example is the core elements of exemplar of academic integrity policy (Bretag et al. 2011, 7), with the second being the six named practices to be included in the academic integrity policy (Bretag and Mahmud 2016) and the third is Pecorari's six common elements of a plagiarism policy. Each of these will be discussed in turn.

The Academic Integrity Standards Project's five core elements of exemplary academic integrity policy can be used as a guide to developing new policies in regional HEIs or as a measuring tool to evaluate existing policies. Figure 19.2 shows the model with its five elements.

Based on figure 19.2, the five policy elements are access, approach, responsibility, detail and support. According to Bretag et al. (2011), access is both intellectual and physical and relates to the ease with which the policy can be located and used. Ease of use will be impacted by the language of the policy, the headings in the policy and whether the policy is well written, clear and concise. Soiferman speaks of the need for academic integrity policies

Figure 19.2. Core elements of exemplary academic integrity policy.

to be written in a language which students can understand as this is likely to promote higher levels of compliance (2016, 29). Although access is so important, Kokkinaki, Demoliou and Iakovidou found only one-third of Cypriot students reported that "policies, procedures and information about policies for plagiarism were available to them" (2015, 8).

Bretag et al. (2011) state that the policy should establish that it takes an educative approach to academic integrity and this should be included in the introduction to establish the context within which the policy will be implemented. There should also be an institutional commitment to academic integrity, reflected throughout the policy which should clearly outline the responsibility for academic integrity by the stakeholder groups and a demonstration of the institution's support for the policy. These stakeholder groups are the university management, the academic and professional staff and the students, and the responsibilities of each group should be detailed in the policy.

Support speaks to strategies for the implementation of the policy. Bretag et al. state that systems must be in place to enable:

- implementation of the academic integrity policy including procedures, resources, modules, training, seminars, and professional development activities to facilitate staff and student awareness and understanding of policy; (2011, 6); and
- proactive measures to educate students about academic writing and referencing conventions; and practical strategies to prevent breaches of academic integrity. (2011, 7)

According to the Bretag et al., the policy should also provide sufficient details about the processes and procedures involved in treating cases of misconduct. The Caribbean policies examined during this research came up short when compared to these guidelines (2011).

From the Exemplary Academic Integrity Project, Bretag and Mahmud list six practices that should be included in the academic integrity policy. These are:

1. academic integrity champions;
2. academic integrity education for all;
3. student engagement;
4. robust decision making systems;
5. record keeping for evaluation; and
6. regular review of policies and processes.

This project was commissioned by the Australian Government Office for Teaching and Learning with the purpose of developing "support materials, systems and resources to address implementation issues associated with assuring academic integrity" (2016, 1). These themes emerged from the qualitative data gathered from senior academic representatives from five Australian universities identified by the Academic Integrity Standards Project as having exemplary policies for academic integrity (Bretag and Mahmud 2016, 3). The six practices identified previously are supported by the literature.

Most institutions seem to be aware of the important role an academic integrity policy can play in helping to address issues of plagiarism. Hu and Sun note that policies can be found on the websites of most universities in the English-speaking world (2017, 57), as is the case for the Caribbean. They cite Pecorari who identified six common elements in plagiarism policies of fifty-five universities in the United Kingdom, the United States and Australia. The common elements are (a) a definition of plagiarism; (b) a discussion of acts that could be characterized as plagiarism; (c) an explanation of the wrongness of plagiarism; (d) a constructive approach focusing on education rather than punishment, procedures and sanctions for suspected plagiarism; (e) recognition of the complex nature of plagiarism; and (f) a statement on the lack of universal standards of what constitutes plagiarism (2017, 4). Lack of agreement among "experts" as to what should be included in a plagiarism policy is symptomatic of the challenge surrounding its study and manifestations. This filters down to students, a fact borne out by the qualitative data presented in chapter 12.

Fundamental Values of Academic Integrity: Siaputra believes the six fundamental values of academic integrity (honesty, trust, fairness, respect, responsibility and courage) which are promoted by ICAI (2014) must be included in the mitigation plan. These are discussed in detail in chapter 2. The belief is that the students' understanding and adoption of these values might decrease their desire to engage in academic misconduct. However, training in these values will be important to ensure that the students adopt and practice them.

Taxonomies of Misconduct: A taxonomy is "the science of classification according to a predetermined system, with the resulting catalog used to provide a conceptual framework for discussion, analysis or information retrieval" (Taxonomy 2020). Chowdhury and Bhattacharyya (2018) support the use of taxonomy in conceptualizing plagiarism and present one with entries divided into textual and source code plagiarism. Joy et al. (2009) believe that once a taxonomy is developed, it can be used to guide the creation of resources to assess students' understanding of plagiarism. Additionally, they believe a taxonomy can inform the implementation of strategies to treat breaches of academic integrity.

Tauginienė, Galžauskaitė and Razi (2019) developed the three most detailed taxonomies relating to academic integrity: one containing positive terms related to integrity, the second having neutral terms and the third comprising terms related to misconduct. The taxonomies are very detailed, and Tauginienė and colleagues explain the reason for this by saying that "a glossary of terms for the study of academic integrity developed through a well-defined conceptual taxonomy is an important contribution to the field." They recommend that the taxonomy can be used as, "source material for teaching students, training scholars and raising the awareness of the general public" (2019, 355). This is a valuable resource that can be utilised in the suggested ways in the Caribbean.

Strategies for Prevention

Ideally, all institutions should aim to develop academic integrity and, thereby, prevent academic misconduct. This can best be done by examining the many factors which lead to academic misconduct and seeking to reduce their influence. Siaputra (2019) advocates capacity building, resource toolkit and assessment as three such prevention strategies.

Capacity Building: Capacity building is a "process that supports only the initial stages of building or creating capacities and assumes that there are no existing capacities to start from" (Capacity Development Group 2009, 54). This contrasts with capacity development, defined as "the process through which individuals, organizations and societies obtain, strengthen and maintain the capabilities to set and achieve their own development objectives over time" (Capacity Development Group 2009, 54). Within the regional context, capacity development would seem to be more feasible than capacity building as students and institutions already have some academic integrity knowledge and structures (Baker-Gardner and Smart 2017; Walcott 2016), though these would need to be further developed. To say there are "no existing capacities" would therefore not be true. In support of the fact that there are existing capacities, East notes that "both staff and students can assume that students arrive at university with existing understanding of academic integrity values and concepts" (2016, 6). Therefore, instead of a focus on capacity building, this author will focus on how institutions can develop the capacity of both the students and the faculty to aid in the development of a culture of integrity.

The institution develops capacity by crafting a programme and assigning qualified personnel to implement and manage it. The capacity of staff needs to be further developed through education and training to enable them to support students in the development and practice of academic integrity while ensuring that the institutional mandate is carried out. Capacity development for students can best be achieved through education and training to include academic literacy, which is supported by Neeley (2005). The content and methodology to be employed in education and training are discussed in chapter 20.

Resource Toolkit: The concept of the toolkit emphasizes the variety of resources required to develop a culture of academic integrity. The University of Notre Dame in Australia is one example of an institution that has a toolkit showing the various components of the programme (see figure 19.3). From observing the graphic organizer, it is clear that Notre Dame University (2020) takes an institutional approach to academic integrity which involves education and participation by lecturers at the course level.

The toolkit has resources for both staff and students and shows the institutional context within which academic integrity is situated as well as identifies both the educational and policy resources available. Based on Figure 19.3, this toolkit includes a partnership with the university library, a recommended practice (Wood 2004; Lampert 2006; Lampert 2008). This multi-pronged approach in partnership with the academic library would be

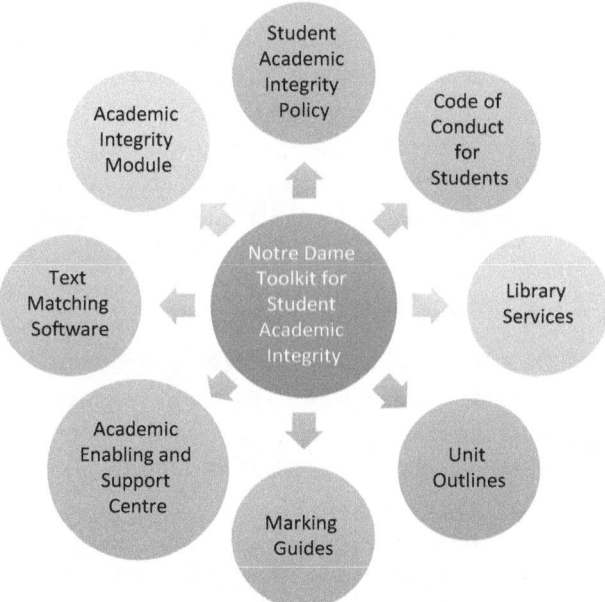

Figure 19.3. Academic integrity toolkit of Notre Dame University.

of value to the Caribbean. Some institutions already utilize this approach as library staff who participate in the teaching of information literacy were listed as sources of assistance in some plagiarism and academic integrity policies and also in the qualitative data. This partnership would need to be clearly established and the role of the academic library carefully thought out.

Assessment: Both personal and institutional assessments are vital components of academic integrity. The ICAI has a rating system called Academic Integrity Rating System that can be used to assess the integrity climate of institutions. The centre notes that this assessment serves to:

- identify benchmarks for institutionalizing academic integrity in schools, colleges, and universities;
- allow colleges and universities to quickly compare themselves to their peer institutions;
- publicize for interested stakeholders the efforts of campuses to curb cheating and empower academic integrity; and
- stimulate and provide data for the international conversation on academic integrity (International Center for Academic Integrity 2020).

This rating system is evidence of the international push for academic integrity within the global education system. It could prove useful to Caribbean institutions in their quest to develop academic integrity as it could provide the preliminary baseline data for programme development.

Personal assessment by students and faculty is important. This should include a realistic evaluation of current skills, knowledge and perception using a reliable instrument. The results from this would be useful in determining what educational interventions need to be pursued.

Managing Allegations of Misconduct

Regardless of the structures in place to develop and promote academic integrity, some breaches are still likely to occur. Siaputra's (2019) third set of sub-elements for managing allegations of misconduct would need to be applied and the allegations managed through reporting procedures, investigation and recommendations.

Reporting Procedures: The procedures for managing allegations of misconduct should be set out in the academic integrity policies, as recommended by Bretag et al. (2011). Faculty and students should be aware of these procedures as is the case at Boise State University (n.d.). In some institutions, alleged breaches can be reported via an online reporting system, for example, at the University of Mary Washington (2021). Some institutions also allow both staff and students to file reports, and there is considerable merit to giving students the opportunity to report as sometimes they might have information regarding the behaviour of their peers that faculty does not. Academic integrity education should include information on the procedure for reporting academic misconduct for both faculty and students.

Within some Caribbean countries, there is very little tolerance from some segments of society for "informers" – persons who make reports on others. Hawthorne describes Jamaica as a country with a strong "anti-informer culture" (2017, 70), and Charles (2013) uses discourse analysis to explain how this phenomenon has become entrenched in the lyrics of dancehall songs. Floyd Green, then minister of state in charge of youths in Jamaica, acknowledged the presence of this anti-informer culture and advised youths of the "importance of their role in changing the country's deeply entrenched anti-informer culture" (Baines 2018), which according to Fitz Bailey, deputy commissioner of police, hinders police investigations (Henry 2020). Trinidad and Tobago also seems to share the anti-informer culture as Gonzales (2019) reports on the murder of an individual allegedly accused of being an informer. Based on the social stigma and the possible negative consequences of making reports on others, any system established for students to make reports will have to guarantee total anonymity, and even then, there might be reluctance on the part of students to make reports on their peers.

Investigation: The burden of providing evidence for reported cases of plagiarism usually rests with the faculty involved (Thomas 2017, 106). The University of Cambridge warns that "[c]ases of suspected academic misconduct should be investigated with care and concern for both the student and the member of staff raising the case" (2021) as there can be reputational damage. Some HEIs include procedures for investigating academic misconduct on their websites, such as the University of British Columbia, Vancouver Campus. The Graduate School requires the submission of two copies of the students' work in addition to the sources from which students have copied. The faculty is required to highlight the copied portions. In cases where the student is suspected to have copied from more than one source document, the faculty member is expected to use different colours to highlight the copied portions (n.d.), a practice followed by the UWI. This activity can now be successfully done using Turnitin and therefore save the faculty member's time.

Nelms presents six questions that might be useful when investigating suspected cases of plagiarism:

1. Were ideas or language of a source or sources employed by the writer without acknowledgment of the source(s) – that is, is it really plagiarism?
2. Does the amount or significance of the plagiarism rise to the level of academic dishonesty – that is, to the level where further investigation is warranted?
3. Was the plagiarism committed within a context where the use of others' ideas and/or language is considered acceptable? Or was the plagiarist under the impression that she or he was writing within a context where plagiarism is accepted, what Brian Martin calls "institutionalized plagiarism."
4. Does it appear that the writer made an effort to adapt the ideas and/or language of the source, rather than merely adopt those ideas and/or language?
5. Does the plagiarism appear to be the result of carelessness or an inadequate understanding of the conventions of the community the writer is attempting to address?
6. If the plagiarism is determined to be intentional, are there extenuating circumstances that might warrant consideration? (2015b)

These questions can be employed by faculty and should help to determine if it is worth proceeding with an allegation of misconduct.

Acts of plagiarism can be classified on a continuum as posited by Carroll (2016). At the lowest level is "misunderstanding" by the student of what is required in academic work. In this case, she suggests that the consequence should be "significant enough to capture the student's attention." She proposed that it should be communicated to students that a repeat of this action could result in more severe penalties. Additionally, there should be support provided to encourage skills development, and this should be "efficient enough to be sustainable." In order for an infringement to be described as "misconduct," which is the middle of the continuum, there should be "evidence of high levels of misconduct." At the third level, incidents were considered "fraud" when there were "extensive attempts to deceive" and "attempts to deceive in significant work products." In addition to these two criteria, the acts must be "severe enough to threaten the university's capacity to assure the value and reliability of its qualification" (2016, 10–12).

Text-matching software can be considered a useful tool in the investigation of plagiarism; however, Caribbean institutions need to be aware of two issues related to its use. Firstly, along with highlighting plagiarized content, the software might also show quoted materials which are correctly cited if settings were not established before the paper was turned in. This means that the faculty will need to scrutinize the document to determine if the student has actually plagiarized. Secondly, material not contained in databases or available online, including those materials which exist only in print, could be plagiarized. This would not be detected since there would be nothing to check against. This is an important consideration especially in the Caribbean since many of our textbooks and primary sources might still be in physical format.

Recommendation: The likely outcome of an investigation is a recommendation for applying a sanction or for the dismissal of the case. The recommendations are likely to depend on the severity of the case and the extenuating circumstances. In some systems, the academic maturity of the student will influence the recommendations (Berlinck 2011, 369). In systems that utilize honour codes, these recommendations are usually made by students who comprise the Honour Council.

Rehabilitation

Siaputra (2019) is of the view that rehabilitation, the final quadrant of the PACT model, includes advocacy, vindication, counselling and training.

Advocacy: This is considered an important feature of any programme in order to obtain a buy-in from stakeholders. Advocacy "can be a challenging concept because there is no one set of instructions about where to begin, how to begin and what constitutes effectiveness" (The Meaning and Actions of Advocacy 2000). The Social Care Institute for Excellence (2020) identifies six types of advocacy based on who is advocating. These are self-advocacy, group advocacy, peer advocacy, citizen advocacy, professional advocacy and non-instructed advocacy. The suggestion presented in a previous chapter to utilize academic integrity champions is a form of peer advocacy that could help to promote the culture of academic integrity.

Vindication: Students involved in alleged acts of plagiarism who have been cleared of allegations ought to be vindicated. This should be done by formally communicating to the student and the faculty involved in the outcome of the case. The University of Arkansas (n.d.) allows undergraduate students the opportunity to have sanctions removed from their files after they have successfully completed a programme of remediation.

Counselling/Training: This should be provided to students who have committed acts of misconduct. Galen University (2016) uses this approach as indicated in its plagiarism policy. Some institutions accomplish this by ensuring that students go through a remediation process which includes education. In cases where students have already taken courses, workshops or seminars but they still plagiarize, they should be required to undergo additional training aimed at helping them to get a better understanding of the dangers of continuing to cheat and strengthening their academic skills, if this is needed. Counselling and training are not a substitute for penalties but should be provided in addition to them. Where it seems as if students continue to plagiarize in spite of this kind of support, institutions will need to act decisively in keeping with the procedures outlined in their policies.

Sanctions: These are a part of any system for developing academic integrity. The literature provides a comprehensive listing of sanctions which, for lesser acts of misconduct, include reduced grade, zero grade for the assignment, resubmission of assignment and warning letter. For the more severe acts of academic misconduct, the sanctions might include a failing grade for the course, and suspension or even expulsion in severe cases (McGrail and McGrail 2015, 30).

Reporting Systems

Fish and Hura suggest the need for a campus-wide reporting system to gather data on plagiarism, which can then be shared with the faculty each semester (2013, 42). Given that students are more likely to plagiarize if they believe others are doing so (Broeckelman-Post 2008, 210), this data could prove helpful in debunking this myth, considering that both faculty and students overestimate the number of students who cheat (Fish and Hura 2013, 36). Bretag and Mahmud agree with the collection and use of data on academic misconduct, stating that centralized record keeping could be used for the evaluation and improvement of educational practice. They further stated that this data could identify which courses, programmes or faculties needed additional academic integrity resources and particular cohorts of students who required support; show critical points in study periods when students are most at risk of breaching academic integrity; and identify gaps in professional development for staff. These authors advocate that even in systems where individual academic units treat academic breaches, this centralized data gathering is important (2016, 11).

Lehigh University (2021) in Pennsylvania, United States, is one institution that has an "open policy" in dealing with academic misconduct, and its statistics are available to the public online. Berlinck and other supporters of this approach (2011, 370) do so from the standpoint that transparency will drive home to students that cheaters actually get caught and might serve as a deterrent in some cases. Caribbean universities tend not to publicize this information possibly out of fear that it might tarnish their reputation.

Honour Systems

One practice in managing academic integrity in the United States is the use of honour councils and honour codes in what is called an honour system. The code is central to this system, and it is defined by Henry as, "a set of ideals governing a group. It is based on what constitutes honorable behavior among group members" (2008). Honour codes are not new, as Stanford University's code was written in 1921 (n.d.), while Rice University in Houston Texas had its honour code from 1912 (Martin 2011, 134). Honour codes require that students regulate their own behaviour and report other students who violate the code (Honour Codes across the Country n.d.).

Students participate in the honour system by signing the honour pledge. Below is one example of the honour pledge from the University of Mary Washington:

> I, as a new member of the University of Mary Washington community, pledge not to lie, cheat, or steal, and to actively contribute to a community of trust. I understand that honor is a way of life at Mary Washington and that my words and deeds impact the lives of others. As a Mary Washington student, I therefore promise to hold myself to the highest standards of honesty and integrity in all that I do and say. I further pledge that I will endeavor to create a spirit of honor, both by upholding the Honor System myself and helping others to do so. (2021)

The Student Honour Council at the University of Mary Washington is a branch of the University Student Judiciary.

The University of Maryland Code of Academic Integrity outlines the following responsibilities of the Honour Council:

- to increase awareness throughout the campus of the importance of academic integrity;
- to designate from its members students to serve as members of Honor Boards, as specified in this Code; and
- to advise and consult with faculty and administrative officers on matters pertaining to academic integrity at the University (2019, 5).

Students at Mary Washington who sit on the Honour Council are given the authority to impose sanctions on students who come before the council, and these are upheld by the university. In order to be a part of the Honour Council, students (undergraduate or graduate) have to be trained. Virginia Polytechnic

Institute and State University (2021) also have student-run honour systems with administrative oversight. In some institutions, students volunteer to be part of the honour system, which in others, such as the University of Mary Washington (2021), students are elected by other students.

Don McCabe, the founder of the Center for Academic Integrity (now ICAI), discovered that honour codes were effective in decreasing cheating in both examination and course work. He observed that on campuses with honour codes, cheating was one-third to one-half times lower than on those without and that cheating on assignments was even less (Bibliography – Academic Honesty 2006). However, research on the effects of honour codes does not always point to a positive outcome. Mason, Gavrilovska and Joyner (2019) found that honour codes by themselves were not effective in decreasing the number of cases of code plagiarism among computer science students. However, providing education in academic honesty within the context where the honour code was used resulted in significant decrease in the number of cases of plagiarism. The research on the use of honour codes is not conclusive, as Barnard-Brak, Schmidt and Wei did not find the reporting of academic violations, according to the honour code, to be more effective than the faculty's reporting (2013, 231).

Martin offers some well-thought-out suggestions aimed at ensuring the effective implementation of honour codes. He believes students must be aware of the code and understand how it operates and why it works (2011, 131). In order for the code to work, it must have support from the authority figures and the students (145). In the latter case, the students must be actively involved in implementing the codes as this provides a sense of ownership and credibility. Martin opines that the context within which the code is implemented is important as it works best when it has a long history (135); students live on campus and know each other (137); there is a climate of cooperation instead of competition; and actual learning is valued over credentials (153). The majority of institutions in the Caribbean do not offer residential facilities to students, so this might be one challenge in the use of honour codes.

Two mentions were made of the use of honour codes in the region. One was by the Northern Caribbean University (2018). However, although mention was made of the code, there was no mention of an honour system within which the code was used. Additionally, there were no details as to how it was implemented. The second mention of the honour code was in response to the allegations of widespread plagiarism at Jamaica College in 2013. One of the measures suggested by the then principal was the implementation of an honour code to ensure there was no further cheating

(Francis 2013). However, even if honour codes were to be implemented in the Caribbean, there would need to be infrastructural support, such as the toolkit suggested by Siaputra (2019), for them to be effective.

The viability of the use of the honour system in Caribbean societies is something that needs to be given consideration and possibly subjected to research. Three findings mentioned previously from the literature on the use of honour codes in the United States are worth noting as it concerns their potential success in the Caribbean region. Firstly, the literature on the efficacy of honour codes is inconclusive, and they are used mainly in the United States so there is no evidence of international acceptance of this practice. Secondly, honour codes work best in institutions that have a long history of its use, and therefore Caribbean institutions would have to implement these and give them time to see if they would be effective. Thirdly, honour codes are most effective when students live on campus and know each other. Given the large size of some regional universities (with enrolment trending up to almost twenty thousand), the fact that many students live off-campus, and there is a large number of part-time students, the use of honour codes might not be effective. To add to these challenges, the fact that most universities are moving to offer courses and programmes online makes for less than ideal situations for the implementation of honour codes.

Another factor which must be considered is whether students will be willing to participate in these honour systems. It could be argued that Caribbean students were already involved in matters of discipline at the secondary levels through the prefect and students' council system. At the tertiary level, there are the student governments and in some HEIs they are already present on some academic integrity panels. However, research into the efficacy of this approach in the region would be required. The Caribbean ranked highly in terms of having a corrupt education system. With this seemingly high level of corruption (Heyneman 2011), selection of students for participation in the honour system would have to be done based on stringent guidelines, and rigorous training would be required. There are many variables that need to be considered, and research would provide an avenue through which these can be investigated.

Ongoing Programme Evaluation

Ongoing evaluation will be important to determine whether the programme is achieving its objectives and to make changes where necessary. Metz states that programme evaluation is useful because it can help the implementation team "find out what works and what does not work; showcase the effectiveness of a program to the community and to funders; improve staff's frontline practice with participants; increase a program's capacity to conduct a critical self-assessment and plan for the future; and build knowledge" (2007, 3). She identifies two types of programme evaluations that are necessary. First, there is process evaluation which determines if the implementation of the programme proceeded as planned and if it reached the target population. This kind of evaluation also examines the major challenges and the strategies that were successful. The second is the outcome evaluation which seeks to determine if the changes are attributable to the programme or its activities (Metz 2007, 1). McNamara (n.d.) mentions goals-based evaluation which seeks to establish whether the goals or objectives of a programme were met. It is suggested that these three types of evaluation should accompany the implementation of the academic integrity programmes in the Caribbean.

McNamara (n.d.) identifies seven considerations that are important for programme evaluation. He poses these as questions that the evaluation team can ask about the programme:

1. For what purposes is the evaluation being done?
2. Who are the audiences for the information from the evaluation?
3. What kinds of information are needed to make the decision you need to make and/or enlighten your intended audiences?
4. From what sources should the information be collected?
5. How can that information be collected in a reasonable fashion?
6. When is the information needed?
7. What resources are available to collect information?

Programme evaluation should identify whether improvements are needed, and should results in changes for greater efficiency.

The University of Waterloo conducted a survey of its academic integrity system, and the report noted only 16 per cent of the academic staff felt that the process for treating academic integrity was effective. This led the university to conclude that there was a need for a more simplified process and more support for the investigation of the allegations of misconduct (2013, 6). This demonstrates the importance of evaluating the effectiveness of the components of an academic integrity system. Many HEIs in the region already have robust evaluation procedures aligned to the requirements of the national accreditation agencies, and the internal quality control systems. These can be utilized to conduct an evaluation for the academic integrity programme.

Conclusion

In order to implement a programme aimed at developing a culture of integrity in any institution, attention needs to be given to ensuring each element of the programme is carefully thought out. Siaputra's PACT model identifies prevention, mitigation, managing allegations of misconduct and rehabilitation, as the four major elements that need to be included. The emphasis, therefore, needs to be placed on mitigation, prevention and rehabilitation in order to move from the current punitive stance to an educative approach. Attention must also be paid to each sub-element in the PACT model to ensure that the programme addresses all the factors that need to be considered. Lastly, programme evaluation is important to ensure that the programme is meeting the needs of students and the institutions and inform changes where needed.

Chapter 20

Education and Training for Academic Integrity

Introduction

This chapter explores the need for training and education in academic integrity in the Caribbean. It then examines attempts in the region to provide education in academic integrity at the pre-tertiary levels and later delves into content and methodologies which can be employed in academic integrity programmes at the tertiary level, drawing on examples of global practices. It concludes by briefly focusing on professional development in academic integrity for faculty.

The Need for Training and Education in Academic Integrity in the Caribbean

The University of Waterloo found that even though students were familiar with academic integrity policies, there was an expressed need for education on academic integrity for teaching assistants, students and faculty. This finding emerged from a comprehensive study with data collected from 3,867 undergraduate students, 394 graduate students, and 277 faculty (2013, 24). A finding like this supports Nushi and Firoozkohi's conclusion that universities provide minimal instructions and information on plagiarism (2017, 13).

There are several factors that speak to the need for systematic academic integrity education for students in the Caribbean. These are:

- research findings internationally, which point to the need for students to receive academic integrity education (Hughes 2006; Hu and Sun 2017; Saddiqui 2016; East 2016; Benson et al. 2019);
- findings from research in the region (though sparse), which recommend education in academic integrity for students in HEIs (Baker-Gardner and Smart 2017; Walcott 2016; Welsh-Unwala 2019; Porter 2016);
- findings from the current research, which indicate students' lack of knowledge of plagiarism;

- lack of systematic programmes for teaching about academic integrity in HEIs resulting in limited opportunities for students to learn about and practice needed skills in a teaching-learning context, before being required to demonstrate competence;
- the students' own recommendations for the provision of education on plagiarism in the qualitative data collected for the current research and the high percentage of responses regarding the need for education on plagiarism in the quantitative data; and
- absence of or inadequate instructions in academic integrity at the secondary level (Baker-Gardner and Smart 2017; Berlinck 2011).

Although faculty agree that plagiarism is a serious offence, Parmley (2000) agrees with Nushi and Firoozkohi's (2017) finding that little teaching is done on this topic at any level of the education system. Given the wealth of literature supporting the difficulty in understanding plagiarism, this is an unacceptable situation.

It should not be taken for granted that students possess an adequate and correct understanding of academic integrity, especially those just entering tertiary education. Ismail noted that one-third of the four hundred undergraduate students in his research did not know what plagiarism was (2018, e199). To further compound the challenge, Eret and Gokmenoglu found that even among research assistants, the majority of whom were PhD students, there was a lack of knowledge of academic integrity (2010, 3306). There is evidence that some regional universities provide basic instructions on academic integrity, but these do not seem to be consistent with the needs of the students and the approach used was not as systematic as that advocated in the literature. Therefore, education and training in academic integrity is needed for students at both the undergraduate and graduate levels and also for faculty.

On the one hand, education has been promoted as the most effective way to develop a culture of academic integrity in HEIs, and it is the most frequently recommended strategy for decreasing cases of academic misconduct. East states, "Effective academic integrity education enables learners to internalize the values of the university, to acquire their own conceptual understanding of academic authorship and to take opportunities to develop their capabilities" (2016, 10). On the other hand, insistence on a punitive system of rules and punishment creates fear among students, who are frightened they will plagiarize unintentionally (Gullifer and Tyson 2013, 13), a finding borne out in the qualitative data for this study.

Education in academic integrity should result in the development of both ethical and academic knowledge and skills. Education and training is also important as it serves as a bridge between staff and students and help staff to better understand the challenges of students with regard to academic integrity, while assisting students to understand the expectations of both faculty and the institution. East notes the disparity between the views of these groups regarding academic integrity, stating that because the staff is knowledgeable about academic conventions, they may not see the necessity of providing explicit instructions on academic integrity. On the other hand, students might not be cognisant of their limited or lack of knowledge of academic integrity and might not see a need to learn about it (2016, 6).

There is consensus among researchers and students about the need for education on academic integrity (Thompsett and Ahluwalia, 2010). The positive impact of education on academic integrity was experienced by Welsh-Unwala (2019), who demonstrated through her action research carried out with students at the University of the Bahamas, that education in academic integrity can be beneficial to regional students. Over the period of five semesters, she engaged five cohorts totaling 110 students in a project, lecture, activity and discussion and they also completed assignments. At the end of the project, the results indicated that the students demonstrated increased knowledge of plagiarism, and were more agreeable to the administering of stricter penalties for breaches, In addition, they were less tolerant of the reuse of assignments (2019, 33), a practice known as double-dipping (Roig 2015).

Academic Integrity Instruction at the Pre-University Level

Although this project focuses on higher education, there is a need for academic integrity education at the pre-tertiary levels. East contends that students enter HEIs with some knowledge of academic integrity (2016, 5), which leads one to deduce that some form of academic integrity education, whether explicit or implicit, took place prior to students entering university. However, research has shown that entry-level students at tertiary institutions tend to lack adequate knowledge of the topic (Tauginienė and Gaižauskaitė 2018). This section explores the need for academic integrity education at the pre-university levels and makes suggestions as to how this can be effectively carried out.

Academic Integrity in Primary Education: There is a paucity of research on academic integrity and academic misconduct at the elementary level internationally because academic integrity tends to receive the most attention at the tertiary level. However, elements of academic integrity are sometimes taught at the primary levels during information literacy sessions. Wan and Scott suggest that academic integrity education should begin at the primary level based on the amount of time students spend online (2016, 1). They note the need to teach information literacy at the primary level; in order to stem plagiarism, and citing research, they explain that cheating behaviours among children begin in pre-school, increase in early childhood and then decrease by ages eight to sixteen (4). In addition, one of the factors which contribute to academic misconduct at the tertiary level are the misconceptions formed by students in the earlier years often as a result of miseducation (Tauginienė and Gaižauskaitė 2018). Therefore some level of academic integrity education in the early years is important.

Academic cheating in children is fuelled by pressure to achieve, lack of education on plagiarism and lack of consequences (Wan and Scott 2016, 4), and these reasons do not differ much from the reasons adults cheat. Wan and Scott advocate for providing students with early education on plagiarism which is likely to have long-term positive effects, but note that for the most part, discussions on plagiarism in primary school are centred around a policy that condemns plagiarism (2016, 7). Berlinck supports this recommendation and states, "Institutions and their professionals have a responsibility to contribute to the education of students and, therefore, students must be informed at an early age about what constitutes plagiarism and the consequences of plagiarizing" (2011, 368). Campbell (2019) suggests the following three ways academic integrity can be integrated at the primary level: teaching and utilizing the vocabulary of integrity; cultivating an environment of kindness and respect; and emphasizing the importance of a growth mindset.

Information literacy has been proposed as a strategy for developing academic integrity at the primary level; however, Wan and Scott (2016, 5) note an absence of a structured approach for teaching these skills at that level. An investigation into the information literacy skills of Australian grade 4 and 5 students revealed that although the majority of the participants understood information literacy concepts, not many students were putting the lessons into practice (Foggett 2002, 6), although these students were close to the exit point of the primary system.

No study that investigated the information literacy skills of primary students was found for the Caribbean, and up to 2005, the majority (70 per cent) of teachers at both the primary and secondary levels in Jamaica did not have any formal instructions on information literacy. This would make them ill-equipped to teach these vital skills to students (McKenzie 2005, 95). The recommendation was that the Jamaican Ministry of

Education should make the teaching of information literacy mandatory in all schools at the primary and secondary levels (McKenzie 2005, 97). Advancement was made in this matter in 2017, when the University of the West Indies (UWI), Joint Board of Teacher Education and UNESCO entered into a partnership to develop materials for the teaching of Media and Information Literacy (MIL) (Jamaica Information Service 2017). This was embedded in the curriculum of teacher training programmes for both primary and secondary teachers island-wide. However, at the time of writing, it was not possible to determine the impact of these programmes on the knowledge and information behaviour of teachers who had completed the programme. It was also not possible to evaluate the impact, if any, on the students taught by these teachers. These fell outside the parameters of this work.

Although there is an absence of plagiarism policies in elementary institutions in the Caribbean, it is expected that teachers possess some knowledge of academic integrity both from the exposure to MIL during teacher training in the case of Jamaica and from having completed at least one research course as part of the preservice training. These should make them aware of the importance of academic integrity and the need to emphasize it in the classroom.

Porter reported that after a series of workshops and discussions it was discovered that the attitude of teachers in training towards plagiarism was "less than desired" (2016, 273). The survey was administered to forty students who were being trained as early childhood and primary educators. Porter further found that "while students could define plagiarism, their application of the knowledge did not consistently bear out this awareness. While admitting that it was wrong to plagiarise, many did not think there should be any consequences" (273). These student-teachers demonstrated the same kind of ambivalence to plagiarism as those who participated in the survey reported in part 2 of this book. Given this kind of scenario, it is unlikely that without further education these teachers were likely to emphasize plagiarism when they begin their teaching careers.

Academic Integrity Education at the Secondary Level: When compared to research on academic integrity at the primary level, the body of research on academic integrity at the secondary level is more robust; however, compared to the vast cache of research on academic integrity in HEIs, the quantity is negligible. Internationally, it has been established that secondary students are cheating (Sureda-Negre, Comas-Forgas and Oliver-Trobat 2015; Yeung et al. 2016). Tauginienė and Gaižauskaitė posit that cheating at the tertiary level is actually a result of practices developed during high school and contend that the level of maturity of students who enter HEIs makes it difficult for these institutions to successfully manage academic misconduct (2018, 105). This makes academic integrity education at the secondary level a critical component of academic integrity development in the Caribbean.

Although academic integrity at the secondary level has not been researched in the Caribbean in any significant way, there is evidence that Caribbean students are also cheating. This assertion is based mainly on the newspaper reports from across the English-speaking Caribbean and the data analysed from the regional examination council as presented in previous chapters. The challenge, therefore, becomes how to provide support at the secondary level to assist students in developing academic integrity since cheating by secondary students seems to point to a lack of instructions on academic integrity. In a study conducted to evaluate the information literacy skills of three thousand secondary students from eight high schools in Singapore, Foo, Majid and Chang found that the overall average score of the students fell well below the minimum acceptable score (2016, 335). This would seem to indicate that even if they were being properly taught, the students were not absorbing the lessons. This is a finding that the Caribbean needs to pay attention to.

Media and Information Literacy (MIL) in the Caribbean: Education has been promoted as the most effective way of helping students to develop academic integrity which would likely have a positive impact on decreasing the number of cases of academic misconduct. Academic integrity education is sometimes subsumed under MIL and in the context of HEIs it is sometimes integrated into academic literacy courses. It must be noted that since studies by McKenzie (2005) and Foo, Majid and Chang (2017) were published, there has been a shift from information literacy to the concept of MIL. According to UNESCO, MIL "constitutes a composite set of knowledge, skills, attitudes, competencies and practices that allow [students to] effectively access, analyze, critically evaluate, interpret, use, create and disseminate information and media products with the use of existing means and tools on a creative, legal and ethical basis" (2019). UNESCO (2019) explains that all the information literacy competencies are included in MIL under which is also subsumed digital and technological literacies to reflect the changing nature of the information environment.

UNESCO has been active in placing MIL on the Caribbean agenda. As early as 2015, two workshops were held in Antigua and Guatemala titled, "Assessment of Media and Information Literacy in Latin America and the Caribbean." These was attended by participants from seven countries who were engaged in pilot testing instruments designed to assess the MIL competencies of Caribbean teachers (Assessment of Media and Information Literacy in Latin America and the Caribbean 2017). In 2017, Kingston, Jamaica, hosted the global MIL conference which saw attendees from as far as Africa. To support its worldwide programme, UNESCO has developed a MIL curriculum which is available online in eleven languages and can be tailored to meet the needs of any country. However, in spite of the efforts by UNESCO, and the fact that there is a need to provide academic integrity education to students in the region, MIL has still not experienced the anticipated level of popularity for various reasons. One of these relates to the state of most of the Caribbean school libraries with many lacking the requisite qualified staff and infrastructure to deliver such a programme on a systematic and consistent basis (Shelley-Robinson 2007, 108).

The teaching of MIL is being promoted as an effective way of developing academic integrity at both the primary and secondary levels. In their recommendations to encourage the teaching of MIL at the primary level, Wan and Scott identified online resources, some of which were free, that could be integrated into lessons by the classroom teachers. Some were based on two of the most popular models for teaching information literacy – the Big6 for older primary students and Super 3 for the lower primary classes. Wan and Scott also suggest the use of the KidsHealth website, in addition to books such as *The Pirates of Plagiarism* and *Plagiarism! Plagiarism: 25 Games and Activities to Teach Documenting and Sourcing Skills to Students*. They recommend an integrated approach to the teaching of MIL (2016, 9) which means embedding it within the curriculum at all levels and including information on the proper citation of sources.

Trinidad and Tobago has demonstrated an awareness of the need to explicitly integrate MIL into its curriculum. In the grade 5 English Language Arts (ELA) curriculum, it states that "the goal of Media and Information Literacy within the ELA curriculum is to develop a literate person who is able to read, analyse, evaluate, and produce communication in a variety of media forms" (Curriculum Planning and Development Division 2013, 26). It must however be noted that there is a greater emphasis on media literacy than on information literacy when, ideally, both should be given equal attention. Nevertheless, this is a positive step in the right direction.

Education for Integrity at the Primary and Secondary Levels

Having discussed the importance of academic integrity at the primary and secondary levels and the challenges that the lack of such instructions pose for HEIs, it is expedient to briefly examine how such a programme can be implemented. Curriculum reform is the responsibility of the Ministry of Education which usually has a unit devoted to this task. For example, the Ministry of Education of Trinidad and Tobago accomplishes this task through its Curriculum Planning and Development Division tasked with "managing the curriculum development process which includes curriculum design/development, implementation, monitoring, evaluation and review, for primary to post-secondary" (Curriculum Development and Planning Division n.d.). The Curriculum and Assessment Unit of the Ministry of Education, Technological and Vocational Training in Barbados is responsible for "the evaluation and revision of curricula in the interest of ensuring relevant content and pedagogically sound practices in our educational institutions at all times" (Curriculum and Assessment 2021). It could be argued that academic integrity is both relevant content and sound practice that needs to be given consideration in the curriculum "evaluation and revision" (Curriculum and Assessment 2021).

Building on the previously proposed regional framework with its glossary which provides the definition of terms as a guide, local ministries of education will need to develop national policies for academic integrity. These policies should outline the need for academic integrity development at all levels, specify the aims and objectives of such a programme and provide a broad framework within which this can be implemented in individual institutions. After conducting an audit of the current curriculum at the primary and secondary levels to determine the extent to which academic integrity is embedded, the Ministry of Education through its curriculum unit needs to use empirical data (such as students' knowledge and perception of academic integrity) and develop a draft syllabus for the teaching of academic integrity. This should be done in consultation with stakeholder groups like the Parent Teachers Association, students' council (at the secondary level), classroom teachers, school librarians and principals.

Training for the teaching of academic integrity is likely to be necessary, and this can be done virtually to decrease cost through the trainer of trainer model. Training can be done at the regional level through an education subcommittee of the Council for Human and Social Development. Using the trainer of model, those persons can in turn train curriculum developers, principals, school librarians and teachers at the national level. CARICOM can acquire training through the International Center for Academic Integrity which has both an international mandate and expertise in academic integrity.

There is no need to develop a curriculum for MIL from scratch as UNESCO has already created one that is suited for adaptation to any environment. The curriculum, which was developed by an international team that included representatives from the Caribbean, was published in 2011 and is currently used in 653 schools in 25 countries. At the time of writing, this curriculum was under review and the Caribbean was represented by persons from The Bahamas, Jamaica, Barbados, Curacao, Sint Maarten, St Lucia, and St Vincent and the Grenadines. This curriculum is important, as the focus on the creative, legal and ethical use of information is vital in the age of technology. The flood of information can be overwhelming, so students need assistance to successfully navigate their way through it. In addition, in an environment where technology seems to be fuelling cheating (Carpenter et al. 2006, 184; Jereb et al. 2018b, 11), it is not enough to provide students with curricula that encourage technology integration without providing opportunities for them to acquire the requisite skills to manage both the technology and the information. After the curriculum is adapted, it will need to be pilot tested to ensure its suitability for implementation in individual territories, and the curriculum development units of ministries of education are the most suitable agencies to accomplish this.

Funding will be required primarily for training and research for this programme, and given the hostile financial climate in the Caribbean, funding will be a critical issue. One significant way the cost of training can be reduced is to use the online medium which has become increasingly popular as a result of the Covid-19 pandemic. This eliminates the need for ground and air travel, given the disperse geographical space of the region. Individual ministries of education could be required to contribute to the cost of the required training. In terms of funding for research, national governments such as those in countries where research universities are located can partner with these institutions to assist in conducting research. Local ministries of education can provide research grants to these institutions which already have the research expertise to conduct baseline studies on which these national programmes can be built.

In systems where school libraries exist, school librarians should be seen as vital partners in implementing a MIL curriculum because they already have the education and training in information literacy. Seeing that some schools, especially at the secondary level, already have personnel in the libraries tasked with the teaching of information literacy, some amount of staff is already in place to deliver the programme. Furthermore, where additional knowledge is needed in media literacy, this can be acquired through ongoing professional development workshops offered through the national library associations and the regional library school located at the UWI, Mona, Jamaica, given that this institution is a member of the Media and Information Literacy and Intercultural Dialogue University Network. At the primary level where there are no school libraries, MIL competencies can be integrated into the curriculum and taught by classroom teachers who are expected to have previous exposure to some of the concepts during teacher training. A newly revised MIL curriculum is also a resource which can be tailored to meet the needs of local schools.

It can therefore be concluded that some of the required structures are already in place for MIL instructions at both the primary and secondary levels so it should be possible to get national programmes operational within four years, and this timeline would include the phase for pilot testing of the programme. MIL should not be seen simply as an addition to the curriculum at these levels but instead should be considered as providing students with the skills to make curriculum implementation more meaningful and student-centred as students gain vital life skills and become empowered learners.

Developing Academic Integrity among Students in HEIs

There is difficulty understanding and defining plagiarism and other types of academic misconduct (Sutherland-Smith 2008; Thompsett and Ahluwalia 2010; Ali, Ismail and Cheat 2012). Coupled with this are students' poor writing skills (Kayaoglu et al. 2015, 1) and a lack of knowledge of how to cite (Clearly 2017). Lack of or limited education on academic integrity, or silence on the topic, might lead students to believe that it is not a serious matter. East (2016), therefore, recommends that any programme which is designed to educate students about academic integrity must:

- be designed to reach students who do not see a need for academic integrity education as well as those who believe acknowledgment conventions are strange and therefore they need explicit directions; and
- take a step-by-step approach moving from simple to complex with feedback provided from simple to complex. It should allow for individualized pathways depending on the needs of the students until completion.

In agreeing, Berklinck (quoting Macdonald and Carroll 2006) states that students should not be left on their own to develop and practise academic integrity. He believes HEIs are responsible: "a) to prepare students for their learning tasks, or show them how necessary [it] is to learn and assimilate the knowledge that they are offered; b) to establish programs and teaching methods that minimize the possibility of student plagiarism, such as memorization, repetition and reproduction in excess; c) to develop programs to prevent plagiarism rather than to apply punitive policies, though these are necessary" (2011, 368).

Lee (2016) presents empirical data to support the need for education on plagiarism, noting that students linked plagiarism with citing and referencing instead of with the appropriate use of previous research in their own writing. He also states that many students were unable to identify plagiarism in their work and in the work of others, and they were confused by the different referencing styles required by faculty from various disciplines. The desire of Caribbean students to be educated about academic integrity should provide the impetus for the region to formally address the issue. Additionally, the influence of technology and the emergence of contract cheating globally have made academic integrity an imperative at this time.

Content of the Programme: There are suggestions from the literature as to the content that should be included in the educational programme on academic integrity so it is relevant to and consistent with students' needs. This section offers some general guidelines about the content; however, it must be noted that individual institutions will need to conduct a needs analysis to determine what should be included in each local programme. Staff competencies and the institutional readiness must also be assessed to decide what needs to be included for programme delivery and the administrative structures that must be in place before implementation. Variations to the content of the programme based on faculty, level of students and gender will be given due consideration later in this chapter.

In keeping with the recommendation to treat academic integrity from an ethical, moral and educational perspective, an infusion of ethics into the curriculum should be considered. Hughes and Gallant posit, "[A]cademe should aspire to teach all students essential ethical decision-making skills, so that they may become well equipped to play an active role in the creation and maintenance of ethical organisational cultures and societies" (2016, 1). They advocate the importance of this, not only for academic integrity but for the students' personal and professional lives. Hughes and Gallant cement their arguments of whether ethics should be taught, by stating that universities were originally established with ethics as a central focus, as they were primarily concerned with matters of ethics and religion (2016, 3). Bertram and Hughes further state that formal education is one of the avenues to providing ethical development, given "declining church enrolments and disintegration of the traditional family unit" (2016, 4).

Barnard, Schurink and de Beer (2008) theorize that the schooling context impacts the development of integrity, strengthening the case for its inclusion in the programme for academic integrity.

Hughes and Gallant noted an increase in the calls for ethics in education globally. They cited the work of international organizations, institutions and disciplinary centres of ethics to show the need for and value of ethical education (2016, 5). They present four components of what they describe as an effective and comprehensive ethics education programme. These are universal standards, philosophical frameworks, embedded curriculum and a personal development plan (6). Hughes and Gallant advises that ethical decision making and training are important as a lack of these means that students have to rely on intuition and feelings which are usually influenced by biases (2016, 8) and are therefore not reliable.

Wangaard agrees that education for academic integrity should not just focus on academics. He instead advocates for education to develop students' moral identity and mentions core ethical values such as fairness, caring, responsibility and integrity as being a part of this moral identity (2016, 10). Elaine Foster-Allen opines that in developing a comprehensive, flexible framework for curriculum development and programme structure for HEIs, special attention needs to be given to the questions of personal and professional ethics (2007, 128). She served as principal of one of the oldest teacher training colleges in the Caribbean and also as permanent secretary in the Ministry of Education in Jamaica. This suggests that there is a recognized need for ethics education in Jamaica which might be possibly a reflection of the need in the wider Caribbean. Meng et al. support the inclusion of ethics education as a vital component of academic integrity education (2014, 134).

Based on the *Framework for Integrity and Integrity Development* postulated by Barnard, Schurink and de Beer (2008), in addition to religious beliefs, other factors essential to the development of integrity are parental and other role models, cultural and schooling context, disciplined upbringing and idiosyncratic life experiences. The role of schooling as a contributor to the development of integrity to include academic integrity is supported by Meng et al.. They opine that through course syllabus, learning materials and codes of conduct, universities can assist students to develop ethical sensitivity (2014, 134). They further advocate that universities can plan compulsory ethics-based workshops and conferences for students. These would help to ensure "students are equipped with fundamental understanding and belief in business values, principles and ethics, apart from possessing an entrepreneurial spirit and the ability to access and manage risk" (Meng et al. 2014, 134). Education in integrity is, therefore, important for any institution that is committed to producing graduates who act ethically.

There are suggestions from the literature about the academic content of integrity programmes, with writing instructions as one of the most common elements proposed. Smedley, Crawford and Cloete (2020) found that an intensive intervention among nursing students resulted in improved knowledge and understanding of plagiarism but had no impact on their ability to paraphrase, one of the vital skills in writing. Thus, Kayaoglu et al. advocate for writing development training programmes to remediate students' writing problems which they believe may be contributing to unintentional plagiarism (2015, 21). East (2016) concurs that education in writing is important and states, "Commencing students come to university to gain knowledge and develop skills, but in order to succeed at this, they need to manipulate academic language so they can construct and demonstrate their academic opinions according to expected communication convention" (3).

Stabingis, Šarlauskienė and Čepaitienė believe that the essential components of a programme aimed at developing student's use of the conventions of writing should include

- teaching and training of bachelor level students on literature search, correct citing and referencing;
- teaching and training of master's level students on correct citing, paraphrasing and proper academic writing;
- consulting with students on correct citing, paraphrasing and referencing through courses, in which written works have been prepared, and during preparation of final works; and
- regularly analyzing the drafts of projects and final works and discussing with students, mistakes of citing, paraphrasing and referencing, found in drafts of these works. (2014, 696)

In institutions where some elements of these already exist, there needs to be an audit of existing practices and inclusion of these in the programmes so as to avoid duplication of efforts and waste of resources (Gilbert 2007). Librarians are equipped with the skills to teach about literature searching and correct citing and referencing. Some regional institutions offer various writing courses. However, a more purposeful and focused approach to academic integrity might be desired. One observation made by students who provided qualitative data in this study was that, although the university had writing courses, the focus on academic integrity was either lacking or inadequate. This strengthens the case for the institutional audit recommended by Gilbert (2007) and supported by this researcher.

East notes that education on academic integrity usually includes a suite of activities aimed at providing support to students as they transition into higher education (2016, 5); hence, Morris supports the need for writing instruction but believes this is not enough. She proposes that academic integrity education and academic writing development are integral to helping students learn about academic integrity (2016, 1). In agreement, East notes the challenge of not informing students about academic integrity and advocates for institutions to engage students in academic integrity education while providing them with opportunities for the development of their scholarship abilities (2016, 2). Berlinck introduces another aspect to the discussion on academic integrity education. He believes that the role of the institution should be to "establish programs of discussion sessions between teachers and students about academic integrity, the nature of the assessments, the value of the acquisition and application of critical analysis and elaboration of the original texts" (2011, 368).

One of the advantages of providing students with a suite of activities is the opportunity to cater to the needs of the various groups within the institution, for example, males compared to females, undergraduates and graduates, and students from various disciplines. The recommendation is that there should be a basic set of resources for all undergraduate students which teach them the rudiments of academic integrity and provide them with resources aimed at helping them to act with integrity. This should include instructional activities such as short courses on how to write and cite, and these can be supplemented with online resources such as videos. Additional resources should be included in the suite such as resources for graduate students which teach more difficult concepts that are required at this level. Within this structure, programme developers could also include information that is beneficial to various disciplines such as how to use Oxford Standard for Citation of Legal Authorities or Oxford referencing which is specific to law. The suite approach would allow institutions to cater to the general population while still meeting the needs of subgroups.

The greatest disadvantages to this approach would be the time required for developing the resources, and for students who are already pressed with a variety of activities to make time to take advantage of these. One recommendation is that programme developers could develop resources over time and supplement these with existing online resources. Where there are copyright issues with hosting these on the library website (which is the place recommended by this researcher in the absence of an academic integrity centre), the staff could provide links to them. Students on the other hand could be encouraged to use the resources based on need or at their convenience.

There is one additional element that could be included in the content of the programme – the use of text-matching software, and this should be guided by a policy which is available to stakeholders in the institution. Turnitin offers a revision assistant for students, and this would be well worth the while in the journey to an ethical academy. Based on the current research, Turnitin is used in the Caribbean mainly as a tool to police plagiarism (Wan and Scott 2016, 5). However, based on previous discussions, students can be taught to use it to check their work so that they can make necessary adjustments before submission (Sachar 2018). Staff and students would also need training in the use of Turnitin, and this can be integrated into research courses or added as part of the offering provided in the suite of activities previously discussed.

Students also weighed in on the content of an educational programme aimed at developing academic integrity. Razera et al. (2009) reported that when asked what could be done to decrease the number of cases of plagiarism, 47 per cent of students and 33 per cent of teachers in their study agreed that "a mandatory introduction course for students on what it is like to study at university, expectations, rules, and so on" would achieve that objective. Students who participated in the survey done for this research also indicated their need for instructions in writing especially in developing skills such as paraphrasing. The content of this course could be up for discussion and there are many models available that can be used as a guide for decision making in this regard.

Methodology for Use in Academic Integrity Education

Academic integrity education can take a variety of forms including non-credit modules that students can take voluntarily, or modules taken for credits during the first year. It can also be embedded as part of courses taken for credits and delivered in an online, face-to-face or blended mode. Instruction can be carried out by faculty, students or both. The most popular suggestion from the literature for education in academic integrity is the workshop (Meng et al. 2014; Ismail 2018; Kayaoglu et al. 2015). Meng et al. (2014) also support the use of conferences, course syllabi, learning materials and the code of ethical conduct, while Ismail (2018) also propose lectures and seminars. Kayaoglu et al. further argue for the use of writing centres and showing students real examples (2015, 21). At least one HEI in the Caribbean utilizes the writing centre approach to develop students' writing skills so this concept is not new to the region. East suggests that universities can apply gamification principles, one of the new trends in education (2016, 6). The Sidney Martin Library at the University of the West Indies, Cave Hill in Barbados offers academic integrity training as one of its support services to researchers. It uses gamification to teach users about academic integrity.

Hughes and Gallant advocate that ethics must be taught in such a manner that students are able to apply what is being taught. They suggest the use of problem-based learning, group discussions and team-based learning (2016, 9), and this method would be beneficial to all instructional components of the programme. With all these suggestions to choose from, HEIs in the Caribbean can be creative in how they deliver the content for their academic integrity programmes.

There are many examples of how universities have organized their education programmes, and a few will be highlighted here. Indiana University, Indianapolis, has a course that is self-enroling and is not taken for credit, yet it has a high percentage of student enrolment, 83 per cent completion rate and an average score of 93 per cent. This programme allows students to do a pre-test and post-test and receive a certificate of completion. This institution also has a course for new faculty and teaching assistants and includes videos on academic integrity done from the perspectives of both staff and students (Indiana University 2019).

The University of Auckland in New Zealand has an online academic integrity course that students are required to complete in their first semester. The course is "designed to increase [students'] knowledge of academic integrity, university rules relating to academic conduct, and the identification and consequences of academic misconduct" (n.d.). Although there is no indication on the university's website as to whether this course has credits attached to it, students are not able to graduate unless it is completed. The University of Maryland has an academic integrity tutorial consisting of six modules and each model can be completed individually. There is also a chat feature on the webpage with the tutorial which provides students the opportunity to seek needed assistance (University of Maryland Global Campus 2021).

There are also several free online academic integrity courses developed by reputable institutions, and these could be used within the academic integrity programme as either one of the basic resources or as an additional resource for students. In addition, there are commercial academic integrity tutorials and courses online that interested persons can access at varying costs.

The model that is being recommended for HEIs in the Caribbean is the tutorial, an example of which is offered by the University of Maryland.

There are several modules, and students can take the modules individually at their convenience, providing them the flexibility needed and requiring limited staff time apart from initially ensuring its development. The course could be compulsory, and like the system implemented at the University of Auckland, students would need to complete the same as a requirement for graduation to ensure maximum participation. The challenge in making this compulsory for completion is that students might complete the same out of routine without experiencing the intended benefits. This tutorial could be the core of the programme for all students. Within the suite, other resources could be offered that are discipline-specific and tailored to the academic levels of students. In addition, lecturers would be expected to include statements on academic integrity in their course outlines and have a discussion on these at the beginning of the semester when they present the course outlines to students. The core tutorial will be supplemented by ongoing seminars for students on specific topics, and these can be considered as part of the library's information literacy offerings. Benson et al. (2019) have shared their experience of how this was done at a Canadian University, and Caribbean institutions can benefit from this.

Some institutions such as the UWI embrace the concept of the writing centre for students who require extensive support beyond what undergraduate foundational writing courses are able to provide. For a minimal fee, students register for the semester and are given individual assistance. This provision is ideal for students who are at risk academically and who might be tempted to cheat to pass, or for those who generally lack adequate writing skills and are unable to use the works of others responsibly. It is therefore a valuable resource that can be used to support students who breached academic integrity rules as a result of poor writing skills. The challenge with the writing centre is the cost factor as both staff and a dedicated facility might be needed. If institutions can get the support of private sector entities to establish these centres, this would still leave them to cover the cost of staff. Even if volunteers are to be used in this type of programme, at least one dedicated full-time staff member would still be needed. Institutions would therefore need to seek ways to overcome this staffing challenge and maybe redeployment could be considered.

Mandatory training in academic integrity for students and staff, in some institutions, will involve student government and unions. However, given the importance of this mandate, it is imperative that institutions pursue whatever course of action is required in order to ensure implementation. Faculty are usually interested in initiatives that benefit students, so it is not expected that getting buy-in from them for the implementation should be difficult. Student governments, which represents the interest of students, are likely to see this as another opportunity to serve their major stakeholders and should welcome the opportunity to participate.

Example of a Multi-Prong Academic Integrity Programme: East and Donnelly describe the educational programme for Latrobe University in Australia which utilizes a collaborative teaching and learning design in educating students about academic integrity. In order to ensure the subject received the attention required for success, it was positioned within the university system as a curriculum issue. The result was that all new students and staff were required to participate in academic integrity programmes. This was implemented as a means of moving away from the following situation. La Trobe University, in 2009, did not have a systematic means to educate students about academic integrity, and the arrangements were ad hoc, with information and inconsistent guides scattered across the university. Furthermore, the citation guides were localized, and the number of styles prescribed by the various faculties nearly equalled the number of disciplines (East and Donnoley 2012).

The response was the development of the following resources aimed at students and faculty:

- a mandatory academic integrity module (AIM) for commencing undergraduate students to educate them about La Trobe University's values;
- academic integrity module for staff (AIMS) that teaches them about their responsibilities and how La Trobe deals with academic misconduct;
- academic referencing module (ARM) that teaches students when to reference and why referencing takes place;
- academic referencing tool (ART) which details examples of how to reference;
- academic integrity site that provides advice and information about where students can get help, in addition to links to policy and related resources.

This is an example of a systematic approach to the development of academic integrity that provides educational support for both staff and students. HEIs in the Caribbean have a number of research-based methodologies to choose from in implementing the educational components of the academic integrity programme. What they choose will depend on both the human and material resources they have at their disposal and the needs of their stakeholders.

Developing Academic Integrity among Faculty

Nelms' (2015a) research points to the need for faculty to be also educated about plagiarism. The majority of faculty are products of the systems in which they currently work, and so any attempt at producing students who practise academic integrity will require partnerships with faculty who are like-minded. Pecorari and Shaw (2010) note with concern that faculty differed in what they considered plagiarism, how they arrived at this conclusion and how they actually treated cases of plagiarism. Based on these findings, they recommended dialogue within and among universities to arrive at some consensus. Latrobe University provides academic integrity training for all commencing staff (Carboon 2013, 4).

East suggests mandatory staff development aimed at helping staff to understand their responsibilities regarding academic integrity. This training would also provide staff with support for teaching referencing and citation (2016, 8). Bjelobaba reports on an academic integrity education project at a Swedish university which aimed to "strengthen faculty members' knowledge on academic integrity, to remind them of their duty to report cases of suspected misconduct, as well as to provide different tools and ideas to improve the academic integrity of their students" (2018, 131). This resulted in an increase in the number of plagiarism infractions reported by staff, suggesting that training for staff can have a positive impact. According to Flint, Clegg and McDonald, the institutions will need to figure out how to come to a common understanding of the varying perspectives among the stakeholders (2006, 154). It is now time for the Caribbean to embrace this challenge and begin to seek solutions.

Within the Caribbean, new staff employed in HEIs usually go through an orientation period. This can be used as the initial forum for the introduction of academic integrity. Some institutions require new faculty to complete sessions, while others require completion of courses aimed at preparing new faculty to teach in higher education. Academic integrity can be further explored through whatever avenue is used to prepare new faculty for their duties whether seminars, courses or programmes for certification. These need to include what is academic integrity and plagiarism; students' perceptions of academic integrity and plagiarism; how to identify plagiarism; and the institution's regulations on academic integrity including procedures for managing allegations of academic misconduct.

Conclusion

This chapter examined the content and methodology that can be employed to educate students at the pre-university and university levels about academic integrity. At the elementary and secondary levels, students should be systematically introduced to academic integrity through MIL sessions. This will help them to acquire skills some of which are currently embedded in the curriculum. At the tertiary level, education in academic integrity should seek to develop students' writing skills while also targeting their ethical and moral development. This can be done through workshops, seminars or courses. It is best to make allowances for the differences in the academic conventions between disciplines, as each one might treat academic integrity in a different way. Faculty also need some education and training in academic integrity, and this should provide them with an understanding of the academy's perspective on and the resources for academic integrity while simultaneously helping them to discover ways in which they can offer support to their students.

Chapter 21

The Way Forward

Introduction

This final chapter provides suggestions which can be implemented to begin the shift away from the present punitive approach to academic integrity currently practised in the Caribbean to a centralized, systematic approach. It outlines the roles to be played by the CARICOM, the ministries of education and the educational institutions.

Background

Academic integrity is very important to the international education system primarily because "as pressures for achievement, selection and qualification grow and examinations increase in importance, academic misconduct has become a matter of serious concern" (Hallak and Poisson 2007, 231). From the literature reviewed, it was observed that academic misconduct is a global issue, affecting developed as well as developing countries, and ivy league universities as well as those at the bottom of the ranking. Much research of significance has been conducted on academic integrity, especially plagiarism, which has been studied from a variety of perspectives as researchers seek to gain a better understanding of the phenomenon so as to implement programmes to reduce its occurrence and to create what Gallant (2011) refers to as the ethical academy.

Within the English-speaking Caribbean, the study of academic integrity is just emerging although there is evidence of the awareness of plagiarism as a societal issue based mainly on newspaper reports. The few empirical studies available have shown evidence of academic misconduct at the tertiary level, with one possible cause being a lack of instruction for students at both the secondary and tertiary levels. This has resulted in ignorance on the part of students which has led to unintentional plagiarism (Baker-Gardner and Smart 2017). The findings of a study done in the Caribbean revealed that teaching students about plagiarism increased their knowledge and which is likely to result in decreased rates of plagiarism (Welsh-Unwala 2019).

The current research aimed to provide an overview of academic integrity in the Caribbean. The objectives of the research were to:

- determine the prevalence of plagiarism in various sectors of Caribbean societies and responses to its manifestation;
- investigate the prevalence of academic integrity in secondary and tertiary education in the Caribbean;
- evaluate HEIs mine presentation and treatment of plagiarism in their policies;
- determine undergraduate students' perceptions of the causative factors and penalties for plagiarism;
- examine undergraduate students' perceptions of the justifications for plagiarism;
- investigate the inclusion of academic integrity in accreditation policies and guidelines of member territories;
- propose strategies aimed at assisting institutions to develop a culture of academic integrity.

The researcher chose to focus on plagiarism because this is the most prevalent form of academic misconduct in other countries.

In an effort to achieve the objectives of the study, content analyses of the plagiarism policies in HEIs, accreditation standards of three territories and articles published in online newspapers over a fifteen-year period were undertaken. In addition, data on the students' perceptions of plagiarism were garnered from a survey conducted among 1,039 undergraduate students. Secondary data on plagiarism obtained from four universities and the Caribbean Examination Council (CXC) were also used to explore the prevalence of plagiarism. The data were analysed using charts, tables and graphs generated by SPSS and Microsoft Excel. In addition, qualitative data captured on the questionnaire were analysed using the Creswell (2007) data analysis spiral. This data analysis is presented in part 2 of this book. The major findings for each objective are reported in the following sections.

Prevalence of Academic Misconduct in Secondary and Tertiary Education: The analysis of newspaper articles revealed that based on the cases reported, plagiarism was most dominant in the education sector. Further analysis showed there was a range of academic misconduct at the secondary level both inside and outside the examination room. Inside the examination room, students cheated by copying from information written on body parts or paper, reproducing sample stories and bringing in cellular phones. Outside of the examination room, plagiarism in School-Based Assessments (SBAs) was the main challenge. Other breaches of academic integrity included the stealing and selling of examination papers and falsifying examination results' certificates. One reason purported for these breaches was having too many SBAs, which resulted in a lack of time for students to focus on each task. The issue of limited time resulting from the need to complete too many assignments was exacerbated by the need for students to search for information in multiple places (Fernandes 2016). Additional factors which might have contributed to plagiarism were the absence of a detection system and "superficial monitoring" (Vázquez-Recio et al. 2016, 5711). Lack of education on plagiarism at the secondary level and dishonest teachers were also identified as factors which contributed to academic misconduct.

There were cases of suspected plagiarism at CXC in both the CSEC and CAPE examinations, with the most popular of these being the case at Jamaica College in 2013. At the CSEC level, the subjects with the highest number of cases of suspected plagiarism between 2006 and 2018 were Principles of Accounts, Social Studies and Music. At CAPE, Information Technology and Caribbean Studies had the highest rates of plagiarism. Outside of the Jamaica College case, the number of suspected cases was highest in 2012 and 2015. The council responded by applying the penalties outlined in its policies. These included a grade of zero for individuals or a class based on the particulars of the case, court cases and the implementation of an electronic detection system.

At the tertiary level, plagiarism was evident based on the analysis of data from four universities. However, the rate of plagiarism was significantly higher in some institutions than in others with the highest number of cases recorded in the academic years 2011–2012 and 2014–2015, and this coincided with the data from CXC. Although the number of cases of plagiarism increased minimally over the period, there were significant fluctuations from year to year. At the tertiary level, males and Year 3 students were more likely to cheat than others.

Presentation of Plagiarism in Accreditation Policies and Guidelines: Accreditation agencies are responsible for safeguarding the quality of education at the tertiary level. At the time of writing, there were ten active agencies operating in CARICOM, and three of these included guidelines for academic integrity in their policies for the accreditation of the tertiary institutions. However, the treatment of academic integrity varied greatly among each, and they presented a punitive approach to the subject requiring institutions to have a policy on plagiarism and other attendant policies without the essential structures for supporting students.

Treatment of Plagiarism in Academic Integrity and Plagiarism Policies: Caribbean universities have given some attention to academic integrity and plagiarism with the majority having a policy online. However, there was great variance in their content, length and emphasis. There were stand-alone policies usually in pdf format, policies embedded in handbooks, and some were presented as web pages. The majority of these policies were named with either positive or neutral wording, for example, "Academic Integrity Policy" or "Academic Honesty Policy." The length of the policies varied from a few sentences to a maximum of eleven pages.

The most common element in all the policies was the definition of plagiarism followed by the sanctions, types and examples of the act. Other elements in the policies were levels of plagiarism, procedures for dealing with it, its electronic detection, faculty responsibilities, sources of assistance and a statement of accountability. The majority of institutions used the generic definition of plagiarism which speaks to the use of another person's work without giving credit, while others were very detailed. The majority of definitions included four of the six objects presented by Nushi and Firoozkohi (2017).

There was an emphasis on sanctions but not a corresponding emphasis on sources of assistance to students. This conforms to the punitive approach which stresses sanctions and penalties without providing students with the assistance necessary to develop the requisite skills (Hu and Sun 2017). The procedures for dealing with cases of plagiarism were clearly set out in some policies, but in others, they were either non-existent or not clearly outlined. Faculty responsibilities also varied as some institutions expected faculty to take full responsibility for the process, while others made the role of faculty optional. Sources of assistance included the academic library or links to other websites. Whereas some institutions presented examples of behaviours which constitute plagiarism, it was evident that there was a lack of clarity as to what behaviours should be classified as such.

Students' Perceptions of Plagiarism: Students showed an interest in the topic, with some expressing the hope that the study will in some ways help them to come to a better understanding of the issue. The majority of students believed plagiarism was wrong but could be justified. They pointed to "instructor-based neutralization" (Carpenter et al. 2006, 192) and the friend factor (Sisti 2007) as a possible justification for plagiarism; however, a significant number of them believed plagiarism could not be avoided. Participants were able to identify challenges which led to plagiarism and these aligned with the literature. These included poor writing skills (Ukpebor and Ogbebor 2013; Charubusp 2015; Kayaoglu et al. 2015) and a lack of education on plagiarism, as they contended they did not receive instructions on plagiarism at the secondary level (Baker-Gardner and Smart 2017; Kam, Hue and Cheung 2018).

The data revealed that the influence of peers (Sisti 2007) referred to here as the friend factor was likely to encourage students to cheat. In addition, students believed other factors influencing plagiarism were the belief that others were cheating, and a heavy workload. They are most likely to justify cheating with the arguments that students can't avoid using other people's work, undergraduate students were just learning and needed leniency and previous descriptions do not change. On the one hand, students believed that plagiarism was a big deal and should be considered a serious offence, and that it undermined independent thought. On the other hand, they also believed that plagiarism should not be considered serious seeing that words were intangible assets and they were not "stealing" tangible items. This demonstrates an ambivalence towards plagiarism that is evident in the literature.

An examination of the impact of age, gender, academic discipline and academic maturity on the students' perceptions of plagiarism had mixed results. There was no difference in the students' perceptions of plagiarism based on academic discipline, but perceptions differed based on gender, age and academic maturity. It was discovered that males had a more positive attitude towards plagiarism than females, and data from one of the four universities showed that males plagiarized more than females. Younger students disagreed more with the factors that caused plagiarism than older students, and those who were at the institution longer tended to disagree more with the the severity of and penalty for plagiarism than those in their first and second years. This negative attitude might indicate an inclination to plagiarize.

Building a Culture of Integrity

After examining plagiarism from a variety of perspectives, the focus now shifts to how to transition from a punitive approach to plagiarism to a culture of academic integrity. To develop academic integrity across the Caribbean, a number of strategies are being proposed. These range from a regional framework to ensuring integrity at the personal level. This section presents a synopsis of these strategies which are presented in detail in the previous chapters.

Regional Framework: Given that CARICOM has two regional educational institutions which have significant influence in the Caribbean, and given the interrelatedness of the education systems of each territory, it seems plausible to begin at the regional level. According to Tewarie, "A regional policy framework is therefore required that will form the basis for the development and implementation throughout the Caribbean of national policies, programmes and action plans in relation to tertiary education" (2009, 11). This regional policy framework is needed to address the matter of academic integrity given the influence of CARICOM generally and the fact that the largest institutions at both the secondary and tertiary levels are directly under the responsibility of CARICOM. In addition, given CARICOM's interest in the quality of education in the region, the inclusion of policies on academic integrity at this level is encouraged.

Tewarie further speaks of the "absence of integrated, harmonized approaches to education issues that are common in the region. What is required, therefore, is a legal framework that is comprehensive in scope, covering all pertinent issues ranging from the powers and responsibilities of Line Ministers and regulatory bodies to the rights and responsibilities of students" (2009, 11). Academic integrity is one of those "pertinent issues" that could be considered under the "rights and responsibilities of students." However, as discussed previously, the responsibility for acting with integrity should not be left up to students without providing them with the structures and education that prescribe the manner in which they should act. CARICOM could provide a framework for academic integrity, which could be used to guide the development of national policies by determining the context for such a policy and adopting agreed-on definitions to be used across the region. This is important, as a lack of common definition of terms was identified as one of the challenges with some of the policies that were analysed. The use of a regional framework is evident in Europe while Australia utilizes a national framework, and so this approach could be adopted for the region.

Council for Human and Social Development, one of the ministerial councils of CARICOM with the responsibility for human resources, including education, is the avenue through which a regional framework for academic integrity could be developed. This council is made up of ministers designated by each member state of CARICOM. One of its responsibilities is to "promote the development of education through the efficient organisation of educational and training facilities in the Community, including elementary and advanced vocational training and technical facilities" (Caribbean Community Secretariat 2001, 13). It would therefore be the appropriate organ to undertake this mandate.

National Policy: With reference to the regional framework for academic integrity, each country needs to develop a national policy which speaks to how it will integrate academic integrity at the national level. This process would be led by the ministries of education. Decisions at this level would include where in the curriculum academic integrity should be taught, the aspects of academic integrity which will be taught at each level and who will be responsible for this. For academic integrity programmes and activities to be successful, they must have a strong educational component. The national policy should also have a research agenda that speaks to areas of academic integrity that will be researched and specify how the results should be disseminated. The Media and Information Literacy curriculum developed by UNESCO which is currently being revised could be adapted for use at both the primary and secondary levels.

Institutional Policies: Each institution from the primary to the tertiary level should have a policy for academic integrity. The complexity of the policy, including the language used, should reflect the requirements at each level. Each policy should clearly outline the role of all stakeholders – the institution, the faculty, the library and students. It should identify and define the behaviours that constitute academic misconduct and provide details on the sanctions for breaches. Each institution should also have a robust programme to promote academic integrity so that it is visible to all stakeholders. These can include celebrations and displays on academic integrity. Faculty should be actively involved in teaching students about academic integrity and creating opportunities for them to practise it across all disciplines.

In order to accomplish this shift, faculty need to be educated about the importance of academic integrity as they are the persons who directly interface with students daily and have the greatest impact on students' perceptions and understanding of plagiarism (Dant 1996). They also need academic integrity education as research shows gaps in faculty knowledge and their varying perceptions of academic integrity (Pecorari and Shaw 2010). Their roles are important as not only do students model their behaviours, but faculty also have opportunities to directly influence students' behaviour through discussions and expectations (Fish and Hura 2013). Buy-in from teaching staff is also important seeing that they are the ones who usually detect the cases of academic integrity and are integral to the reporting process.

Change takes time, and the process described above might require discussions at various levels, policy changes and additional research to inform practice. In the meantime, institutions can begin to evaluate their academic integrity structures using the Academic Integrity Rating Scales produced by the International Center for Academic Integrity. Many institutions are already aware of where weaknesses lie, and so measures to address these can be established. These can be tailored to meet the national policy when one becomes available. Principals at the primary and secondary levels need to make academic integrity an agenda item for their meetings. They need to begin to seek collective ways of dealing with the issue so that students do not end up in tertiary institutions without the knowledge that is required for them to make ethical choices.

Conclusion

The face of education is constantly changing, but regardless of this, there is the need to ensure quality. Each region has the responsibility to ensure that the quality mandate is not compromised as this is likely to have implications for the regional and global education system. The Caribbean has made significant strides in its attempt to develop a system that embraces the quality assurance strategies that are necessary. The time has come to now further the quality mandate by the introduction of a robust system for academic integrity which involves CARICOM, national governments, accreditation bodies and institutions. To fail to respond to this call in a timely and appropriate manner is to compromise the region's ability to deal with threats to the integrity of its education systems by those who knowingly or out of ignorance commit acts of academic misconduct.

Appendices

Appendix 1

Questionnaire

An Examination of Undergraduate Students' Perceptions of Plagiarism at a Regional University

> The purpose of this questionnaire is to gather information on your perceptions of plagiarism. Kindly tick the box which best reflects your response to the statements, or write your answers on the lines where appropriate.

DEMOGRAPHIC DATA

1. Registration status: ☐ Full time   ☐ Part time

2. Faculty: ☐ Humanities and Education   ☐ Medical Science

    ☐ Law   ☐ Social Sciences

    ☐ Science and Technology

3. Year: ☐ Year 1   ☐ Year 2

    ☐ Year 3   ☐ Year 4

4. Gender: ☐ Male   ☐ Female   ☐ Prefer not to say

5. Employed: ☐ Full time   ☐ Part time   ☐ Not employed

6. Age: ☐ Below 25 years   ☐ 26–35   ☐ 36–45   ☐ Above 45

SA – Strongly Agree; A – Agree; U – Undecided; D – Disagree; SD – Strongly Disagree

Factors that exacerbate plagiarism	SA	A	U	D	SD
7. Short deadlines or a heavy workload give me the right to plagiarize a bit.					
8. A plagiarized paper does no harm to the value of a university degree.					
9. Those who say they have never plagiarized are lying.					
10. Plagiarism can be justified if I currently have more important obligations or tasks to do.					
11. Sometimes, it is necessary to plagiarize.					
12. I am tempted to plagiarize if I have permission from a friend to copy his or her work.					
13. I am tempted to plagiarize if I currently have more important obligations or tasks to do.					
14. I am tempted to plagiarize because, even if caught, the punishment will be light (the reward outweighs the risk).					
Justification for plagiarism	SA	A	U	D	SD
15. Sometimes you cannot avoid using other people's words, because there are only so many ways to describe something.					
16. It is justified to use previous descriptions of a concept or theory, because they remain the same.					
17. Undergraduate students, because they are just learning the ropes, should receive milder punishment for plagiarism.					
18. Self-plagiarism is not punishable because it is not harmful (you cannot steal from yourself).					
19. It is justified to use your own previous work, without providing citation, in order to complete the current work.					
20. Since plagiarism is taking other people's words rather than tangible assets, it should not be considered a serious offence.					

Severity and penalty	SA	A	U	D	SD
21. Plagiarised parts of a student's paper should be ignored if the paper is otherwise of high quality.					
22. Self-plagiarism should not be punishable in the same way as plagiarism is.					
23. If you cannot write well because of unfamiliarity with the topic area, it is justified to copy parts of a paper already published in that area in order to accurately represent those ideas.					
24. Given a commonly perceived decline in moral and ethical standards, it is important to discuss issues like plagiarism and self-plagiarism.					
25. Plagiarism is as bad as stealing an exam.					
26. Plagiarism undermines independent thought.					
27. Since plagiarism is taking other people's words rather than tangible assets, it should not be considered a serious offence.					
28. Plagiarism is not a big deal.					

Additional Comment are welcomed:

_____
_____
_____

Thank you for taking the time to complete this survey.

Appendix 2

Confessions of a Plagiarist

This narrative was written in the student's voice. The researcher wanted to preserve its originality and thus did not edit.

In my early years of high school, more specifically from the 7th to 8th grade, I failed at almost every subject. I guess one could say my transition from primary to high school was not a very smooth one. I was however able to turn my high school life around in the first term of third form, for now I was determined to make my parents proud. I did make them proud as I graduated from high school with nine Caribbean Secondary Education Certificate (CSEC) subjects at the Fifth form level and two years later with eight Caribbean Advanced Proficiency Education (CAPE) units. Up to this point I had never had a brush with plagiarism so severe.

The conversation at high school about plagiarism is not as current and ongoing as it is in university. I cannot recall hearing people repeat phrases like "intellectual property and copyright" during my high school tenure, except in my final years when we had to submit our School Based Assessments (SBA) which had to be sent to the Caribbean Examination Council (CXC). It was at that point close attention had to be paid to properly citing the sources in our bibliographies. Before that, simply copying and pasting where you got the information from and sometimes adding the date and time was all that was needed. I had never been seriously penalized for plagiarism nor had I ever been threatened with any related penalty. So one can imagine my disbelief when hearing from my lecturers at the University of the West Indies (UWI) that I could be expelled for not citing or better yet not properly citing a source. I was beyond appalled especially by the not properly citing part. At the high school level we are made familiar with the American Psychological Association (APA) and the Modern Language Association (MLA) format but that's about as far as it went. Anything else would be a bit extra. I believe the most popular form of citation at that point was MLA as it was what was preferred for our SBA's.

The preferred citation style for students pursuing a degree in law is Oxford Standard for Citation of Legal Authorities (OSCOLA), a format with which I was unfamiliar. Also in first year the authority for most of the work that is required of us comes from cases which are pretty easy to cite. With the understanding that citation was pretty for me and all I needed was the cases cited properly I embarked on the journey of completing my very first assignment which was an outline. This unfortunately was not during one of my best seasons of life. I was emotionally exhausted due to family and personal issues taking a turn for the worst. In addition, my tuition was not yet finalized and I was again not transitioning smoothly, this time from high school into university. On top of all that, my laptop stopped working and I was too full of pride to sit in the library and do my assignment on the library's computer while the other rich kids were around. Fortunately even when we are stubborn as Christians God shows us favour knowing that eventually we will realize the error in our ways and change. I had two friends in the law faculty at the time. One offered to help me with the assignment and the other upon my request agreed to let me use her laptop.

It was all going well until the final days for the assignment to be submitted. It came down to the three of us having to be basically fighting over one laptop to edit and submit our assignments. I ended up using case summaries and not the actual cases themselves, so I had no sources to cite in my references. For the information that I had sources, I was not able to properly cite them because I had not done the study of OSCOLA which the tutor had suggested. So evidently I became a thief. I was found guilty of plagiarism which at UWI carried the sentence of failure of that assignment or course or expulsion from the institution. At this time, I was basically in panic mode. Knowing I had not intended to plagiarize, I immediately emailed the tutor and explained to her what had happened hoping that she would respond favourably. To my surprise the tutor was extremely understanding and lenient especially due to the fact that this was my first year and first assignment for this course. For a short while, I gave sighs of relief. I had crossed over my first law school hurdle. The grade I was awarded for that assignment was a B. Excitement filled my heart when I saw it; however, a strong warning was issued with that B instructing me never to plagiarize again.

This incident left me with several lessons. Firstly, I learnt from this experience never to plagiarize again. Plagiarism is not yet a criminal offence; however, a civil suit can be brought against a person for stealing and using another person's intellectual property. I also realized that you can get expelled from school for plagiarizing. Secondly, I learnt that I must have faith in God and always try to correct my mistakes if I can. Depending on the approach I take people may surprise me with their response. Honesty is truly the best policy. I will most definitely be doing my best to never plagiarize again.

In ensuring that other students don't have these stressful experiences it would be a good idea for the University to introduce a plagiarism foundation course. This could be a course with no credits designed to run alongside our academic tenure. At the undergraduate level, we must enrol in a beginner's course on plagiarism and as we advance in our studies we do refresher courses each semester. This course could have additions of the practices we need to learn in relation to the papers we will be required to submit with references. This of course should be tailored to the citation needs of each faculty.

The View from the Other Side

It is often felt that plagiarism negatively impacts the students, but not many persons consider the impact of plagiarism on the faculty involved. I hope my experience will help to shed some light on the range of emotions that faculty go through when they are required to treat with cases of plagiarism. Here is my story.

Today was like any other Tuesday morning towards the end of the semester. I had a batch of essays to mark for my final year undergraduate class. For me, teaching was the most enjoyable part of my job. The interactions with the students and the questions and answers and occasional laughs made the adrenaline rush through my veins. This was what I was born to do. My childhood dream of becoming a lawyer paled in the distance as I revelled in the joy of teaching, moulding and shaping lives, and learning some very important lessons from the next generation in spite of the generational gap that sometimes felt as wide as the Caribbean Sea.

My greatest desire was to see students learn and succeed. To see them move from one year level to the next and sometimes even from undergraduate to postgraduate studies gave me utmost delight. To watch them come into the institution unsure of themselves and leave full fledged professionals who had so much confidence they felt they could take on the world warmed my spirit and made me feel that I had been a part of their success story. The job of marking was the part of the job that I wished I could outsource, but since it had to be done, I launched into it with gusto.

The paper was an essay that was worth 20 per cent of the course grade. Marking was going well. I had two As and a B+. A sigh of satisfaction accompanied the setting aside of the third paper and I reached for the fourth to tackle it. I was in high spirits as nothing makes a teacher's heart rejoice than when students are getting high grades. Two sentences into the fourth paper, I came up short. This just did not sound like the voice of an undergraduate student. The writing was very polished and precise. That was what jumped out at me. I turned to my trusted friend Google to inquire if it was familiar with what I was reading. I typed the second sentence into the search box and a peer-reviewed journal article came up which suspiciously resembled the one I had started to mark. I stopped to read the article online, and that was when I realized that although the majority of the student's assignment matched the article, there were parts that did not. However, these parts that did not match still did not sound like the voice of a student at the undergraduate level. I repeated the process of searching Google and another peer-reviewed article came up that contained the segments I was searching for.

It was as if the earth shifted. I could not come to the understanding that a student would do something like this. My years in the primary system never prepared me to deal with plagiarism, and I sat at my desk lost in Wonderland just like Alice. I never knew incidents like this happened. I thought all students followed the protocol for writing and citing. Not knowing what to do, I spoke to my supervisor, who instructed me to go to the Examination Section and get instructions on how to treat the matter. With a heavy heart I walked across the campus. For me it was a tough decision. It is obvious that this student had done something unacceptable, but I did not want my student to be in trouble. I had a long debate with myself as to whether or not to report the student, but then ethics won. I felt it was the student's decision to try to trick the system and since she had taken that decision, I had to be responsible and do what I believed to be the right thing.

Examination instructed me to highlight the parts of the document that were copied and submit both the student's paper and the articles from which she copied. I was also required to write a letter outlining the case. With a heavy heart I proceeded as instructed, vacillating between the need to do what was right and my sympathy for the student who had so blatantly broken one of the sacred laws of academia. I chose two different colour highlighters and to my amazement when I was finished highlighting, only a few sentences were left that could be identified as the original work of the student. Interestingly, the in-text citations did not match as the student had changed every one of them and had written new works cited list to reflect these changes. Based on my reading after the incident I learnt that based on the Plagiarism Spectrum these types of plagiarism were called Remix and 404 Error. Remix is the taking of parts from more than one source and combining these to form a cohesive whole. 404 Errors is the use of non-existent citations. These are two of the top 10 most often occurring types of plagiarism (The Plagiarism Spectrum).

With mixed emotions I submitted the required documents to the Examination Section and weeks later I received a letter to attend a hearing. I sat in the waiting room with the same student that I reported, while they completed deliberations on another case. This was indeed an uncomfortable experience. What do you say to your student when you are going to be a witness against her in a few minutes? After that case was completed I was ushered into the room. This hearing was very formal. I was invited in to make my case before the panel.

Examinations came before the case was closed, and the student called repeatedly to find out if she should sit the examination. Since I was not aware of any prohibition forbidding her to do so, I advised her to go to examination. The outcome of the hearing came after the examination. A letter was sent to inform the Department that the student was found guilty of Level 2 plagiarism, and was given a failing grade for the course (incidentally she had failed the examination already). She was also fined and given a warning. She did not choose to register for that course again, so she took an optional course that I taught. This too was a very uncomfortable experience for me, and I am sure it could not have been easy for her either.

This experience changed my life. It changed the way I treat students and the assumptions I make about them understanding the nature of plagiarism and the need to ensure that they avoid its far-reaching consequences. In addition, I have become a champion for academic integrity. I have become an avid researcher on the subject as I seek to get a better understanding so I can help students. Every class that I have gets some formal instructions on plagiarism and I have also devised ways to do mini-series on writing so as to help students who have difficulty in this area. For me, it is more expedient to help students stay on the straight and narrow than to risk having to go through the trauma of having to report a student and go to another "trial" for plagiarism.

References

"Academic Integrity." 2020. *Wikipedia, The Free Encyclopedia*. Accessed 3 April 2020. https://en.wikipedia.org/w/index.php?title=Academic_integrity&oldid =936279434.

"Academic Integrity Standards: Aligning Policy and Practices in Australian Universities." 2013. Australian Government Office for Teaching and Learning. https://ltr.edu.au/resources/PP10_1783_Bretag_report_2013.pdf.

"Academic Librarian." 2020. Prospects. Graduate Prospects Ltd. https://www.prospects.ac.uk/job-profiles/academic-librarian.

"Academic Misconduct Cases Disclosed." 2013. Accessed 25 August 2018. http://usa.chinadaily.com.cn/china/2013-08/02/content_16864333.htm.

"Accreditation Agencies and Quality Assurance in Belize." 2021. *Belize Education*. https://www.belizeeducation.info/education-system/accrediting-agencies.html.

Adelphi University. n.d. "Academic Honesty Awareness Week." Accessed 21 March 2020. https://students.adelphi.edu/au_event/academic-honesty-awareness-week/.

Admin. 2017. "How to Detect Plagiarism." SEO Tool Station. https://seotoolstation.com/blog/manually-detecting-plagiarism.

Ahearne, John F. 2011. "Honesty." *American Scientist* 99 (2): 120–22. doi:10.1511/2011.89.120.

Ahmad, Irfan. 2018. "How Much Data is Generated Every Minute? [Infographic]." *Social Media Today*. https://www.socialmediatoday.com/news/how-much-data-is-generated-every-minute-infographic-1/525692/.

Ali, Asim M., Hussam M. Abdulla, and Václav Snášel. 2011. "Overview and Comparison of Plagiarism Detection Tools." *Dateso*, 161–72. http://ceur-ws.org/Vol-706/poster22.pdf.

Ali, Wan Zah, Habsah Ismail, and Tan Tien Cheat. 2012. "Plagiarism: To what Extent is it Understood?" *Procedia - Social and Behavioral Sciences* 59: 604–11. Accessed 12 May 2018. doi: https://doi.org/10.1016/j.sbspro.2012.09.320.

Alleyne, George. 2018. "Education Relief in Barbados." *Caribbean Life*. https://www.caribbeanlifenews.com/education-relief-in-barbados/.

Alleyne, Ruby S. 2015. "A Critical Look at the Legislative Framework for External Quality Agencies in CARICOM." In *Quality in Higher Education in the Caribbean*, edited by Anna Kasafi Perkins, 86–109. Kingston: University of the West Indies Press.

Almeida, Renan, Karina Rocha, Fernanda Catelani, Aldo Fontes-Pereira, and Sonia Vasconcelos. 2016. "Plagiarism Allegations Account for Most Retractions in Major Latin American/Caribbean Databases." *Science and Engineering Ethics* 22: 1447–56. https://doi.org/10.1007/s11948-015-9714-5.

American University of Washington DC. 2019. "Students' Rights and Responsibilities." https://www.american.edu/academics/integrity/rights-and-responsibilities.cfm.

Andrews, Kenneth G., Linda A. Smith, David A. Henzi, and Elaine Demps. 2007. "Faculty and Student Perceptions of Academic Integrity at U.S. and Canadian Dental Schools." *Journal of Dental Education* 71 (8): 1027–39.

Anney, Vicent, and Mary Mosha. 2015. "Student's Plagiarisms in Higher Learning Institutions in the Era of Improved Internet Access: Case Study of Developing Countries." *Journal of Education and Practice* 6 (13): 203–16.

Archie, P. "Organisational Culture: Definitions, Features, Significance, Elements, Types." *Business Management Ideas*. https://www.businessmanagementideas.com/organisation/organisational-culture/organisational-culture/21161.

Ary, Donald, Lucy Cheser Jacobs, Asghar Razavieh, and Christine Sorensen. 2005. *Introduction to Research in Education*. Belmont: Wadsworth.

ASBPE Staff. 2014. "Even at Graduate School Level Plagiarism Reaches New Heights." http://www.asbpe.org/blog/2014/05/06/even-at-graduate-school-level-plagiarism-reaches-new-heights/.

"Assessment of Media and Information Literacy in Latin America and the Caribbean." 2017. UNESCO. https://en.unesco.org/events/assessment-media-and-information-literacy-latin-america-and-caribbean.

Association of College and Research Libraries. 2016. "Framework for Information Literacy for Higher Education." http://www.ala.org/acrl/standards/ilframework.

Atkinson, Doug, and Yeoh Sue. 2008. "Student and Staff Perceptions of the Effectiveness of Plagiarism Detection Software." *Australasian Journal of Educational Technology* 24 (2): 222–40.

Babbie, Earl. 2013. *The Practice of Social Research*. Belmont: Thomson Wadsworth.

Bahadori, Mohamadkarim, Morteza Izadi, and Mohammadjavad Hoseinpourfard. 2012. "Plagiarism: Concepts, Factors and Solutions." *Iranian Journal of Military Medicine* 14, no. 3 (Autumn): 168–77. http://militarymedj.ir/article-1-1049-en.pdf.

Bailey, Jonathan. 2011a. "Why Plagiarism Is on the Rise." *Plagiarism Today*. Last modified 11 November 2011. https://www.plagiarismtoday.com/2011/11/11/why-plagiarism-is-on-the-rise/.

———. 2011b. "The World's First 'Plagiarism Case.'" *Plagiarism Today*. Accessed 21 August 2018. https://www.plagiarismtoday.com/2011/10/04/the-world per centE2 per cent80 per cent99s-first-plagiarism-case/.

———. 2013. "The Two Types of Plagiarism Detection Tools." *Plagiarism Today*, 19 September 2013. https://www.plagiarismtoday.com/2013/09/19/two-types-plagiarism-detection-tools/.

———. 2014. "New Turnitin Study on the Impact of Plagiarism Detection in Higher Education." *Plagiarism Today*. Accessed 12 May 2018. https://www.plagiarismtoday.com/2014/02/05/turnitin-release-study-impact-plagiarism-detection-software-higher-education/.

———. 2015. "Do Men Plagiarise More than Women?" https://www.plagiarismtoday.com/2015/03/30/do-men-plagiarize-more-than-women/.

———. 2017. "5 Ways the Internet Changed Plagiarism." *Plagiarismtoday.com*. Accessed 17 May 2018. https://www.plagiarismtoday.com/2017/05/30/5-ways-the-internet-changed-plagiarism/.
———. 2017. "Top Ten Plagiarism Stories of 2016." *Ithenticate*, 27 February 2017. https://www.ithenticate.com/plagiarism-detection-blog/the-top-10-plagiarism-stories-of-2016#.YTKcM45Kh1s.
Baines, Syranno. 2018. "Change 'informer fi dead culture', Green Tells Youth." https://jamaica-gleaner.com/article/lead-stories/20180920/change-informer-fi-dead-culture-green-tells-youth.
Baker-Gardner, Ruth, and Cherryann Smart. 2017. "Ignorance or Intent? A Case Study of Plagiarism in Higher Education among LIS Students in the Caribbean." In *Handbook of Research on Academic Misconduct in Higher Education*, edited by Donna M. Velliaris, 182–205. Hershey: IGI Global.
Bakhtiari, Sadegh, and H. Shajar Isfahan. 2006. "Globalization and Education: Challenges and Opportunities." *International Business and Economics Research Journal (IBER)* 5 (2). https://pdfs.semanticscholar.org/bc08/f574ffaf59a26d81b00fb7d2a2105482c50c.pdf?_ga=2.88883739.1462409920.1582738912-1070940892.1581082899.
Bamford, Jan, and Katerina Sergiou. 2004. "International Students and Plagiarism: An Analysis of the Reasons for Plagiarism among International Foundation Students." *Investigations in University Teaching and Learning* 2, no. 2 (Spring 2005). https://core.ac.uk/download/pdf/36771682.pdf.
"Barbados." n.d. *International Labour Organisation*. Accessed 15 January 2021. https://www.ilo.org/caribbean/countries-covered/barbados/lang--en/index.htm.
Barbados Accreditation Council. 2021. Institution Accreditation Standards. https://bac.gov.bb/downloads-and-forms/.
Barnard, Antoni, Willem Schurink, and Mariè de Beer. 2008. "A Conceptual Framework of Integrity." *SA Journal of Industrial Psychology* 34 (2): a427. https://doi.org/10.4102/sajip.v34i2.427.
Barnard-Brak, Lucy, Marcelo Schmidt, and Tianlan Wei. 2013. "How Effective is Honor Code Reporting over Instructor- Implemented Measures? A Pilot Study." *Journal of College and Character* 14 (3): 231–40. https://doi.org/https://www.tandfonline.com/doi /abs/10.1515/jcc-2013-0030?journalCode=ujcc20.
Barnes, Godfrey. 2018. "Government Presents Budget of $773.6 Billion for 2018/19." Jamaica Information Service. Accessed 16 February 2019. https://jis.gov.jm/government-presents-budget-773-6-billion-2018-19/.
Barrett, Ruth, James Malcolm, Anna Cox, and Carolyn Lyon. 2004. "Plagiarism Prevention is Discipline Specific: A View from Computer Science." *Journal for the Enhancement of Learning and Teaching* 3 (1): 48–56. Accessed 5 January 2020. https://uhra.herts.ac.uk/bitstream/handle/2299/6143/902158.pdf?sequence=1.
Bates College. 2020. "Plagiarism and Academic Honesty: Politics: Bates College." Bates Wordmark, 23 March 2020. https://www.bates.edu/politics/plagiarism-and-academic-honesty/.
Bavaharji, Madhubala, Thiba Naraina Chetty, Zalina B. Ismail, and Krishnaveni Letchumanan. 2016. "A Comparison of the Act and Frequency of Plagiarism

between Technical and Non-Technical Programme Undergraduates." *English Language Teaching* 9 (4): 106. https://doi.org/10.5539/elt.v9n4p106.

Beale, Sarah Sun. 2003. "Governmental and Academic Integrity at Home and Abroad." *Fordham Law Review* 72 (2): 405–14. https://ir.lawnet.fordham.edu/cgi/viewcontent.cgi?article=3934&context=flr.

Becker, D'Arcy A., and Ingrid Ulstad. 2007. "Gender Differences in Student Ethics: Are Females Really More Ethical?" *Plagiary: Cross-Disciplinary Studies in Plagiarism, Fabrication, and Falsification*, 77–91.

Benson, Lyle, Kristin, Rodier, Rickard Enström, and Evamdrp Bocatto. 2019. "Developing a University-Wide Academic Integrity E-learning Tutorial: A Canadian Case." *International Journal for Educational Integrity* 15 (5). https://doi.org/10.1007/s40979-019-0045-1.

Berlinck, Roberto G. 2011. "The Academic Plagiarism and Its Punishments - A Review." *Revista Brasileira De Farmacognosia* 21 (3): 365–72. Accessed 25 February 2018. http://doi:10.1590/s0102-695x2011005000099.

Beyerstein, Lindsay. 2010. "Plagiarism is a Big Moral Deal." *Big Think*. Last modified 11 August 2010. https://bigthink.com/focal-point/plagiarism-is-a-big-moral-deal.

"Bibliography – Academic Honesty: CAI Research." 2006. The Center for Academic Integrity. Duke University. https://www.waunakee.k12.wi.us/hs/departments/lmtc/Assignme nts/McConnellScenarios/AcadHonesty_5Article.pdf.

Bilić-Zulle, Lidija, Vedran Frković, Tamara Turk, Josip Azman, and Mladen Petroveck. 2005. "Prevalence of Plagiarism among Medical Students." *Croatian Medical Journal* 46 (1): 126–31.

Bjelobaba, Sonja. 2018. "Academic Integrity Skill Development amongst the Faculty at a Swedish University." In *Towards Consistency and Transparency in Academic Integrity*, edited by Salim Razı, Irene Glendinning, and Tomáš Foltýnek, 131–46. Berlin: Peter Lang. doi: 10.3726/b15273.

Blake, Byron. 2000. "The Caribbean - Geography, Culture, History and Identity: Assets for Economic Integration and Development." In *Contending with Destiny: The Caribbean in the 21st Century*, edited by Kenneth Hall and Denis Benn, 45–52. Kingston: Ian Randle Publishers.

Bland, J. Martin, and Douglas G. Altman. 1997. "Statistics Notes: Cronbach's Alpha." *BMJ* 314: 275. 10.1136/bmj.314.7080.572.

Bleeker, Karen C. 2008. *To Be Honest: Championing Academic Integrity in Community Colleges*. Washington, DC: Community College Press.

Blum, Susan D. 2009. "Academic Integrity and Student Plagiarism: A Question of Education, not Ethics." *The Chronicle of Higher Education*. Last modified 20 February 2009. https://www.chronicle.com/article/Academic-IntegrityStudent/32323.

Bowdoin College. n.d. "The Common Types of Plagiarism." *Bowdoin College*. Accessed 21 May 2021. https://www.bowdoin.edu/dean-of-students/judicial-board/academic-honesty-and-plagiarism/common-types-of-plagiarism.html.

Boise State University. n.d. "Faculty Responsibility to Address Student Academic Misconduct." Accessed 6 July 2020. https://policy.boisestate.edu/academic-affairs-faculty-administration/policy-title-faculty-responsibility-to-address-student-academic-misconduct/.

Boyle, Douglas M., James F. Boyle, and Brian W. Carpenter. 2016. "Accounting Student Academic Dishonesty: What Accounting Faculty and Administrators Believe." *The Accounting Educators' Journal Special Edition*, 39–61. http://www.aejournal.com/ojs/index.php /aej/article/view/329/171.

Bretag, Tracey. 2013a. "Challenges in Addressing Plagiarism in Education." *Plos Medicine* 10 (12). https://doi:10.1371/journal.pmed.1001574.

———. 2013b. "Short Cut Students: From Academic Misconduct to Academic Integrity." In *Global Corruption Report: Transparency International*, 171–77. New York: Routledge.

———. 2018a. "Academic Integrity." *Oxford Research Encyclopedia of Business and Management*. https://doi.org/10.1093/acrefore/9780190224851.013.147.

———. 2018b. "The Rise of Contract Cheating in Higher Education: Academic Fraud Beyond Plagiarism." https://www.biomedcentral.com/collections/cche.

Bretag, Tracey, Saadia Mahmud, Margaret Wallace, Ruth Walker, Colin James, Margaret Green, Julianne East, Ursula McGowan McGowan, and Lee Partridge. (2011). "Core elements of exemplary academic integrity policy in Australian higher education." *International Journal for Educational Integrity*, 7(2): 3–12.

Bretag, Tracey, and Saadia Mahmud. 2016. "A Conceptual Framework for Implementing Exemplary Academic Integrity Policy in Australian Higher Education." In *Handbook of Academic Integrity*, edited by Tracey Bretag. https://link.springer.com/referenceworkentry/10.1007/978-981-287-098-8_24.

Brigham Young University. 2019. "Using Alternative Assessments." https://ctl.byu.edu/using-alternative-assessments.

Briney, Amanda. 2018. "Caribbean Countries by Land Area." ThoughtCo. Last modified 25 July 2018. https://www.thoughtco.com/caribbean-countries-by-area-4169407.

Broeckelman-Post, Melissa. 2008. "Faculty and Student Classroom Influences on Academic Dishonesty." *IEEE Transactions on Education* 51 (2): 206–11. https://ieeexplore.ieee. org/stamp/stamp.jsp?arnumber=4472093.

Bryman, Alan. 2016. *Social Research Methods*. 5th ed. Oxford: Oxford University Press.

Burns, Robert. 2000. *Introduction to Research Methods*. London: Sage Publications.

Byron, Jessica. 2000. "Migration, National Identity and Regionalism in the Caribbean: A Leeward Islands Case Study." In *Contending with Destiny: The Caribbean in the 21st Century*, edited by Kenneth Hall and Denis Benn, 80–90. Kingston: Ian Randle Publishers.

Caldwell, Cam. 2010. "A Ten-Step Model for Academic Integrity: A Positive Approach for Business Schools." *Journal of Business Ethics* 92: 1–13.

Campbell, Audrey. 2019. "3 Ways Academic Integrity Can Start in Primary School." Turnitin. https://www.turnitin.com/blog/3-ways-academic-integrity-can-start-in-primary-school.

Campbell, Wayne. 2013. "What If CSEC Cheating Widespread?" *The Gleaner*, 14 October 2013. http://jamaica-leaner.com/gleaner/20131014/cleisure/cleisure2.html.

Capacity Development Group. 2009. "Capacity Development: Frequently Asked Questions: The UNDP Approach to Supporting Capacity Development." United Nations Development Programme. http://content-ext.undp.org/aplaws_assets/2072460/2072460.pdf.

Carboon, Bruce. 2013. "Academic Integrity at La Trobe University." La Trobe University. https://lo.unisa.edu.au/file.php/6751/Roundtable/Carboon_La_Trobe.pdf.

"Caribbean." 2019. *New World Encyclopedia*. Accessed 7 April 2020. https://www.newworldencyclopedia.org/entry/caribbean.

Caribbean Area Network for Quality Assurance in Tertiary Education. n.d. "Constitution of the Caribbean Area Network for Quality Assurance in Tertiary Education (CANQATE)."

Caribbean Community Secretariat. 2001. "Revised Treaty of Chaguaramas Establishing the Caribbean Community Including the CARICOM Single Market and Economy." PDF file. https://caricom.org/documents/4906-revised_treaty-text.pdf.

Caribbean Examinations Council. 2012. "Electronic Document Preparation and Management Syllabus." Caribbean Examinations Council. https://www.cxc.org/SiteAssets/syllabusses/CSEC/CSEC_Electronic_Document_Preparation_and_Management.pdf.

———. 2013a. "Guidelines for Candidates Writing Examinations Offered by CXC." https://www.cxc.org/SiteAssets/GUIDELINES/GUIDELINESTOCANDIDATESRevised2013.pdf.

———. 2013b. "SBA Handbook for Teachers." PDF file. https://www.cxc.org/SiteAssets/MANUALS/SBA _Handbook_for_Teachers4Feb13.pdf.

———. 2015. "School Based Assessment Manual for Principals: Caribbean Secondary Education Certificate (CSEC)." https://www.cxc.org/SiteAssets/MANUALS/MAN_ per cent20EAS per cent20SBA per cent20Manual2015v2.pdf.

———. 2016. "School Based Assessment (SBA)." Last modified 5 May 2016. https://www.cxc.org/school-based-assessment-sba/.

———. 2018. "Annual Report 2018." *Caribbean Examinations Council*. https://www.cxc.org/annual-reports/2018/7.html.

———. 2019. "2020 Strategic Goals." *Caribbean Examination Council*. https://www.cxc.org/100-support-for-cxcs-2020-strategic-goals/.

———. 2020a. "About CXC." https://www.cxc.org/about/about-cxc/.

———. 2020b. "History." https://www.cxc.org/about/history/.

———. 2021. "Governace." *Caribbean Examination Council*. https://www.cxc.org/about/structure/governance/.

Caribbean Maritime University. 2018. "Caribbean Maritime University Student Handbook 2018-2019." https://srs.cmu.edu.jm/web_student_information/static/src/pdf/CMU StudentHand book_ 2018_2019.pdf.

"Caribbean Population (Live)." 2019. *Worldometer*. Accessed 24 March 2020. https://www.worldometers.info/world-population/caribbean-population/.

CARICOM. 2018. "CARICOM Human Resource Development 2030 Strategy: Unlocking Caribbean Human Potential." https://caricom.org/documents/16065-caricom-hrd-2030-strategy-viewing.pdf.

CARICOM. 2019. "Education: Overview." Last modified 2019. Accessed 31 July 2019. https://CARICOM.org/work-areas/overview/education.

———. n.d. "CARICOM Regional Guidelines for Developing Policy, Regulation and Standards in Early Childhood Development Services." PDF file. Accessed 10 March 2021. https://caricom.org/documents/12069-regional_guidelines_-_early_childhood_development_services.pd.

Carnero, Andres M., Percy Mayta-Tristan, Kelika A. Konda, Edward Mezones-Holguin, Antonio Bernabe-Ortiz, German F. Alvarado, Carlos Canelo-Aybar, Jorge L. Maguiña, Eddy R. Segura, Antonio M. Quispe, Edward S. Smith, Angela M. Bayer, and Andres G. Lescano. 2017. "Plagiarism, Cheating and Research Integrity: Case Studies from a Masters Program in Peru." *Science and Engineering Ethics* 23 (4): 1183–97. doi: 10.1007/s11948-016-9820-z.

Carpenter, DonaldD., Trevor S. Harding, and Cynthia J. Finelli. 2006. "The Implications of Academic Dishonesty in Undergraduate Engineering on Professional Ethical Behavior." *Proceedings of the 2006 World Environmental and Water Resources Congress*. doi: 10.1061/40856(200)341.

Carpenter, DonaldD., Trevor S. Harding, Cynthia J. Finelli, Susan M. Montgomery, and Honor J. Passow. 2006. "Engineering Students' Perceptions of and Attitudes towards Cheating." *Journal of Engineering Education* 95 (3): 181–94.

Carrington, Edwin W., and Caribbean Community Secretariat. 1993. "The Future of Education in the Caribbean: Report of the CARICOM. Advisory Task Force on Education." Georgetown, Guyana: ERIC Clearinghouse. https://CARICOM.org/documents/ 12090-the_future_of_education_in_the_caribbean.pdf.

Carroll, Jude. 2016. "Making Decisions on Management of Plagiarism Cases Where There Is a Deliberate Attempt to Cheat." In *Handbook of Academic Integrity*, edited by Tracey Bretag. https://link.springer.com/referenceworkentry/10.1007/978 981-287-098-8_54.

Carroll, Jude, and Jon Appleton. 2001. "Plagiarism a Good Practice Guide." *Oxford Brookes University*. https://i.unisa.edu.au/siteassets/staff/tiu/documents/plagiarism---a-good-practice-guide-by-oxford-brookes-university.pdf.

"Challenges in Higher Education: Annual Report 2010-2011." n.d. University of the West Indies. Accessed 15 June 2020. Mona. https://www.mona.uwi.edu/opair/reports/20102011/highered.pdf.

Chaney, Jerry, and Tom Duncan. 1985. "Editors, Teachers Disagree About Definition of Plagiarism." *Journalism Educator* 40: 13–16. https://doi.org/10.1177/107769588504000204.

Chapman, Kenneth J., Richard Davis, Daniel Toy, and Lauren Wright. 2004. "Academic Integrity in the Business School Environment: I'll Get by with a Little Help from My Friends." *Journal of Marketing Education* 26 (3): 236–49. https://doi.org/10.1177/0273475304268779.

Charles, Christopher. 2013. "The Anti-Informer and Anti-Snitch Discourses in Dancehall and Rap Songs." Available at SSRN: https://ssrn.com/abstract=2372209 or http://dx.doi.org/10.2139/ssrn.2372209.

Charubusp, Sasima. 2015. "Plagiarism in the Perception of Thai Students and Teachers." *Asian EFL Journal Professional Teaching Articles* 87: 61–80. https://www.academia.edu/16450883/Plagiarism_in_the_Perception_of_Thai_Students_and_Teachers.

"Cheating at Examinations." 2015. *Stabroek News*, 21 April 2015. https://www.stabroeknews.com/2015/04/21/opinion/editorial/cheating-at-examinations/.

Chen, Quan. 2018. "Plagiarism is Rampant in China, and Its Media Companies Are Raking in Billions." *CNBC*, 3 January 2018. https://www.cnbc.com/2018/01/23/ip-plagiarism-is-rampant-in-china-and-media-companies-profit-from-it.html\.

Cheng, Ming. 2016. *Quality in Higher Education Developing a Virtue of Professional Practice*. University of Wolverhampton: Sense Publishers. https://www.sensepublishers.com/media/2877-quality-in-higher-education-1.pdf

Cherry, Kendra, and Amy Morin. 2019. "Gardner's Theory of Multiple Intelligences." *Verywell Mind*. https://www.verywellmind.com/gardners-theory-of-multiple-intelligences-2795161.

Chickering, Arthur W., and Zelda F. Gamson. 1987. "Seven Principles for Good Practice in Undergraduate Education." *AAHE Bulletin* 39 (7): 3–7. https://files.eric.ed.gov/fulltext/ED282491.pdf.

———. 2019. "Chickering and Gamson 7 Rules for Undergraduate Education." Center for Instructional Technology Training. http://citt.ufl.edu/tools/chickering-and-gamson-7-rules-for-undergraduate-education/.

Choemprayong, Songphan, and Barbara Wildemuth. 2009. "Developing New Measures." In *Applications of Social Research Methods to Questions in Information and Library Science*, edited by Barbara Wildermuth, 278–93. Westport: Libraries Unlimited.

Chowdhury, Hussain A., and Dhruba K. Bhattacharyya. 2018. "Plagiarism: Taxonomy, Tools and Detection Techniques." *Paper of the 19th National Convention on Knowledge, Library and Information Networking (NACLIN 2016) held at Tezpur University, Assam, India from October 26-28, 2016*. https://doi.org/arXiv:1801.06323 [cs.IR].

Chrysler-Fox, Pharny. 2017. "Who Will Perpetrate Plagiarism? Predictors of Student Plagiarism." *29th SAIMS Annual Conference Proceedings*. https://www.researchgate.net/publication/319650833_Who_will_perpetrate_plagiarism_Predictors_of_student_plagiarism.

Clarke Roger. 2006. 'Plagiarism by Academics: More Complex Than It Seems." *Journal of the Association for Information Systems* 7 (1): 91–121. https//doi.10.177705/1JAIS.00080.

Clayton, Anthony. 2003. "Current Trends in Higher Education and the Implications for the UWI." In *Contending with Destiny: The Caribbean in the*

21st Century, edited by Kenneth Hall and Dennis Benn, 137–46. Kingston: Ian Randle Publishers.

Cleary, Michelle Navarre. 2017. "Top 10 Reasons Students Plagiarize & What Teachers Can Do about it (with Apologies to David Letterman)." *Phi Delta Kappan* 99 (4): 66–71. https://doi.org/10.1177/0031721717745548.

Cohen, Louis, Lawrence Manion, and Keith Morrison. 2000. *Research Methods in Education*. 5th ed. London: Routledge-Falmer.

Collins, Mary Elizabeth, and Maryann Amodeo. 2005. "Responding to Plagiarism in Schools of Social Work: Considerations and Recommendations." *Journal of Social Work Education* 41 (3): 527–43. http://www.jstor.org/stable/23045023.

Comas, Ruben, and Jaume S. Negre. 2008. "Academic Cyberplagiarism: Tracing the Causes to Reach Solutions." *Digithum*, no. 10. https://doi.org/10.7238/d.v0i10.505.

Commission on Dental Accreditation. 2021. "Definitions and Purposes of Accreditation." https://www.ada.org/en/coda/policies-and-guidelines/training-resources/new-site-visitor-training/unit-1-accreditation/definitions-and-purposes-of-accreditation#:~:text=Accreditation%20in%20higher%20education%20is,every%20five%20to%20ten%20years.

"Concerns at UWI Over Plagiarism Claim." 2014. *Trinidad Express*, 15 May 2014. https://trinidadexpress.com/news/concern-at-uwi-over-plagiarism-claim-25048665.html.

Conzemius, Anne, and Jan O'Neill. 2001. *Building Shared Responsibility for Student Learning*. Association for Supervision and Curriculum Development: Alexandria, 2001. http://www.ascd.org/Publications/Books/Overview/Building-Shared-Responsibility-for-StudentLearning.aspx#:~:text=Shared%20responsibility%20is%20something%20school,how%20all%20students%20learn%20.%20.%20.%20&text=Reflection%2D%2DThe%20commitment%20to,data%2C%20and%20adjust%20practices%20accordingly.

Coren, Arthur. 2011. "Turning a Blind Eye: Faculty Who Ignore Student Cheating." *Journal of Academic Ethics* 9 (4). https://doi.org/10.1007/s10805-011-9147-y.

Cornell University. 2018. "The Essential Guide to Academic Integrity at Cornell Office of the Vice Provost for Undergraduate Education." https://ccengagement.cornell.edu /sites /ccengagement.cornell.edu/files/rnsp/documents/2018_ai_guide_08_30_18.pdf.

Craig, Robert, and David Dalton. 2013. "Understanding First Year Undergraduate Student Perceptions of Copying and Plagiarism: Developing a Platform for a Culture of Honest Inquiry and the Academic Construction of Knowledge." *Plagiarism across Europe and Beyond—Conference Proceedings*, 103–14. http://academicintegrity.eu/conference/ proceedings/2013/Craig_Understanding.pdf.

———. 2014. "Developing a Platform for a Culture of Honest Inquiry and the Academic Construction of Knowledge in First-year Students." *International Journal for Educational Integrity* 10 (1): 56–69. https://www.ojs.unisa.edu.au/index.php/IJEI/article/viewFile/934/657.

Creswell, John W. 2007. *Qualitative Inquiry & Research Design: Choosing among Five Approaches*. Second ed. Thousand Oaks: Sage Publications.

"Curriculum and Assessment." 2021. *Ministry of Education, Technological and Vocational Training.* https://mes.gov.bb/Departments/Curriculum-Assessment/.

"Curriculum Planning and Development Division." n.d. *Government of the Republic of Trinidad and Tobago Ministry of Education.* Accessed 15 April 2021. https://www.moe.gov.tt/curriculum-planning-and-development-division-cpdd/.

Curriculum Planning and Development Division, Ministry of Education Trinidad and Tobago. 2013. "Curriculum Guide English Language Arts Infants 1 – Standard 5." https://www.moe.gov.tt/wp-content/uploads/2019/06/2-CURRICULUM-GUIDE-ELA.pdf.

Curtis, Guy J., and Lucia Vardanega. 2016. "Is Plagiarism Changing Over Time? A 10-year Time-lag Study with Three Points of Measurement." *Higher Education Research and Development* 35 (6): 1–13. https://doi.org/10.1080/07294360.2016.1161602.

"CXC 1998 – 2008: A Period of Consolidation and Expansion." 2013. *The Caribbean Examiner* 11 (1). https://www.cxc.org/SiteAssets/Examiners/CXC40thexaminerJune2013.pdf.

"CXC Aiming to Reduce Disqualification at Upcoming Exams." 2012. *Kaieteur News.* Last modified 7 May 2012. https://www.kaieteurnewsonline.com/2012/05/07/cxc-aiming-to-reduce-disqualification-at-upcoming-exams/.

"CXC Fraud Pp." 2012. *Kaieteur News.* Last modified 18 March 2012. https://www.kaieteurnewsonline.com/2012/03/18/cxc-fraud-up/.

"CXC Touts Introduction of Software to Arrest Plagiarism." 2012. *Kaieteur News.* Last modified 8 May 2012. https://www.kaieteurnewsonline.com/2012/05/09/cxc-touts-introduction-of-software-to-arrest-plagiarism/.

"Cyber Plagiarism & Statistics." 2020. CheckForPlagiarism.net. https://www.checkforplagiarism.net/cyber-plagiarism.

Dames, Candia. 2014. "Reappointing Rodney Smith: A Bad Signal." *The Nassau Guardian,* 1 September 2014. https://www.bahamasb2b.com/news/2014/09/reappointing-rodney-smith-a-bad-signal.

Daniel, John. 2016. "Advisory Statement for Effective International Practice Combatting Corruption and Enhancing Integrity: A Contemporary Challenge for the Quality and Credibility of Higher Education." https://www.chea.org/userfiles/PDFs/advisory-statement-unesco-iiep.pdf.

Danielson, Charlotte. 2006. "Schoolwide Policies and Programs." In *Teacher Leadership That Strengthens Professional Practice.* Heatherton: Hawker Brownlow Education. http://www.ascd.org/publications/books /105048/chapters/Schoolwide-Policies-and-Programs.aspx.

Dant, Doris R. 1986. "Plagiarism in High School: A Survey." *The English Journal* 75 (2): 81–84. https://www.jstor.org/stable/817898.

Davies, Laura J., and Rebecca Moore Howard. 2016. "Plagiarism and the Internet: Fears, Facts, and Pedagogies." In *Handbook of Academic Integrity,* edited by Tracey Bretag. https://doi.org/https://link.springer.com/referenceworkentry/10.1007/ 978-981-287-09 8-8_16.

Dias, Pulo C., and Ana Sofia Bastos. 2014. "Plagiarism Phenomenon in European Countries: Results from GENIUS Project." *5th World Conference on Educational*

Sciences - *WCES 2013: 2526-2531*. Rome: Procedia. Accessed 12 May 2018. doi:10.1016/j.sbspro.2014.01.605.
"DNO Poll: How Important is the Issue of Plagiarism in Deciding for Whom You Vote?" 2014. *Dominica News Online*, 17 September 2014. https://dominicanewsonline.com/news/homepage/news/polls/dno-poll-issue-plagiarism-really-important-dominica-right-now/.
"Does Turnitin Detect Plagiarism?" 2013. Turnitin. https://www.turnitin.com/blog/does-turnitin-detect-plagiarism.
Dottin, Bea. 2013. "Plagiarism Worrying CXC." *Nation News*. https://www.nationnews.com/nationnews/news/50933/plagiarism-worrying-cxc.
Drinan, Patrick. 2011. "Expanding the Radius of Trust to External Stakeholders." In *Creating the Ethical Academy: A Systems Approach to Understanding Misconduct and Empowering Change in Higher Education*, edited by Tricia Bertram Gallant, 183–98. New York: Routledge.
Duke University. n.d. "Duke University Plagiarism Tutorial: Intentional Plagiarism." Accessed 25 August 2018. https://plagiarism.duke.edu/intent/.
East, Julianne. 2016. "Educational Responses to Academic Integrity." In *Handbook of Academic Integrity*, edited by Tracey Bretag, 1–13. https://doi.org/https://link.springer.com/referenceworkentry/10.1007/978-981-287-098-8_33.
East, Julianne, and Lisa Donnelly. 2012. "Taking Responsibility for Academic Integrity: A Collaborative Teaching and Learning Design." *Journal of University Teaching and Learning Practice* 9 (3). https://doi.org/https://ro.uow.edu.au/jutlp/vol9/iss3/.
Eaton, JudithS. 2018. "Combating Academic Corruption: Quality Assurance and Accreditation." *International Higher Education* 2 (93): 8–9. https://doi.org/10.6017/ihe.0.93.10426.
Eckersley, Bill, Helen Borland, and Fiona Henderson. n.d. "Culture of Academic Integrity." Victoria University. Accessed 12 July 2020. https://lo.unisa.edu.au/file.php/6751/Roundtable/Henderson_VU.pdf.
Edna Manley College of the Visual and Performing Arts. 2017. "College Handbook 2017-2018." http://emc.edu.jm/wpcontent/uploads/2017/08/EMCVPA_College_Handbook_2017_18.pdf.
"Education Ministry Implements Stricter Measures for CXC SBAs." 2015. *Jamaica Observer*, 1 January 2015. http://www.jamaicaobserver.com/news/Education-Ministry-implements-stricter-measures-for-CXC-SBAs.
"Education Rankings by Country 2020." Accessed 20 March 2020. https://worldpopulationreview.com/countries/education-rankings-by-country/.
"Education Spending, Percent of GDP - Country Website 2021 Rankings." *The Global Economy*. https://www.theglobaleconomy.com/rankings/Education_spending/.
"Education System in Trinidad and Tobago." 2018. Scholaro Pro. https://www.scholaro.com/pro/Countries/Trinidad-and-Tobago/Education-System.
Enago Academy. 2018. "The Difference Between Honorary and Ghost Authorship in Scientific Research." https://www.enago.com/academy/difference-between-honorary-and-ghost-authorship-in-scientific-research/.

Eret, Esra, and Tuba Gokmenoglu. 2010. "Plagiarism in Higher Education: A Case Study with Prospective Academicians." *Procedia Social and Behavioral Sciences* 2: 3303–07. https://doi.org/https://core.ac.uk/download/pdf/82632126.pdf.

Eriksson, Li, and Tara R. McGee. 2015. "Academic Dishonesty amongst Australian Criminal Justice and Policing University Students: Individual and Contextual Factors." *International Journal for Educational Integrity* 11 (5). https://doi.org/https://doi.org/10.1007/s40979-015-0005-3.

ETH Zurich. "Plagiarism." 2021. https://ethz.ch/students/en/studies/performance-assessments/plagiarism.html.

European Union and the Council of Europe. "Academic Integrity - Achievements and Future Perspective for Montenegro." Held in Bečići, Montenegro, 16–17 May 2017. Budva: European Union and the Council of Europe. Accessed 20 March 2020. http://etico.iiep.unesco.org/sites/default/files/akademski_integritet-izvjestaj-eng-feb_2018_0.pdf.

Evans-Tokaryk, Tyler. 2014. "Academic Integrity, Remix Culture, Globalization: A Canadian Case Study of Student and Faculty Perceptions of Plagiarism." *Across the Disciplines* 11 (2): 1–40. https://wac.colostate.edu/atd/articles/evans-tokaryk2014.cfm.

Farahian, Majid, Farshad Parhamnia, and Farnaz Avarzamani. 2020. "Plagiarism in Theses: A Nationwide Concern from the Perspective of University Instructors." *Cogent Social Sciences* 6 (1): 1–17. doi: 10.1080/23311886.2020.1751532.

Fass, Richard A. 1986. "By Honor Bound: Encouraging Academic Honesty." *Educational Record* 67: 32–35.

Fawzy, Farida. 2016. "From Speeches to Ph.D.'s: Politicians Called Out for Copying." *CNN Politics, CNN*. Updated 19 July 2016. https://edition.cnn.com/2016/07/19/politics/politicians-plagiarism/index.html.

Ferguson, Melissa J., and John A. Bargh. 2004. "How Social Perception can Automatically Influence Behavior." *Trends in Cognitive Sciences* 8 (1): 33–9. doi:10.1016/j.tics.2003.11.004.

Fernandes, Autry A. 2016. "There Are Too Many School-Based Assignments for CXC." *Stabroek News*. Last modified 9 February 2016. https://www.stabroeknews.com/2016/opinion/letters/02/09/many-school-based-assignments-cxc/.

Fish, Reva, and Gerri Hura. 2013. "Students' Perceptions of Plagiarism." *Journal of the Scholarship of Teaching and Learning* 13, no. 5 (December): 33–45. https://files.eric.ed.gov/fulltext/EJ1017029.pdf.

Fish, Stanley. 2010. "Plagiarism Is Not a Big Moral Deal." *The New York Times Opinionator*, 9 August 2010. https://opinionator.blogs.nytimes.com/2010/08/09/plagiarism-is-not-a-big-moral-deal/?mtrref=www.google.com&assetType=REGIWALL.

Fishman, Teddi, and Jason Chu. 2017. "Policy to Practise: Developing Effective Academic Integrity Policies." *Plagiarism.Org*. https://www.plagiarism.org/video/policy-to-practice.

Fiszbein, Ariel, and Sarah Stanton. 2018. "The Future of Education in Latin America and the Caribbean: Possibilities for United States Investment and Engagement." http://www.observatorioeducacion.org/sites/default/files/usaid-layout-6.12.2018-final_pdf.pdf.

Flinders University. 2021. "Student Academic Integrity Procedures." https://www.flinders.edu.au/content/dam/documents/staff/policies/academic-students/student-academic-integrity-procedures.pdf.

Flint, Abbi, Sue Clegg, and Ranald Macdonald. 2006. "Exploring Staff Perceptions of Student Plagiarism." *Journal of Further and Higher Education* 30 (2): 145–56. https://doi.org/https://www.researchgate.net/publication/228764924_Exploring_staff_perceptions_of_student_plagiarism.

Floyd, Emily, Rebecca Taylor, and Edward Queen. 2019. "Cultivating a Community of Integrity." *International Center for Academic Integrity 27th Annual Conference*, March 8–10, New Orleans, Louisana.

Foggett, Tracy. 2002. "Information Literacy at the Primary School Level?" *The Australian Library Journal* 52 (1): 55–63. https://doi.org/10.1080/00049670.2003.10721496.

Foo, Schubert, Shaheen Majid, and Yun Ke Chang. 2017. "Assessing Information Literacy Skills Among Young Information Age Students in Singapore." *ASLIB Journal of Information Management* 69 (3): 335–53. https://doi.org/10.1108/AJIM-08-2016-0138.

Fordham University. n.d. "The Academic Integrity Committee." Fordham University. https://www.fordham.edu/info/25380/undergraduate_academic_integrity_policy/6939/the_academic_integrity_committee.

Forstall, Melanie. 2019. "Definition of School Policies." *The Classroom*. Last modified 6 May 2019. https://www.theclassroom.com/definition-school-policies-5943931.html.

Foshay, Arthur W. 1991. "The Curriculum Matrix: Transcendence and Mathematics." *Journal of Curriculum and Supervision* 6. Accessed 17 June 2019. https://www.ascd.org/ASCD/pdf/journals/ed_update/eu201207_infographic.pdf.

Foster-Allen, Elaine. 2007. "Prospects for Tertiary Education in Jamaica." In *Higher Education: Caribbean Perspective*, edited by Kenneth O. Hall and Rose Marie Cameron, 119–31. Kingston: Ian Randle Publishers.

Foust, Cathy. 2016. "Plagiarism: What It Is and Why It Is Wrong." *Brighthub*. https://www.brighthub.com/education/online-learning/articles/35421.aspx.

Fowler, FloydJ. 2009. *Survey Research Methods*. Thousand Oaks: Sage Publications.

Fraenkel, Jack, and Norman Wallen. 2009. *How to Design and Evaluate Research in Education*. 7th ed. Boston: McGraw-Hill Higher Education.

France-Presse, Agence. 2021. "Austrian Minister Resigns Amid Thesis Plagiarism Scandal." *The Guardian*, 9 January 2021. Accessed 1 March 2021. https://www.theguardian.com/world/2021/jan/09/austrian-minister-resigns-amid-plagiarism-scandal.

Francis, Jermaine. 2013. "Plagiarism in Schools Likely Widespread - JTA President." *The Gleaner*, 23 October 2013. http://jamaicagleaner.com/gleaner/20131023/lead/lead2.html.

Francis, Kimone. 2019. "Participants Hail Tour of Canadian Universities as Informative." *Jamaica Observer*, 4 October 2019. http://www.jamaicaobserver.com/news/participants-hail-tour-of-canadian_176356?profile=1470.

Furedi, Frank. 2017. "Universities Blame Others for Plagiarism. They Need to Look at Themselves." *The Guardian*, 27 February 2017. https://www.theguardian.com/education/2017/feb/27/universities-blame-plagiarism-frank-furedi.

Gabriel, Trip. 2010a. "Plagiarism Lines Blur for Students in Digital Age." *The New York Times*, 1 August 2010. Accessed 25 March 2018. https://www.nytimes.com/2010/08/02/education/02cheat.html.

———. 2010b. "Under Pressure, Teachers Tamper with Tests." *New York Times*, 10 June 2010. https://www.nytimes.com/2010/06/11/education/11cheat.html.

Galen University. 2017. "Academic Policies." https://galen.edu.bz/academic-policies/.

Gallant, Tricia Bertram. 2011. "Building a Culture of Academic Integrity." PDF File. Accessed 1 April 2021. https://www.depts.ttu.edu/tlpdc/Resources/Academic_Integrity/files/academicintegrity-magnawhitepaper.pdf.

———. 2015. "Leveraging Institutional Integrity for the Betterment of Education." In *Handbook of Academic Integrity*, edited by Tracey Bretag, 979–93. https://link.springer.com/referenceworkentry/10.1007/978-981-287-098-8_52.

Gallant, Tricia Bertram, and Patrick Drinan. 2008. "Toward a Model of Academic Integrity Institutionalization: Informing Practice in Postsecondary Education." *Canadian Journal of Higher Education* 38 (2): 25–43. https://journals.sfu.ca/cjhe/index.php/cjhe/article/view/508/557.

Gallant, Tricia Bertram, and Lester Goodchild. 2011. "Introduction." In *Creating the Ethical Academy: A Systems Approach to Understanding Misconduct and Empowering Change in Higher Education*, edited by Tricia Bertram Gallant. 27–44. New York: Routeledge.

Gallant, Tricia Bertram, and Michael Kalichman. 2011. "Academic Ethics: A Systems Approach to Understanding Misconduct and Empowering Change." In *Creating the Ethical Academy: A Systems Approach to Understanding Misconduct and Empowering Change in Higher Education*, edited by Tricia Bertram Gallant. 3–11. New York: Routeledge.

Gamage, Kelum, Erandika K. de Silva, and Nanda Gunawardhana. 2020. "Online Delivery and Assessment during COVID-19: Safeguarding Academic Integrity." Multidisciplinary Digital Publishing Institute, 25 October 2020. https://doi.org/10.3390/educsci10110301.

Garrett, Jennifer. 2011. "Academic Integrity: Examining Two Common Approaches." *Faculty Focus*. Last modified 22 September 2011. https://www.facultyfocus.com/articles/edtech-news-and-trends/academic-integrity-examining-two-common-approaches/.

George, Nancy. 2016. "Education in the Caribbean." *Caribbean Journal*. Last modified 22 May 2016. https://www.caribjournal.com/2016/05/22/education-in-the-caribbean/.

Gilbert, Greg, Bernie Day, Alice Murillo, Jane Patton, Andrea Sibley-Smith, and Beth Smith. 2007. *Promoting and Sustaining and Institutional Climate of Academic Integrity.* PDF file. https://files.eric.ed.gov/fulltext/ED510583.pdf.

Gillis, Charlie. 2011. "When Professors Plagiarize: Star Academics Get Light Punishments for Lifting Ideas." *McLean's University*, November 8. Accessed 15 May 2018. https://www.macleans.ca/education/uniandcollege/when-professors-plagiarize/.

Gilpin, Jodi-Ann. 2013. "Principal Wants Kids to be Taught About Plagiarism." *The Gleaner*, 8 October 2013. http://jamaica-gleaner.com/gleaner/20131008/lead/lead8.html.

Glendinning, Irene. 2013. "Comparison of Policies for Academic Integrity in Higher Education Across Europe (IPPHEAE)." IPPHEAE Project Consortium. http://plagiarism.cz/ippheae/files/D2-3-00%20EU%20IPPHEAE%20CU%20Survey%20EU-wide%20report.pdf.

———. 2014. "Responses to Student Plagiarism in Higher Education Across Europe." *International Journal for Educational Integrity* 10 (1): 4–20.

———. n.d. "Promoting Maturity in Policies for Plagiarism across Europe and Beyond." https://rm.coe.int/168069226e.

Global Monitoring Education Review: Meeting our Commitments to Gender Equality in Education. 2018. https://resourcecentre.savethechildren.net/library/global-education-monitoring-report-gender-review-2018-meeting-our-commitments-gender.

Gnanavel, Sundar. 2014. "Self-plagiarism: The Latest Ethical Dilemma in Biomedical Research." *Indian Journal of Psychological Medicine* 36 (4): 448–49. doi:10.4103/0253-7176.140763.

Goh, Edmund. 2013. "Plagiarism Behavior among Undergraduate Students in Hospitality and Tourism Education." *Journal of Teaching in Travel & Tourism* 13 (4): 307–22.

Gonzales, Gyasi. 2019. "Family Flees Sea Lots as Gangsters Kill 'informer'." *Daily Express*, 12 February 2019. https://trinidadexpress.com/news/local/family-flees-sea-lots-as-gangsters-kill-informer/article_519729f8-2ef9-11e9-9aef-8fee6b76c6fa.html.

Grant-Woodham, Jeanette. 2007. "Accessing Higher Education: Transitions Within an Era of Change in Jamaica." In *Higher Education: Caribbean Perspective*, edited by Kenneth O. Hall and Rose Marie Cameron, 132–65. Kingston: Ian Randle Publishers.

Greenburg, David. 2008. "Friends, Romans, Countrymen, Lend Me Your Speech." *The New York Times*, 24 February 2008. www.nytimes.com/2008/02/24/weekinreview/24greenberg.html.

Greenland, Philip, and Phil B. Fontanarosa. 2012. "Ending Honorary Authorship." *Science* 337 (6098). https://doi.org/10.1126/science.1224988. https://science.sciencemag.org/content/337/6098/1019.summary.

Grieneisen, Michael, and M. Minghua Zhang. 2012. "A Comprehensive Survey of Retracted Articles from the Scholarly Literature." *Plos One* 7 (10): e44118. https://doi.org/10.1371/journal.pone.0044118.

Griffith, Stafford. 2009. "The Caribbean Examinations Council: Leading and Facilitating Transformation in Secondary Education." *Journal of Eastern Caribbean Studies* 34, no. 2 (June): 40–55. Ebscohost.

———. 2013. "The Impact and Influence of CXC on the Regional Education Landscape." *The Caribbean Examiner* 11, no. 1 (May): 16–19. https://www.cxc.org/SiteAssets/Examiners/CXC40thexaminerJune2013.pdf.

———. 2015. *School-based Assessment in a Caribbean Public Examination*. Kingston: The University of the West Indies Press.

"Guidelines for Managing School-Based Assessments (SBA) in Trinidad and Tobago." n.d. Ministry of Education. http://moe.gov.tt/Documents/Curriculum/SBAGuidelines.pdf.

Gullifer, Judith. 2013. "Students' Perceptions of Plagiarism." PhD diss., Charles Sturt University.

Gullifer, Judith, and Graham A. Tyson. 2010. "Exploring University Students' Perceptions of Plagiarism: A Focus Group Study." *Journal of Studies in Higher Education* 35 (4): 463–81.

———. 2014. "Who has Read the Policy on Plagiarism? Unpacking Students' Understanding of Plagiarism." *Studies in Higher Education* 39 (7): 1202–18. https://doi.org/10.1080/03075079.2013.777412.

Halgamuge, Malka N. 2017. "The Use and Analysis of Anti-Plagiarism Software: Turnitin Tool for Formative Assessment and Feedback." *Wiley Online Library*, 13 June 2017. doi: https://doi.org/10.1002/cae.21842.

Hall, Kenneth O. 2013. "The Caribbean Examinations Council: An Instrument of Decolonisation." *The Caribbean Examiner* 11, no. 1 (May): 6–7. https://www.cxc.org/SiteAssets/ Examiners/CXC40thexaminerJune2013.pdf.

Hall-Hertel, Catherine, Christine Davis, and James Birkett. 2018. "Academic Integrity is Not Just an Academic Concern: Supporting Success for International and Graduate Students." Presented at the NASPA Annual Conference, 3–7 March 2018, Philadelphia.

Hallak, Jacques, and Muriel Poisson. 2007. *Corrupt Schools, Corrupt Universities: What Can Be Done?* Paris: UNESCO. https://unesdoc.unesco.org/ark:/48223/pf0000150259.

Hank, Carolyn, Mary Wilkins Jordan, and Barbara Wildermuth. 2009. "Survey Research." In *Applications of Social Research Methods to Questions in Information and Library Science*, edited by Barbara Wildermuth, 256–59. Westport: Libraries Unlimited.

Hansen, Robin F., and Alexandra Anderson. 2015. "Law Student Plagiarism: Contemporary Challenges and Responses." *Journal of Legal Education* 64, no. 3 (February): 416–27.

Harding, Trevor, Donald Carpenter, Cynthia Finelli, and Honor J. Passow. 2004. "Does Academic Dishonesty Relate to Unethical Behavior in Professional Practice? An Exploratory Study." *Science and Engineering Ethics* 10 (2): 311–24.

Harding, Trevor S., Honor J. Passow, Donald D. Carpenter, and Cynthia J. Finelli. 2003. "An Examination of the Relationship between Academic Dishonesty and Professional Behavior." *33rd ASEE/IEEE Frontiers in Education Conference*, Boulder, CO, 5 November 2003. http://citeseerx.ist.psu.edu/viewdoc/download?doi=10.1.1.922.9396&rep=rep1&type=pdf.

Harris, Andrew. 2014. "Jamaicans Making the Most of Overseas Studies." *The Gleaner*, 21 November 2014. http://jamaica-gleaner.com/article/lead-stories/20141121/jamaicans-making-most-overseas-studies-0.

Harvard University Extension School. 2017. "*Tips to Avoid Plagiarism* 2017-2018." Accessed 12 May 2018. https://www.extension.harvard.edu/resources-policies/resources/tips-avoid-plagiarism.

Hawthorne, Omar. 2017. "Protected Disclosures Act—Whistleblowing in an Anti-Informer Culture." In *Global Encyclopedia of Public Administration, Public Policy, and Governance*, edited by Ann-Marie Bissessar and Ali Farazmand. London: Springer.

Heater, Derek Benjamin. 1999. *What Is Citizenship?*. Malden: Polity Press. http://public.eblib.com/choice/publicfullrecord.aspx?p=1209614.

Heitman, Elizabeth, and Sergio Litewka. 2011. "International Perspectives on Plagiarism and Considerations for Teaching International Trainees." *Urologic Oncology* 29 (1): 104–08. https://doi.org/10.1016/j.urolonc.2010.09.014.

Hendry, Graham. n.d. "Practical Assessment Strategies to Prevent Students from Plagiarising." Accessed 15 June 2019. https://sydney.edu.au/education-portfolio/ei/news/pdfs/Practical per cent20assessment per cent20strategies per cent20to per cent20prevent per cent20students per cent20from per cent20plagiarising3.pdf.

Henry, Balford. 2020. "'Informer fi dead' Culture Hindering Police Investigations, Says DCP." *Jamaica Observer*, 24 January 2020. https://www.jamaicaobserver.com/news/-informer-fi-dead-culture-hindering-police-investigations-says-dcp_185412?profile=&template=PrinterVersion.

Henry, Catherine. 2008. "Honour Codes: From Honourable Intentions to Honest Behaviour." Compliance and Ethics Institute. Last modified 14–17 September 2008. https://assets.hcca-info.org/Portals/0/PDFs/Resources/library/Honor_Codes.pdf.

Hepburn, Kerry-Ann. 2017. "Caribbean Society and Culture." *The Gleaner*, 26 September 2017. https://www.pressreader.com/jamaica/jamaica-gleaner/20170926/textview.

Heyneman, Stephen P. 2011. "The Concern with Corruption in Higher Education." In *The Ethical Academy: A Systems Approach to Understanding Misconduct and Empowering Change in Higher Education*, edited by Tricia Bertram Gallant, 13–26. New York: Routeledge.

"Higher Education." 2016. *Encyclopaedia Britannica*. https://www.britannica.com/topic/higher-education.

Hodges, Amy, Troy Bickham, Elizabeth Schmidt, and Leslie Seawright. 2017. "Challenging the Profiles of a Plagiarist: A Study of Abstracts Submitted to an International Interdisciplinary Conference." *International Journal for Educational Integrity* 13 (7). https://doi.org/10.1007/s40979-017-0016-3

Holding, Rheima, and Olivene Burke. 2005. "Mona Declaration on Tertiary and Higher Education." In *Revisiting Tertiary Education Policy in Jamaica: Towards Personal Gain or Public Good*, edited by Rheima Holding and Olivene Burke, 416–19. Kingston: Ian Randle Publishers.

"Honesty in Conduct." n.d. *Josephson's Business Ethics*. Accessed 18 January 2019. http://josephsononbusinessethics.com/2011/01/honesty-in-conduct/.

Honig, Benson, and Akanksha Bedi. 2012. "The Fox in the Hen House: A Critical Examination of Plagiarism among Members of the Academy of Management." *Academy of Management Learning and Education* 11 (1): 101–23. EBSCOhost.

Honore-gopie, Venus, and Felicia Rampersad. 2009. "Student Cheats on CXC Maths." *Trinidad and Tobago Newsday*, 22 May 2009. https://archives.newsday.co.tt/2009/05/22/student-cheats-on-cxc-maths/.

"Honor Codes Across the Country." n.d. Accessed 15 June 2020. https://cs.stanford.edu/people/eroberts/cs201/projects/2000-01/honor-code/honorcodes.html.

Hooker, Brad. 2005. "Fairness." *Ethical Theory & Moral Practice* 8 (4): 329–52. doi:10.1007/s10677-005-8836-2.

Hoskin, Rob. 2012. "The Dangers of Self-report." Science for Brainwaves. Last modified 3 March 2012. Accessed 27 June 2019. https://www.sciencebrainwaves.com/the-dangers-of-self-report/0.

Hosny, Manar, and Shameem Fatima. 2014. "Attitude of Students towards Cheating and Plagiarism: University Case Study." *Journal of Applied Sciences* 14: 748–57.

"How Many Languages Are Spoken in the Caribbean." 2019. *Reference.com*. Last modified 2019. https://www.reference.com/geography/many-languages-spoken-caribbean-60870df7dddae26a.

Howard, Stephen J., John F. Ehrich, and Russel Walton. 2014. "Measuring Students' Perceptions of Plagiarism: Modification and Rasch Validation of a Plagiarism Attitude Scale." *Journal of Applied Measurement* 15 (4): 372–93.

Hoy, Wayne K., and Cecil G. Miskel. 2005. *Education Administration: Theory, Research, and Practice*. 7th ed. Boston: McGraw-Hill.

Hu, Guangwei, and Jun Lei. 2012. "Investigating Chinese University Students' Knowledge and Attitudes toward Plagiarism from an Integrated Perspective." *Language Learning* 62 (3): 813–50. doi:10.1111/j.1467-9922.2011.00650.x.

Hu, Guangwei, and Xiaoya Sun. 2017. "Institutional Policies on Plagiarism: The Case of Eight Chinese Universities of Foreign Languages/International Studies." *System* 66 (March): 56–68. https://doi.org/DOI: 10.1016/j.system.2017.03.015.

Hughes, Julia C., and Tricia B. Gallant. 2016. "Infusing Ethics and Ethical Decision Making into the Curriculum." In *Handbook of Academic Integrity*, edited by Tracey Bretag, 1–20. Singapore: Springer.

Hughes, Julia C., and Donald L. McCabe. 2006. "Understanding Academic Misconduct." *Canadian Journal of Higher Education Revue* 36 (1): 49–63. https://www.researchgate.net/publication/268254674_Understanding_Academic_Misconduct.

Husain, Rushdi, Ghayth K. Al-Shaibani, and Omer H. Mahfoodh. 2017. "Perceptions of and Attitudes toward Plagiarism and Factors Contributing to Plagiarism: A Review of Studies." *Journal of Academic Ethics* 15: 167–95. doi:10.1007/s10805-017-9274-1.

Hussein, Norashikin, Syezreen D. Rusdi, and Siti, S. Mohamad. 2016. "Academic Dishonesty Among Business Students: A Descriptive Study of Plagiarism Behavior." In *7th International Conference on University Learning and Teaching (InCULT 2014) Proceedings*, edited by C. Fook, G. Sidhu, S. Narasuman, L. Fong, and S. Abdul Rahman, 639–48. Singapore: Springer.

Indiana University. 2019. "Learning with Integrity." https://expand.iu.edu/browse/gateway/courses/learning-with-integrity.

International Center for Academic Integrity. 2014. "Fundamental Values of Academic Integrity." https://www.chapman.edu/academics/academic-integrity/_files/the-fundamental-values-of-academic-integrity.pdf.

International Center for Academic Integrity. 2019. "About the Center." *International Center for Academic Integrity*. https://academicintegrity.org/about/about-the-center.

———. 2020. "Academic Integrity Rating System." https://academicintegrity.org/site-search?q=academic+integrity+rating+system.

International Organisation on Migration. 2017. "Migration In the Caribbean: Current Trends, Opportunities and Challenges." Reliefweb. https://reliefweb.int/report/haiti/migration-caribbean-current-trends-opportunities-and-challenges.

Ismail, Kameran H. 2018. "Perceptions of Plagiarism Among Medical and Nursing Students in Erbil, Iraq." *Sultan Qaboos University Medical Journal* 18 (2): e196–e201. http://doi.org/10.18295/squmj.2018.18.02.012.

Ison, David C. 2012. "Plagiarism among Dissertations: Prevalence at Online Institutions." *Journal of Academic Ethics* 10 (3): 227–36. https://link.springer.com/article/10.1007/s10805-012-9165-4.

———. 2015. "The Influence of the Internet on Plagiarism Among Doctoral Dissertations: An Empirical Study." *Journal of Academic Ethics* 13: 151–66. https://doi.org/10.1007/s10805-015-9233-7.

Ithenticate. n.d. "6 Consequences of Plagiarism." Accessed 3 May 2018. http://www.ithenticate.com/resources/6-consequences-of-plagiarism.

———. 2011. "White Paper: The Ethics of Self Plagiarism." Ithenticate. https://www.ithenticate.com/hs-fs/hub/92785/file-5414624-pdf/media/ith-selfplagiarism-whitepaper.pdf.

Jahangier, Azam 2017. "PhD-students' Views on Honorary Authorship – MSc-student Internship." https://www.nrin.nl/ri-collection/ri-enterprises/research-consortia/phd-students-views-on-honorary-authorship/.

"Jamaica: History and Background." n.d. Stateuniversity.com. Accessed 1 February 2019. https://education.stateuniversity.com/pages/725/Jamaica-HISTORY-BACKGROUND.html #ixzz5eHhgSprA.

Jamaica Information Service. 2017. "Student Teachers to Learn Media, Information Literacy." *Jamaica Observer*, 29 October 2017. http://www

.jamaicaobserver.com/career-education/student-teachers-to-learn-media-information-literacy_115280&template=MobileArticle.

Jamaica Theological Seminary. 2020. "Plagiarism Policy." https://www.jts.edu.jm/current-students/plagiarism-policy/.

James, Colin. 2016. "Academic Integrity in Legal Education." In *Handbook of Academic Integrity*, edited by Tracey Bretag, 1–14. Singapore: Springer.

Jereb, Eva, Marko Urh, Janja Jerebic, and Polona Šprajc. 2018a. "Gender Differences and the Awareness of Plagiarism in Higher Education." *Social Psychology of Education* 21: 409. https://doi.org/10.1007/s11218-017-9421-y

Jereb, Eva, Matjaž Perc, Barbara Lämmlein, Janja Jerebic, Marko Urh, Iztok Podbregar, and Polona Šprajc. 2018b. "Factors Influencing Plagiarism in Higher Education: A Comparison of German and Slovene Students." *Plos One* 13 (8): e0202252. https://doi.org/10.1371/journal.pone.0202252.

Johnson, Lamech, 2014. "Plagiarism 'Was Not Intentional.'" *The Tribune*, 4 March 2014. http://www.tribune242.com/news/2014/mar/04/plagiarism-was-not-intentional/.

Johnson, Nancy, 2020. "How to Choose the Best Plagiarism Checker for Teachers: The Complete Guide 2020." Accessed 21 January 2020. https://97unique.com/.

Josephson Institute of Ethics. n.d. "Making Ethical Decisions." PDF file. Accessed 15 March 2021. https://web.engr.uky.edu/~jrcheeo/CE%20401/Josephson%20EDM/Making_Ethical_Decisions.pdf.

———. 2009. "Josephson Institute of Ethics Releases Study on High School Character and Adult Conduct: Character Study Reveals Predictors of Lying and Cheating." Josephson Institute. Last modified 29 October 2009. http://josephsoninstitute.org/surveys/.

Joy, Mike, Georgina Cosma, Jane Sinclair, and Jane Yau. 2009. "A Taxonomy of Plagiarism in Computer Science." *1st International Conference on Education and New Learning Technologies*, 6–8 July 2009. Barcelona, Spain. https://library.iated.org/view/JOY2009ATA.

"Junius Quotes." 2020. *BrainyMedia Inc.* Accessed 3 April 2020. https://www.brainyquote.com/quotes/junius_406319.

Kam, Chester, Ming Hue, and Hoi Cheung. 2018. "Plagiarism of Chinese Secondary School Students in Hong Kong." *Ethics and Behavior* 28 (4): 316–35.

Karasz, Palko. 2012. "Hungarian President Resigns Amid Plagiarism Scandal." *New York Times*, 2 April 2012. https://www.nytimes.com/2012/04/03/world/europe/hungarian-president-pal-schmitt-resigns-amid-plagiarism-scandal.html.

Kayaoglu, Mustafa N., Sarkine Erbay, Cristina Flitner, and Dogan Saltas. 2015. "Examining Students' Perceptions of Plagiarism: A Cross-cultural Study at Tertiary Level." *Journal of Further and Higher Education* 40 (5): 682–705. https://doi.org/10.1080/0309877X.2015.1014320.

Keith-Spiegel, Patricia, Barbara G. Tabachnick, Bernard E. Whitley Jr., and Jennifer Washburn. 1998. "Why Professors Ignore Cheating: Opinions of a National Sample of Psychology Instructors." *Ethics & Behavior* 8 (30): 215–27. https://doi.org/10.1207/s15327019eb0803_3.

Kelly, Tara. 2011. "College Plagiarism Reaches All Time High: Pew Study." *Huff Post*, 1 November 2011. https://www.huffpost.com/entry/college-plagiarism-all-ti_n_944252?guccounter=1.

Keuskamp, Dominic, and Regina Sliuzas. 2007. "Plagiarism Prevention or Detection? The Contribution of Text-Matching Software to Education about Academic Integrity." *Journal of Academic Language & Learning* 1 (1): A91–A99. https://www.researchgate.net/publication/228614309_Plagiarism_prevention_or_detection_The_contribution_of_text-matching_software_to_education_about_academic_integrity.

Kezar, Adrianna J., and Cecile Sam. 2011. "Enacting Transcendental Leadership: Creating and Supporting a More Ethical Campus in Creating the Ethical Academy: A Systems Approach to Understanding Misconduct and Empowering Change." In *Creating the Ethical Academy: A Systems Approach to Understanding Misconduct and Empowering Change in Higher Education*, edited by Tricia Gallant, 153–68. New York: Routledge.

King, Ruby. n.d. "Education in the British Caribbean: The Legacy of the Nineteenth Century." Accessed 23 March 2020. http://www.educoas.org/Portal/bdigital/contenido/interamer/BkIACD/Interamer/Interamerhtml/Millerhtml/mil_king.htm#*.

"Know The Emerging Plagiarism Trends To Keep Your Content Unique." 2021. Copyleaks. https://copyleaks.com/blog/know-the-emerging-plagiarism-trends-to-keep-your-content-unique/?doing_wp_cron=1630926096.2203609943389892578125.

Kokkinaki, Angelika I., Catherine Demoliou, and Melpo Iakovidou. 2015. "Students' Perceptions of Plagiarism and Relevant Policies in Cyprus." *International Journal for Educational Integrity*, 30 June 2015. https://doi.org/ https://doi.org/10.1007/s40979-015-0001-7.

Kovtun, Lesia. 2016. "8 Important Features of a Top Quality Plagiarism Checker." *Emerging Education Technology*, 15 September 2016. https://www.emergingedtech.com/2016/09/8-important-features-of-a-top-quality-plagiarism-checker/.

Kremmer, Michael L., Mark A. Brimble, and Peta Stevenson-Clarke. 2007. "Investigating the Probability of Student Cheating: The Relevance of Student Characteristics, Assessment Items, Perceptions of Prevalence and History of Engagement." *International Journal for Educational Integrity* 3 (2): 3–17.

Krippendorff, Klaus. 2013. *Content Analysis: An Introduction to its Methodology*. Thousand Oaks: Sage Publications.

Kucharska, Wioleta. 2017. "Relationships between Trust and Collaborative Culture in The Context of Tacit Knowledge Sharing." *Journal of Entrepreneurship, Management and Innovation* 13 (4). https://www.jemi.edu.pl/vol-13-issue-4-2017/relationships-between-trust-and-collaborative-culture-in-the-context-of-tacit-knowledge-sharing.

Kupferschmidt, Kai. 2018. "Tide of Lies: Researcher at the Center of an Epic Fraud Remains an Enigma to those Who Exposed Him." *Science*. Last modified

17 August 2018. Accessed 27 June 2019. https://www.sciencemag.org/news/2018/08/researcher-center-epic-fraud-remains-enigma-those-who-exposed-him.

Lai, Kwok-Wing, and Jenny J. Weeks. 2009. *High School Students' Understanding of E-plagiarism: Some New Zealand Observations*. Dunedin: University of Otago College of Education.

Lamallari, Besfort, Gentiola Madhi, and Miada Shpuza. 2016. *Academic (Dis)Honesty in Albania: Concerns on Plagiarism*. Swiss Agency for Development and Corporation. http://idmalbania.org/wp-content/uploads/2017/02/Academic-Dishonesty-In-Albania-concerns-on-Plagiarism.pdf.

Lampert, Lynn D. 2008. *Combatting Students' Plagiarism: A Librarian's Guide*. Oxford: Chandos.

———. 2006. "The Instruction Librarian's Role in Discussing Issues of Academic Integrity." *LOEX Quarterly* 32 (4): 8–9. https://doi.org/https://www.researchgate.net/publication/27327493_The_Instruction_Librarian's_Role_in_Discussing_Issues_of_Academic_Integrity.

Lancaster, Thomas, and Robert Clarke. 2016. "Contract Cheating: The Outsourcing of Assessed Student Work." In *Handbook of Academic Integrity*, edited by Tracey Bretag, 639–54. Singapore: Springer.

LaTrobe University. 2021. "Academic Integrity." https://www.latrobe.edu.au/students/admin/academic-integrity.

Lederman, Dough. 2010. "A Study of Self-Plagiarism." Inside Higher Ed. 3 December 2010. https://www.insidehighered.com/views/2010/12/03/Zirkel.

Lee, Adam. 2016. "Student Perspectives on Plagiarism." In *Handbook of Academic Integrity*, edited by Tracey Bretag. https://link.springer.com/referenceworkentry/10.10 07/978-981-287-098-8_67.

Lee, Christine. 2019. "5 Ways to Include Academic Integrity in Your Institution's Strategic Plan." *Turnitin.com*. Last modified 11 March 2019. https://www.turnitin.com/blog/5-ways-to-include-academic-integrity-in-your-institutions-strategic-plan.

Lee, Juwan, Sanghun Park, Seokhwan Jo, and Chang Dong Yoo. 2011. "Music Plagiarism Detection System." https://slsp.kaist.ac.kr/paperdata/ITC_2011_ljw.pdf.

Leedy, Paul, and Jeanne Ellis Ormrod. 2019. *Practical Research*. 12th ed. Boston: Pearson.

Lehigh University. 2021. "Statistics, Reports, & Training Materials." https://studentaffairs.lehigh.edu/content/statistics-reports-training-materials.

Leo-Ryhnie, Elsa. 2007. "Prospects and Challenges of the Tertiary Education Sector in Jamaica." In *Higher Education: Caribbean Perspective*, edited by Kenneth O. Hall and Rose Marie Cameron, 11–20. Kingston: Ian Randle Publishers.

Leonard, Michael, Denise Bennett, Margeaux Johnson, Medody Royster, and Amy Buhler. 2013. "Seeds of Change: Pruning Perceptions of Plagiarism into Ethical Behavior for STEM Students." In *ALA Annual Conference 2013-STS Research Program*. Chicago: Institutional Repository at the University of

Florida (IR@UF) University of Florida. https://ufdc.ufl.edu/IR00004149/00001.

Lepera, Christine, and Michael Maneulin, 1999. "Music Plagiarism: Notes on Preparing for Trial, 17." *Entertainment and Sports Law* 10, no. 11 (Fall).

Lewis, Norman P., and Bu Zhong. 2013. "The Root of Journalistic Plagiarism: Contested Attribution Beliefs." *Journalism and Mass Communication Quarterly* 90, no. 1 (March): 148–66. doi:10.1177/1077699012468743.

Lim, Louise. 2011. "Plagiarism Plague Hinders China's Scientific Ambition." NPR, 3 August 2011. https://www.npr.org/2011/08/03/138937778/plagiarism-plague-hinders-chinas-scientific-ambition.

"Literary Discourse: Plagiarism in Academic Writing." 2014. *The Multimedia Group*. https://www.myjoyonline.com/literary-discourse-plagiarism-in-academic-writing/.

Löfström, Erika. 2016. "Academic Integrity in Social Sciences." In *Handbook of Academic Integrity*, edited by Tracey Bretag. https://link.springer.com/referenceworkentry/10.1007/978-981-287-098-8_47.

Longcroft, Adam. 2016. "Future Use of Text-Matching Systems (TMS) in the Investigation of Plagiarism and Collusion Cases – A Comparative Evaluation of SafeAssign and Turnitin." University of East Anglia. https://portal.uea.ac.uk/documents/6207125/13238938/ltc15d188 divider c Text Matching Sofrware TMS.pdf/ob16c2b9-5856-4619-99cd-fdc7beb0404b.

Louw, Henk. 2017. "Defining Plagiarism: Student and Staff Perceptions of a Grey Concept." *South African Journal of Higher Education* 31 (5): 116–35. Accessed 22 March 2020. http://dx.doi.org/10.28535/31-5-580.

Lunenburg, Fred C. 2010. "Schools as Open Systems." *Schooling* 1 (1): 1–5.

Lynch, Jack. 2006. "The Perfectly Acceptable Practice of Literary Theft: Plagiarism, Copyright, and the Eighteenth Century." Accessed 10 May 2018. http://www.writing-world.com/rights/lynch.shtml.

Lynch, Joan, Bronwyn Everett, Lucie M. Ramjan, Renee Callins, Paul J. Glew, and Yenna Salamonson. 2017. "Plagiarism in Nursing Education: An Integrative Review." *Journal of Clinical Nursing* 26: 2845–64. doi:10.1111/jocn.13629.

Madden, M. 2015. "Fraud among Teachers, Says CXC." *Barbados Today*, 31 January 2015. https://www.barbadostoday.bb/2015/01/31/fraud-among-teachers-says-cxc/.

Mansoor, Faiqa, and Kanwal Ameen. 2018. "Perspectives on the Role of University Libraries in Preventing Plagiarism among Research Scholars." In *Towards Consistency and Transparency in Academic Integrity*, edited by Salim Razı, Irene Glendinning, and Tomáš Foltýnek, 241–50. Berlin: Peter Lang. doi: 10.3726/b15273.

Marchalleck, Raynaldo. 2015. "CXC Makes Changes to Five Syllabi - SBA Introduced For English Exams." *The Gleaner*, 24 July 2015. http://jamaica-gleaner.com/article/news/20150724/cxc-makes-changes-five-syllabi-sba-introduced-english-exams.

Marklein, Mary Beth. 2018. "Universities Look South to Recruit International Students." *University World News*, 18 June 2018. https://www.universityworldnews.com/post.php?story=20180618140437935.

Marsden, Rhodri. 2014. "The Big Steal: Rise of the Plagiarist in the Digital Age." *The Guardian*, 21 March 2014. Accessed 12 May 2018. https://www.theguardian.com/technology/2014/mar/21/rise-plagiarism-internet-shia-labeouf.

Marsh, Sarah. 2018. "Cheating at UK's Top Universities Soars by 40%." *The Guardian*, 29 April 2018. https://www.theguardian.com/education/2018/apr/29/cheating-at-top-uk-universities-soars-by-30-per-cent.

Martin, Brian. 1994. "Plagiarism: A Misplaced Emphasis." *Journal of Information Ethics* 3 (2): 36–47. https://www.uow.edu.au/~bmartin/pubs/94jie.html.

———. 2011. *Doing Good Things Better*. Sweden: Irene Publishing. http://www.bmartin.cc/pubs/11gt/.

Mason, Tony, Ada Gavrilovska, and David A. Joyner. 2019. "Collaboration versus Cheating." *Proceedings of the 50th ACM Technical Symposium on Computer Science Education - SIGCSE 19*. https://doi.org/10.1145/3287324.3287443.

Maurer, Hermann, Frank Kappe, and Bilal Zaka. 2006. "Plagiarism - A Survey." *Journal of Universal Computer Science* 12, no. 8 (June): 1050–84. https://pdfs.semanticscholar.org/2093/02b33726db59303707186707bd080e68fe59.pdf.

McCabe, Don. 2011. "Academic Integrity and Graduate Students." University of Florida Ethics Symposium. http://ufdc.ufl.edu/IR00003925/00001.

McCabe, Don, Kenneth D. Butterfield, and Linda Trevino. 2006. "Academic Dishonesty in Graduate Business Programs: Prevalence, Causes, and Proposed Action." *Academy of Management Learning & Education* 5 (3): 294–305.

McCabe, Donald L., and Linda Klebe Trevino. 1993. "Academic Dishonesty: Honor Codes and Other Contextual Influences." *The Journal of Higher Education* 64 (5): 522. https://doi.org/10.2307/2959991.

McGrail, Ewa, and Patrick J. McGrail. 2015. "Exploring Web-Based University Policy Statements on Plagiarism by Research-Intensive Higher Education Institutions." *Middle and Secondary Education Faculty Publications* 85. https://scholarworks.gsu.edu/mse_facpub/.

McKenzie, Eunice Letitia. 2005. "Teachers' Perception of Information Literacy Skills and Instructions in a Select Primary and High School." University of the West Indies, Mona.

McNamara, Carter. n.d. "Basic Guide to Program Evaluation (Including Outcomes Evaluation)." Free Management Library. Accessed 24 March 2020. https://managementhelp.org/evaluation/program-evaluation-guide.htm.

"The Meaning and Actions of Advocacy." *Non Profit Quarterly*. Last modified 21 September 2000. https://nonprofitquarterly.org/the-meaning-and-actions-of-advocacy/.

Meng, Ling, Jamilah Othman, Jeffrey Lawrence D'Silva, and Zoharah Omar. 2014. "Ethical Decision Making in Academic Dishonesty with Application of Modified

Theory of Planned Behavior: A Review." *International Education Studies* 7 (3). https://files.eric.ed.gov/fulltext/EJ1068950.pdf.

Metz, Allison J.R. 2007. "Why Conduct a Program Evaluation? Five Reasons Why Evaluation can Help an Out - of- School Time Program." Last modified October, 2007. https://cyfar.org/sit es/default/files/Child_Trends- 2007_10_01_RB _WhyProgEval.pdf.

The Mico University College. 2017. "The Mico University College Undergraduate Student Handbook 2017 – 2020." https://themico.edu.jm/documents/handbooks/Undergraduate%20Student%20Handbook%202017-20%20v1%2020190614.pdf.

Middleton, David. 2004. "Why We Should Care about Respect." *Contemporary Politics* 10 (3–4): 227–41. https://doi.org/10.1080/1356977042000316691.

"Migration in the Caribbean: Current Trends, Opportunities and Challenges." 2017. International Organization for Migration. Accessed 24 March 2020. https://reliefweb.int/sites/reliefweb.int/files/resources/ Working per cent20papers_ per cent20en_baja_20.06.17.pdf.

Miller, Errol. 1999. "Education in the British Caribbean: the legacy of the Nineteenth century in Educational Reform in the Commonwealth Caribbean." edited by Errol Miller. Washington, D. C.: Organization of American States.

———. 2005. "The University of the West Indies, Mona, and Tertiary Education in Jamaica." In *Revisiting Tertiary Education Policy in Jamaica: Towards Personal Gain or Public Good?* edited by Rheima Holding and Olivene Burke, 60–103. Kingston: Ian Randle Publishers.

Moffatt, Barton. 2011. "Responsible Authorship: Why Researchers Must Forgo Honorary Authorship." *Accountability in Research* 18 (2): 76–90. doi: 10.1080/08989621.2011.557297. https://www.tandfonline.com/doi/abs/10.1080/08989621.2011.557297 ?scroll=top&needAccess=true&journalCode=gacr20.

Moore, Roy L., and Michael D. Murray. 2008. *Media Law and Ethics.* New York: Lawrence Erlbaum Associates.

Morris, Ainsworth. 2013. "CXC Warns against Cheating in Exams." *Jamaica Observer*, 12 May 2013. http://www.jamaicaobserver.com/magazines/career/CXC-warns-against-cheating-in-exams_14222067.

Morris, Erica J. 2016. "Academic Integrity: A Teaching and Learning Approach." In *Handbook of Academic Integrity*, edited by Tracey Bretag, 1037–53. Singapore: Springer. https://doi.org/10.1007/978-981-287-098-8_11.

Morris, Erica J., and Jude Carroll. 2016. "Developing a Sustainable Holistic Institutional Approach: Dealing with Realities 'on the Ground' When Implementing an Academic Integrity Policy." *Handbook of Academic Integrity*. https://link.sprin ger.com/referenceworkentry/10.1007/978-981-287-098-823.

Moskovitz, Cary. 2016. "Self-Plagiarism, Text Recycling, and Science Education." *BioScience*, January: 5–6. Accessed 16 May 2018. doi: https://doi.org/10.1093/biosci/biv160.

Moulton, Janice, and George Robinson. 2002. "Plagiarism." In *Encyclopedia of Ethics*, edited by Lawrence Becker and Charlotte Becker. 2nd ed. New York: Garland Publishing. https://sophia.smith.edu/~jmoulton/plagiarism.pdf.

Mudrack, Ben. 2018. *Self-Plagiarism: How to Define It and Why You Should Avoid It*. Accessed 12 May 2018. https://www.aje.com/en/arc/self-plagiarism-how-to-define-it-and-why-to-avoid-it/.

Murray, Susan, Amber M. Henslee, and Douglas K. Ludlow. 2016. "Evaluating Engineering Students' Understanding of Plagiarism." *Quality Approaches in Higher Education* 7 (1): 5–11. http://asq.org/edu/2016/05/evaluating-engineering-students-understanding-of-plagiarism-vol-7-no-1-march-2016.pdf.

Nahas, Mahmoud Nadim. 2017. "Survey and Comparison between Plagiarism Detection Tools." *American Journal of Data Mining and Knowledge Discovery* 2 (2): 50–53. doi: 10.11648/j.ajdmkd.20170202.12.

Naik, Ramesh Ram, Maheshkumar B. Landge, and Namrata Mahender C. 2019. "Plagiarism Detection in Marathi Language Using Semantic Analysis." *Scholarly Ethics and Publishing*, 473–82. https://doi.org/10.4018/978-1-5225-8057-7.ch023.

National Accreditation Board S.V.G. n.d. "Criteria for Institutional Accreditation."

National Accreditation Council of Guyana. n.d. "A Manual for Quality Assurance of Post-Secondary and Tertiary Education Institutions and Programmes in Guyana." https://drive.google.com/file/d/196Grqj9h9uzB4sJcNDRFvcGVmGUQW-KZ/view.

Neeley, Stacia D. 2005. *Academic Literacy*. Pearson Longman: Texas Wesleyan University. http://wps.pearsoncustom.com/wps/media/objects/2834/2902129/writing/pdf/long_neeley2e.pdf.

Nelms, Gerald. 2015a. "50 Ways of Addressing Student Plagiarism Pedagogically." Last modified 2015. https://teachingandlearninginhighered.files.wordpress.com/2015/07/nelms-50-ways-of-addressing-student-plagiarism-pedagogically-1.pdf.

———. 2015b. "Investigating Student Plagiarism Responsibly." Last modified 2015. https://teachingandlearninginhighered.files.wordpress.com/2015/07/nelms-investigating-student-plagiarism-responsibly-1.pdf.

Neuman, Lawerence W. 2006. *Social Research Methods: Qualitative and Quantitative Approaches*. Boston: Pearson.

Newton, Philip M. 2018. "How Common Is Commercial Contract Cheating in Higher Education and Is It Increasing? A Systematic Review." *Frontiers in Education*, 3. https://doi.org/10.3389/feduc.2018.00067.

Nicosia, Lara. 2019. "Starting Conversations and Building Resources: Libraries as Partners in Promoting Academic Integrity." *International Center for Academic Integrity 26th annual Conference*. New Orleans, 8–10 March 2019. Accessed 21 March 2020. https://www.academicintegrity.org/.

Nilsson, Lars-Erik. 2016. "Technology as a Double-Edged Sword: A Promise Yet to Be Fulfilled or a Vehicle for Cheating?." In *Handbook of Academic Integrity*, edited by Tracey Bretag. https://link.springer.com/referenceworkentry/10.1007/978-981-287-098-8_21.

Nonis, Sarath, and Cathy Owens Swift. 2010. "An Examination of the Relationship between Academic Dishonesty and Workplace Dishonesty: A Multicampus Investigation." *Journal of Education for Business*, 69–77. doi:10.1080/08832320109599052.

Northern Caribbean University. 2018. "The Bulletin of Graduate Studies and Research 2018 - 2020." https://www.ncu.edu.jm/ncu_bulletins/GraduateBulletin2018_2020.pdf.

Notre Dame. 2020. "Academic Integrity at Notre Dame." https://www.notredame.edu.au/about/schools/notre-dame-study-centre/academic-integrity-at-notre-dame-2020.

Nushi, Musa, and Amir Hossein Firoozkohi. 2017. "Plagiarism Policies in Iranian University TEF Teachers' Syllabuses: An Exploratory Study." *International Journal for Educational Integrity* 13 (12). https://doi.org/https://link.springer.com/article/10.1007/s40979-017-0023-4.

Office of Research Integrity. 2018. "Plagiarism of Ideas." Accessed 25 August 2018. https://ori.hhs.gov/plagiarism-ideas.

O'Grady, Emmanuel. 2016. "Research as a Respectful Practice: An Exploration of the Practice of Respect in Qualitative Research." *Qualitative Research in Education* 5 (3): 229–54. doi:10.17583/qre.2016.2018.

Ohio State University Libraries. 2020. "Why Use Newspapers?." Accessed 21 July 2019. https://guides.osu.edu/newspapers/why_use.

Olson, Kristen R., and Alex Shaw. 2011. "No Fair, Copycat!': What Children's Response to Plagiarism Tells us about Their Understanding of Ideas." *Developmental Science* 14 (2): 431–39. doi: 10.1111/j.1467-7687.2010.00993.x. PMID: 22213911.

O'Malley, Brendan. 2017. "What Are QA Bodies Doing to Tackle Academic Corruption?." *University World News*. Last modified 6 October 2017. https://www.universityworldnews.com/post.php?story=20171006145505882.

Oransky, Ivan, and Adam Marcus. 2016. "Politicians Seem to Have a Problem with Dishonest Credentials." STAT, 27 October 2016. https://www.statnews.com/2016/10/27/plagiarism-politicians-dissertations/.

Oxford University Press. 2018. "Plagiarism." Accessed 9 May 2018. https://en.oxforddictionaries.com/thesaurus/plagiarism.

Parmley, William W. 2000. "Plagiarism—How Serious Is It?." *Journal of the American College of Cardiology* 36 (3): 953–54. Accessed 12 May 2018. http://www.onlinejacc.org/content/accj/36/3/953.full.pdf.

Parnther, Ceceilia. "It's On Us: A Case Study of Academic Integrity in a Mid-Western Community College." PhD diss., Western Michigan University, 2016.

Patterson, Chris. 2018. "$2.7- Billion Hike in Education Budget." *Jamaica Information Service*. Accessed 16 February 2019. https://jis.gov.jm/2-7-billion-hike-in-education-budget/.

Patterson, P.J. 2003. "Mobilising Human Resources in Support of Caribbean Development." In *Contending with Destiny: The Caribbean in the 21st Century*, edited by Kenneth Hall and Dennis Benn, 7–11. Kingston: Ian Randle Publishers.

Pavela, Gary, Donald L. McCabe, and DeForest McDuff. 2017. "Ten Principles of Academic Integrity for Faculty." Last modified, 2017. http://integrityseminar.org/wp-content/uploads/2018/02/AIS-Ten-Principles-2017.pdf.

Pecorari, Diane, and Philip Shaw. 2010. "University Teachers Discussing Plagiarism: Divided Perspectives on Teaching Writing and Shaping a Culture of

Honesty." *Plagiarism Today*. Last modified 2010. https://www.plagiarism.org/paper/university-teachers-discussing-plagiarism.

Penn State University. 2021. "Students' Responsibilities Regarding Academic Integrity." https://berks.psu.edu/student-responsibilities.

Perkins, Anna Kasafi. 2015. "Ethics and Quality Assurance: Purpose, Values and Principles." In *Quality in Higher Education in the Caribbean*, edited by Anna Kasafi Perkins, 110–118. Kingston: University Press of the West Indies.

Perry, Janett. 2010. "Is Plagiarism a Moral Problem?." iThenticate. Last modified 1 September 2010. http://www.ithenticate.com/plagiarism-detection-blog/bid/52962/Is-Plagiarism-a-Moral-Problem#.XmKWdHJKhxB.

Pettigrew, Todd. 2010. "All Your Profs are Wrong About Plagiarism." Last modified 10 August 2010. https://www.macleans.ca/education/uniandcollege/all-your-profs-are-wrong-about-plagiarism/.

Pincus, Holly Seirup, and Liora Pedhazur Schmelkin. 2003. "Faculty Perceptions of Academic Dishonesty." *The Journal of Higher Education* 74, no. 2 (March/April): 196–209. https://www.southalabama.edu/mathstat/personal_pages/mulekar/BUS622/Pincus-2003.pdf.

"Plagiarism." 2018. Thesaurus.com. Accessed 21 August 2018. https://www.thesaurus.com/browse/plagiarism.

"Plagiarism Consequences: Student Plagiarists: Napolitano." n.d. *Checkforplagiarism*. Accessed 10 July 2019. https://www.checkforplagiarism.net/plagiarism-consequences.

"Plagiarism Fact and Stats." 2017. Plagiarism.org. Last modified 2017. Accessed 3 July 2019. http://www.plagiarism.org/article/plagiarism-facts-and-stats.

"Plagiarism in Politics: 6 Cases of Political Plagiarism." 2016. https://plagiarismsearch.com/blog/6-cases-of-plagiarism-in-politics.html.

Pompey, Ayodele. 2016. "CAPE Results 2016." Caribbean Examinations Council. https://www.cxc.org/cape-results-2016/.

Porter, Jacqueline. 2016. "The Perception of Plagiarism among Students in one Teachers' College." In *60th Yearbook of Teacher Education: 60th World Assembly Teachers for a Better World: Creating Conditions for Quality Education - Pedagogy, Policy and Professionalism*, edited by Carol Hordatt Gentles, 273–82. Kingston: The University of the West Indies.

Power, Lori G. 2009. "University Students' Perceptions of Plagiarism." *The Journal of Higher Education* 80, no. 6 (November–December): 643–62. https://www.jstor.org/stable/27750755?seq=14#metadata_info_tab_contents.

Prensky, Marc. 2001. "Digital Natives, Digital Immigrants." *On the Horizon* 9 (5): 1–6. Retrieved from KWWSZZZPDUFSUHQVN\FRPZULWLQJ3UHQVN\'LJLWDOiDWLYHV'LJLWDO,PPLJUDQWV3DUWSGI.

"Primary Data and Secondary Data." 2015. *At Work*, 82. https://www.iwh.on.ca/sites/iwh/files/iwh/at-work/at_work_82.pdf.

Proffitt, Brian. 2012. "The Dark Side of the Online Struggle against Plagiarism." ReadWrite. https://readwrite.com/2012/10/05/the-dark-side-of-the-online-struggle-against-plagiarism/.

Pupovac, Vanja, Lidija Bilic-Zulle, Martina Mavrinac, and Mladen Petrovecki. 2010. "Attitudes toward Plagiarism among Pharmacy and Medical Biochemistry Students – Cross-Sectional Survey Study." *Biochemia Medica*, 307–13. https://doi.org/10.11613/bm.2010.039.

The Quality Assurance Agency for Higher Education, UK. 2018. "Self-Assessment Report for Review by ENQA." https://dera.ioe.ac.uk/31611/1/ENQA-2018-self-assessment-report.pdf.

Razera, Diana, Harko Verhagen, Teresa Cerratto Pargman, and Robert Ramberg. 2009. "Plagiarism Awareness, Perception, and Attitudes." Last modified 2009. https://www.researchgate.net/profile/Harko_Verhagen/publication/242738794_Plagiarism_awareness_perception_and_attitudes_among_students_and_teachers_in_Swedish_higher_education_-_a_case_study/links/0c9.

Ramzan, Muhammad, Muhammad Asif Munir, Nadeem Siddique, and Muhammad Asif. 2012. "Awareness about Plagiarism amongst University Students in Pakistan." *Higher Education* 64 (1): 73–84. http://www.jstor.org/stable/41477920.

Ramzan, Muhammad, Muhammad Asif, and Hina Adeeb. 2018. "Insights into University Students' Perceptions about Plagiarism." In *Towards Consistency and Transparency in Academic Integrity*, edited by Salim Razı, Irene Glendinning, and Tomáš Foltýnek, 77–87. Berlin: Peter Lang. doi: 10.3726/b15273.

"Reform Approaches and Experience." 2019. Curbing Corruption. Last modified 2019. Accessed 25 March 2020. https://curbingcorruption.com/reform-approaches-2/.

Reid, Tyrone. 2012. "Caught! Employees with Bought CXC Passes Identified." *The Gleaner*, 23 September 2012. http://jamaica-gleaner.com/gleaner/20120923/lead/lead7.html.

———. 2013d. "Ban Them!." *The Gleaner*, 27 October 2013. http://jamaica-gleaner.com/article/news/20150814/students-should-do-sbas-under-exam-conditions-educator.

———. 2013a. "Charged for Fake CXCs." *The Gleaner*, 27 October 2013. http://jamaica-gleaner.com/gleaner/20131027/lead/lead84.html.

———. 2013b. "Dunce Move - Teacher Causes CXC to Cancel Grades For 70 JC Sixth-Formers." *The Gleaner*, 6 October 2013. http://jamaicagleaner.com/gleaner/20131006/lead/lead1.html.

———. 2013c. "Jamaica's Reputation Intact - Head of The OEC Says Jamaica's Image at CXC Not Damaged by SBA Cheating." *The Gleaner*, 20 October 2013. http://jamaica-gleaner.com/gleaner/20131020/lead/lead3.html.

"Responding to Migration Challenges in the Caribbean 2009." IOM UN Migration. Last modified 3 December 2009. https://www.iom.int/news/responding-migration-challenges-caribbean.

Roanoke College. 2012. *Information for Students Aware of an AI Violation*. Inside Roanoke. https://www.roanoke.edu/inside/a-z_index/academic_affairs/academic_integrity/resources_for_students/information_for_students_aware_of_an_ai_violation.

Roberts, Vivienne. 2007. "Accreditation and Evaluation Systems in the English-Speaking Caribbean." In *Higher Education : Caribbean Perspectives*, edited by Rose Marie Cameronm and Kennith O. Hall, 45–94. Kingston: Ian Randle Publishers.

Robinson-Zañartu, Carol, Elizabeth Peña, Valerie Cook-Morales, Anna Peña, Rosalyn Afshani, and Lynda Nguyen. 2005. "Academic Crime and Punishment: Faculty Members' Perceptions of and Responses to Plagiarism." *School Psychology Quarterly* 20: 318–37.

Rogers, Tony. 2019. "The Top 12 Journalism Scandals since 2000." ThoughCo. Last modified 25 May 2019. Up https://www. thoughtco.com/the-top-journalism-scandals-2073750.

Roig, Miguel. 2015. "Avoiding Plagiarism, Self-Plagiarism, and Other Questionable Writing Practices: A Guide to Ethical Writing." Office of Research Integrity. https://ori.hhs.gov/content/avoiding-plagiarism-self-plagiarism-and-other-questionable-writing-practices-guide-ethical-writing.

Roka, Yam Bahadur. 2017. "Plagiarism: Types, Causes and How to Avoid This Worldwide Problem." *Nepal Journal of Neuroscience* 14, no. 3 (January): 2–6. https://doi.org/10.3126/njn.v14i3.20517.

Roller, Matthew. 2018. "Record Number of Oxford Students Found Guilty of Plagiarism." *Cherwell*. Last modified 2 April 2018. https://cherwell.org/2018/04/02/record-number-of-oxford-students-found-guilty-of-plagiarism/.

Rosentiel, Tom. 2006. "Getting a Grad Degree in Cheating." Pew Research Center. https://www.pewresearch.org/2006/09/26/getting-a-grad-degree-in-cheating/.

Roser Max, and Esteban Ortiz-Ospina. 2016. "Global Education." Published online at OurWorldInData.org. Retrieved from: https://ourworldindata.org/global-education.

Rothschild, David. 2011. "International Research Community Stands up to Plagiarism." *Ithenticate*. http://www.ithenticate.com/plagiarism-detection-blog/bid/52937/International-Research-Community-Stands-up-to-Plagiarism#.XntzLYhKiM9.

Sachar, Cassandra O. 2018. "How to Use Turnitin to Teach Students not to Plagiarize." *Inside Higher Ed*. https://www.insidehighered.com/advice/2018/04/10/how-use-turnitin-teach-students-not-plagiarize-opinion.

Saddiqui, Sonia. 2016. "Engaging Students and Faculty: Examining and Overcoming the Barriers." In *Handbook of Academic Integrity*, edited by Tracey Bretag, 1–23. https://link.springer.com/ref erenceworkentry/10.1007/978-981-287-098-8_18.

Sarlauskiene, Lina, and Linas Stabingis. 2014. "Understanding of Plagiarism by the Students in HEIs of Lithuania." *Social and Behavioral Sciences* 110: 638–46.

"The School as an Open System." 2014. *Edutrends*. https://euniceacheampong.wordpress.com/2014/11/26/the-school-as-an-open-system/.

Schlesinger, Walesska, Amparo Cervera, and Carmen Pérez-Cabañero. 2017. "Sticking with your University: The Importance of Satisfaction, Trust, Image, and Shared Values." *Studies in Higher Education* 42 (12): 2178–94. https://srhe.tandfonline.com/doi/abs/10.1080/03075079.2015.1136613#.YFC7x51KjIV.

Schrier, Karen, and David Gibson. 2011. "Using Games to Prepare Ethical Educators and Students." In *Society for Information Technology & Teacher Education International Conference*, 1372–79. https://www.researchgate.net/publication/279480785_Using_Games_to_Prepare_Ethical_Educators_and_Students.

"Second Czech Government Minister Resigns over Plagiarism." *Associated Press*, 7 July 2018. Accessed 10 March 2021. https://www.businessinsider.com/ap-second-czech-government-minister-resigns-over-plagiarism-2018-7.

"Secondary School Officials Charged with Fraud." 2017. 6 TV CCN. Last modified 16 November 2017. https://www.tv6tnt.com/news/local/secondary-school-officials-charged-with-fraud/article_42dfd758-cb12-11e7-a14c-27e7f3ef99c6.html.

Segal, Scott, Brian J. Gelfand, Shelley Hurwitz, Lori Berkowitz, Stanley W. Ashley, Eric S. Nadel, and Joel T. Katz. 2010. "Plagiarism in Residency Application Essays." *Annals of Internal Medicine* 153 (2): 112–20. doi: 10.7326/0003-4819-153-2-201007200-00007

Sentleng, Mapule Patricia, and Lizette King. 2012. "Plagiarism Among Undergraduate Students in the Faculty of Applied Science at a South African Higher Education Institution." *South African Journal of Libraries and Information Science* 78 (1): 57–67. doi:http://dx.doi.org/10.7553/78-1-47.

Sheets, Brenda, and Paula Waddil. 2009. "E-Cheating among College Business Students: A Survey." *Information Technology, Learning, and Performance Journal* 25 (2): 4–19.

Shelley-Robinson, Cherrell. 2007. "School Libraries in the Caribbean, a Jamaican Case Study." In *Caribbean Libraries in the 21st Century: Changes, Challenges, and Choices*, edited by Cheryl Peltier-Davis and Shamin Renwick, 95–118. Medford: Information Today.

Shreiber, David. 2018. "Avoiding Unintentional Plagiarism: Implementing a Programmatic Self-Check." *Turnitin*. Accessed 21 April 2018. http://turnitin.com/en_us/awards-json/item /avoiding-unintentional-plagiarism.

Siaputra, Ide B. 2019. "Promoting Academic Integrity in Indonesia." PowerPoint Presentation. s.id/ICAI_Siaputra_2019<http://s.id/ICAI_Siaputra_2019><http://s.id/ICAI_Siaputra_2019.

Simon, Beth. 2016. "Academic Integrity in Non-Text Based Disciplines." In *Handbook of Academic Integrity*, edited by Tracey Bretag. https://link.springer.com/referencework entry/10.1007/978-981-287-098-8_61.

Sisti, Dominic A. 2007. "How Do High School Students Justify Internet Plagiarism?." *Ethics and Behavior* 17 (3): 215–31. doi: 10.1080/10508420701519163.

Smedley, Alison, Tonia Crawford, and Linda Cloete. 2020. "An Evaluation of an Extended Intervention to Reduce Plagiarism in Bachelor of Nursing Students." *Nursing Education Perspectives* 41 (2): 106–08. doi:10.1097/01.NEP.0000000000000492.

Social Care Institute for Excellence. 2020. "Types of Advocacy." n.d. *Care Act 2014, Social Care Institute for Excellence*. https://www.scie.org.uk/advocacy/commissioning/inclusion.

"Social System." 2020. *BusinessDictionary.com*. WebFinance, Inc. Accessed 31 March 2020. http://www.businessdictionary.com/definition/social-system.html.

Soiferman, L. Karen. 2016. "Problems of Policing Plagiarism and Cheating in University Institutions Due to Incomplete or Inconsistent Definitions." University of Manitoba. Last modified 2016. https://files.eric.ed.gov/fulltext/ED569164.pdf.

Spence, Omarsha. 2011. "CXC Regulations for Cell Phones in the CXC Exam Room - May/June 2011." CaribExams.org. Accessed 8 April 2020. https://caribexams.org/node/1481.

St. Petersburg College. 2019. "Plagiarism and Academic Integrity." Accessed 3 July 2019. https://spcollege.libguides.com/c.php?g=2543 83&p=1695452.

Stabingis, Linas, Lina Šarlauskienė, and Neringa Čepaitienė. 2014. "Measures for Plagiarism Prevention in Students' Written Works: Case Study of ASU Experience." *Procedia Contemporary Issues in Business, Management and Education*, 689–99. https://doi.org/doi:10.1016/j.sbspro.2013.12.913.

Stanford University. n.d. "What is the Stanford Honor Code?." https://undergrad.stanford.edu/academic -planning/cardinal-compass/your-questions-answered/what-stanford-honor-code.

Statistical Institute of Jamaica. 2017. "Labour Force Statistics." STATINJA. Accessed 15 January 2019. http://statinja.gov.jm/labourforce/newlfs.aspx.

"Statistics." 2017. International Center for Academic Integrity. https://academicintegrity.org/statistics/.

Stenmark, Cheryl K., and Nicolette A. Winn. 2016. "Ethics in the Humanities." In *Handbook of Academic Integrity*, edited by Tracey Bretag. https://doi: 10.1007/978-981-287-098-8_43.

Stowe, Susan. 2017. "Will They or Not? Online Faculty Intentions to Report Student Plagiarism." *Academy of Educational Leadership Journal* 21 (1). https://www.abacademies.org/articles/will-they-or-not-online-faculty-intentions-to -report-student-plagiarism-6724.html.

Stripling, Jack. 2008. "Student vs. Faculty Plagiarism." *The Gainesville Sun*, 26 April 2008. https://www.gainesville.com/news/20080426/student-vs -faculty-plagiarism.

"Students Should Do SBAs Under Exam Conditions - Educator." 2015. *The Gleaner*, 14 August 2015. http://jamaica-gleaner.com/article/news/20150814/students-should-do-sbas-under-exam-conditions-educator.

SUNY Empire State College. 2021. The Assignment Calculator. https://www.esc.edu/learning-support/assignment-calculator/.

Sureda-Negre, Jaume, Rubén. Comas-Forgas, and Miquel Oliver-Trobat. 2015. "Academic Plagiarism among Secondary and High School Students: Differences in Gender and Procrastination." *Comunicar* 44 (22): 103–10.

Sutherland-Smith, W. 2008. *Plagiarism, the Internet and Student Learning: Improving Academic Integrity*. Routledge.

———. 2010. "Retribution, Deterrence and Reform: The Dilemmas of Plagiarism Management in Universities." *Journal of Higher Education Policy and Management* 32 (1): 5–16. https://doi.org/10.1080/13600800903440519.

———. 2011. "Crime and Punishment: An Analysis of University Plagiarism Policies." *Semiotica* 1 (4): 127–39. https://www.researchgate.net/publication/275691527_Crime_and_punishment_An_analysis_of_university_plagiarism_policies.
Tabor, Erin. 2013. "Is Cheating Always Intentional? The Perception of College Students toward the Issues of Plagiarism." Capella University. doi:https://eric.ed.gov/?id=ED552854.
Tanacković, Sanjica F., Maja Krtalić, and Darko Lacović. 2014. "Newspapers as a Research Source: Information Needs and Information Seeking of Humanities Scholars." https://www.ifla.org/files/assets/newspapers/Geneva_2014/s6-lacovic-en.pdf.
Tauginienė, Loreta, and Inga Gaižauskaitė. 2018. "Integrity Management in High Schools: Paving a Way to Misconduct?." In *Towards Consistency and Transparency in Academic Integrity*, Bern, Switzerland. https://doi.org/10.3726/b15273/19.
Tauginienė, Loreta, Inga GaižauskaitėSalim Razi, Irene Glendinning, Shivadas Sivasubramaniam, Franca Marino, Marco Cosentino, Alla Anohina-Naumeca, and Julius Kravjar. 2019. "Enhancing the Taxonomies Relating to Academic Integrity and Misconduct." *Journal of Academic Ethics* 17: 345–61. https://doi.org/10.1007/s10805-019-09342-4.
Tauginienė, Loreta, Inga Gaižauskaitė, Irene Glendinning, Július Kravjar, Milan Ojteršek, Laura Ribeiro, Tatjana Odiņeca, Franca Marino, Marco Cosentino, and Shiva Sivasubramaniam. 2018. "Glossary for Academic Integrity Report." European Network for Academic Integrity. www.academicintegrity.eu/wp/wp-content/uploads/2018/02/GLOSSARY_final.pdf.
"Taxonomy." Techtarget. Last modified 2020. https://searchcontentmanagement.techtarget.com/definition/taxonomy.
Taylor-Bianco, Amy, and Dawn Deeter-Schmelz. 2007. "An Exploration of Gender and Cultural Differences in MBA Students Cheating Behavior." *Journal of Teaching in International Business* 18 (4): 81–99. https://doi.org/10.1300/j066v18n04_05.
Tbilisi. 2019. "National Center for Educational Quality Enhancement." https://eqe.ge/res/docs/ დასკვნიანი ლისური.pdf.
Tennant, Peter, and Fiona Duggan. 2008. "Academic Misconduct Benchmarking Research Project: Part 2: The Range and Spread of Penalties Available for Student Plagiarism Among UK Higher Education Institutions." https://marketing-porg-statamic-assets-us-west-2.s3-us-west-2.amazonaws.com/main/Tennant_amber2.pdf.
Tewarie, Bhoendradatt. 2007. "Tertiary Education and Development in the Knowledge Economy in the Twenty-First Century." In *Higher Education: Caribbean Perspectives*, 27–44. Kingston: Ian Randle Publishers.
———. 2009. "Concept Paper for the Development of a CARICOM Strategic Plan for Tertiary Education Services in the CARICOM Single Market and Economy (CSME)." *CARICOM Regional Symposium on Services, Antigua*. Accessed 25 May 2020. https//caricom.org/documents/9524-concept_paper_tertiary_education.pdf.

Thomas, Adele. 2017. "Faculty Reluctance to Report Student Plagiarism: A Case Study." *African Journal of Business Ethics* 11 (1): 103–19. doi: 10.15249/11-1-148.

Thompsett, Andrew, and Jatinder Ahluwalia. 2010. "Students Turned Off by Turnitin? Perception of Plagiarism and Collusion by Undergraduate Bioscience Students." *Bioscience Education* 16 (1): 1–15. https://doi.org/10.3108/beej.16.3.

Thornton, Linda Fisher. 2014. "Ethics and Trust Are Reciprocal." Leading in Context. Accessed 15 December 2018. https://leadingincontext.com/2014/06/18/ethics-and-trust/.

Tomas, Foltýnek Tomáš, and Glendinning Irene. 2015. "Impact of Policies for Plagiarism in Higher Education across Europe: Results of the Project." *Acta Universitatis Agriculturae et Silviculturae Mendelianae Brunensis* 63 (1): 207–16.

"Top 10 Retractions of 2017." 2017. *The Scientist Magazine*. Accessed 18 January 2019. https://www.the-scientist.com/research-round-up/top-10-retractions-of-2017-29834.

"Top Universities in the World 2018." 2018. *Top Universities.com*. https://www.topuniversities.com/university-rankings-articles/world-university-rankings/top-universities-world-2018.

Tran, Ut T., Thanh Huynh, and Trịnh Thanh Hòa. 2018. "Academic Integrity in Higher Education: The Case of Plagiarism of Graduation Reports by Undergraduate Seniors in Vietnam." *Journal of Academic Ethics*, 1–9. https://doi.org/10.1007/s10805-017-9279-9.

"Translation Plagiarism: A Modern Day Concern." Plagramme. Accessed 5 May 2018. https://www.plagramme.com/translation-plagiarism-modern-day-concern.

"Trinidad and Tobago." 2021. *International Organisation for Migration*. https://www.iom.int/countries/trinidad-and-tobago.

Tull, Matthew. 2018. "CXC Annual Report 2018." Caribbean Examinations Council. Last modified 13 December 2018. https://www.cxc.org/cxc-annual-report-2018/.

Turner, Camilla. 2017. "University Lecturers Are Topping up Earnings by Helping Students Cheat, Review Suggests." *The Telegraph*, 7 October 2017. https://www.telegraph.co.uk/education/2017/10/07/university-lecturers-topping-earnings-helping-students-cheat/.

Turnitin. 2013a. "Does Turnitin Detect Plagiarism?." https://www.turnitin.com/blog/does-turnitin-detect-plagiarism.

———. 2013b. "Turnitin Studies Impact of Plagiarism Detection Software in High Schools." *Plagiarism Today*. Accessed 12 May 2018. https://www.plagiarismtoday.com/2013/09/26/turnitin/.

———. 2021. "About Us." https://www.turnitin.com/regions/apac/about.

Turnquest, Ava. "Smith Chosen As CoB President After 'Accepting Plagiarism Responsibility'." *The Tribune*, 21 August 2014. http://www.tribune242.com/news/2014/aug/21/smith-chosen-cob-president-after-accepting-plagiar/.

Uberti, David. 2014. "Journalism has a Plagiarism Problem. But It's Not the One You'd Expect." *Colombia Journalism Review*. https://www.cjr.org/behind_the_news/journalism_has_a_plagiarism_pr.php.

Ukpebor, Christopher O., and Abieyuwa Ogbebor. 2013. "Internet and Plagiarism: Awareness, Attitude and Perception of Students of Secondary Schools." *Journal of Library & Information Science* 3 (2): 254–67. https://www.researchgate.net/publication/281282362_Internet.

UNESCO. 2014. "Regional Report about Education for All in Latin America and the Caribbean: Global Education for All Meeting Muscat, Oman, May 12 and 14 of 2014." PDF file. http://www.unesco.org/new/fileadmin/MULTIMEDIA/HQ/ED/ED_new/pdf/LAC-GEM-2014-ENG.pdf.

———. 2019. "Media and Information Literacy." UNESCO, 19 November 2019. https://en.unesco.org/themes/media-and-information-literacy.

UNESCO Institute for Statistics. 2019. "School Enrollment, Secondary." The World Bank. Accessed 31 January 2019. https://data.worldbank.org/indicator/SE.SEC.ENRR ?locations=BZ-BM-VG.

UNICEF. 2019. "A World Ready to Learn: Prioritizing Quality Early Childhood Education. Global Report." https://www.unicef.org/media/57926/file/A-world-ready-to-learn-advocacy-brief-2019.pdf.

United States International Trade Commission. 2008. "Caribbean Region: Review of Economic Growth and Development." Last modified May 2008. https://www.usitc.gov/publications/332/pub4000.pdf.

University Council of Jamaica. 2017. "Manual for the Visiting Team: Institutional Accreditation." The University Council of Jamaica.

———. 2018. "Standards for Institutional Accreditation." The University Council of Jamaica.

———. 2019. "Manual for the Visiting Team: Programme Accreditation." The University Council of Jamaica.

———. 2021. "What is Accreditation." https://www.ucj.org.jm/accreditation/what-is-accreditation/.

University of Arkansas. n.d. "Academic Initiatives and Integrity." https://honesty.uark.edu/policy/index.php.

University of Auckland. n.d. "Academic Integrity Course." *University of Auckland*. Accessed 30 March 2021. https://uoa.custhelp.com/app/answers/detail/a_id/3474/~/academic-integrity-course.

University of Belize. 2018. "Handbook of Academic Policies." https://www.ub.edu.bz/download/academic-policies/.

University of British Colombia. n.d. "Investigating and Documenting Suspected Plagiarism." Accessed 15 January 2021. https://www.grad.ubc.ca/faculty-staff/policies-procedures/investi gating-documenting-suspected-plagiarism.

University of Cambridge. 2018. *The University's Definition of Plagiarism*. Accessed 1 May 2018. https://www.plagiarism.admin.cam.ac.uk/what-plagiarism/universitys-definition-plagiarism.

———. 2021. "Procedures and Policy for Investigating Academic Misconduct." Last modified 2019. https://www.plagiarism.admin.cam.ac.uk/information-staff/procedures-and-policy-investigating-academic-misconduct.

University of Central Florida. n.d. "Job Opportunities." Accessed 15 May 2019. https://www.jobswithucf.com/postings/5 6668.

University College of London. n.d. "Plagiarism: Advice to Departments and Faculties." Accessed 22 March 2020. https://www.ucl.ac.uk/academic-manual/sites/academic-manual/files/appendix_42_-_plagiarism_.pdf.

University of Guyana. 2016. "Rules and Regulations ... Useful Student Information more about what Students should know... 2017-2018 Academic year." https://www.uog.edu.gy/sites/default/files/documents/Rules per cent20and per cent20Regulations per cent202017-2018 per cent20final.pdf.

University of Indiana. 2019. "Best Practices for Teaching with Turnitin." Indiana University. Accessed 7 April 2020. https://kb.iu.edu/d/asxq.

University of Leeds. 2011. "Role Description: Academic Integrity Officer." PDF file. https://www1.maths.leeds.ac.uk/school/staff/teaching/AIO_Role.pdf.

University of Mary Washington. 2020a. "Overview of University of Mary Washington." Last modified 2020. https://www.usnews.com/best-colleges/mary-washington-3746.

———. 2020b. "Academic Integrity: 2015 – 2016 Case Summaries." https://academics.umw.edu/academicintegrity/academic-integrity/hc/case-summaries/2015-2016-case-summaries/.

———. 2021. "Academic Integrity: Student Resources." https://academics.umw.edu/academicintegrity/academic-integrity/student-resources/.

University of Maryland. "Code of Academic Integrity." 2019. Last modified January, 2019. https://president.umd.edu/sites/president.umd.edu/files/files/documents/policies/III-100A.pdf.

University of Maryland Global Campus. 2021. Academic Integrity Tutorial. https://www.umgc.edu/current-students/learning-resources/academic-integrity/tutorial/index.cfm.

University of Oxford. 2021. "Facts and Figures." University of Oxford. https://www.ox.ac.uk/about/facts-and-figures

University of Oxford Gazette. 2016. "Oration by the Demitting Proctor and Assessors." https://gazette.web.ox.ac.uk/files/orationbythedemittingproctorsandassessor-1ton05127pdf.

University of Tasmania. 2018. "Minimising Plagiarism and Cheating." Last modified 2018. https://www.teaching-learning.utas.edu.au/assessment/choosing-and-designing-assessment-tasks/minimising-plagiarism-and-cheating.

University of Technology. 2019. "UTech Ja Student Handbook 2019– 2020." http://www.utechjamaica.edu.jm/publications/undergradhandbook/2/.

University of the Bahamas. 2018. "The Interactive Student Handbook 2018." PDF file. https://www.ub.edu.bs/wp-content/uploads/2018/08/Student-Handbook-2018-2019-Draft.pdf.

University of the Commonwealth Caribbean. 2018. *Student Handbook 2018-2019.* https://ucc.edu.jm/sites/default/files/files/docs/UCC per cent20Student per cent20Handbook per cent20- per cent2020182019.pdf.

University of Toronto. n.d. "University's Plagiarism Detection Tool – FAQ." *University of Toronto*. https://teaching.utoronto.ca/ed-tech/teaching-technology/pdt/pdt-faq/.

The University of the West Indies. 2011. "University Regulations on Plagiarism (First Degrees, Diplomas and Certificates)." https://www.mona.uwi.edu/socsci/sites/default/files/socsci/uploads/university_regulations_on_plagiarism.pdf.

———. 2013. "University Regulations on Plagiarism Graduate Diplomas and Degrees." Last modified 26 May 2013. https://www.mona.uwi.edu/socsci/sites/default/files/socsci/uploads/university_regulations_onplagiarism_graduate_diplomas_and_degrees_final_approved_4-10-2013.pdf.

———. 2018. "Statistical Digest 2012/13 to 2016/17: A Statistical Review of 5 Year Trends in Student Enrolment and Graduation Statistics at the UWI during the Period 2012/13 to 2016/17 for Selected Datasets." The University of the West Indies, Office of Planning. Last modified April 2018. https://www.mona.uwi.edu/opair/statistics/2016-2017/C.P6d per cent20- per cent20The per cent20UWI per cent20Statistical per cent20Digest per cent202012-13 per cent20to per cent202016-17.pdf.

———. 2021a. "About the UWI Mona." https://www.mona.uwi.edu/about.

———. 2021b. "History." The University of the West Indies At Mona, Jamaica. https://www.mona.uwi.edu/uwimona-history

———. n.d. "History." The University of the West Indies at St. Augustine, Trinidad and Tobago. https://sta.uwi.edu/history/.

University of Waterloo Office of Academic Integrity. 2013. "Report on the Findings of the 2012 Academic Integrity Survey." https://uwaterloo.ca/academic-integrity/sites/ca.academic-integrity/files/uploads/files/Report%20on%20the%20Findings%20of%20the%202012%20Academic%20Integrity%20Survey_0.pdf.

———. n.d. "Academic Integrity 101." https://uwaterloo.ca/academic-integrity/integrity-students/academic-integrity-101.

University of Wollongong. n.d. "Academic Integrity Officers." University of Wollongong, Australia. https://www.uow.edu.au/about/governance/academic-integrity/aios/.

URKUND. 2005. "Why is Plagiarism a Problem?." Accessed 5 May 2018. https://www.urkund.com/en/about-urkund.

UWI Alumni Online. n.d. "Heads of Government." Accessed 8 January 2019. https://www.uwi.edu/alumnionline/points-pride/heads-government.

The UWI Open Campus. 2019. "About The UWI Open Campus." https://www.open.uwi.edu/about.

Vargas, Viera, and R. Hugo. 2017. "The Caribbean: An Overview." Enciclopedia De Puerto Rico. Accessed 6 January 2019. https://enciclopediapr.org/en/encyclopedia/the-caribbean-an-overview.

Vázquez-Recio, Rosa, Guadalupe Calvo-García, Mónica López-Gil, Marina Picazo Picazo-Gutiérrez, Aurora María Ruiz-Bejarano, and Pilar Calvo-Gutiérrez. 2016.

"Conceptions and Causes of Plagiarism among University Students of the Degree in Infant and Primary Education." INTED2016 Proceedings, 5705–13.

Virginia Polytechnic Institute and State University. 2021. "Office of Undergraduate Academic Integrity." https://honorsystem.vt.edu/.

Walcott, Paul. 2016. "Attitudes of Second Year Computer Science Undergraduates Toward Plagiarism." *Caribbean Teaching Scholar* 6: 63–80. https://journals.sta.uwi.edu/ojs/index.php/cts/article/view/1649.

Walker, Christopher, and Melanie White. 2014. "Police, Design, Plan and Manage: Developing a Framework for Integrating Staff Roles and Institutional Policies into a Plagiarism Prevention Strategy." *Journal of Higher Education Policy and Management* 3 (6). Accessed 28 February 2020. https://doi.org/10.1080/1360080X.2014.957895.

Walker, John. 1998. "Student Plagiarism in Universities: What Are We Doing About It?." *Higher Education Research and Development* 17 (1): 89–106.

———. 2010. "Measuring Plagiarism: Researching what Students Do, Not What They Say They Do." *Studies in Higher Education* 35 (1): 41–59.

"Walter Weighs in on Plagiarism Allegations." 2014. *Da Vibes*, 17 September 2014. https://www.dominicavibes.dm/news-143134/.

Wan, Guofang, and Michael R. Scott. 2016. "Start Them Early and Right: Creating a Culture of Academic Integrity in Elementary Schools." In *Handbook of Academic Integrity*, edited by Tracey Bretag. Singapore: Springer.

Wangaard, David B. 2016. "Practices to Support Developing Academic Integrity in Secondary School Students." In *Handbook of Academic Integrity*, edited by Tracey Bretag. https://link.springer.com/referenceworkentry/10.1007/978-981-287-098-8_34.

Watters, Audrey. 2011. "Plagiarism Differences in High School and College Students." KQED, 3 November 2011. https://www.kqed.org/mindshift/16612/plagiarism-tactics-differ-between-high-school-and-college-students.

Weber-Wulff, Debora. 2016. "Plagiarism Detection Software: Promises, Pitfalls, and Practices." In *Handbook of Academic Integrity*, edited by Tracey Bretag. https://link.springer.com/referenceworkentry/10.1007/978-981-287-098-8_19.

Wees, David. n.d. "The Role of Immediacy of Feedback in Student Learning." Last modified 2010. https://davidwees.com/content/role-immediacy-feedback-student-learning/.

Welsh-Unwala, Kristen. 2019. "Plagiarism Education in Science: The Effect of Instruction on Student Attitudes." *International Journal of Bahamian Studies* 25: 33–44. http://journals.sfu.ca/cob/index.php/files/article/viewFile/319/pdf_65.

"What is Copyright." n.d. *Black's Law Dictionary*. Accessed 2 May 2018. https://thelawdictionary.org/copyright/.

"What If CSEC Cheating Widespread?." 2013. *The Gleaner*, 14 October 2013. http://jamaica-gleaner.com/gleaner/20131014/cleisure/cleisure2.html.

Wheeler, Debbie, and David Anderson. 2010. "Dealing with Plagiarism in a Complex Information Society." *Education, Business and Society: Contemporary Middle Eastern Issues* 3 (3): 166–77.

"White Paper: The Plagiarism Spectrum: Instructor Insight into the 10 Types of Plagiarism." 2012. *iParadigms*. https://www.ed.ac.uk/files/atoms/files/10-types-of-plagiarism.pdf.

Whitley, B. 1998. "Factors Associated with Cheating Among College Students: A Review." *Research in Higher Education* 39 (3): 235–65.

"Why Does Academic Integrity Matter?." 2015. https://www.plagiarism.admin.cam.ac.uk/what-academic-misconduct/why-does-academic-integrity-matter.

Whyte, Millicent. 1977. *A Short History of Education in Jamaica*. London: Hodder and Stoughton.

Wilkinson, Jenny. 2009. "Staff and Student Perceptions of Plagiarism and Cheating." *International Journal of Teaching and Learning in Higher Education* 20 (2): 98–105.

Williams, Laurel V. 2008. "CXC Official to Testify in Fraud Case." *Newsday*, 28 October 2008. https://archives.newsday.co.tt/2008/10/28/cxc-official-to-testify-in-fraud-case/.

Wilson, Nadine. 2014. "Teachers Said to be Aiding Student Cheating: CXC Again Warns Against Practice." *Jamaica Observer*, 6 April 2014. http://www.jamaicaobserver.com/ magazines/career/Teachers-said-to-be-aiding-student-cheating_16406434.

Wood, Gail. 2004. "Academic Original Sin: Plagiarism, the Internet, and Librarians." *The Journal of Academic Librarianship* 30 (3): 237–42.

Woodard, Cooper R., and Cynthia L. S. Pury. 2007. "The Construct of Courage: Categorization and Measurement." *Consulting Psychology Journal: Practice and Research* 59 (2): 135–47. doi: 10.1037/1065-9293.59.2.135.

The World Bank. 2019. "Population Total." https://data.worldbank.org/indicator/SP.POP.TOTL.

———. 2021. "Expenditure on Education, Total (as % of GDP)." 2021. https://data.worldbank.org/indicator/SE.XPD.TOTL.GD.ZS?locations=BZ-BM-VG.

Wrobel, Shiela. 2011. "Plagiarism: Literary Theft." University of Nebraska. Accessed 5 May 2018. https://www.unmc.edu/vcr/education/rug/Plagiarism_Presentation_Feb_2011-2.pdf.

Xavier University Library. n.d. *Why Is Plagiarism Wrong?* Accessed 5 May 2018. https://www.xavier.edu/library/xu-tutor/Why-is-Plagiarism-Wrong1.cfm.

Xinhau. 2013. "Academic Misconduct Cases Disclosed." *China Daily*, 2 August 2013. Accessed 16 May 2018. http://www.chinadaily.com.cn/china/2013-08/02/content_16864299.htm.

Yeo, S. 2007. "First-year University Science and Engineering Students' Understanding of Plagiarism." *Journal of Higher Education Research & Development* 26 (2): 199–216.

Yeung, Alice H.W., Connie B.L. Chu, Samuel Kai-Wah Chu, and Charmaine K.W. Fung. 2016. "Exploring Junior Secondary Students' Plagiarism Behavior." *Journal of Librarianship and Information Science* 50 (4): 361–73. https://doi.org/10.1177/0961000616666625.

Yusof, Dahlia Syahrani. 2009. "A Different Perspective on Plagiarism." http://iteslj.org/Articles/Yusof-Plagiarism.html.

Žalec, Bojan. 2013. "Trust, Accountability, and Higher Education." *Synthesis Philosophica* 28: 65–81. https://hrcak.srce.hr/119712.

"Zero Tolerance for Cheaters, Cell Phones CXC Lays Down the Law; Warns Pupils." 2012. *Daily Express*, 7 March 2012. http://www.trinidadexpress.com/news/Zero-tolerance-for-cheaters-cellphones-141839303.html.

Zong, Jie, and Jeanne Batalova. 2019. "Caribbean Immigrants in the United States." Migrationpolicy.org. Last modified 28 February 2019. https://www.migrationpolicy.org/article/caribbean-immigrants-united-states.

Index

Note: Page numbers in *italic* indicate figures and tables.

404 Error, 321–322

Abdulla, Hussam M., 52
academic discipline/faculty, 213, 308; difference in knowledge, 188; line graph, factor of plagiarism scale on, 190, *193–194*; mean differences, *192*; null hypothesis, 178, 194; objectives, study, 178; perceptions of plagiarism, 177–178, 188, 190, 192, 194–195; plagiarism across all, 179–183, *180*; undergraduate students, data analysis, 177, 183–184
academic dishonesty, 5, 13; academic fraud, 14–15, 100; causes, among secondary students, 101–104; CXC's response to, penalties, 104–105; defined, 14; faculty involved in, 56; forms of, 16–17; impact of, 15–16; plagiarism, popular form of, 17, 19, 36; reported cases, 15–16, 101; retraction of papers, 15, 57; among scholars, 15; by secondary students, practised types, 98, 100–101; workplace behaviour connect, 16
academic fraud, 14–15, 100, 142
academic honesty, 57
academic institutions, as social systems, 12; failure and feedback, 13; open system with, reference to, *12*

academic integrity, 112–113, 130, 140, 304; in accreditation policies, guidelines and, 137, 140–143, 149–150, 214; approaches to, 222. *See also* integrity culture, approaches to; Caldwell's ten steps for, 232; for California Community Colleges, 114; CANQATE constitution, 140; Caribbean policies, 116; in Caribbean, research, 207, 209; centralized institutional approach, 237–240; challenges with, 253; compliance and, 227–228; as core value of institution, 251–253; culture development, 215–216, 222–223, 308–311; curriculum reform, 291; defined, 1, 3–4; developing among students/faculty, 293–298, 302; development among HEIs students, 293–298; education in, strategies, 143, 216. *See also* training/education, in academic integrity; educative approach, 228; elements of, in accreditation guidelines, 140–143; factors supporting, need for education, 284–285; faculty and students, roles and responsibilities of, 215–216, 248–258; findings and recommendations, 217–219; fundamental values of, and responsibilities for, 3, 5, 7; and higher education institutions

(HEIs), 1, 12, 99, 293–298;
ICAI's approach, holistic, 228;
information literacy, as strategy,
287; institutional perspective, to
approach, 235–237; institutions
with online, policies, 115; justice
and rule of law approaches, 222;
lack of knowledge/understanding,
253, 285–286; lessons on,
209; library/librarians, role
to develop, 241–247, 245–246;
limited education on, 293.
See also training/education, in
academic integrity; location of,
policies, 115, *116*; MIL integration,
into curriculum for, 288–290;
monitoring approaches, 222;
moral courage, 8; multi-prong
academic integrity programme,
301; national policy on, 224–226,
309–310; officer, duties for, 239;
or academic honesty committee,
239; people-centred approaches,
222; plagiarism, breaches, 29, 31,
306. *See also* plagiarism; plagiarism
policies and, 219–223; policy for,
112; poor practices, at secondary
level, 98–99; pre-university
level, instruction at, 286–290;
in primary education, 286–288;
principles of, *252*; programme,
elements. *See* elements of
academic integrity programme;
punitive or regulatory approach
to, 116, 226–229; purpose of
education, 9, 13–14, 19; rating
system, assessment, 274; regional
approach to, 223–224, 308–309;
relevance of research, 60, 214;
research in Caribbean, objectives,
59–60, 305; role of institutions,
223, 310–311; at secondary level,
education, 288–289. *See also*
secondary education, in Caribbean;
self-regulatory approach, 228;
support for graduate students,
258–259; Tauginiene defined,
3–4; taxonomies relating to, 272;
toolkit, of Notre Dame University,
273–274, *273*; training for teaching,
291; training or education, need.
See training/education, in academic
integrity; transparency approaches,
222; treatment of plagiarism in,
307; whistleblowing approaches,
222
academic integrity community, 232–233
academic integrity module for staff
(AIMS), 301
Academic Integrity Standards Project,
220, 269, 271
academic library/librarians, role,
241–247, *245–246*
academic maturity, 147, 196, 209,
213–214; impact on plagiarism,
196, 198–199, 206, 209; mean
differences, relates to years in
school, *204*; overall perspective of
plagiarism, 202–203; severity of
and penalty for, *203, 205*
academic misconduct, 1, 3, 137, 208,
253, 259, 304; academic issue
as, 229; articles on, in secondary
education, 99, 100; behaviours, 17;
challenge with, in Caribbean, 101;
CXC sanctions for, 96, 209; focus
on students, problem, 227–228;
Jamaica College case, 108–110,
209; managing allegations of, 274–
277; plagiarism, common form of,
1, 36; prevalence in, secondary/
tertiary education, 305–306;
prevention strategies, 272–274;
reporting procedures, 274–275,
278; university's approach to
dealing with, 237
Academic Misconduct Benchmarking
Research Project (AMBeR), 55
academic referencing module (ARM),
301
academic referencing tool (ART), 301
academics, plagiarism among, 44–45
access to education, 11
accidental plagiarist, 230
accountability, 130–131
accreditation, defined, 135
accreditation, policies and guidelines,
80, 149–151, 306; in Caribbean,

138–140; cases of plagiarism, HEIs, 143, *144, 145,* 147–148, 149–150; examples of corruption, 137–138; functions, 135–136; link with academic integrity and, 136–137, 140–143, 220; mandate for, 139; as stamp of approval, 220
Adeeb, Hina, 153
age factor, and plagiarism, 196–198, 205, 213, 308; data analysed, questionnaire, 199, *200;* factors perception, 201, *202;* justification for plagiarism, *202, 203;*participants, age groups, 199–200, *200, 201;* post hoc analysis, 201
Ahearne, John F., 5
Ahluwalia, Jatinder, 169, 182, 196, 198, 205
Ali, Asim M., 52
Ali, Wan Zah, 41, 170
Allen, Elaine Foster, 103
Alleyne, Ruby S., 139
Almeida, Renan, 57
Ameen, Kanwal, 246
American Psychological Association (APA) format, 130, 318
Amodeo, Maryann, 181
Anderson, Alexandra, 182
Anderson, David, 86
Andrews, Kenneth G., 57, 128, 150, 153–154
anti-informer culture, 275
Aschbucher, Christine, 29
Asif, Muhammad, 153
assessments, personal and institutional, 263, 274
Association of College and Research Libraries' (ACRL), 243–244
Atkinson, Doug, 53
Avarzamani, Farnaz, 41

Babbie, Earl, 82–83
Bailey, Fitz, 275
Bailey, Jonathan, 20, 24, 29, 43, 50, 194, 254
Baker, Phillip, 57
Bakhtiari, Sadegh, 221

Barbados Nation, 104
Barnard, Antoni, 295
Barnard-Brak, Lucy, 280
Barrett, Ruth, 255
Bastos, Ana Sofia, 28, 56
Batalova, Jeanne, 73
Bavaharji, Madhubala, 178
Beale, Sarah Sun, 230–231
Beale's categorization, 230–231
Becker, D'Arcy A., 179, 186
Beckles, Hilary, 68
Bedi, Akanksha, 47
Benson, Lyle, 241, 249, 300
Berlinck, Roberto G., 28, 42, 54–55, 126, 134, 170, 227, 249, 278, 293, 297
Beyerstein, Lindsay, 230
Bhattacharyya, Dhruba K., 271
the Big6, 290
Biliæ-Zulle, Lidija, 177, 178, 181
Birkett, James, 268
Bjelobaba, Sonja, 302
Blake, Byron, 61, 62
Blum, Susan D., 39–40, 226, 229, 240–241, 247
Boyle, Douglas M., 56
Boyle, James F., 56
Bretag, Tracey, 29, 35, 43, 46, 123, 138, 149, 171, 178, 196, 198, 232, 235–236, 252, 269–270, 274, 278
Brimble, Mark A., 198
Briney, Amanda, 62
Broeckelman-Post, Melissa, 38, 39
Burke, Olivene, 11
Burns, Robert, 78

Caldwell, Cam, 232, 240, 247
Campbell, Audrey, 287
Campbell, Wayne, 103, 105
Carboon, Bruce, 240
Caribbean: academic integrity in, 209, 217–219; accreditation structures in, 138–140; CXC institutions, 68–70, *70;* data on plagiarism, from universities, 209–210; defining, 61–63, 73; educational institutions, regional, 68–73; education overview in, 64–66;

four-tiered education system, 64, 73; funding education in, 66–68; G.D.P. percentage, spent on education, 67; institutional accreditation in, 138–140; map of, 62; Media and Information Literacy (MIL), in agenda, 96–97, 288–290; plagiarism prevalence, in education, 85–87, 88, 89, 93, 207–210
Caribbean Advanced Proficiency Examination (CAPE), 69, 94, 105, 306; suspected plagiarism, by subjects, 106–108, 107
Caribbean Area Network for Quality Assurance in Tertiary Education (CANQATE), 139–140, 224
Caribbean Community (CARICOM) institutions, 61–64, 68–70, 86, 223, 291, 304
Caribbean Examination Council (CXC), 53, 61, 68–70, 88, 94, 207, 305; definition for plagiarism, 96; documents, for guidance, 96; sanctions, for academic misconduct, 96
Caribbean Maritime University (CMU), 121
Caribbean Secondary Examination Certificate (CSEC), 68–69, 70, 94, 105, 306, 318; suspected plagiarism, by subjects, 105–106, 106, 107
Carnero, Andres M., 55, 236
Carpenter, Brian W., 56
Carpenter, Donald D., 35, 38, 40, 175
Carroll, Jude, 39, 248, 276
Center for Academic Integrity. *See* International Centre for Academic Integrity (ICAI)
Čepaitienė, Neringa, 296
Cervera, Amparo, 6
Chaney, Jerry, 86–87
Chang, Yun Ke, 289
Chapman, Kenneth J., 53, 155, 181
Charles, Christopher, 275
Charubusp, Sasima, 154
cheating: academic in children, 287; in adulthood, 16; in all academic

disciplines, 179–183, 180, 208–209; behaviours prevalence, 28–29; education system, as factor, 41; in examination, and technology use, 100–101, 110, 208; faculty, 57; among graduate students, relative levels, 180; harmful, and impacts, 15–16, 32; in high school, 16; for institution and society, impact, 32; internet use, to facilitate, 18, 29, 35; justification for, 57; plagiarism, commonly practised form of, 45, 208; private schools, 101; reasons for, 38–39, 58; School-Based Assessments (SBAs), 90; among students, undergraduate/graduate, 45–46; at tertiary level, 288–289
Cheat, Tan Tien, 41, 169
Checkforplagiarism.net, 56
Check for Plagiarism website, 45
Cheng, Ming, 66
Cheung, Hoi, 99
Chickering, Arthur W., 215, 248, 251–255, 257
China, plagiarism issue in, 33
Choemprayong, Songphan, 81
Chowdhury, Hussain A., 271
Chrysler-Fox, Pharny, 197
Clarke, Robert, 34–35, 181
Clarke, Roger, 86–87
Clayton, Anthony, 11, 12
Cleary, Michelle Navarre, 174
Clegg, Sue, 302
Cloete, Linda, 296
College of Science, Technology and Applied Arts of Trinidad and Tobago (COSTAATT), 115–117
College of the Bahamas, 92
Collins, Mary Elizabeth, 181
Comas-Forgas, Rubén, 43, 98, 102, 149, 178
committed plagiarist, 230
confessions of students, 318–322
content analysis, 76–77; accreditation policies and guidelines, 80–81; advantages of, 78; contents of policies, 80; of newspaper articles, 78–79; of plagiarism policies, 79–

80; procedures, 77–78; purposive sampling, 78; relevance sampling, 84; wide scope of, 77
continuum, intentionality levels in plagiarism and decentralised approach, 227
contract cheating, 1, 18, 36; business students, 180–181; challenges, 35–36; dangerous, and ramifications, 35; defined, 34; driving factors, 34–35; plagiarism *vs.*, 35, 43; products of, 34; source of, third parties, 34
Conzemius, Anne, 8
copyediting services, 34
copyright, 24
Council for Higher Education Accreditation and International Network for Quality Assurance Agencies, 220
Council for Human and Social Development (COSHOD), 223, 309
Council for International Quality Group (CIQG), 137, 220
courage, 8
Craig, Robert, 251
Crawford, Tonia, 296
Cunningham, Don, 221
Curriculum Planning and Development Division, 291
Curtis, Guy J., 146
cyber-plagiarism, 42–43

Dalton, David, 251
Daniel, John, 137
Danielson, Charlotte, 112
Dant, Doris R., 39, 42
Davies, Laura J., 44
Davis, Christine, 268
de Beer, Mariè, 295
Deeter-Schmelz, Dawn, 179
Demoliou, Catherine, 113, 126, 236, 270
descriptive survey. *See* survey, descriptive
detection of plagiarism: assessing projects, SBA, 100–101; detection tools, types of, 50–51; features, to be checked, 51–52; in music, 87; possible ways for, 50; text-matching software, use and evaluation, 51–54; threat of discovery, 53; training for both students and faculty, 54; use of electronic systems, 127–128; use of Turnitin, 52–54
Dias, Pulo C., 28, 56
direct plagiarism, 25, 26–27
dishonest behaviour, 16
Dissernet network, 86
"double dipping," 28
dual publications, 28
Duncan, Tom, 86–87
Duns, Jeremy, 56

East, Julianne, 240, 293, 297
Eaton, Judith, 136
Edna Manley College for the Visual and Performing Arts (EMCVPA), 117–118
education, in Caribbean: academic integrity, prescribed norm, 13, 19; early childhood, 64; ethics inclusion in, 294–295; examinations, importance, 11; funding/expenditure in, 66–68, 67; G.D.P. spent on, by territory, 67; globalization of, 220–221; goal of employability, 10; higher education, 11, 65–66; high investment, in sector, 10–11; for integrity, primary/secondary levels, 290–293; maintaining quality of, 11–12; open social system, 12, 13–14; plagiarism prevalence in, 207–210; primary or elementary, average enrolment in, 64–65; regional institutions role, The CXC/UWI, 68–73, 70, 72; role/purpose of, 9; secondary, 65; transformation process, critical nature of, 10, 11, 14. *See also* academic integrity; plagiarism
Ehrich, John F., 33, 81, 155–159, 161–162, 170, 195
elements of academic integrity programme, 216, 267; allegations, investigation, 274–277; five

policy elements, core, 269, 270; fundamental values, 271; honour systems, 279–281; mitigation strategies, 268–272; ongoing programme evaluation, 281–282; PACT model, 267, 268; prevention strategies, 272–274; recommendations, 277; regulations, well-defined, 268–271; rehabilitation, 277–278; reporting system, data on plagiarism, 278–279; strategies for policy implementation, 270–271; taxonomies of misconduct, 271–272

employability, skills for, 10
Enago Academy, 29
entertainment, plagiarism in, 87
Eret, Esra, 285
Eriksson, Li, 237, 257
essay writing services, 34
ethics-based workshops, 295
ethics in academic pursuits, 140
ETH Zurich, about plagiarism, 23
European Network for Academic Integrity project, 223
Evans-Tokaryk, Tyler, 221
examinations, importance, 11

factors contributing, to plagiarism: academic reasons, for plagiaristic behaviours, 38; context importance as, 38; external factors, or social factor, 41; ignorance or lack of understanding, 41–42; institutional, 40–41; personal, 37–38; student-related, 37–39; teacher-related, 39–40; in theses, 41
faculty: academic integrity training for, 302; barriers to engagement, 263–266; cheating on part of, 57; consequences for plagiarism, 56–57, 288; cooperative effort, to learning, 258; as critical partners, 248; developing academic integrity among, 302; encourage active learning and creative assessment, 255–256; as guides and mentors, 257; implementation of programmes, for academic integrity, 248–249; importance of role, reasons, 249–250; librarians teaching, role, 241–247, 245; lifelong learning, commitment to, 258; maintain vigilance, and high-quality assessment, 254; plagiarism among, 39–40, 44, 46–48; plagiarism impact on, 320–322; plagiarism, unwillingness to report, 56, 150, 210; providing feedback, 254–255; responses to plagiarism, 249–250; responsibilities, plagiarism as, 128–129. *See also* policies or guidelines, of plagiarism; role in academic integrity, 215; strategies for developing integrity, 251–254; support for academic integrity, 250–251; time management, 256–257
fairness, 6
Farahian, Majid, 41
Fatima, Shameem, 33
Fernandes, Autry A., 101, 102
Finelli, Cynthia J., 35, 38
Firoozkohi, Amir Hossein, 128, 152, 210, 284–285, 307
Fish, Reva, 248, 278
Fish, Stanley, 229
Fiszbein, Ariel, 66
Flint, Abbi, 302
Floyd, Emily, 237, 250
Fontanarosa, Phil B., 48
Foo, Schubert, 289
Forstall, Melanie, 112
Foshay, Arthur W., 9
Foster-Allen, Elaine, 295
Foust, Cathy, 32
Fowler, Floyd J., 81
Fraenkel, Jack, 77–78
Francis, Jermaine, 109
Francis, Kimone, 109
Furedi, Frank, 40

Gabriel, Trip, 26, 38
Gaižauskaitė, Inga, 98, 272, 288

Galen University, 116, 118, 127, 130, 277
Gallant, Tricia B., 218, 222, 224–226, 228–229, 233–235, 260, 294–295, 299, 304
Gamson, Zelda F., 215, 248, 251–255, 257
Gardner, Howard, 255
Garrett, Jennifer, 227, 237
Gavrilovska, Ada, 280
gender, impact of, 148–149, 209, 213, 308; demographic data on, 183–184, *184*; null hypothesis, 178, 194; objectives of study, 178; perceptions of plagiarism, females/males, 177–178, 184–188, *185–189*, 194–195; severity of and penalty for plagiarism, 188, *190*
geographical location, and plagiarism, 45
ghostwriters, 29
Gibson, David, 245
Gilbert, Greg, 114, 246, 264–265, 296
Giles, Susan, 100, 104, 106
Gillis, Charlie, 47
The Gleaner, 101, 103, 109
Glendinning, Irene, 113, 125, 128, 168, 219, 225
globalization: of education, 220–221; international migration and, 221; online learning, 221; study overseas, 222
Global Monitoring Education Review, 65
Gnanavel, Sundar, 27
Goh, Edmund, 53, 147
Gokmenoglu, Tuba, 285
Gonzales, Gyasi, 275
Goodchild, Lester, 229, 235
Grammarly benefits, 52
Grayson, Stephenson, 100
Greenburg, David, 86, 92
Green, Floyd, 275
Greenland, Philip, 48
Grieneisen, Michael, 57
Griffith, Stafford, 68, 94–95
Guidelines for Managing School-Based Assessments (SBA), 103
Gullifer, Judith, 131, 154, 165, 219, 253, 262

Hallak, Jacques, 14, 15, 100, 110, 168
Hall-Hertel, Catherine, 268
Hall, Kenneth, 68, 69
Hansen, Robin F., 182
Harding, Trevor S., 16, 35, 38, 168
Hawthorne, Omar, 275
health professionals, plagariasim among, 181–182
Heater, Derek Benjamin, 9
Henry, Balford, 279
Henslee, Amber M., 198
Hexham, Irving, 47, 57
Heyneman, Stephen P., 97, 223, 229
higher education institutions (HEIs), 1, 112, 132–134, 136; academic integrity policy, 210; approach to academic integrity, 112–113, 119, 219–220, 222; cases of plagiarism, 131, 132, 143–149, *145*, *147–148*; contract cheating, 34–36; to educate students, 293–294; institutional framework, to academic integrity in, 233–234; issue of plagiarism, separation based on severity, 29, 210; plagiarism policies in, 113, 114, 122, 126, 210–212, 305; quality framework, public pressure and, 66; rates of plagiarism in, 143, *144*, *145*, *147–148*; societal factors, influence, 234–235; developing academic integrity among students in, 293–298. *See also* academic integrity; plagiarism
Holding, Rheima, 11
Holly Seirup, Pincus, 14
honesty, dimensions of, 5–6, 237
Honig, Benson, 47
honorary authorship, 47–48
honour systems, 262, 279–281; honour codes, 279–280; honour pledge, 279
Hooker, Brad, 6
Hosny, Manar, 33
Howard, Rebecca Moore, 44
Howard, Stephen J., 33, 81, 155–159, 161–162, 170, 195
Hoy, Wayne K., 12, 13
Hue, Ming, 99
Hughes, Julia C., 45, 294–295, 299

Hugo, R., 61
Hu, Guangwei, 112, 113, 118–119, 122–124, 133, 170, 177, 179, 188, 228, 271
humanities, plagarisim and, 182–183
Hura, Gerri, 248, 278
Hussein, Norashikin, 177–178, 180

Iakovidou, Melpo, 113, 126, 236, 270
ideas plagiarism, 26
Impact of Policies for Plagiarism in Higher Education across Europe (IPPHEAE), project, 113, 220
Information Literacy and Integrity Model, 244, 245
institutional academic integrity programmes, 215, 232; Blum's model, 240–241; Caldwell's Ten Step Model, 240; centralized institutional approach, 237–240; components of, 235; establishment of ethical culture, 232; framework, 235–241; holistic approach, 232; information literacy sessions, 244; integrity officers and integrity centre, 239; role of library/librarians in, 241–247, 245–246; stakeholders, 233, 238–239, 241; strategies, 251; systems approach, 240; triadic approach to, 233–235, 234
institutional factors, for plagiarism, 40–41
integrity culture, approaches to, 222; four stages in, 223; globalization and, 220–221; national policy/programme, 224–226, 309–310; need for institutional accreditation, 219–220; regional approach to, 223–224, 308–309; rule compliance, 226. *See also* academic integrity
integrity, defined, 3
International Centre for Academic Integrity (ICAI), 1, 3, 4–5, 179, 228; Academic Integrity Rating System, 274; courage, 8; fairness, 6; founded by Don McCabe, 4, 179; fundamental values, academic integrity, 5, 8, 271; honesty, 5; respect for self and others, 7; responsibility or responsible actions, 7–8; trust, 5–6
International Journal of Occupational and Environmental Health, 15
international students, 220–221
internet, and plagiarism connection, 29, 42–44, 101, 107–108, 181
Isfahan, H. Shajar, 221
Ismail, Habsah, 41, 169
Ismail, Kameran H., 170, 178, 181, 188, 298
Ison, David C., 42, 43
iThenticate, 51, 55, 56

Jahangier, Azam, 48
Jamaica College case, 101, 108–110, 208, 209
Jamaica Observer, 109, 110
Jamaica Teachers' Association, 109
James, Colin, 182
Jereb, Eva, 40, 43, 88, 177–179, 194
Josephson Institute Center for Youth Ethics, 98
Josephson Institute of Ethics (2009), 3, 5; caring, 9; citizenship, social facet of, 9; pillars of character, Aspen Declaration, 8–9; respect, 7, 9; trustworthiness, 5–6, 9
journalism, plagiarism in: definition of, 90; among journalists, 86–87; no written policies for, 87
Joyner, David A., 280

Kaieteur News, 102
Kalichman, Michael, 218, 222, 225, 229, 233–235, 260
Kam, Chester, 99
Kayaoglu, M.N., 43, 170, 296, 298
Keohane, Nannerl, 8
Keuskamp, Dominic, 54
Kezar, Adrianna J., 233
KidsHealth website, 290
King, Lizette, 39, 46, 183
Kokkinaki, Angelika I., 113, 126, 236, 270

Kovtun, Lesia, 51
Krcal, Petr, 29
Kremmer, Michael L., 198
Krippendorff, Klaus, 77–78
Krtalić, Maja, 85
Kupferschmidt, Kai, 16
Lacović. Darko, 85
Lai, Kwok-Wing, 97
Lamallari, Besfort, 44
Lampert, Lynn, 226, 241–242
Lancaster, Thomas, 34–35, 181
law students, plagarisim among, 182
Lee, Christine, 248
Leedy, Paul, 81
Lee, Juwan, 87, 294
Lei, Jun, 177, 179, 188
Leo-Ryhnie, Elsa, 10, 16
Lepera, Christine, 87
Lewis, Norman P., 87
Lim, Louise, 33
Lincoln, Lennox, 92
Löfström, Erika, 44, 180–181
Ludlow, Douglas K., 198
Lynch, Jack, 181

Macabe, Don, 3, 17, 28, 34, 39, 43, 88, 106, 179–181, 183, 280
Macdonald, Ranald, 302
Madhi, Gentiola, 44
Mahmud, Saadia, 46, 235, 270, 278
Majid, Shaheen, 289
Mala, Tatna, 29
mandatory academic integrity module (AIM), 301
Maneulin, Michael, 87
Mansoor, Faiqa, 246
Marcus, Adam, 86
Marklein, Mary Beth, 221
Martin, Bland, J., 280
Mason, Tony, 280
Mavrinac, Martina, 81
Max, Roser, 9
McCabe, Donald L., 45, 110, 145, 215, 233, 248, 251–258
McDuff, DeForest, 215, 233, 248, 251–258
McGee, Tara R., 237, 257

McGrail, Ewa, 114, 116–117, 119, 121, 123–124, 126, 128, 132, 168, 230
McGrail, Patrick J., 114, 116–117, 119, 121, 123–124, 126, 128, 132, 168, 230
McKenzie, Eunice Letitia, 289
McNamara, Carter, 282
Medford, Dianne, 101, 104
Media and Information Literacy (MIL), 96–97, 288–290
Medical Literature Analysis and Retrieval System Online (MEDLINE), 15
medical students, plagarisim among, 181–182
Meng, Ling, 295, 298
mentoring, 257
methodology, for research. *See* research, and methodology for
Metz, Allison J.R., 281
Mico University College (MUC), 118, 130
Middleton, David, 7
migration, Caribbean persons, 73, 74
Miller, Errol, 9
misconduct, taxonomies of, 271–272
Miskel, Cecil G., 12, 13
mitigation strategies, 268; fundamental values of academic integrity, 271; regulations, 268–271; taxonomies of misconduct, 271–272
Modern Language Association (MLA) format, 318
Mohamad, Siti S., 177–178, 180
Moore, Roy L., 86
moral identity, 295
Morris, Ainsworth, 105, 298
Morris, Erica J., 248, 249
Moskovitz, Cary, 177
Moulton, Janice, 21
Mudrack, Ben, 27
Murray, Michael D., 86
Murray, Susan, 198
music plagiarism, 87

Napolitano, Gabrielle, 56
national accreditation agencies, 139

National Natural Science Foundation of China, 33
National Parent Teacher Association of Jamaica, 109
Neeley, Stacia D., 273
Negro Education Grant of 1835, 64
Nelms, Gerald, 302
Neuman, Lawerence W., 77, 79
newspaper articles, content analysis of, 78–79, 208; identifying key events, 79; Caribbean Community (CARICOM) territories, 86; online articles, limitation to, 79; published on plagiarism, increase in, 88, 89, 93; responses to plagiarism, 92–93; in secondary education, on academic misconduct, 99–100, 99; by sectors, 89–90, 91; territories, cases of plagiarism, 87–89, 88, 93; types of plagiarism, 90, 92
Nicely, Mark, 109
Nushi, Musa, 128, 152, 210, 284–285, 307

Ogbebor, Abieyuwa, 99
O'Grady, Emmanuel, 7
Oliver-Trobat, Miquel, 43, 98, 102, 149, 178
Olson, Kristen R., 197
O'Neill, Jan, 8
online education/learning, 220–221
open social system model, 12, 13, 19, 89
opportunistic plagiarist, 230
Oransky, Ivan, 86
organizational culture, 264
Ormrod, Jeanne Ellis, 81
Ortiz-Ospina, Esteban, 9
outsourcing assignments, practice of, 24, 34
Oxford referencing, 297
Oxford Standard for Citation of Legal Authorities (OSCOLA) format, 297, 318
Oxford University Press, 22, 23

Parhamnia, Farshad, 41
Parmley, William W., 44, 45, 285

Parnther, Ceceilia, 250–252
Patterson, P.J., 11
Pavela, Gary, 215, 233, 248, 251–258
Pecorari, Diane, 24, 152, 271, 302
penalties for plagiarism, 54–55, 168–169, 198
perceptions of plagiarism, 152–153, 307–308; academic discipline role, students'. *See* academic discipline/faculty; age and academic maturity, role, 196–199, 205–206, 308; factors exacerbate, 155–157, 156, 316; friend factor, 155, 161, 308; gender, students'. *See* gender, impact of; justification, responses for, 157–159, 158, 171–172, 175, 316; punishment, severity of, 154, 157, 162; qualitative data from respondents, 163–164, 164; questionnaires used, 154, 163, 315; rates of, in HEIs, 85, 143, 144, 145, 147–148; self-plagiarism, 173–174; severity of and penalty, responses, 159–161, 160, 162, 165–169, 317; students, 307–308; themes, qualitative responses by, 164, 165; topic relevance or importance, 174–175; undergraduate students' study for, 152–154, 161–162, 175–176, 212–214, 315; unintentional plagiarism, 173–174. *See also* students, and plagiarism
Pérez-Cabañero, Carmen, 6
Perkins, Anna Kasafi, 140
Perry, Janett, 230
pharmacy and medicine, plagiarisim and, 181–182
Pincus, Holly Seirup, 42, 119
The Pirates of Plagiarism and *Plagiarism!*, 290
plagiarism: 404 Error, 321; in academia, 28–29, 31–32, 44–45, 48, 57–58, 92; academic dishonesty, popular form, 17, 19, 36; academic maturity impact, 196, 198–199; academic reasons for, 38; academics, consequences among, 56–57; accountability and,

130–131; accountability statement, 211; across academic disciplines, 179–183, *180*, 188, 194–195; actual *vs.* reported cases, 210; age factor and, 197–198; agreed-on definition, 21; approaches to, 131–132; articles, reports in. *See* newspaper articles, content analysis of; in articles, types of, 25–28, 90, *92*; behaviours lists, ETH Zurich, 23; Beyerstein's position, 230; cases of, 1, 16–17; categorization of, 26; causes and prevalence of, 37–42; challenges in, 23, 24, 36; challenge to education systems, 18–19, 28–29, 31; citation rules, 25; complex notion, 41; confessions of, 318–322; contract cheating *vs.*, 35–36; contributing factors to students', 1, 37–39, 45–46; copyright violation and, 24; CSEC and CAPE examination, suspected cases, 105–107, *106*, *107*; detection of, 1, 50–54; deterrents to, 57–58; discipline-specific approach to, 259; distinction, undergraduate and graduate students, 133; educative approach to, 44, 162, 169–170, 286–288 elements of, 152–154, 161; elements of, 1, 21–22, 24–25, 119, 133, 210; in entertainment and music, 87; ethical, moral or educational issue, 32, 57, 229–231; factors contributing to, 41, 171; by faculty, 46–48; as faculty responsibilities, 128–129; frequency of suspected cases, 107–108, *108*; genders, perception in carrying out, 178–179, 184–188, 194–195; among graduate and undergraduate students, *18*, 42, 45–46; in grant proposals and research writing, 33; ignorance or lack of understanding, 26, 41–42, 219, 287; impact on faculty, 320–322; institutional factors, influencing, 40–41; intentional *vs.* unintentional, 26–27; internet connection and,

29, 42–44, 101, 107–108, 147, 181; investigation of, 276; issue in China, 33, 57; Jamaica College, case of, 108–110; in journalism, no written policies for, 86–87; justifications for, 171–172, 212; lack of reporting by faculty, 56; language used, 131; legal representation for hearing, 132; levels of, 122; as necessary evil, 171; newspapers, cases of, 85–86, 88; outsourcing assignments, practice of, 24, 34; penalties for, 54–55; perceptions of factors, exacerbating, 152–153, 155, *156*; policies, content analysis, 79–80, 210–211; in politics, 86; presentation in, accreditation policies and guidelines, 306; prevalence, type of, 17–18, 45–48, 88; problem, global, 28–29, 31, 49; procedures for treating, 123–125; punitive approach, 132; rates of, in HEIs, 85, 143, *144*, *145*, 147–148; Remix, 321; sanctions and consequences for, 56, 125–127; secondary education, reasons, 18, 97–103; self-, 27–28; social factor contributing to, 41; sources of information, 129–130; Spectrum, advocated by Turnitin, 25, *26*; student plagiarists, kinds of, 230; students and, 33–34, 37–39, 54–56, 152–153; study of policies, institutions with online, 113–114, *115*; synonymous terms, 22, 23; teacher-related factors, 39–40; in theses, reasons for, 41; top ten cases of 2016, 29, *30–31*; types and examples, 25–28, 90, 92, 122–123; ubiquitous, 28–29, 85; undergraduates' perception of, 152–154, 161–162, 175–176, 212–214. *See also* perceptions of plagiarism; unintentional, 20, 40; use of electronic detection systems, 127–128; UWI defines, 22; varying interpretation of, 21; weak academic writing skills, 38;

"what" of, focus on, 21–22; word, etymology of, 20–21; work types, 23; wrong, reasons, 29, 31–34; zero-tolerance approach to, 27. *See also* contract cheating
Plagiarism: 25 Games and Activities to Teach Documenting and Sourcing Skills to Students, 290
Plagiarism Advisory Service, 51
Plagiarism Facts and Stats, 46, 98
Plagiarism Is Not a Big Moral Deal, 229
PlagiarismSearch.com, 90
Plagramme, 52
Playscan, 52
Poisson, Muriel, 14, 15, 100, 110, 168
policies or guidelines, of plagiarism, 113–114, 134, 219; academic integrity and, 219–223; accountability in, 130–131; analysis of, and data presentation, 114, 116–119; approaches to, 131–132; common elements in, 271; content analysis of, 307; search strategies, 79–80; units of analysis, 80; electronic detection system, 119, 127–128; elements of, 119, 121–122; Hu and Sun's eight codes, 118–119, *118*, 133, 228; institutions with online, 115; levels in, 122; location of, 115, *116*; popular element of, 119, *120*; procedures for treating, allegations of, 123–125; reference to sources, 129–130; responsibilities of faculty, 128–129; sanctions for, 125–127, 133; studies/ analysis, 113–114; types and examples in, 122–123
policy, defined, 112
politics, plagiarism in, 86, 90, 92
Porter, Jacqueline, 85, 170
positive labels, 116
Power, Lori G., 153–154
prevention strategies, PACT model, 272; assessments, 274; capacity building, 272–273; resource toolkit, 273–274
Prevention, Mitigation, Assessment and Curation of Academic Integrity Based on Values and Taxonomy (PACT) model, 216, 267, *268*, 277, 283
primary education, academic integrity in, 286–288
Principles of Academic Integrity for Faculty, 251
Proffitt, Brian, 52
psychometric testing, 81
"publish or perish" mandate, 44
Pupovac, Vanja, 181
Pury, Cynthia L. S., 8

Quality Assurance Agency for Higher Education, 34
Queen, Edward, 237, 250
Ramzan, Muhammad, 42, 46, 153
Rasch validation technique, 81
Razera, Diana, 298
Razi, Salim, 272
Reddock, Rhoda, 44
Regulations for the Conduct of the Council's Examinations, 96
rehabilitation, PACT model: advocacy, 277; counselling and training, 277–278; sanctions, 278; vindication, 277
Reid, Sharon, 103
Reid, Tyrone, 109
Remix, 321
research and methodology: content analysis, procedure, 76–78; data collection and analysis, 75, 84; data sources, 76; descriptive survey, 81–83; design, 76; ethical standards/ concerns, 84; informed consent, 84; misconduct, 33; objectives, 75; purposive sampling, 78; qualitative and quantitative methods, 76; secondary data defined, 84. *See also* content analysis; survey, descriptive
respect for self and others, 7
respectful person, defined, 7
results, falsification of, 101
retraction of articles, 15, 57
Retraction Watch, 15
Roberts, Vivienne, 139
Robinson, George, 21

Rogers, Tony, 90
Roig, Miguel, 28
Rosentiel, Tom, 180, 182
Rothschild, David, 33
Rusdi, Syezreen D., 177–178, 180

Sachar, Cassandra, 54
Saddiqui, Sonia, 227–228, 233
SafeAssign, 52
Sam, Cecile, 233
sanctions, 211, 278; for plagiarism, 125–127, 133
Sarath, Nonis, 16
Šarlauskienė, Lina, 225, 296
Sato, Yoshihiro, 16, 57
SBA Handbook for Teachers, 96
Schlesinger, Walesska, 6
Schmelkin, Liora Pedhazur, 14, 42, 119
Schmidt, Marcelo, 280
Schmitt, Pat, 29
School Based Assessment Manual for Principals, 96
School-Based Assessments (SBAs), 90, 208, 305; component of examination, 94; role and variety of forms, 95; significant feature of CXC, 94; time problem issue, 102
schools, open systems, 12, 13–14
Schrier, Karen, 245
Schurink, Willem, 295
science and technology, plagiarisim and, 183
Scott, Michael R., 53, 287, 290
secondary data, defined, 84
secondary education, in Caribbean, 94, 110–111, 288–289; academic dishonesty causes, 101–104; academic integrity in/at, 94–97, 288–289; cheating in exams, 100–101; CXC, processes and practices of, 96, 97; educators role in SBAs, 101; fraudulent certificate, sale/creation, 104–105; Jamaica College case, 108–110; penalties for cheatings, 104; plagiarism among secondary students, 98–99; quality assurance in, 95–97; reason for plagiarism in, 102–104; suspected cases, of plagiarism, 105–108, 106–108. *See also* academic dishonesty; plagiarism
Segal, Scott, 44, 47
self-plagiarism, 173–175, 212; defined, 27–28; specific behaviours, 28; students' justification, 153–154
Sentleng, Mapule Patricia, 39, 46, 183
SEO Tool Station website, 50
Seven Principles for Good Practice in Undergraduate Education, 251
Shaw, Alex, 197
Shaw, Philip, 302
Sheets, Brenda, 179
Shpuza, Miada, 44
Siaputra, Ide B., 216, 267–268, 272, 274, 277, 281, 283
Siaputra's PACT model. *See* elements of academic integrity programme
Simon, Beth, 183, 189, 259
Sisti, Dominic A., 39, 58, 98, 153–154, 175
Skerritt, Roosevelt, 92
Sliuzas, Regina, 54
Smart, Cherryann, 21, 26, 85, 121, 131, 169, 208
Smedley, Alison, 296
Snášel, Václav, 52
social sciences, plagiarisim and, 180–181
social systems: boundaries and normative nature, 13–14; defined, 12
Stabingis, Linas, 225, 296
Stabroek News, 101
Stanton, Sarah, 66
Stenmark, Cheryl K., 182
Stephenson, Hector, 103, 104
Stevenson-Clarke, Peta, 198
Student Conduct Coordinator, 238
students and plagiarism: academic discipline impact. *See* academic discipline/faculty; academic maturity impact, 196, 198–199, 206; age factor impact, 196–198, 205; applied science, 183; Attitude Towards Plagiarism Survey, 152; challenges, 213; confessions

of, 318–322; consequences, 54–56, 288; epidemiology and pharmacology, 181; ethical decision-making skills/ethics, teaching, 294–295; factors contributing, 171, 212; friend factor, 155, 161, 175, 308; gender and perceptions of. *See* gender, impact of; independent variables, impact of, 213; "instructor-based neutralizations," 153, 171, 175, 307; justification for, 153, 157, 171–172; kinds of plagiarists, 230; lack of understanding, severity of, 26, 41–42, 154, 168, 213, 288; law, 182; learning and shared responsibility, 8; need for education on, 162, 169–170, 174, 294; nursing and medical, 181–182; perceptions of factors, 152–154, 212–213, 307–308. *See also* perceptions of plagiarism; prevalence among, 45–46, 48, 152; related factors, 37–39; responses, justification, 33–34, 157–159, 158; social sciences and humanities, 182–183; social work, 181; summarizing and paraphrasing skills, 172; top ten reasons, 38–39; writing difficulties, 172–173, 213, 307

students role in academic integrity, 215–216, 259–263; barriers to engagement, 263–266; challenges, 260; creative assessment, 254–256; high expectations, 253–254; getting information on, 261–262; participation in programmes and activities, 262; reinforcement of existing knowledge and skills, 263; responsibilities, 260–261, 263; strengths and weaknesses, assessing, 263. *See also* academic integrity

Sue, Yeoh, 53
Sun, Xiaoya, 112, 113, 118–119, 122–124, 133, 170, 228, 271
Super 3, 290
Sureda, Jaume, 35, 38, 41

Sureda-Negre, Jaume, 43, 98, 102, 149, 178
survey description: data collection, 81–82; plagiarism scale, items in, 83; sample distribution, across faculties, 82; statistical analysis, 83
Sutherland-Smith, W., 26–27, 41, 42, 114, 121, 123, 125, 131–133, 233
Swift, Cathy Owens, 16
Tanacković, Sanjica F., 85
targeted assistance, 130
Tauginienė, Loreta, 3, 98, 272, 288
taxonomy, defined, 271
Taylor-Bianco, Amy, 179
Taylor, Rebecca, 237, 250
teaching factor, for plagiarism, 39–40
tertiary institutions, Caribbean, 11
Tewarie, Bhoendradatt, 65, 309
text-matching software, 31, 35, 50–54, 58, 276, 298
Thesaurus.com, 22, 23
Thomas, Adele, 56
Thompsett, Andrew, 169, 182, 196, 198, 205
Thornton, Linda Fisher, 6
threat of discovery, 53
time management, 256–257
Tomas, Foltýnek Tomáš, 225
toolkit, concept of, 273
training/education, in academic integrity, 143; ethical decision-making skills/ethics, teaching, 294–295, 299; factors supporting, 284–285; funding and research, 292; integrity programmes, 294–298; La Trobe University, resources, 301; mandatory for students and staff, 300; methodology for variety of forms, 298–301; MIL in curriculum for, 289–290, 292; moral identity development, 295; multi-prong academic integrity programme, 301; need for, 284–286. *See also* academic integrity; online academic integrity courses, 299; plagiarism, approach to, 44, 162, 169–170, 286–287; self-enroling

courses, 299; for teaching, 291; text-matching software, 298; use of conferences/seminars, 298; writing centre approach, 298, 300; writing conventions, 296–297
Trevino, Linda Klebe, 110, 145
Trump, Melania, 90
trust: defined, 5; ethics and, 6; honesty integral component, 5–6; importance in education, 6
Turner, Camilla, 47
Turnitin, popularity of, 25, 26, 35, 46, 51–53, 90, 298
Tyson, Graham A., 131, 219, 253, 262

Uberti, David, 90
Ukpebor, Christopher O., 99
Ulstad, Ingrid, 179, 186
undergraduate students. *See* students, and plagiarism
Unicheck, 52
unintentional or accidental plagiarism, 25–27, 29, 173–174
United Nations Educational, Scientific and Cultural Organization (UNESCO), 288
United Nations International Children's Emergency Fund, 64
universities role, in plagiarism, 40–41
University Council of Jamaica (UCJ), 80, 135–136
University of Belize, 116, 123, 126, 129
University of California-Berkeley, 45, 126, 149
University of Cambridge, 22, 23; categories of materials, 23; intent and defining plagiarism, 22
University of Maryland, Code of Academic Integrity, 238, 279, 299
University of Mary Washington, 124, 127, 145–146, 275, 279, 280
University of Oxford, 28, 146
University of Technology (UTECH), 115, 118, 120, 122–124, 125, 131–132
University of the Bahamas, 117, 119, 125, 286
University of the Commonwealth Caribbean (UCC), 116
University of the West Indies (UWI), 22, 61–63 84, 69, 73, 131, 139, 222,
318; academic integrity training, 299; allegations of plagiarism, 126–127; began in 1948, establishment of, 70–71; Campus Committee, 124; enrolment by nationalities, 72; enrolment by nationalities, total number, 71, 72; graduate and undergraduate policies, 117, 124–125; information literacy in, 288; mandatory reporting by faculty, 129; Open Campus and physical campuses, 71; penalties for plagiarism, 168–169, 198. *See also* perceptions of plagiarism; plagiarism defined, 22, 122; student's confession, 318–320
University of Waterloo, 256, 258, 259, 282, 284
URKUND company, 31
US Council for Higher Education Accreditation (USCHEA), 136

Vardanega, Lucia, 146
Vargas, Viera, 61
Vázquez-Recio, Rosa, 37, 39–41, 102, 170, 249
video clip, generation, 41

Waddil, Paula, 179
Walcott, Paul, 85, 152, 155–162, 170, 183, 212
Walker, Christopher, 148, 227
Walker, John, 198, 199
Wallen, Norman, 77–78
Walton, Russel, 33, 81, 155–159, 162, 170, 195
Wangaard, David B., 32, 295
Wan, Guofang, 53, 287, 290
Watters, Audrey, 46
Weber-Wulff, Debora, 52
Weeks, Jenny J., 97
Wei, Tianlan, 280
Wei, Yang, 33
Welsh-Unwala, Kristen, 85, 170, 286
Wheeler, Debbie, 86
White, Melanie, 148, 227
Whitley, B., 179, 197
Whyte, Millicent, 64
Wildemuth, Barbara, 81
Wilkinson, Jenny, 148, 198, 250

Wilson, Nadine, 101
Winn, Nicolette A., 182
Woodard, Cooper R., 8
Wood, Gail, 242, 244
writing skills, difficulties, 172–173

Yeo, S., 154

Yeung, Alice H.W., 43

Žalec, Bojan, 6
zero-tolerance approach, 27, 55
Zhang, M. Minghua, 57
Zhong, Bu, 87
Zong, Jie, 73

www.ingramcontent.com/pod-product-compliance
Lightning Source LLC
Chambersburg PA
CBHW021815300426
44114CB00009BA/182